MY HOLLYWOOD, WHEN BOTH OF US WERE YOUNG

STREET SCENE IN HOLLYWOOD

Thousands buck the line on every call issued for a few movie picture extras. This is a sample of the customary massed assault on the employment bureaus resulting from an ad for a very few men and women to work in an insignificent scene. The wage is meagre for a day or night of hard work.

Don't Try To Break Into The Movies
IN HOLLYWOOD

Until You Have Obtained Full, Frank and Dependable Information

FROM THE

HOLLYWOOD CHAMBER OF COMMERCE
(Hollywood's Great Community Organization)

It May Save Disappointments

Out of 100,000 Persons Who Started at the Bottom of the Screen's Ladder of Fame
ONLY FIVE REACHED THE TOP

MY HOLLYWOOD:

When Both Of Us Were Young

Previous pages:
(Top left) Thomas Ince and crew.
(Bottom left) The Hollywood Hotel, 1920.
(Top right) Prof. Jomier, Bessie Love, John Gilbert, Patsy Ruth Miller, Leatrice Joy, Charles Chaplin, Max Linder, Barbara Bedford, Gaston Glass, Ruth Nightman-Morris, Gouverneur Morris, 1925.

Patsy Ruth Miller - January 17, 1904 - July 16, 1995

The Memories of
PATSY RUTH MILLER

Published in the USA by

BearManor Media

P. O. Box 71426
Albany, GA 31708
bearmanormedia.com

Philip J. Riley – Editor

Decorative sketches by Al Herschfeld

Since the original plates were not available, this volume is presented as a facsimile of its original form.

ISBN—1-59393-489-0
978-1-59393-489-7

ACKNOWLEDGEMENTS

The majority of photographs that appear in this volume are from the personal collection of Miss Patsy Ruth Miller. The author and publishers wish to thank the following individuals and institutions for their generous assistance:

MARC WANAMAKER, Bison Archives

MARY CORLISS, The Museum of Modern Art, New York City

Universal Studios

The American Heritage Center - University of Wyoming

Princeton University Library - Jean Preston

The Billy Rose Theater Collection - N.Y. Library at Lincoln Center and Dorothy Swerdlove

Tod Firetag, Poster City

John C. Van Doren

Mon Ayash

Jeffrey Carrier

Cinemabilia Books, New York City

Kevin Brownlow and The British Film Institute

William K. Everson

George Theophilis

Wes Shank

John Kobal

John Springer

National Community Bank, David Middlebrook, Jeffrey Cooper

Design and Art Direction: Marisa Donato-Riley

Michael Hawks Collection

The Atlantic City Library - reference division

Richard and Marion Sonderegger

Rebecca Dunn

Patricia Bishop

Patrick J. Doran

Matthew Doran

Patrick Joseph Doran

9

Although no formal dedication was suggested for this limited collectors edition of MY HOLLYWOOD-WHEN BOTH OF US WERE YOUNG, we received not only permission but the blessing of the author for the following:

We respectfully dedicate this book to Mr. & Mrs. Oscar Miller. The greatest gift that we, the citizens of this great country, have is the family unit. It has been our foundation and it will be our future. Anyone who has met Patsy Ruth Miller and her brother Winston Miller would never forget the great light of love surrounding them. A light that can only begin at birth, be nurtured throughout childhood and grow to touch all those who have been lucky enough to have met them in their lifetime. May all the blessing be to the children of America—and the rest of the world to have parents like them.

To say that Patsy Ruth Miller was simply a star of the Silent Screen is not enough! She certainly was a star when we appeared together in a dreadfully corny film entitled *Broken Hearts of Hollywood* for Warner Brothers, in 1926. It was one of my very early films—and one of the first in which I had the "romantic lead" (what a description!)—but it was her *fortieth*! Even though she made her last film in 1931, Patsy Ruth Miller has always remained part of the magical land and movie capital, Hollywood.

In the film, Patsy played a small-town girl who had won a beauty contest and I played a small-town boy who had won a popularity contest. We, the girl and the boy, meet on a train to Hollywood, both of us sharing the same goal of making it in the movies. Naturally we became "screen lovers"—in the most innocent interpretation of the phrase. Typical of Patsy Ruth Miller's films, she got in with "the wrong crowd" and found herself in jail after a raid on a wild party. To bail her out I take a job as a stuntman—and proceed to injure myself in a dangerous jump. Patsy then manages to get a small job in a movie in order to earn the money to pay my medical bills. Meanwhile we learn that Louise Dresser, whose character is really Patsy's mother and who once had a drinking problem and had been a star herself. Now she is cast in the same film as Patsy as mother and daughter. When a sleazy type villain tries to seduce Patsy she is saved by Louise, but the villain is accidentally shot and Louise goes on trial for murder. Naturally, in the last suspenseful courtroom scene I rush in with the evidence to prove Louise's innocence and the picture fades out on a happy ending.

Variety, the famous "show-biz" paper, had this to say: "Patsy Ruth Miller and Douglas Fairbanks, Jr. contribute corking juvenile performances. Here is a picture that should be supported by the parents and mothers' association in every town that it plays. It is a picture produced with a purpose, the purpose being that youngsters must not expect to go to Hollywood and become screen stars overnight."

In this wonderful book you will find just how Patsy Ruth Miller became a star. In all her 71 pictures she played a wide range of parts, from a prostitute to characters of goody-goodness and super-purity. She acted with such movie immortals as Lon Chaney and Alla Nazimova in melodramas, with Tom Mix and Hoot Gibson in Westerns and then clowned her way through comedies with Glen Tryon, Douglas Maclean and Edward Everett Horton.

She probably will always be remembered by her most famous role, that of Esmeralda the Gypsy girl opposite Lon Chaney in *The Hunchback of Notre Dame* and why not! The picture has been remade four times and the original is still the best version.

Speaking for myself, I remember her first of all as a charmer. She often visited my father's and stepmother Mary Pickford's house, Pickfair, and was part of my stepmother's "girls' club." We also had some pleasant afternoons swimming in the sea or someone's pool. Even though Patsy was a very well-known star, she never put on airs. It was as if she was just enjoying her job of making movies and when she had had enough she just quit.

The charm of her memoirs reflects, as it should, her attitude on life, her gratitude for life itself! You won't find a list of her many accomplishments in this book but rather delightful behind-the-scenes stories of some of the best known names in film, theater, society and literature. It was probably this intelligent detachment that made it possible for her to switch from comedy to tragedy, from an "epic" film to a standard feature, from silents to delightful early talkies and still remain popular with the public. Had she wanted to remain in the profession, we would no doubt be seeing her today playing character parts on television as well as films.

We find in this volume that even though she retired from acting, she always remained part of the theatrical profession. Sometimes she wrote and acted in plays, and in her three marriages, first to the famous director Tay Garnett (with whom I made a film entitled *The Joy of Living*), then to the great MGM writer, John Lee Mahin and finally throughout a loving 40 year marriage to E.S. Deans, a Scottish clothing manufacturer, the friendships that she made during her Hollywood days endured, some even to this day. Clark Gable, Mischa Auer, Gloria Swanson, Colleen Moore, Leatrice Joy, and John Gilbert are all here, alive in these pages. There aren't many still with us, except for Helen Hayes, whom Patsy admires greatly.

In this "Collector's Edition" you also get a list of all her films plus another of the Ackerman Archives historic filmbooks restoring the lost footage of *The Hunchback of Notre Dame*.

Congratulations to you, dear Patsy Ruth and herewith I record my confidence in the reader's enjoyment of your memories.

Douglas Fairbanks, Jr.
August 1988

Hollywood and Vine, 1918

PREFACE

This book came into being because of the urging, pleading insistence and nagging of a young newspaper man from Tennessee named Jeffrey Carrier. For two years he kept after me to write about "My Hollywood" as it was back in the twenties and thirties. "Do you realize", he said, "that you're just about the oldest living actress—except for Lillian Gish—who remembers when Vine Street had wooden sidewalks and pepper trees lined both sides of the dirt road?

"Who cares?" was my snappy retort.

"Lots of people," he insisted. "They'd love to read about all those actors you knew—Rudolph Valentino, Clark Gable, Mary Pickford..."

"Never mind the roll call," I said. "There have been books galore by practically everybody who ever set foot in a studio, even if it was to deliver the mail."

But nothing I said convinced young Jeffrey. He continued to write, to phone, and to nag. I finally explained to him that I had been told by a reputable publisher that all the reading public wanted was dirt and scandal. The publisher said very frankly that nasty stories about parents were the "in" thing... such as *Mommy Dearest* and the one about Bette Davis. "To be honest with you" he said, "Good taste is definitely OUT these days."

Jeff simply didn't believe the publisher. He pointed out that *he* was interested, and so were his friends and his classmates in college—and, how about all the youngsters who watched old films on TV and how about their parents who used to have "crushes" on some of the actors of those days... especially if they were as likeable and as interesting as you found them to be.

So I began to think about nice young people like Jeff and his friends, and about older people whom I knew, and about all the fine decent men and women in this country, and I thought maybe that publisher is wrong. I've been told that sometimes they are.

Of course, if he was right, then I have two strikes against me before I even step up to bat; I don't like dirty words, and I can't write nasty things about the people I knew in Hollywood because I liked most of them, even the producers, and how can you write nasty things about people you like?

Well, here goes. Not an autobiography—no baring of my soul—just some stories about Hollywood and its people as I knew them back in those golden days—and a bit about myself, too, while I'm about it.

So, dear reader, I hope you will enjoy these reminiscences... and that you won't mind the lack of scandal.

Don't say I didn't warn you.

CHAPTER ONE

To begin with, I'll answer the first question people always ask: "How did you get started in the movies?"

According to a Peoria Illinois newspaper article from 1923, this is how it happened, and I quote: "From drudgery at the kitchen sink to the sovereignty of the silent screen, from stolen visits to the Peoria nickelodeon when having a Thursday off, to supreme stardom in the Million Dollar production of The Hunchback of Notre Dame, went Patsy Ruth Miller in one swift splendid bound." (How's that for purple prose?). "If you see Patsy Ruth Miller at the Madison Theatre this week, go home and remember that ten years ago she was a maid in a household here." (But, wait—there's more...) "By what steep and tortuous paths she rose to be the star of Universal's greatest picture does not appear at the moment." Notice, there isn't even a mention of Lon Chaney, who happened to be the real star of the picture. But, of course, he wasn't a Peoria boy!

But, then, neither was I a Peoria girl! That's a slight flaw in the story. I've never been in Peoria in my life. If it had been true, I'd have been the youngest housemaid in America—all of nine years old!

I remember Mother being rather upset when she read that story, but my Father's only comment was, "If you're such a good housemaid, why don't you straighten up your room some time?"

The other "how I got started" story was an article in a fan magazine, written by Adela Rogers St. Johns, a well-known and highly respected writer of the time. Here's what Adela told a palpitating public:

"Patsy Ruth Miller and her parents came to California for a vacation. Patsy Ruth was in school but it was summertime. She was sitting on the sands watching the waves with a demure and pensive gaze. (Really, that's what it says). Little did she dream that the man watching her so intently was a motion picture director—in fact she didn't see him at all. Douglas Gerrard, the director, watched her for some time. Then he offered her a job in pictures."

Kind of like the Lana Turner story, isn't it? Me, on the beach in a bathing suit, Lana at a lunch counter in a tight sweater.

So which one was true? Neither one was the real story, although there was a grain of truth no bigger than a mustard seed, in the beach version.

I did indeed meet Douglas Gerrard on the Santa Monica Beach.

In those days there was nothing on the Santa Monica but sand. The only building was a wooden bathhouse which always smelled of wet bathing suits. I think you paid a quarter—or maybe fifty cents—to use one of its cubicles for changing. At the far end of the beach an amusement pier jutted out into the Pacific, on which were soft drink stands and fresh fish stalls, and the eternal optimists leaning over the railing, dangling their lines in the water.

Santa Monica Beach was like a club to us young people. You had to bring your own beach chairs and picnic lunch; the chairs were for the parents, of course. We young people scorned them. Some of us were visitors, some natives; a few of us were trying to get into the movies, a few were already in. You could tell which were the visitors from back East; they sat under umbrellas; at least the parents did. We were respectful of their right to be there, but the beach was ours.

The boys did their handstands and gymnastics, showing off much as they do today. The older ones played volley-ball, batting the ball at each other over a high ragged net while we girls, sprawled on the hot sand in clusters, cheered them on while covertly eyeing our own favorite lean brown young man.

There were no bikinis, of course; we wore one-piece bathing suits with little skirts, and thought them very daring. Some of the older women wore black silk stockings and bathing slippers held on by ribbons, which were actually very attractive, and set off a well shaped leg most becomingly, but we free souls were bare legged, and scorned bathing slippers even when the hot sand burned our feet.

On the Santa Monica Beach with Douglas Gerrard

The Californians were all good swimmers; we visitors did a good deal of jumping up and down in the surf and screaming when a wave tumbled us, laughing and sputtering, up on the shore. In time, many of us actually learned to swim well.

One day, when Mother and I were sitting alone, a rather distinguished-looking man approached us, introduced himself as Douglas Gerrard, and asked if he could join us. Mother smiled and said, "Of course. I'm Mrs. Miller, and this is my daughter, Pat," so he sat down beside her. After some light chit-chat, in which I had no part, he said that he was connected with the motion picture business, that he had been watching me, and that he thought I had possibilities for the screen. I don't think for one moment that he had selected me out of that bevy of young girls because of my beauty, or whatever; I think he was trying to impress my Mother, who had that effect on most men. She was impressed, all right, and probably to his own surprise, he went on to suggest a screen test for me, leading us to assume that he was a director, or someone equally important. When he said that he would arrange a screen test at the Douglas Fairbanks studio, to *my* surprise, Mother agreed to it, asking where and when. Poor Mr. Gerrard; he was cornered! So he set it up for the next day, took his leave and left us floating on Cloud Nine.

To me, it was the possible entry into a new world - the world of acting. To Mother, it was nothing so pretentious; it was merely the opportunity to actually see the inside of a movie studio. It must be remembered, that back in 1920, Hollywood wasn't the open book it is today. It was a mysterious, fairy tale place which only a handful of people had ever seen, except for those who worked there, and to the average American they were a breed apart. Today, my teen-age granddaughter and all her friends know how movies are made and would probably feel right at home in front of a motion picture camera,...but, not in 1920.

It was tacitly understood that we couldn't mention this adventure to Daddy. We knew instinctively that he would have considered it nonsense; he might even have forbidden my going. (Oh, yes, Fathers in those days could forbid things).

So we waited until he had left for his golf game, then off Mother and I drove to the Fairbanks Studio. Mr. Gerrard was there as promised, but to my disappointment Fairbanks was in Europe. I think Mother was disappointed too, although she didn't say so. However, Mr. Gerrard was affability itself; he ushered us in and introduced us to the casting director, a bosomy lady named Mrs. Wood. Then, explaining that it was better not to have spectators when a test was being made, he wafted Mother off to the commissary for a cup of coffee. As I saw Mother disappear, I felt like a six year old on her first day at school.

Mrs. Wood escorted me to the studio, which was not what I had expected; it was more like a big barn, almost deserted. Someone then took me into a little cubicle smelling of grease paint and glue. That was the make-up room, with the make-up man waiting for me. He looked at me gloomily, shook his head, and told me to sit in front of a small table which had a mirror surrounded by bright lights. I stared at myself in the mirror, and the make-up man stared at me. Then, with a sigh he said "We gotta get that mouth down. It's much too big. Lillian Gish, that's what we want. Lillian Gish." And, he started covering my face with pink grease paint.

Of all the actresses in the world, both here and abroad, the one I am least like is Lillian Gish. But I didn't protest; I just sat there while he valiantly attempted to reduce my "generous" mouth to a Gish Rosebud. Then he drew black circles around my eyes and handed me a cube of something black, telling me to spit on it. I thought he was making fun of me. With another deep

Mary Pickford - Douglas Fairbanks Studios

sigh he explained that it was mascara and I was to put it on my eyelashes with the little brush. So I dabbed some on, making a few lashes stick together, which gave me rather a startled look.

Then the hairdresser came in, picked up my long mass of hair, shook her head sadly, and said, "Gee, I dunno, honey. How do you usually put it up?".

I had to tell her I didn't know either; I had never worn it up. I must say for her that she tried. She made the damnedest coiffure I've ever seen, with rolls and curls, and as a final touch, she stuck a large Spanish comb in the top roll. When I followed her out to what I heard them call "the set", I felt as though I was balancing a bowl of fruit on my head. Thus, I entered that alien land of cameras and Klieg lights and reflectors, hearing jargon that to me was a foreign language—"Hit the lights"— "Kill the reflector"—"O.K., we're rolling"—and wondered what I was doing there. I even wished that I were at home or back on the beach or in school, or anywhere else but there."

The set was a street scene, and in addition to the lights, there was a bright sun directly overhead. The cameraman said, "Look, sweetheart, I'm getting a halation from your dress. Somebody find her something else." From somewhere, someone brought a heavy embroidered Spanish shawl and draped it across my shoulders. It kept slipping, so I clutched it tightly over one hip which more or less held it in place.

Someone yelled "Quiet! We're rolling!", and someone else said "Okay, start walking." So, I did, but then he yelled, "No, Sweetheart, toward the camera," so I looked around and walked toward where I thought the camera was, but I couldn't see it; the sun was in my eyes.

I was almost beginning to enjoy myself by the time the test was over. Mother drove me back home in a hurry, so we would have time to get the makeup off before Daddy got home. I asked her if she had had a nice time with Mr. Gerrard, but all she said was that he was a very nice man who talked a great deal—mostly about Mr. Gerrard! One thing she had learned about him; he wasn't actually a director, more sort of a friend and trusted advisor to Douglas Fairbanks. Years later I learned he was more of a court jester to Fairbanks, who gave him an occasional part in a picture, but mostly used him as the butt of his jokes. I still don't know how he had the authority to order the test for me. Anyway, we were told to be back the next day at three o'clock, and we were there promptly and told to go to the projection room, whatever that was. Off Mother and I went, back to the studio where a woman showed us into a small room with seats much like a theatre. Mr. Gerrard wasn't there but some other men in dark business suits, many puffing on cigars, strolled in and seated themselves. Then the lights went out, a hum came from behinds us, a shaft of light struck the screen and there it was, the street, the lamp post, the fronts of buildings... and then, this girl started walking from the far end of the street toward the camera. She was awkward and wore a Spanish shawl which she couldn't manage. The fringe trailed in the dust, and once, her legs got tangled in it and she stumbled.

Now, she was close to the camera. A grimace distorted the rosebud mouth; that's where the director had said, "Pretend you're flirting with someone behind the reflector." There was a panicky glance toward the camera and a flutter of smudged eyelashes. The convolution of rolls and curls made the head of that girl look so out of proportion she seemed deformed. And when the Spanish comb slipped and hung at an impossible angle, someone in that lethal chamber finally laughed.

All I wanted to do was get away, but it's hard to find your way around a studio when you're not familiar with it. But I grabbed Mother's arm and pulled her out, and on our search for the exit, Mrs. Wood, the bosomy lady, caught sight of us. She pulled us into her office and said what I already knew—the test was awful! Speaking over my head to Mother, she said, "My advice to you, Mrs. Miller, is to take your daughter home, wherever that is, and put her back in school. I believe in being frank; that's what I'm known for. I don't beat around the bush. In my opinion your daughter has nothing in her favor, and it's better to know it now than later!"

"Mark my words," she said. "It will save you a lot of heart break in the long run. She'll never be an actress. She'll never make it, not in a million years!" Mother murmured something and we left. My understanding Mother had the good sense not to say a word on the interminable ride home.

The infamous screen test.

And that is how I was discovered on the beach by a motion picture director and made overnight into a star. In a pig's eye! The moral to this gruesome tale is: Don't Believe Everything You Read—especially about movie actors.

There is a postscript to the story: about two years later, in the Fall of 1922, the first WAMPAS Ball was held. WAMPAS stands for Western Association of Motion Picture Advertisers—imagine my remembering that! The party was to honor the young actresses whom they thought would become stars. They called us The Stars of Tomorrow. I was one of the thirteen they had voted on as most likely to succeed, and I was in Seventh Heaven. Some of the others whom I remember were Lila Lee, Bessie Love, Colleen Moore—some of us made it and some didn't. But that night we all felt like stars.

The affair was held at the new Ambassador Hotel and was really quite elegant. We girls were presented much as debutantes at a Society Cotillion, taking our bows from the stage amid much applause.

As I was wending my way through the tables to rejoin my family, a hand reached out and grabbed me. It was none other than Mrs. Wood, the bosomy Dragon Lady, seated with several couples.

"Patsy dear," she cooed. "Do stop and meet my guests." She rattled off their names, the men rose, the women nodded. Then, patting my hand which she still held, she said, "This is the dear child I was telling you about, the one who made the test at our studio. I saw her talent immediately, I told her mother so, I said, 'Don't take this child away.' Didn't I, dear? I am so glad your mother took my advice, I daresay it is largely due to my encouragement that you are here tonight, isn't it, dear?"

This was the moment I had rehearsed in my mind a thousand times—my Walter Mitty dream of revenge come true. With what slashing phrases, what biting sarcasm, would I bring the bosomy Dragon Lady to her knees? Sobbing contritely, she would implore forgiveness...

These are the slashing phrases with which I heaped coals of fire on her marcelled head: "Thank you, Mrs. Wood. I'll give Mother your regards. Nice to have met you all."

And then I joined my family at our table.

Strangely enough, I didn't regret my lost opportunity. Thinking it over, I decided that getting even is probably more fun to dream about than to do. I've heard it said that "Revenge Is Sweet"—but I'll bet it leaves a bitter after-taste.

The Ambassador Hotel

CHAPTER TWO

Now to tell the real story, I have to go back a bit. I was born and raised in St. Louis, where I attended Mary Institute, a girl's school, until I was sixteen. Every summer our family - Mother, Daddy, my younger brother and I-went to Walloon Lake, in Michigan, where we had a cottage and small outboard motor boat.

The summer of 1920, the pattern changed; It was decided to go instead to Los Angeles to visit my Mother's family who had moved there some years before. My uncle had rented a house for us in Hollywood, and there Mother, my brother Winston and I settled in to await the arrival of my father, who was driving across the country with a baseball pal of his named Mike Donlin.

Today driving across the country is hardly worth a paragraph in the local newspaper; then, it was almost comparable to Columbus crossing the ocean without a chart. There were no Auto Club maps to consult; in fact, there was no Auto Club. Nor were there any highways; only road going from town to town. Sometimes what started out as a road became merely a country lane, sometimes the lane stopped abruptly at someone's farm.

Of course there were very few service stations; you had to carry cans of extra gas, plus jugs of water, not just for drinking, but to fill the radiator. There was no such thing as anti-freeze to keep the motor cool - and if the radiator went dry the car stopped and that was that. You'd be stuck in the desert until some prospector ambled by with his burro. When it was just too hot to travel, Daddy and Mike slept in the shade of the car during the day and drove at night.

Somewhere en route they came upon a camp of railroad workers who were laying the tracks for the Union Pacific, and that was a very welcome respite. The railroad gang thought they were crazy, but made them welcome with food and drink, gave them blankets to sleep under, and sent them on their way with rousing farewells and a bottle of Red-Eye.

They eventually arrived in Hollywood after some arduous three weeks of travel. Meanwhile, I had met some boys and girls my age, and about two months later one of the boys, whose name I don't remember, invited me to a dance at the Hollywood Hotel which was the gathering place for the movie colony. It was rather eyed askance by mid-Western families such as mine, but after some persuasion and assurance that my escort would not carry a pocket flask, and that he would have me home by midnight, I got permission to go. I must explain that pocket flasks were a "must" in those days of Prohibition. Even kids who didn't drink carried them; it was the "in" thing to do. It proved you were sophisticated to order a "set-up" in a hotel or restaurant then secretly (?) pour whiskey in the glass from the pocket flask. Since everybody did it, and everybody knew everybody did it, the whole thing was pretty much of a farce; it would have been funny, except that it started a lot of kids drinking who otherwise wouldn't, and it led to a new form of crime in this country - Bootlegging! Which led to Gangsterism. Which led to Organized Crime. But, enough of that Noble Experiment.

My escort had given me the impression that he was on

After 6 years of Visitation convent school I attended Mary Institute.

LaBrea Avenue, 1920

a first-name basis with lots of celebrities, but the best he could do was point out various stars—Wallace Reid, Viola Dana, Bebe Daniels, Rod la Roque—and although I was thrilled to see them in the flesh, it was becoming something like a studio tour. Then, with a happier note in his voice, he said, "There's Madame!".

I turned and saw a woman seated queen-like in a monstrous pseudo-Spanish chair, her courtiers on each side, and suddenly recognizing her, fairly shouted, "That's Nazimova!". She was wearing a sort of Chinese brocade gown, and looked just as she had in *The Red Lantern*, a picture I had sat through three times.

The Hollywood Hotel, 1920

"We call her Madame," he said, stressing the last syllable. "Everyone who knows her calls her Madame."

"Oh, gosh," I breathed. "Do you really know her?"

"I worked on her set once," he said loftily.

I had no idea what kind of work he had done - I realized later that he must have been an extra—but that didn't matter. He actually knew my idol! I begged so dramatically to be introduced to Madame that he reluctantly plowed through the Palace Guard surrounding her and got close enough to say something which I couldn't hear. She turned and looked at him in such surprise that my heart sank, and I can imagine what his did. But she spoke to him, he said something in reply, and then she waved him aside and leaned forward to look at me. Whatever she saw in my face - admiration, fear, maybe sheer idolatry - it seemed to amuse her, because she smiled and beckoned to me with her long cigarette holder.

My heart was pounding and my knees were trembling as I approached the throne. I don't remember what I said, if anything. I think she asked me the routine questions—where are you from, do you like Hollywood, that sort of thing. I was too fascinated by her incredibly blue eyes, her long red fingernails, and her Russian accent to be aware of what I answered.

I may seem to be overdramatizing this, but it must be remembered that not only was Nazimova the very first movie actress I had ever met, she was far and away my favorite. All the girls at school were movie-mad; their bedroom walls were covered with pictures of their favorite stars, the cute ones - Marguerite Clark, Viola Dana, Mary Pickford. I liked them too, but it was Nazimova who thrilled me. When she suffered, she really suffered, no holds barred. When her love was betrayed, as it frequently was, our collective hearts were broken. In one

23

picture she bore an illegitimate child, which was very daring in those days. In the sub-title it was referred to as a bastard—and, I felt her shame as though I had borne the child myself, though to tell the truth, I had no idea what made the child a bastard.

Anyway, there I was, sitting on a stool at the feet of Hollywood's greatest tragedienne, while my escort hovered unhappily nearby; gradually I lost my self-consciousness and was able to reply to her questions with some degree of intelligence. Something I said made her chuckle - she had a lovely throaty chuckle - and she leaned forward and tapped my cheek with her forefinger.

"You have answered my questions very prettily," she said, "but I think there is something more." Then, seeing my bewilderment, she smiled, showing an unexpected dimple. "I think you would prefer not to return to your very nice girls' school. I think you have a great desire to remain here and become an actress. Am I not right?".

I was absolutely speechless—a condition I seldom suffer from. Since that horrible test I had determined never to even think of such a thing again. I swore to myself that never would I step foot in front of a movie camera - never would I subject myself to another Mrs. Wood. And now this wondrous star had penetrated deep into my innermost soul. "Oh, yes, Madame," I cried, with the fervor of a Bernhardt—or a Nazimova. "Oh, yes."

Madame chuckled again, then she said something in Russian to a man standing beside her. He looked at me with a frown, then he half smiled, shrugged, and said, "Da. Why not?". There was some more talk in Russian, and then, quite seriously, Madame turned back to me and said, "It is possible—not a promise, but possible—that you shall have a small part, a very small part, in my next picture." She chuckled again and said, "Close your mouth. You look like a fish waiting to be caught."

There was some more talk in Russian, than Madame told me to come to the Metro Studio on Santa Monica Boulevard the next day. "You are to be there at three o'clock," she told me. "I may be late, but you are not to be. Understood?"

"Yes, Madame," I said, "and thank you."

"That remains to be seen," she said.

I suppose I danced the rest of the evening with my young escort, and that he got me home safely before the witching hour, but I actually have no recollection of it. Nor do I recall ever seeing that anonymous young man again. I daresay it wasn't the best date he had ever had.

At breakfast the next day I regaled Mother and Daddy with an account of the party, the stars I had seen, and my meeting Nazimova, but I left it at that. I didn't mention the semi-promise of a part in her picture. Mother was thrilled to hear about all the movie stars. Daddy was reluctantly impressed by my description of Madame, and I quit while I was ahead.

By bus and by street car I was at the Metro Studio by two o'clock. It was quite unlike the Fairbanks Studio; it was a labyrinth of cables, lights, and people, bristling

Alla Nazimova in "Camille".

with activity. When Madame arrived, not too long after three, again I was made up, but this time under Madame's supervision. There were no black lines drawn around my eyes, nor was my mouth made into a Cupid's bow. On the set, no one told me to flirt with the camera. They just said, "Look right." "Now look left." " Turn into the camera and smile.". That was easy. When the cameraman asked me which was my good side, before I could tell him I didn't know, Madame said, "Don't be stupid. She doesn't have a bad side." Although I wasn't sure what he had meant, I was relieved to hear that.

Later, when I was taking off the makeup, I heard Madame say, "If she can act at all, she's the perfect Nichette." I didn't know what a Nichette was, but I hoped it was something good.

Metro Studios, 1921.

24

CHAPTER THREE

It was something good, the role of the little shopgirl, Camille's friend, in the coming production of that sad lady's life. Although a very small part, and it became even smaller in the cutting room, it was a beginning.

It would be lovely to say that I played Nichette, was an overnight sensation, and rocketed to fame and fortune. It would be lovely, but it wouldn't be true. In the first place Camille wasn't nearly ready to go into production, and in the second place, according to Madame, I wasn't ready either.

A few days after the test, Madame summoned me to her office to tell me that the test was quite good; I was the right size and the right age, but woefully lacking in experience. But that could be corrected, she said. What I must do now was get work as an extra. Then, with a reassuring smile, she told me that she would be interested to hear of my progress and that I should report to her every now and then. If she was not at the studio, she said, I had permission to come to her house on Sunset Boulevard to make my report which, knowing me, she was sure would be amusing, if not informative.

Of course I had to let Mother in on it, and she was thrilled. Naturally, she said, she would chaperone me if I ever did get work as an extra; naturally, I agreed, some of my enthusiasm dampened. "We won't mention it yet to Daddy," she said, and again I agreed.

The first step was to get professional photos taken, so we picked the name of a photographer out of the telephone book, who turned out to be very cooperative when we told him what the pictures were for. He draped me in tulle, posed my hands in impossible positions, and made several plates, chatting all the while, and explaining to us how to register with the Central Casting Bureau, what information to put on the back of the photos, and other such professional details.

I had a mental picture of the Central Casting Bureau, perhaps from something I had read; it would be a sad place where would-be actors sat around day after day, waiting for a day's work, hoping for that big break—but, it wasn't at all like that. It was more like a big club; they all seemed to know each other, and most of the talk was about what they had been doing last night, or what they planned to do tonight. I didn't hear any discussions about acting, but they did sometimes exchange information about which assistant director was a good one to know, or which studio was putting out a call for a mob scene.

I got quite a bit of work during the next few months, and although I didn't learn much about acting, I did learn how to put on my own makeup, and how to avoid getting tangled in the cables. It still surprised me that the other extras seemed to have so little interest in anything but being called back the next day. I wonder if it's still like that—if most extras are content to be just a face in the crowd, or do some of them yearn for stardom, as I did?

I recall one who did. I first saw him on the set of a comedy I was doing with Cullen Landis. I noticed him because of his interest in everything that was going on. He didn't sit around playing cards between scenes; he watched and listened intently. You could almost feel

William Hays visits Central Casting, 1922

Alla Nazimova's bungalow at Metro Studios.

him storing up knowledge. He was young, probably not much older than I, but at first I didn't realize it, as he was made up to look older. He had asked permission to make up that way, he told me, because he wanted to play character parts and this seemed a good way to practice.

Several times that week I sat between scenes and chatted with him. I learned that he had served overseas in the War; that he was glad to be home in one piece, that he would volunteer again if our country ever got into another war, and that he hoped some day to be more than an extra. I sincerely hoped he would make it, because he was a truly nice young man.

He did make it. His name was Walter Brennan.

One thing I did learn from working as an extra was how strongly my father felt on the subject. One day he returned home unexpectedly from a fishing trip and caught me in my makeup before my Mother and I had had a chance to break it to him tactfully. He fairly erupted.

"This is the damndest nonsense I've ever heard," he said—and he was a man who did not swear in front of his family—"To think that my own wife and daughter would deceive me like this!" There was more along the same line; an eavesdropper might well have thought he had just discovered I was with child by C.B. deMille.

When he finally wound down, Mother went into her calming act. First she reminded him that he had been off golfing and fishing; she had had no chance to tell him anything. And when he was home in the evening, it had simply slipped her mind. Before he could think of an answer she hastily assured him that she had been on the set with me every moment—which was true—and that not one ungentlemanly word had ever been uttered in

Walter Brennan far left.

my presence—which was perhaps not quite true. Furthermore—this was the clincher—several of the directors for whom I had worked were terrific baseball fans, and were greatly impressed to learn that Ty Cobb was a personal friend of ours.

That did it. No baseball fan could be all bad!

William Crane, Patsy Ruth Miller and Buster Keaton. We were just tourists watching the Keaton company shooting on a street corner. Despite the look Buster is giving me, it was my Mother to whom he said. You oughtta be in pictures. My Father said, No she aughtn't—and that was the end of her career. A few years later I met Buster in the studio commissary and he said, with that famous dead-pan. "It looks like I bet on the wrong horse, didn't I?" I thought that was very cute of him.

Mrs. Miller, Patsy Ruth, Ty Cobb, Mrs. Cobb and son

It was true that Mother had been with me on every set, sitting demurely behind the camera and flirting mildly with the director. No one ever objected to her presence; apparently she was not considered a typical pain-in-the-neck Movie Mother, as was the mother of Mary Miles Minter.

And, I daresay that Daddy (and even Mother) thought of it as a Summer frivolity to be forgotten in September when we would all return to St. Louis, and I would go back to Mary Institute.

Patsy Ruth Miller, Lois Wilson and May McAvoy

The comedy team of Lyons and Moran welcome Mr. Miller, Winston and Patsy Ruth

27

There was one incident of my "extra" days that still makes me giggle when I think of it. I was working on the set of a Wallace Reid movie. Wallace Reid was—how to describe him?—the Robert Redford of his day, one of the most popular stars, young and handsome, and with a certain flair which so few of the young actors today seem to have.

Just a week or so before we left for California, Wallace Reid had made a personal appearance at our local outdoor movie theatre in St. Louis, and of course we all went to see him—Mother, Daddy, my kid brother and myself. My brother Winston, who was then about ten years old, bore a truly remarkable resemblance to Wallace Reid. People often commented on it.

Reid made a nice little speech, expressing the hope that we would enjoy the picture which would follow; then he stepped down from the stage and made his way down the aisle, greeting his fans as he went. We were at the very back, too thrilled to do anything but look at him, but as he approached, my brother Winston said "Hello, Mr. Reid."

Reid stopped, looked at my brother, and did a doubletake. Turning to the man with him, probably his P.A., he said, "Irving, have I ever played St. Louis before?".

My father grinned, my mother said "Well, really!" and then she giggled, and I sat there naively thinking it was pretty dumb of him not to know if he had ever been in St. Louis before.

This is leading up to the day I was an extra on his set. He had made some funny remark to Bebe Daniels, who was playing opposite him. At least, I supposed it was funny, because she laughed and said, "Oh, Wallie, you're terrible!" Then he noticed me and said, "Oh, Oh, kindergarten's in session" which offended me. I was terribly sensitive about my youth, which he must have realized, because he came over to me, smiled his adorable smile, and said "I don't believe I've seen you before, have I?"

"Not exactly," I said, "But I've seen you before." Then I told him about seeing him when he made his personal appearance in St. Louis a few months before. "You said hello to my brother," I told him. "He's only ten, but he looks exactly like you, everybody says so. Do you remember? You asked somebody if you played St. Louis before."

"Now I remember" he said, and broke into a grin— and at that moment, at the age of sixteen going on seventeen, it dawned on me what had made Daddy chuckle and Mother giggle. I could feel a blush starting at my neck and going right up to my forehead.

Do you know what that darling man did? He managed to refrain from laughing, and he said very seriously, "When you go home you tell your father that I had never been in St. Louis before in my life."

When, after some deep thought, I decided to tell Daddy what had happened, he laughed and said, "What a relief!"

That was my only contact with Wallace Reid, and yet when he died, so young, I felt bereaved.

After some hesitancy, one day I took Madame up on

Winston Miller

Wallace Reid

28

her invitation to drop in and report on my progress, if any. She made me so welcome that soon I was making a habit of it, going to see her two or three times a week when I wasn't working, instead of going to the beach. She seemed to enjoy my descriptions of the various directors, and my sometimes rather cruel imitations of the female stars. Other times, I had tid-bits of gossip, the real reason shooting was held up for an hour on the deMille set, what the cameraman said to the leading lady when he didn't know I was within earshot; what the assistant director threatened to do to the heavy if he didn't lay off whatever it was he was doing.

Sometimes Madame made me laugh myself into the hiccups with her pithy descriptions of some of Hollywood's Great and Near Great. She was contemptuous of the baby-faced blondes who were flooding the screen. The quivering lip, the downcast eye, filled her with nausea, she claimed. Such pallid emotions, such saintly sufferings were not for her. Nor for me, I vowed to myself. When my turn came I would spare no one's feelings... I would suffer as Nazimova had suffered in *The Red Lantern*.

I remember once complaining that with all my work as an extra I didn't seem to be learning very much, and her crisp comment—"On the contrary, I think you are learning rather too much."

Finally, late in the summer, Madame called a meeting at the studio to which I was summoned; it was for the cast to meet the director—and vice versa—and to be given some idea of when *Camille* would go into production. The director, a gentle, depressed-looking man named Ray Smallwood, became even more depressed when he met me and learned that he was going to have another inexperienced member of the cast, the first being a young Italian with the improbable name of Rudolph Valentino. He was to play Armand to Nazimova's *Camille*, an important role for a beginner.

Valentino had at least gained some experience in a picture being made at the same studio. It was called *The Four Horsemen of the Apocalypse*, and the rumor was that it was better than its title. It had not yet been released, but the front office reported that this newcomer had possibilities. Mr. Smallwood obviously didn't believe this report, and the only ray of light in his gloomy world was that mine was a very small part.

Rudy, as I soon came to call him, having finished *The Four Horsemen*, was waiting, as I was, for *Camille* to start. I, at least, had occasional extra work to fill the void. He was in limbo. So both of us spent as much time as possible at Madame's house and in her enormous swimming pool. There were many golden days, that late summer, when Madame's house was filled with people and the garden swarmed with Russian emigres, but the days I loved best were when only Rudy and I were there. We swam and ducked each other and vied for Madame's attention. His persistent but unsuccessful attempts to teach me to dive amused her so much that I cheerfully got water up my nose and turned blue with cold to be rewarded us her hearty laugh.

But there were other days when she was all alone in the big house, and those were the days I liked the best.

Frequently I would find her at work on the *Camille* script. June Mathis, a very competent writer, was doing the screenplay, and it must have irked her to feel Nazimova treading on her literary heels, with a cut here and a revision there. Madame may not have known much about writing, but she knew what she liked. And at that time she knew what the public liked. Later the two tastes didn't always coincide.

Dave Thompson, Dick Butler, C. Shulter and Ray Smallwood, Metro California, 1921.

Valentino, June Mathis and Rex Ingram during "The Four Horsemen of the Apocalypse."

June Mathis working on the "Camille" script.

Nazimova's house on Sunset Boulevard.

I can't recall that her comments ever spoiled my appetite.

When she put on her glasses—which she never wore in public—and seated herself at the desk always untidy with papers and ledgers, I knew I was to be quiet. I'd sprawl on the floor, reading, or watching her, or just day-dreaming; often we would sit in silence for an hour or more. Then finally she would push the papers away with a wry grimace, take off her glasses, and throw her arms in the air like a child released from class. Lessons were over—the time had come to talk.

"I'm not learning very much," I complained one day. "I watch, and I listen —and that's hard to do when you're an extra, you know—but I don't feel that I'm really *learning* anything. About acting, I mean."

"Why is it hard when you're an extra?" she wanted to know.

She'd look at me over the script, shake her head sadly, and ask me if I was hungry. I always was. She claimed to be awed by my appetite; "Pure peasant", she called my taste in food, being herself a hearty eater, but discriminating. "Go ask the cook if there's any desert left from last night," she'd say with a resigned air. "You'll love it. It is horrible. Rich, sweet, fattening, *degoutant*. And by all means have a pickle with it. You wouldn't look natural without a pickle. . . and when I would return with a heaping plateful— and the pickle—she would say severely," Not only is your head hollow, but both legs as well. You will have the figure of a barrel before you are my age." Or, very grumpily, "You are eating me out of house and home—but at least you don't talk so much when you're full, so it's worth it."

"Because they're not interested in acting. They make fun of you if you are. . . all they're interested in is getting called back the next day. They never pay any attention to what's going on. Sometimes they don't even know the name of the picture; all they know is that it's a job. All they talk about is what set is using extras, and who the assistant is - he's the one who calls them, you know. Honestly, they think you're silly if you ask questions, or try to watch the scenes you're not in."

"So they are extras," she said. "What has that to do with you? You are either going to become an actress—or go back to school. Is that not so?"

I agreed rather doubtfully.

"Then, as you have no intention of making extra work your career, how can it possibly matter what they think of you? So you must go on watching, listening, asking questions—not stupid ones, though—and you will learn a little bit every day, even if you don't know you are learning. And maybe by the time you play Nichette you will know something."

We were in the downstairs music room; a small room, less formal than the others, though hardly what one would call cozy. Dominating the room was a larger-than-life portrait of Nazimova, as Hedda Gabler. She looked very tall, the Gibson Girl costume accentuating her height; the high boned collar, the long tight sleeves coming down over the wrists, the tiny waist swirling out into a skirt which swept the floor were most becoming in an odd way. Looking down at her from my magnificent height of five feet almost-two inches, I said, "The clothes must have fooled the artist. He painted you too tall."

"The artist was not fooled," she said. "He painted me as he saw me... as everyone saw me. I *was* tall. When I played Hedda Gabler I was very tall and stately."

I glanced down at the little flat Chinese slippers she was wearing.

"No, you ninny," she said. "Not because I wore high heels—because I *felt* tall. I *thought* tall. I happen to be an actress. A very good actress."

"Yes," I murmured, "I've heard rumors."

"Contrary to most Hollywood rumors," she said solemnly, "They're quite true. And being a good actress, I am neither tall nor short, fat nor thin, ugly or beautiful. I am what the part demands of me. So when I played Hedda Gabler I was tall."

"I see," I said—although I didn't, quite. "Makeup has a lot to do with it, too—hasn't it?"

She shrugged. "It helps—but it is not the most important thing. Mind you, I am speaking of a true actress; an artist. Offstage she may be a nothing—a zero. But on stage—ah, then she is whatever the author has written that she is. If he has written that she is beautiful, then she believes herself to be beautiful, and so does the audience. It is a form of mass hypnosis."

"Like when you played "The Brat," I agreed wisely—but not tactfully. "That was only last year, but you looked awfully young."

"I was Youth Incarnate," she said, "and I do not need a reminder from you that last year I was twenty years past my teens. The lesson is over for today. Now we shall have our tea—although you don't deserve any."

A few days later, after we had finished our glasses of hot, strong tea, I led her back to the subject of acting—a subject I never tired of. This time I approached it a little more diplomatically by exclaiming that it had been hard to believe that she was Richard Barthelmess' mother in *War Brides*, a picture which had reduced me to a sodden pulp, although I frankly hadn't understood it completely.

"I should think not," she said. "I'm surprised you were even allowed to see it."

I let that pass. "You were so different in *Revelation*," I said. "And *The Red Lantern*." And *Out Of The Fog*.

She flashed me an impish grin. "Another lesson?"

"Tell me about stage acting,"I begged. "I wish I had seen you on the stage."

"Listening," she said thoughtfully. "To listen is as important as to speak. Not to twiddle, you understand; not to use tricks to get the attention of the audience. No—merely to listen, as though you were hearing the words for the first time. Did I ever tell you about Duse?"

"No, I don't think so. What about her?"

"You know who Duse is?"

Did I know who Duse was! I scorned to answer.

"She is a great one for listening," Nazimova said with a reminiscent smile. "I shall tell you what happened a few years ago in Paris..."

Duse was playing in Paris, she told me, and sent Nazimova tickets for the show. In the first act, the great Italian actress captured the hearts of her audience. As the curtain went up on the second act it disclosed a street scene before a cathedral. On the steps of the cathedral crouched an old beggar woman muffled in rags, her face hidden by a tattered shawl. Various minor characters entered and left the scene, their bits of dialogue furthering the plot, but the old beggar woman said nothing. She simply sat, huddled in her rags—but aware of everyone who passed. One felt that her unseen eyes missed nothing, that she heard every word that was spoken—storing it away in her memory, perhaps for future use.

The eyes of the audience turned to her again and again, and all, including Nazimova, expected her to return in the ensuing scenes with a dramatic role. She did not re-appear, however; the play went on, Duse scored her usual triumph, and the curtain fell on an enthusiastic but strangely disappointed audience.

When Nazimova went backstage to visit her friend, she found the director in Duse's dressing room. He was in a fine Gallic rage, threatening dire punishment to the beggarwoman, should he find her.

"That was not the actress who always plays the part?" Nazimova asked.

"Of course not!" the director fumed. "It was an imposter! A substitute! She ruined the scene. Everyone watched her... everyone waited for her to come on again. I was in the back of the house—I could sense their disappointment. It was a disaster!"

He appealed to Duse, who seemed singularly unperturbed, "My apologies, Signora Duse. No one admits to knowing who she was, but I shall find her! And when I do—I shall either kill her—or offer her a role in my next production."

Duse burst out laughing. "I beg of you, Signor, don't kill her. She only meant it as a little joke—" she turned to Nazimova; "I thought it would amuse, you, Alla. I wondered if you would recognize her."

For of course the beggar woman had been Duse herself.

Years later, watching Nazimova in a performance of Ibsen's "Ghosts", I recalled that story. There were three people on stage: the doctor, the son, and Nazimova. The scene—a very dramatic one—was between the two men. She sat quietly on the far side of the stage, with not

31

a line to speak; she made no movement, she seemed hardly to breathe, yet she gave the impression of being passionately concerned with what was being said. So intently did she listen that the audience seemed to hear the words through her ears, understand them through her mind.

Duse, indeed!

Until I learned to defend myself—verbally, that is—Rudy Valentino and I didn't get along very well. He teased me so unmercifully that on several occasions, unable to think of a cutting retort, I resorted to attempted mayhem. These skirmishes amused Madame very much, although she pretended to deplore our constant bickering.

Once, I remember, he accused me of becoming boy-crazy, and I haughtily replied that I hadn't just discovered boys—I'd known about them for a long, long time. he repeated this simple statement of fact to Madame as though it were a great witticism, to my rather pleased bewilderment.

The Valentino whom I knew isn't at all the one I've since read about—the Great Lover. He was really an outdoor man; he loved sports and horses and was a truly magnificent rider. The fact that he never saw me as anything but an obstreporous kid doesn't mean that he didn't have an eye for the ladies, but conquest was not an obsession, as implied by the fan magzines.

Rudy was 25 years old but from the very beginning his attitude toward me was that of a stern Italian older brother, so I never saw the side that attracted such sophisticates as Pola Negri.

Perhaps it was the public image, as much as the man himself, which intrigued them. That image, created by the Press, certainly did him no harm, and he may even have tried to live up to it, but I don't think his heart was in it. Not, at least, when I knew him.

Despite the Charleston, the Flapper vogue, Prohibition and its gangsters, the 1920's was an age of innocence—and I was one of the most innocent. Rudy seemed determined to keep it that way. Maybe I could have had a crush on him if he hadn't treated me with the tolerant amusement of an older brother, but as it was, we swam in Madame's pool like two happy otters. He tried to teach me Chess, which I never mastered. He was extremely critical of everything I wore, particularly my one-piece bathing suits—with skirts, mind you—and deplored the unattractive style of wearing stockings rolled below the knee—a style which, thank goodness, has not yet returned.

Horses were his first love, but good food was definitely his second, good food meaning Italian. In that respect I was also a disappointment to him, as the only Italian food I had ever heard of was spaghetti. Rudy was shocked at my lack of understanding of gourmet cooking; in fact, at my lack of understanding of *any* cooking. Not that we didn't eat well at home, but it was more the simple Southern-American style than French or Italian.

I explained to Rudy that I came from a long line of non-cookers; neither of my grandmothers knew how to boil an egg, and the most my Mother had ever achieved in the culinary arts was to make burnt fudge. It was hardly my fault, I told Rudy quite simply, that I had never learned how to broil spaghetti. Or do you fry it?

He was horrified to the depths of his Latin soul.

"You know what will happen you?" he said in a voice of doom. "You have any idea what will become you?"

"No," I said, "What will become me?"

"You will never get a husband is what! Don't be laughing. I tell you true. Lovers, maybe, when you grow up. No husband, never."

I fooled him, three times. Poor Rudy, he also fooled himself. He married Natacha Rambova, nee Winifred Hudnut, (of the perfume Hudnuts) who cared only for "Art" with a very Capital A, and who, I am sure, never even made burnt fudge. Rambova did the sets for *Camille*, as well as having a hand in designing Madame's costumes. It was all frightfully avant garde and to my eye almost grotesque. It was Madame's idea to bring *Camille* up to the Twentieth Century, which might have worked, but Rambova went far beyond that—which didn't work. She leaned rather heavily on the bizarre, both in decor and personal appearance. Having been a ballerina, she wore her hair parted in the center and pulled back into the typical ballerina knot. She wore flat shoes, walked with her toes pointed out, and went in heavily for floaty draperies and long beady necklaces. I never saw her dance, but I'm sure it was "interpretive".

Why Rudy fell for her I could never figure out. But then, so did Madame. Perhaps she was an artist after all—a con artist.

Valentino with Natasha Rambova.

CHAPTER FOUR

By the weirdest of coincidences I *did* find out how he happened to come to America and why he had been left waiting at the boat. But it was too late to tell Rudy about it; he had been dead for many years.

It was on a bleak day in Scotland, just after the Second World War. I was there with a charming Scotsman. There was still a program of austerity, which meant food rationing, as well as shortages of almost everything that makes life enjoyable, so we had flown over laden with foodstuffs, rashers of bacon, Hershey bars, fresh oranges, whatever we could carry. I even managed to juggle a half carton of eggs in my oversized handbag, and landed without having made it into an omelet, which my charming Scot had warned me would happen.

In return for a pound of butter and a few fresh lemons, a friend had asked me to tea. I gallantly insisted I liked my scones butterless, not having the heart to use any of the butter I had given her. The tea was served by a gaunt middle-aged woman who looked more Slavic than Scottish, but all she said was "Yes, Modom," in the typically English way, with no perceptible accent, so I didn't give it another thought.

When the maid had left the room, Doreen, my hostess, leaned over and whispered, "Do you remember a cinema star named Valentino?" I did indeed, I told her. "Well," said Doreen, nodding toward the door, "she knew him personally."

I thought this very unlikely, but just said, "Really? How amazing."

When we had had our tea—with powdered milk—Doreen begged me to excuse her for half an hour or so; petrol was being dispensed at the local filling station and she had to be there on the dot for her ration, or she wouldn't get any until next week. She hurried off, and the housekeeper came in to take the tea tray.

"I understand you knew Rudolph Valentino," I said.

"Yes, Modom," she said, picking up the tray and starting to leave the room.

"I knew him too."

"Did you now. Would you be wanting anything further?"

By now I had concluded that the only way she knew him was from a shilling seat in the cinema, but for some reason I said, "I worked with him once, in Hollywood."

Her manner changed completely; her whole face seemed to loose it angularity. "You were in the theatre? You were an actress?"

"Yes, I was. For many years."

"I, too. You were in the cinema with him?"

When I nodded, she shook her head in wonderment. "You knew Rodolpho... I also. And we meet here."

By now I was beginning to believe that perhaps she had known Rudy, unlikely as it seemed. "Tell me about it," I said. "I'm really interested."

She frowned thoughtfully, then with sudden decision she said, "You wait a moment, I return." and she took the tray out of the room. In less than a minute she was back. "I shall tell you," she said, "because you are of the theatre." And, leaning against the doorway, in slightly accented English with a few Scottish expressions thrown in, she told me this story:

She was a Ballerina, a great Ballerina, in the days before the First World War. Although Polish, she had studied in Russia and had danced before the crowned heads of Europe. In those days, she reminded me, there had been quite a number of them. One of her admirers had been a German Prince, high in the diplomatic service, and in an exchange of favors she sent his Government certain information as she danced her way across the Continent. She took chances, but she was amply repaid, she assured me with a smile of surprising warmth. He was a generous men, her Prince.

She danced in Italy—Milano, I believe she said—and there a young Italian student fell in love with her. He was much younger than she, but so ardent. She had not intended to be unfaithful to her Prince, but there it was. Every night the young student watched from the audience, every night he came backstage... It was a scandal and his family was upset, but what could one do. These things occur...

When the troupe left Italy, the young student left also, left the University, left his family, left the life he had always known. He wanted only to be with her, so she trained him to be a dancer; it was not difficult, he had natural grace he was accepted into the troupe. In the chorus only, of course.

For six months, perhaps longer, he traveled with her. It was in Paris that the blow fell. She received secret word from her German Prince that the French were not unaware of her activities, that it was not safe for her in France; there would soon be a war, the message said; all Europe might be involved. She would be safest in Germany.

She did not want to return to Germany. Poles were not welcome in Russia. The long arm of the French Surete reached far. Then where to go? If there was to be a war in Europe, the best place to go would be America. She could dance there, she had already had offers...

So it was decided. Through the influence of friends in certain high places she obtained the necessary papers. She bought passage on a ship and sent her young student on ahead to make sure all was arranged. Then suddenly, all was kaput. The police took her papers—her ticket, her passport—it was only through the kindness of a former lover that she escaped into Spain...

There was no way to get word to the young student. Perhaps he was already on board the ship, waiting... perhaps he had gone back to Milano... How was one to know that when she did not arrive he would go on to

33

Occasionally I was allowed to stay for one of Madame's dinner parties, a privilege Rudy often enjoyed. She seemed to feed half the Russina emigres in Hollywood. They were a fascinating group, some of whom became actors, some directors, some took whatever jobs they could get. Many, however, merely remained White Russians; to dine out when they could, to go hungry when they couldn't or, if lucky, to marry an heiress.

I remember Leopold Godowski, the famous pianist, and his film actress daughter, Dagmar. Dagmar was not much older than I in actual years, but in sophistication, she made me feel like a kindergarten tot.

For instance, it was mandatory in those days of prohibition, to have cocktails before dinner, but none were ever offered to me, although Dagmar could have one if she wanted it. I was permitted a glass of wine with my dinner; Madame claimed that I had a distressing appetite for all the wrong foods, so she felt it her duty to give me one civilized taste. Eventually, I learned to enjoy wine with my meals, although my preference then would have been Root Beer or Coca Cola.

There were also people of the theatre, of course, among whom I remember Eva LeGallienne. One evening she started to tell an anecdote of the theatre then abruptly, with a wry glance at me, switched smoothly into French, whereupon Madame said, "She speaks it abominably but she understands it quite well," which stopped Miss LeGallienne in mid-sentence.

Another time Rudy began the story of how he happened to come to America. As far as it went it bore no resemblance to the many stories later published in the fan magazine. But Madame said something to him in Italian, and he said, "Oh, scusi" and that was the end of that story.

Later I protested to Madame. Rudy was only a few years older than I, as I pointed out with devastating logic; if he could tell it, why couldn't I hear it? But my irrefutable logic had no effect; Madame would take no nonsense, and that was that. I felt aggrieved. It had sounded fascinating, as far as it went. There had been something about a ballerina, something about being left waiting at the boat, and now I would never find out how Rudy happened to come to America.

Cameraman Paul Ivano, Nazimova, Valentino, Natasha Rambova, and Patsy Ruth on a picnic break during the shooting of "Camille".

Courtesy Tod Firetag, Poster City

America without her? But why not? The passage was paid for; America was everyone's dream; he would have been foolish to have done otherwise.

When the war came, as her Prince had said it would, she was at least safe in Spain. It was not too bad. She survived, with the help of an admiring Spaniard... and after that, there were her jewels to be sold.

Seven years later she saw her young student again—on the screen. He was called Valentino.

I had been expecting this, of course, but still for a moment I couldn't think of anything to say.

"If that will be all, Modom" she said, and started out.

"Wait a minute," I burst out. "Didn't you try to reach him? Didn't you write or anything?".

She turned and looked at me again angular and expressionless. "Why should I? I was no longer the beautiful young ballerina he had known."

At that moment we heard Doreen come in the house. With a typically British "Thenk you" she left the room, just as Doreen entered. Waiting until the housekeeper was out of earshot, Doreen said, "Tell me all about it. Did you ask her about Valentino?"

"No," I said, "I didn't think to mention it."

At some time during that period when I was waiting for *Camille* to start, my father had financial problems of some sort, probably to do with his business in St. Louis. I just gathered that because Mother would occasionally say, "No, dear, we can't afford a new dress for the party, wear the one you have, it looks fine", or "Let's not go to Santa Barbara this weekend, it's so expensive." I had never heard her say anything like that before; she was not a spendthrift, but she did like to go shopping, and she loved buying new clothes for me. Money was never discussed in front of the children, but I overheard enough to worry me; I think I had visions of going to the poorhouse, or standing in front of a theatre with a tin cup. I also had a sense of guilt. Maybe it was my fault; maybe if we hadn't stayed in California it wouldn't have happened.

(To relieve the reader's mind, whatever the problem was, it apparently was solved; by the next year Mother was again taking me on shopping binges, and Daddy renewed his membership in the golf club.)

I thought I was very careful not to say anything about money—or the lack of it—in front of Madame. I felt it would be disloyal to my Father to have let anyone know that we couldn't afford a new car... or anything we wanted. Mostly, I daresay, anything I wanted.

How naive I was to think that I had fooled Madame; that those strange blue eyes, which had seen so much, had not looked through my pitiful pretenses and seen the worried girl behind them. I seldom left her house without a gift of some sort, but never presented as a gift; rather, in such a way that it seemed I was doing her a favor by accepting it. So well did she understand my youthful pride that she never gave me anything practical, only the fripperies so dear to a young girl's heart, so impossible to fit into our limited budget.

I remember a dinner hat, the first I ever owned, a frothy bit of nonsense in which I felt so *soignee* I could quite forget that the dress I was wearing was Mother's, taken in a bit at the waist. Madame had just happened to be trying it on one day when I stopped by. She tore if off impatiently, exclaiming that she must have been mad when she bought it, that it was much too *jeune fille* for her.

"It's for someone like you," she said. "God knows you're *jeune fille* enough."

Somehow it never occurred to me to wonder why she had bought it for herself, it being well known that Nazimova never wore hats. There were countless other things; earrings which, she claimed, pinched her ears—but didn't pinch mine. Scarves which matched nothing she had, but matched a dress of mine perfectly. Gloves from Paris, too small for her—or too large. Whatever it was they always seemed to be just my size.

There was a turquoise-colored necklace, not particularly valuable, but a luscious color. "It dresses up black," Madame said. "That little black frock of yours—it needs something like this, if you happen to like turquoise. For myself, I am frightfully bored with it."

Dear Madame—I no longer wear little black frocks; black is not so becoming at my age. But I still love turquoise, and I still have the beads of that necklace, tucked away in a box with other bits and pieces that I never wear but cannot bear to part with.

37

CHAPTER FIVE

Camille finally got under way in January, just after my seventeenth birthday. That we were still in California was not because of my possible career, but because my parents had fallen in love with it, and kept putting off a return to St. Louis. It seems that Daddy had gone back on business during one of the worst Autumns they had ever had: rain, humidity and more rain. (God was on my side). So, it was decided to stay in the golf-and-tennis climate until Christmas. He went back to St. Louis in December, with the understanding that we would join him there for Christmas, but again, bless its little heart, my hometown put on a real display of bad weather; snow, sleet, slush, and more snow.

It ended with Daddy selling his business and our house, and Lo and Behold, we became Californians, with a house in Beverly Hills and a roadster for me.

So when the call came to be made up and ready to shoot at nine, I was there at eight. But Madame was already at the studio, a very different Madame, cold and business-like, a tiny Czarina with an eye on every detail. When I came on the set, made up, Madame took one look at me and called for the make-up man in a tone which made it clear that she was not going to compliment him. "Look at her," she demanded. "Very well—she is not beautiful, but neither does her face resemble a pudding with raisins in it."

The make-up man mumbled something about "Yeah, maybe it's a little too light," to which Madame replied that he would do well to remember who was dying of consumption, Camille or Nichette. To his credit, he didn't take it out on me; he put darker powder on my face, muttering "So okay, she's the boss, I thought you looked okay, but she's the boss."

In my first scene I was to be a bride, wearing a high-waisted satin wedding dress which I considered far too youthful, but which Madame had personally selected. When I passed inspection, I was introduced to Rex Cherryman, the very fair, handsome young man who was to play opposite me. He had just come out from New York where he had scored a great success in *The Trial of Mary Dugan*. This was to be his first time before a camera, and he was more nervous than I, if that was possible. Another neophyte to direct seemed almost more than Mr. Smallwood could bear, and he made it quite apparent which did not help to ease my tension.

The set was a small chapel, the scene, the wedding of Gaston (Rex) and Nichette (me). Nazimova wasn't in it; she was supposed to be home, dying as we were being married. The morning was spent on long shots, in which I successively got tangled in my long skirt, tripped on the step to the alter, and dropped my bouquet.

Even the character actor robed as a priest allowed himself a look of pained forbearance as Rex and I alternated in doing things wrong, so that it was nearly noon before we were ready for the closeups.

Poor Mr. Smallwood, looking like a pallbearer at his own funeral, placed us in position before the altar and retreated behind the camera. All we were to do, we were told, was to rise from our knees and go into the traditional embrace after being pronounced man and wife.

The camera would dolly to a close shot of the kiss. Rex and I very selfconsciously rehearsed the embrace a few times for lighting, faking the kiss... on my part, dreading it. My first scene in my first part and I had to kiss a perfectly strange man—and in front of all those people! I wondered if I could go through with it.

Just before the camera started rolling Madame came up to us with an encouraging smile. "You will be lovely, both of you," she said. "Remember, you are very much in love, so it must be a real kiss this time. Hold the kiss until you hear Mr. Smallwood say 'Cut'. Don't move—just hold the kiss until we fade out, understand?".

We two strangers looked at each other and nodded. I tried for a smile, but couldn't make it.

Then, "Lights! Camera! Quiet, we're rolling!"

Rex and I stood there, our backs to the camera but our faces alight with love even though they weren't seen, as the camera dollied up to a close shot. I was the young bride being married to a man I loved with every fiber of my being. At the words, "I now pronounce you man and wife," we turned toward each other, embraced as rehearsed, and kissed.

I could hear the creak of the camera as it rolled up for a tight shot. Then silence. We held the kiss. The lights were hot on my back but no voice cried, "Cut!", so we continued to kiss. I could feel the perspiration trickling down between my shoulder blades. Rex's hands on my back were burning through the white satin wedding gown. I was becoming breathless, but Madame had said to hold the kiss until the director said "Cut", so we held it. It was undoubtedly the longest kiss in screen history.

Finally I could stand it no longer. At the risk of giving up my career before it got off the ground, I pulled away, drew a deep breath, and turned toward the camera, prepared to face Mr. Smallwood's wrath. There was no wrath to face because there was no Mr. Smallwood. In fact, there was no one. The set was deserted. Everyone, even the priest, had sneaked away, presumably to lunch. Rex and I were the only two people in the vast cavernous stage.

For one horrible moment I was shocked and mortified then, as surely as though I had seen it written in letters of fire, I knew that this was Madame's doing, and I started to laugh. Rex obviously thought I had gone stark raving mad until he looked around and saw the empty set, then the expression on his face started me laughing again. I could see a flush of anger creep up his fair skin under the makeup and for a moment I wasn't sure what he was going to do.

"Madame," I said, still laughing. "Oh, Rex... It's Madame."

He still glared for a second, then as realization dawned, he began to chuckle, then to laugh aloud, and at this, Madame came out of hiding, clapping her hands in glee because her plan had worked; this silly gag that she had hoped would break the ice, release the tension, and make us both relax. One by one the members of the crew reappeared, with the exception of Mr. Smallwood, who really had gone to lunch.

There was a lot of good-natured banter, the camera-

39

man telling us we were good sports, the assistant director saying to Rex that he was one lucky guy to which Rex, now in the spirit of the thing replied that if that kiss had been in the script he'd have taken a cut in salary. The head gaffer said, you can sure take a kidding, Miss Miller, and the script girl whispered to me, "You too looked cute up there. They oughtta keep it in the picture."

Later, Madame admitted to me that she had some qualms, wondering how we would take her little joke. "Of you," she said, tapping me lightly on the cheek, "I thought I was sure. Still, one never knows. As for our darling Rex, I could only pray that his sense of humor would be greater then his sense of dignity, and that he would not take the first train back to New York.

"It was touch and go there for a moment," I told her. "You must admit it was a rather extreme remedy."

"It worked didn't it? She gave one of her impish smiles. "The butterflies are gone, no?"

It was true, They had been swept away in a gale of laughter. From then on I felt like a professional, one of the gang. It was a wonderful feeling.

And so I became an actress - a real live movie actress. As smoothly as a seal sliding into water, I entered that alien world of long shots, close ups, quiet! we're rolling!.

In becoming an actress I also became a highschool dropout. I don't like the sound of that, and prefer to merely say, my formal education came to an end... but my real education has continued to this very day. Learning doesn't necessarily stop when you leave school; in fact, it shouldn't. As long as you can read, and think, you can go on learning every day of your life. Drop out indeed!

Nichette - Patsy Ruth Miller

One day, something went wrong on the set; I never knew what it was. It seemed that someone's mistake had caused a delay which, in turn cost the company money. Madame was keenly interested in saving production money as a good deal of it was her own. She was one of the first stars in Hollywood, I believe, who put her own money into her pictures.

Well, Madame fairly blew her top. After blistering everyone, even poor Mr. Smallwood, the director, she dismissed the company for the day, threatening to call off the whole production if the mistake was not promptly rectified or if it ever happened again.

I was so embarrassed at being a witness to the scene that I tried to escape notice by hiding behind a flat, but as she swept out she saw me and motioned imperiously for me to come with her. Feeling like a teacher's pet, I trailed along behind her, out to the waiting limousine where, to my astonishment, she pushed me in ahead of her. She was in a foul mood, she said—that was pretty obvious—and didn't want to talk to anyone. Apparently I didn't count. Not a word was spoken in the car. When we got to her house she went straight up to her big round bedroom with me still trailing along, and threw herself down on the bed. I sat nearby, my hands folded in my lap, and waited, Finally she sat up, gave me one of her winsome smiles, and said in a syrupy sweet little-girl voice... "You think I behaved badly, don't you?"

I just sort of shrugged, and looked down at my hands.

"Come now," she said. "You are one of the few people I know who doesn't bother to lie to me. Tell me truly what you think." "Well..." I took a deep breath. "You made Mr. Smallwood miserable."

"He's always miserable. Come now, what else?"

"All right I'll tell you. You weren't really very nice. You bawled everybody out. You had them all scared to death...". I sat there waiting for the sky to fall on me.

"They were, weren't they?" An impish grin spread over her face. "I gave quite a performance, didn't I? And close your mouth before you catch a fly in it."

"You mean... you didn't mean it?" I croaked. "You were just acting?"

"Perhaps I overdid it a little today." she said, then went on in a conversational tone, to explain she sometimes had to use temperament as a weapon; being not only a woman, but a small one, people tended to forget that her knowledge and her experience were vast? If she merely attempted, in a reasonable manner—and God knows she was a reasonable woman—to point out mistakes to directors, production managers and so forth, they had a tendency to speak to her in soothing tones, looking down at her kindly, trying to pacify her as though she were a child. So—to get their attention, you might say, she had to throw a temper tantrum. Sometimes she was so inwardly amused by the picture of her tiny-self stomping up and down, making strong men quail, that it was hard to keep from laughing.

Perhaps, she admitted, she had gone a bit too far today; she had almost allowed the acting to become real. Not that her annoyance wasn't justified—but to let temper take over was exhausting, and therefore stupid.

"Tomorrow I shall apologize very prettily to everyone, and they shall all say, what a great woman is Nazimova, that she can say she is sorry. And they will tell everyone what a character I am. But, mind you, there will be no more such mistakes made on *Camille*!" and sure, enough, there weren't.

40

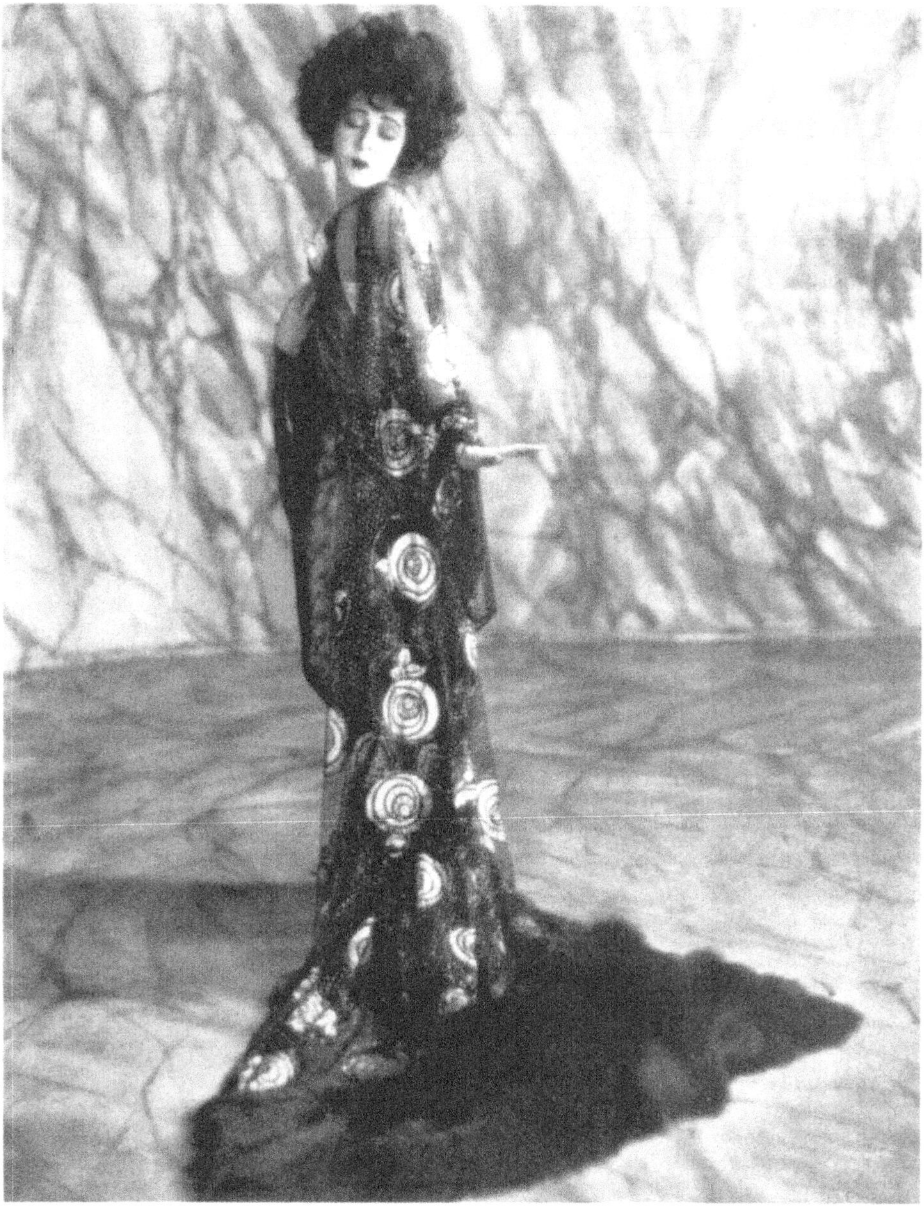

I am recounting this incident because of something that occurred some four years later, during the shooting of a picture I was in called Broken Hearts Of Hollywood, which despite its title was a pretty good movie. Douglas Fairbanks, Junior, was my leading man. he was tall—much taller than his father—was good looking, and pleasant to work with; the trouble was that he was too young, only about my own age. Males my own age seemed children to me. I preferred playing opposite older men, say, twenty-six or twenty-seven. . . maybe even thirty! I will say this for young Douglas, at 18 he was becoming his own man, even with the tough job of overcoming his father's name and image. Eventually his acting style alternated between the lusty swashbuckler and the smooth, suave man of the world. . . but I got to know him as the sweet, rather self-conscious boy he really was.

It was a hot summer, and sometimes after work Doug would invite me for a swim in the Pickfair pool, Pickfair being the home of his father and Mary Pickford, his stepmother. She always accepted him—and me—very cordially, and then left us to our own devices. To my regret, Douglas Senior was never there; maybe he was in Europe again. I never did get to meet the man.

One day Mary joined us, not to swim, just to sit on the edge of the pool and chat. Doug soon became restive and went up to the house, probably to phone one of his lady loves. I stretched out on a mattress and Mary and I talked of this and that and somehow we got into the subject of temperment, with which she claimed to have little sympathy. I ventured the opinion that most so called temperament was probably just plain bad temper, and Mary gave one of her bubbly little chuckles.

"Don't tell me you've never heard of my temper tantrums. You must have," she insisted. When I claimed I had never heard any such thing, she said, well, it was perfectly true, she had 'em—but only when it was absolutely necessary, only when things had not been done the way she thought they should be, only when logic and sweet reason had failed to prevail.

"It's because I'm so darn short," she said. "I've had more experience than most of my directors, but when they can look down on the top of your head, they're more inclined to pat you on it than to appreciate what's inside it."

"I just can't imagine you throwing your weight around," I couldn't help saying. "You haven't enough weight to throw." She stood up, taking a typical "Sweetheart of America" stance, fists on hips, toes turned in, lower lip pouting. "I can work up a fine rage," she said. "Can't you just see me, my blond curls bouncing, my starched pinafore switching, as I march up and down in my little flat shoes?" She started pacing back and forth like Rebecca of Sunnybrook Farm on a rampage.

I burst out laughing. "How do you keep a straight face?"

"Sometimes it's all I can do. If I ever passed a mirror I'd break myself up. But it's very effective, let me tell you. They all run for cover, but when they come back I get the scene done the way I want it."

I was bemused and enchanted by the picture of these two women, Nazimova and Mary Pickford, as far apart in looks, character, background and personality as it was possible for two women to be, having this one thing in common: they knew how to use temperament to get what they wanted, and they used it.

It never worked for me, alas. Perhaps I wasn't big enough professionally, or small enough physically, or perhaps because, like my mother, I have a tendency to giggle. . .

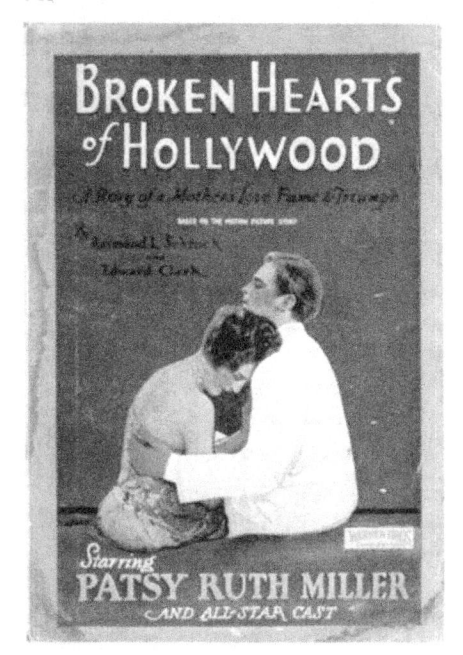

Pickfair

42

CHAPTER SIX

But getting back to *Camille*, six months after we finished shooting, *Camille* opened in New York to rather lukewarm notices. My part, small to begin with, had become even smaller in the cutting-room. I don't recall any mention of me in the reviews, so apparently I made little impact on the critics or, I daresay, on the public. But on the strength of having been in a Nazimova picture, I got another job. But this time not as an extra. I could hardly go back to extra work after actually having my name on the screen! Frankly, I think I got the part because I would work cheaper than any other young actress in Hollywood. It was the ingenue role—second in importance, or was it third, or maybe fourth—to the star, a pleasant if not talented young lady named Grace Darmond. The name of the picture was *Handle With Care*.

The picture was being shot at the L.B. Mayer Studio, before L.B. became a part of Metro-Goldwyn-Mayer. To call it a Studio was stretching a point. Actually, it was a dismal clump of buildings way out of town, past all bus or trolley lines. To add to its charm, it adjoined the Selig Zoo, making the stages smell faintly like a Lion's cage. At feeding time, conversations became a shouting match. Novice though I was, I think I soon suspected that this was not the picture that would propel me to fame and fortune. The story was utterly inane, our star was no great shakes as an actress, and the director couldn't have directed his way out of a hotel lobby. To further confirm my suspicion, the "juvenile" lead playing opposite me was a most charming gentleman named William Courtleigh, who had been a matinee idol on the stage when my mother was a girl. To say that he looked old enough to be my grandfather is not being unkind, merely factual; he probably was. I can only suppose that Mr. Courtleigh needed the job and would work for as little as I would... which was very little indeed.

43

L.B. Mayer Studio, 1921.

The Neighboring Selig Zoo.

With William Courtleigh in "Handle With Care".

To keep our love scenes from appearing more incestuous than romantic, I had to give the impression of being the oldest ingenue extant. My limited wardrobe did not include the sophisticated clothes necessary to disguise my youth, so when Mother had nothing suitable to lend me, I had to rent a few outfits, as the picture's budget did not allow for a studio wardrobe. This rental, plus taxi fare twice when the good old Chalmers failed me, swallowed up my munificent salary of $50 a week without a hiccup.

It was also the rainy season, or, as Southern Californians describe it, "unusual weather." It rained practically every day of the three weeks I worked on the picture; it was a six day working week in those days. My dressing room, completely without heat, almost without light, was blocks away from the stage, which was surrounded by a swamp through which I had to pick my way without ruining my makeup or rented clothes. To top it all, the director was a sadistic son of a bitch.

Looking back on it from this distance, I can see that he was probably very unhappy about the story, the cast, and the studio, as he had every right to be; what made him so insufferable to me, I daresay, was that, as low man on the totem pole I was the only one on whom he could vent his frustration. Miss Darmond was, technically anyway, a star, and must be treated as such; he was a little in awe of Mr. Courtleigh and directed him with exaggerated courtesy; Harry Myers, the leading man, viewed the whole thing with disdain and would probably have walked off the set if provoked—and that left me.

Phil Rosen—that was his name—might have been attractive under other circumstances; he was tall, lean, and not bad looking in a dark sneery way. But to me he was the Marquis de Sade; he made my three weeks so miserable that I was never able, thereafter, to fall in love with a tall dark man.

My first free day—it must have been a Sunday, as in those days we worked on Saturdays—I rushed out to see Madame, to tell her about the picture, but mostly to get a little sympathy. I was deeply aggrieved when the butler, whose name I don't recall, but who was a darling, whispered confidentially that Madame wasn't feeling very well but would cut his throat out if he told anyone. (She hated illness and would seldom even acknowledge fatigue.) In my mood of the moment, this seemed a personal affront.

"Don't disturb her on my account," I said, probably with a quivering lip, possibly even a tear in my eye.

The butler, bless his sweet heart, gave me a little pat on the shoulder, then, resuming his formal Jeeves manner, said that if I would kindly wait, he would inform Madame that I was there, and with stately tread climbed the stairs. In a moment Nazimova came flying down the stairs clad in Chinese silk pajamas, with cream on her face, and her coarse hair pulled into a net.

"Tragedy!" she cried. "Kindly remember that I am the tragedienne in this house." Then, seeing that I really was on the verge of tears, she said, "I am tired today and not too happy. Come upstairs and cheer me up a little."

Meekly I followed her to the big, round tower room. Like a child, she leaped into the huge round bed, pulling the lace coverlet up to her chin. Surrounded by the little lacy pillows that she loved, she really did look like a precocious infant, and I had to smile.

"That's better," she said. "The tragic muse must wait until you've lost your baby fat." Then, as she saw that I was again on the verge of tears, she pulled me down on the bed and said quietly, "Now, sit here and tell me about it. The work is not going well?"

So I told her about Mr. Rosen. I wouldn't mind, I said, if he corrected my acting, I'd be glad, I want to give a good performance, even if it is only a stupid little B picture and the studio is a mess. But all he does is make fun of me; he makes sarcastic remarks about my clothes. Well, some of them are Mother's, and maybe they are a little long, some of the skirts. I didn't have time to have them shortened. And when I wore Mother's fur piece, two Marten skins, really nice ones, put together by holding the other in its mouth, he said "Put that piece of Tomcat or whatever it is on the nearest chair when you come in; we don't want its glass eyes staring at us."

I went on and on, remembering all the slights which I couldn't tell my parents; it would have made Mother unhappy and Daddy would probably have yanked me off the picture. "It's the humiliation," I kept repeating. "You don't know what it's like... in front of everyone... it's so humiliating."

Finally, after I had cried myself out, and blown my nose, and put cold water on my eyes, Madame said, "Now it is over. You will go to work tomorrow and you will do the best you can even if it is a stupid little B picture, and you will make other pictures in good studios with good directors, and this will some day only be a funny experience which you will laugh at."

"I'm not going to make any more pictures if it is like this," I said. "I'm going back to St. Louis. I don't have to stay here and be humiliated."

Madame looked at me thoughtfully for a long moment, as though trying to make up her mind about something. Finally she said, "You think I do not understand humiliation? I am a Jewess, you know. I understand it."

To me that had no meaning, and she must have seen that, for she shifted in her bed, plumped up the pillows, and said, "You will not go back to St. Louis anymore than I went back to Yalta."

"Yalta?" I had never heard of it.

"It is a city in the Crimea... a beautiful city. I was born in the Crimea."

I refrained from asking where the Crimea was.

"I went from there to St. Petersburg, to study in the Conservatory. It was a long journey to St. Petersburg from Yalta—longer than any I have taken since. I was very young, as young as you, when they accepted me. It was most unusual for them to take a Jewess. I was, perhaps, the first one. Ah, we students worked hard... and ate little. For my scholarship I must do other things than act; I must work on costumes, make the tea, write out parts, oh, many, many things. And study, of course... languages, speech, everything. I was always busy, always tired... sometimes hungry... but it was a happy time. Yes, I was often quite, quite happy. Until the summer I was discovered by the Countess Debrovnik."

She fell into a brooding silence, and I sat quietly, waiting. Then, gazing into space, she told me the story.

The Count and Countess took pride in furthering the careers of young artists and having heard of Nazimova, they came to see her perform. Whether she really impressed them so favorably that they could overlook her background, or whether they thought to prove their devotion to the arts by sponsoring, not only a Jewess, but a Jewess of humble origin, is not clear. Whatever the reason, they came to see her perform.

They did offer her their patronage, and invited her to spend her vacation with them at their summer Dacha in a little village not far from Novgorod.

There she met their two sons, one about eighteen, the other a little older. The family treated her very kindly; she had her own room, she dined with them except when they were entertaining formally, and she revelled in the luxury of her surroundings. Then, the inevitable happened. She and the younger brother fell in love.

They became sweethearts... lovers, possibly, but the word she used was sweethearts. It was hopeless, of course, but the boy refused to admit it; he was determined to marry her, but being the younger son he had to get his parent's consent or do without his heritage. That would have meant starvation, as there was no way in which a young Russian nobleman could earn money.

After weeks of furtive meetings, stolen moments together, and all the unhappy subterfuge of such star-crossed lovers, he evolved a plan to overcome the family opposition. It was a forlorn hope, born of the desperation of first love; perhaps she never really believed that it would succeed, but she would have done anything that he suggested.

The greatest barrier was that she was a Jewess, therefore she would remove that barrier by being baptized into the Greek Orthodox Church! So they went to the village priest, a gentle old man, and sought his aid. A simple man of the people, he was easily persuaded that it was no less than his duty, as a man of God, to bring an unbeliever into the Church. The date was set for the following Sunday.

The Debrovnik Family services, which the boy had to attend, were held in their own private chapel on the estate, so that Sunday, clad in a simple white dress, Nazimova went alone to the village church. When the priest announced that there was to be a baptism, every head turned toward her; she felt their eyes on her as she walked timidly down the aisle... blank eyes, showing no open hostility, but no friendliness either.

Then a difficulty arose. To the old priest, to baptize meant to immerse in the small basin near the altar. It was large enough to hold the average baby—and, babies were all he had ever baptized. Obviously this girl could not be immersed in it. After a moment of deep thought the priest motioned her to follow him. In silence she did so. In silence the congregation rose and followed her.

The priest led them to the village square, and stopped before the town drinking fountain. There was a stone platform beside the well; the water overflowed into a trough, some three feet square, at which the peasants watered their stock. This was to be her batismal font.

The priest mounted the platform. She followed him, her legs trembling. The people gazed up at her with the suspicious curiosity of animals regarding an unfamiliar object. The old priest, his brow furrowed, seemed to be puzzling something out in his mind. Finally he reached a decision; she could not be baptized wearing that dress; she could not be baptized wearing anything. The custom was to dip the naked child into the water. She came as a child into the Church; she must therefore be naked.

She searched the heavy gaping faces for help; she tried to think of the boy, of their love; she could think of nothing. Her mind was as numb as her body, she wanted to run, to hide, but she was powerless to move. As though in a trance, she felt herself being stripped... There were some snickers, a loud braying laugh. A man said something in an undertone and a woman's voice rebuked him. Some eyes filled with pity. Some turned away. She stepped into the trough. The old priest put a shaking hand on her head and pushed her under...

Through the pounding of blood in her ears she heard a clatter of hooves as a horseman galloped down the hill toward the Church. He drew up at the sight of the crowd just as she emerged, dripping. She met her lover's eyes over the heads of the peasants. Even at that distance she could see the shock, the horror in his face. The horse reared at his savage tug, he dug in the spurs and galloped back up the hill.

A kindly old woman covered her with a shawl and led her away.

The boy was not at the dinner table that night. The next day she was given a note. He had had to leave so unexpectantly there was no time to say good-bye. He would see her in St. Petersburg that winter. It was signed, "All my love, forever."

On the surface, nothing was changed in the great Dacha. The Count and Countess were, as always, coolly pleasant, the thoughtful hosts, the kindly benefactors. The older brother's attitude was subtly different; his eyes were bolder, he found excuses to touch her, once he complained whimsically that the villagers had certain amusements unfairly denied him.

She left before the summer was over. It had ended for her anyway. Of course, she never saw the boy again.

Her voice trailed off. By now the daylight was gone, the room was in deep shadow, Nazimova's face only a white blur. I gave a long shuddering sigh, and she turned on the lamp by the bed, and handed me a handerchief. "Tears again, my God" she said. "You are a regular Niobe."

"I'm crying for you," I said. "I couldn't have borne it. I would have died."

"Don't cry for me, Little Mother," she said. "I didn't die—neither would you. We would go on, and soon it is a nothing, a pfui!—to all the Debrovniks and the Rosens of the world."

The was she said "pfui" with a whee sound at the end, made me laugh. Twilight had suffused the room, shadowing her face, then a late ray of sun darted in the window touching her with a rosy glow that erased the years, and I saw her as she must have been that dreadful day, so young, so vulnerable... what it must have cost her to reopen that old wound.

The talk had helped me a little bit, but I still cherished the dream of myself as a great star, rich, famous, glamorous and passing Mr. Rosen standing humbly in the cheering crowd, in rags and tatters, a three day growth of beard on his hollow cheeks.

One day, about three years later, Mother called me to the sun porch where she had a desk at which she took care of my mail. Without saying a word she handed me a letter. It went something like this:

Dear Patsy:

No one could be more delighted than I by your success, and I am sure you recall, as I do, the warm relationship we had when we worked together. You will be sorry to hear that I have had some professional reverses and some personal problems as well. This has put me in a difficult financial position and I wondered whether, for the sake of old times, you could advance me a few dollars, strictly as a loan, of course. I will pay you back as soon as some prospects I have work out...

Best of luck etc., etc.

Signed, (of course)

Yours sincerely,
Phil Rosen

Mother sat there watching me as I was reading the letter. When I replaced it carefully on the desk she simply said, "How much?"

I don't remember what the amount was. Of course he didn't repay me; I don't think he even thanked me. But it didn't matter I was finally able to say "pfui" to the Phil Rosen's of the world.

One final mention of Rudy and Madame...

At first my parents were concerned about my spending so much time at Madame's house—not that they feared for me—they feared for Nazimova. Daddy said she must be a lot stronger than she looks on the screen to have survived my visits this long, and Mother even called Madame to tell her that if I became a pest she was to send me home. I probably was a pest sometimes, but she never sent me home.

One day Madame said to me, "You so often complain of your father who makes you come home by midnight, and who will not allow you to go out with a boy he has not met - I am curious. I should like to meet this ogre." Only she pronounced it "og-ra."

So she extended an invitation, and Mother and Daddy and I had tea with her, which in Daddy's case was Bourbon and water, I having told her that all Kentucky men drank Bourbon or Rye. According to Daddy, Bourbon was real whiskey; Scotch was a lady's drink.

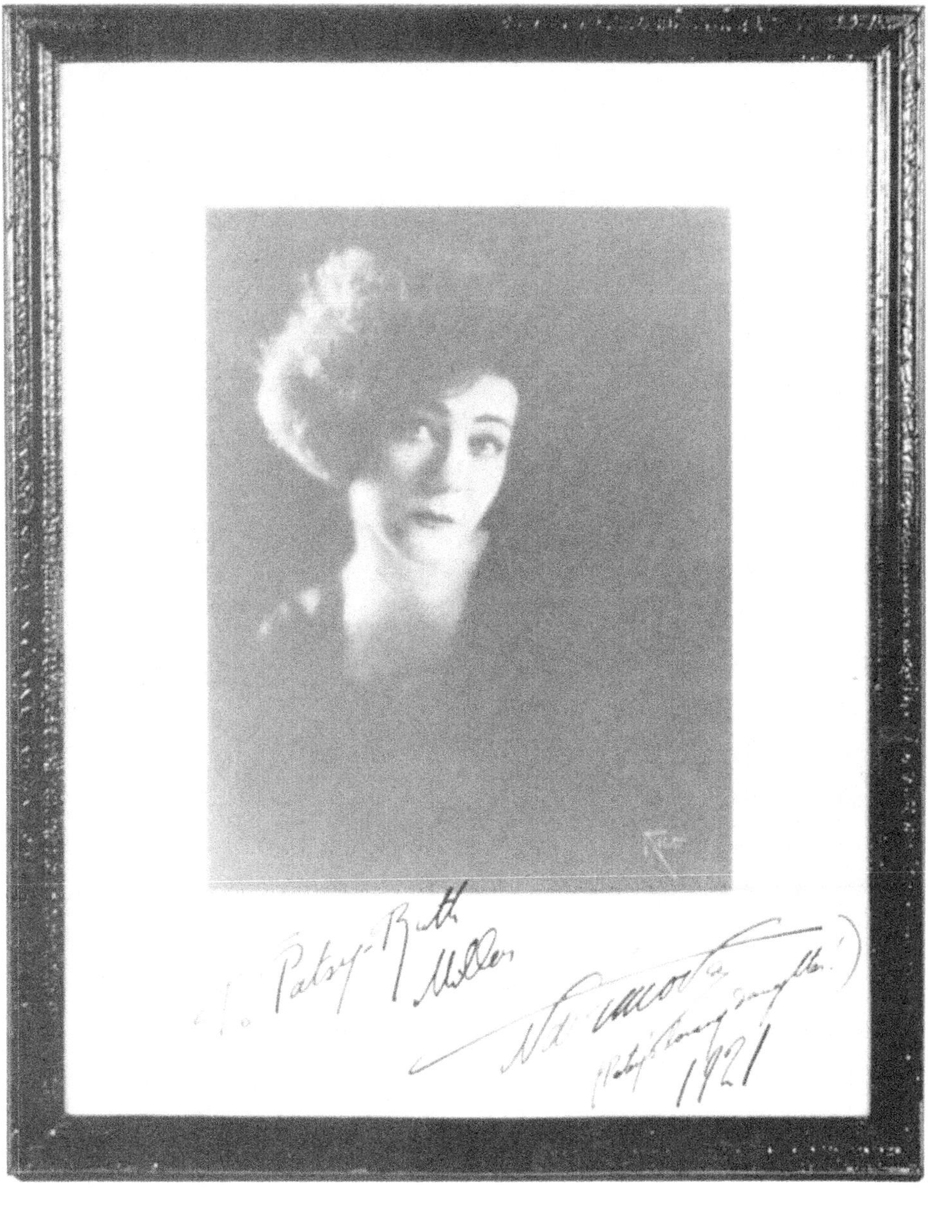
Patsy-Ruth
Miller
1921

Mother rather gingerly sipped her strong hot tea out of a tall glass, trying to look as though that's what she did every day at four. Daddy was in top form, and he and Madame got along like a house afire. He even urged her to try a snort of Bourbon, which she did, screwing up her face and pretending to choke on it. He assured her that if she persisted she would eventually learn to like it. "Why, I must have been at least fourteen years old," he said, "Before I was able to appreciate good Whiskey."

Madame was most impressed and promised to apply herself assiduously to the task of learning to enjoy good American liquor. Mother giggled and warned Madame not to believe a word Daddy said. Then he described a golf game he had had on the public course with an excellent but eccentric golfer who turned out to have escaped from a mental institution -or, in other words, a nut farm., making Madame laugh so hard she got a stitch in her side. So all in all it went very well.

As we were leaving, Daddy made her promise to kick me out if I became a nuisance. Madame said, No, she would do better than that, she would call him to come and get me. Mother said, Oh, oh, she should have listened to her friends; they had warned her about movie actresses. We finally went out in that warm laughing glow that means everyone has liked everyone and it has been a good party.

On the way home I realized that nothing had been said about *Camille* or my acting career; in fact, I hadn't been discussed at all, yet I instinctively knew that Daddy's resistance had been lowered. Mother said that Nazimova had been everything I said she was: charming and interesting, with the cutest accent. Daddy said better not ask him what he thought of her—why make your Mother jealous?

Oscar Miller, Patsy Ruth and Mrs. Miller.

I wonder what I would have done if they hadn't liked Madame and had forbidden my visits. I don't think I ever actually disobeyed a direct order from either my father or my mother, odd as that may sound today. It wasn't odd then at all. I must have had the usual rebellious thoughts common to all adolescents, but I'm sure I never even contemplated open defiance; direct confrontation was to be avoided at all costs, as there was no doubt as to who would win. Despite an occasional restiveness, due to the firm conviction that my parents had never been young themselves, I don't think I would have had it otherwise. It gave me a comforting sense of security.

As Mother hadn't been on the set with me, she had never met Valentino. After the preview of *Camille*, to which we were invited, she said to me in some surprise, "Well, my goodness, Pat—he's not at all what I expected from your description of him."

When *The Sheik*, starring Rudy and Agnes Ayres, opened in L.A. a girl friend and I went to a matinee. I sat there entranced. That fierce, fascinating man on the screen, who captured and captivated Agnes Ayres was no one I had ever known. Cathy and I left the theatre still breathless. On the drive home she broke a long reflective silence. "Gosh, Pat," she said in a feverential tone, "To think you were actually in a movie with him. You never told me he was so - you know - like that."

"He wasn't" was all I could say. "At least. . . well, I guess I never noticed it. . . I mean. . . that he was like that."

"I'd certainly have noticed it," Cathy said. "You can just bet I would have!"

Perhaps I sort of did notice it. There was one time...

It was on my 18th birthday. I was leaving Madame's house with a scarf she had given me and I met Rudy as he was coming in. Holding up the scarf I said, "Isn't it pretty? It's a birthday present."

"Your birthday?" he said. "Well, then. . ." and, putting his arms around me, he lifted my face to his and gave me a long, lovely kiss. Then, still holding me, he said, "Happy Birthday, Bambina, and here is one—how do you say—one to grow on." And he kissed me again.

Yes, I suppose you could say there was one time I noticed he was, you know. . . like that.

Filming "Fortune's Mask". Oliver Hardy is standing in the shadows behind Patsy.

49

CHAPTER SEVEN

Some two years and seven pictures later, I was cast as Esmeralda, the Gypsy girl, in *The Hunchback of Notre Dame*, starring Lon Chaney which was, to coin a phrase, a turning point in my career.

Seven pictures sounds like a lot of movies to make in such a short time, but in those days we didn't spend a year on one picture; we shot them in a few weeks, at most a few months. As I heard Jimmy Stewart once say, when asked how he had been able to make so many pictures during his career, "Well, we were actors, so we acted." That's about how it was. We finished one picture, took a deep breath, and started another.

Two of those pictures were Tom Mix westerns, and although it didn't take great histrionic ability to play the leading lady in a "oater," as we called them, it was great exposure. You had a ready-made audience as Mix westerns were box-office gold, real family entertainment. One thing that made them so popular was that the Good Guys always won.

When I was interviewed for the part, one of the questions was, Could I ride? Technically I could. I had been on a horse several times back in St. Louis, when I was about fourteen. We had a riding class, with an instructor, and four or five of us, riding English saddle, walked slowly, or sometimes trotted slowly, around the bridle path of Forest Park without falling off. So without going into detail, I answered Yes to the question.

Tom Mix was a real character, with a peculiar charm all his own. Daddy went on several locations with us and got to know Tom very well. He loved to listen to the yarns Tom spun about his past, but said he never could decide which of them to believe. According to Tom, he had, in his time been a sheriff, a Texas Ranger, and a plain ol' cowhand before he became a movie star. Who knows? Maybe they were all true.

One thing is certain: he knew his business. He was a damn good rider, a good shot, and a good roper. He was also very kind and understanding, as I found out my first day on the set. I didn't have to ride that first day, but they had my horse all ready and saddled for me to get acquainted with. The saddle was nothing like the one I had sat upon in Forest Park; it was a huge thing with long stirrups that scared me just to look at. I wasn't so much afraid of falling off as I was of making a fool of myself. Gritting my teeth, I climbed up, with the help of a friendly cowboy, managed to get my feet into the stirrups after they were shortened for me, picked up the reins and just sat there, not knowing what to do next.

Tom rode up beside me, made a soothing sound to my horse, who seemed to be getting a little nervous, and said, "You haven't rode much, have ya?"

"Not much," I admitted.

"I kinda thought so." He smiled, a comforting smile. "Well, now, ya see that thing there in front of ya? That's the pommel. You can kinda hang on to it as we're startin' out, but in two or three days, I don't wancha touchin' it."

I followed his directions and off we went. For two or three days, between scenes, he took me riding like that. Doing it in easy stages gave me confidence and sure enough, by the end of the third day, I didn't have to hang on. By the end of the week I was sitting in the saddle without bouncing and had learned that you don't post to a trot, as in an English saddle, you sort of push your fanny against the cantle and let the horse trot under you. That was the beginning of my long love affair with horses.

I could have loved Tony, Tom's horse, had he permitted me to, but he was a one-man horse, and Tom Mix was that man. He graciously accepted an occasional lump of sugar, a gentle rub on the nose, or friendly slap on the flank, but his attitude said clearly, No sloppy sentimentality, PLEASE and I respected his feelings and didn't push it.

One day on location there was a scene in which the heavies kidnapped me and tied me to a tree—probably a Yucca—out on the lone prairie. Then the villains rode off, setting fire to the underbrush as they went... accidentally, of course, I forget just how. Probably by carelessly tossing away a lighted match. Anyway, they galloped off without looking back, and there was I, tied to the stake, a bright blaze coming slowly toward me. Before the fire could reach me, Tom would come tearing in, cut me loose with one sweep of his knife, swing me up on the saddle behind him, and go galloping off before the villains spotted him.

The scene was carefully timed and rehearsed. One of the bad guys was shown how to tie a slip knot, so that Tom, while appearing to cut me loose would actually only have to pull the loose end of the rope and it would fall off, freeing me. The only flaw in the plan was that the bad guy who tied me was not a quick learner; he didn't catch on to how to tie a slip knot in one easy lesson, and he tied a real knot - a true Gordian knot. My struggle (acting) to free myself only made the knot tighter. Then the wind shifted a little, and my frantic struggle was no longer acting; I was getting too warm; the fire was uncomfortably close. The director and crew thought I was just hamming it up a bit, I suppose.

By the time Tom came dashing in to the rescue I was getting a little scared. He pulled Tony to a rearing halt then, wielding the knife with a flourish, pretended to cut the rope while really pulling on the loose end as in the rehearsal. But instead of falling free, the rope just got tighter; it would have taken three hands to untie it, and Tom barely had one. His left hand holding the reins, he was having all he could do to keep Tony from bolting. Horses have a terrific fear of fire. They panic, and Tony was no exception.

Tom reacted quickly and with great presence of mind. Realizing that if he slashed the rope he would probably also slash me, he slid the knife under the rope where it bound my shoulders. I scrunched my arms back to give him some leeway, and he sawed through it in a matter of seconds. It was a feat of great horsemanship and quick thinking. As soon as I was free, I reached up, he grabbed me, and somehow I was on the saddle behind him clinging like a limpet, and we were galloping off to safety....Not, however, completely unscathed or unsinged. My long, flowing hair was on fire and so was Tony's long, flowing tail. The fire didn't reach the camera truck; either they put it out or it burned itself out. But Tom's rage wasn't that easily extinguished. He raised holy hell with everyone - not, mind you, because his leading lady might have been barbecued - there are always more leading ladies, but because Tony had lost a good part of his tail.

I wasn't too upset about losing some of my flowing mane - they say singeing is good for the hair. But it meant that Tony and I had to have switches made for us to wear for the rest of the picture in order to match up with the scenes already shot. I didn't mind, but Tony did. He had a sheepish look each time they pinned his phony tail on him, and he eyed me reproachfully, as though it were all my fault. In time he forgave me, and we resumed our rather formal friendship.

Tom and the boys also got a kick out of teaching me to shoot, and I became a pretty good marksman—no Annie Oakley, but I could have brought down a varmint at fifty paces. (I was going to say a mugger, but we didn't have muggers in those days.)

52

The Tom Mix company on location, Victorville filming "The Fighting Streak", 1922

I've noticed today, on TV, that the cops take a two-handed stance, facing their quarry. I learned to shoot with one, but maybe if I ever have to shoot a bad guy I'll try it that way.

Another reason I enjoyed working with Tom Mix was his brother-in-law who was the assistant director. He was only a few years older than I. I think his name was Eugene Ford; I'm sure of the Ford part, but not of the Eugene. After all, this was more than sixty years ago, and a girl can't remember every man she had a crush on. But I do remember that he was very cute and I was dying for him to ask me for a date... but he never did.

One Sunday Tom and his wife invited my family down to Malibu for a barbeque. I was hoping young Mr. Ford would be there, but to my disappointment, he wasn't. There was Tom, his wife and mother-in-law, a highly respected character actress named Eugenia Ford, my parents, and Lynn Reynolds, the picture's director, and his wife, but no one my age.

The surf was rather high and no one seemed to want to go swimming; they were all just sitting around on the beach waiting for the grill to get hot enough to broil hamburgers, and I was bored by their grown-up talk, so I wandered off down the beach alone hoping to run into someone more my own age—preferably male—but being spring, the water was cool and the beach empty of everything but shells and sea gulls.

The sun was bright and warm, and even though the surf was rather high, the ocean looked quite calm beyond the breakers. It seemed a shame not to go for a swim on such a lovely day. I had once heard someone mention a riptide, but I saw no evidence of anything unusual so, seeing that no one back at the house was watching me, I plunged in, dove under the waves, and came up in the calm water past the breakers.

After a bit of splashing around, floating on my back, trying to swim like a mermaid, and doing the dead man's float, I decided I had better head for the shore, so I started in with my best Australian crawl. After a minute or two of swimming hard and breathing properly as I had been taught, I looked up to see how close to the shore I was—but I wasn't. I was farther out than when I had started. I was surprised, but not really frightened. I just thought that I had not been heading in the right direction, so I took careful aim at the beach, put my head down, and started to swim again with all my might... kick, kick... stretch out the arms, right, left... breath out under water... come up every fourth stroke for air... I swam like that for what seemed like a long time before raising my head to see how close to the shore I was. But the beach seemed further away than ever, and I was down past three neighboring houses. In fact, I could hardly see the little group of friends and family on the beach which I had just left a few minutes before...

Panic hit me. I knew I was caught in the famous riptide which took its toll of swimmers every year. I tried to remember what I had heard, what you were supposed to do... don't fight it, go with it... but how far would you go? Relax... lie on your back and float... I tried to relax on my back, but I had the sensation of being carried at breathtaking speed... carried where? Out to sea? Onto rocks?

I couldn't stand not seeing where I was going, so I turned over awkwardly and got water up my nose. The more I struggled to get my face out of water, the more I seemed to swallow. The salt was burning my throat, my arms felt as though they had lead weights tied to them, and I just didn't feel as though I could kick my tired legs one more time.

Then a strange thing happened. A sort of peace came over me. I don't believe I actually said a prayer, I just sort of said a thought: Dear God, help me. That's all, just Dear God, help me.

At that moment a voice said, "Give me your hand." I opened my eyes—I hadn't realized they were closed—and there on a large rock, right in front of me, was a man in a bathing suit holding out his hand. I held my hand out, he grasped it firmly, and with a little pull, he had me up on the rock beside him. "Rest here for a minute," is all I remember him saying.

I sat there getting my breath. He smiled at me. It was very sort of companionable. I don't know how else to describe it, nor can I describe the man. I never could, even the next day when I tried to tell my best friend about it. He was just a man, maybe twenty, maybe thirty, maybe not. I couldn't describe him and I found that I didn't want to talk about it anyway, so I never did, until now.

Well, I sat there on the rock, I stopped shivering, and then the man smiled at me in that companionable way and he said, "You can make it now, can't you?" I said yes, I could. Then he said, "Head for that piling the sea gull is sitting on. Do you see it?" I saw it. It seemed the wrong direction to head for if I wanted to hit the shore, but I dove in and headed for it as I had been told.

The swimming seemed a little easier. I looked back and the man raised his hand. I swam more and more and soon I could feel the difference in the water; it wasn't pulling at me. I was going through it easily. I looked back again, but the man was gone. Only the tip of the rock was visible.

When I felt the sand under my feet, I stood up. I just stood there, my feet firmly dug into the sand, the water lapping gently around my ankles. Then I waded ashore, took a deep breath, and walked back.

They were all sitting around the barbeque grill, waiting for the hamburgers to be ready. Someone asked where I had been, and I said that I had had a little swim out to the rock.

"What rock?" Tom asked, "They ain't no rocks around here."

"It was down there," I pointed.

"I don't see no rock," Tom said.

I shaded my eyes and looked again, but I couldn't see a rock.

With director Art Rosen

54

CHAPTER EIGHT

One of the things I miss today is a love story—a true love story. I made one in 1923.

Charles Ray was the star, and a real STAR; I was his leading lady in a picture called *The Girl I Loved*, which had received glowing reviews. It was named Picture of the Month by *Screenland Magazine* and had cleaned up at the box office; always the final accolade.

Recently I received a letter from Kevin Brownlow, the noted film scholar of England, mentioning the very same picture. He had just returned to London from a Film Festival in Brussels, where they had shown what was believed to be the last surviving print of *The Girl I Loved*. Even though the subtitles were a combination of different languages (they speak French, Flemish, and a sort of low Deutsch in Belgium) it didn't matter because the picture was so moving. At the end, the audience did something he had never seen before—they stood up and applauded.

In a footnote, Kevin added that he had forgotten to look for a discrepancy in the last scene which I had once told him about. He said his eyes were so full of tears by that time that he wouldn't have been able to see it had he remembered to watch it. Proving what? That a true love story is a true love story—today just as it was in 1922.

The Girl I Loved, I truly believe, was the loveliest of all the pictures I was in. It was a period picture, set in the 1890's and made just before The Hunchback.

It was a gentle story, filled with interesting characterizations, a little humor, a few very dramatic scenes, and Love. Mostly it was about Love. No SEX. Just Love.

The storyline was this: I was adopted by Charles Rays' parents when I was about twelve and Charles was fifteen. We had a warm, sister/brother relationship until we both matured, then Charles fell in love with me, but I still thought of him as a brother. I was in love with Charles' best friend, and after some beautiful but harrowing scenes, Charles, standing in for his father, has to give me in marriage to the other man.

The final scene is the wedding, with Charles standing there as I come out of the church with his best friend, now my husband, get into a buggy, and drive away. There was a flaw in that scene which apparently no one ever noticed, not even the critics. When I came out of the church, I was wearing a little jacket over my tight bodice and full skirt, but when I got into the buggy, the jacket was gone. I had taken it off between scenes, as it was an unusually hot day, and the script girl, who was supposed to keep track of such things, didn't catch it. Although it was probably caught in the rushes, I daresay they decided it wouldn't be worth bringing back the whole crew just to re-take that one scene. It would have cost a fortune.

As it happened, they made the right decision. Everyone was crying so hard by that time that I could have been wearing a harem costume and no one would have noticed.

55

Charles Ray   Photo: Ruth Harriet Louise

That was what I had told Kevin Brownlow, and he said if he ever saw the picture he would look for the missing jacket. But even *he* didn't see it... Speaks well for my favorite movie, doesn't it?

It does seem a shame that Charles Ray has been forgotten by the industry of which he was such an important part. Not only was he a big star, and a box office draw, he was, to my mind, one of, if not *the* best actor I ever worked with. And yet as a person he was completely un-actorish. I enjoyed every moment of acting with him—it was not only fun, it was exhilarating. As the twelve and fifteen-year-old, we romped in the fields, teased each other, and felt like kids. At least I did, thanks to him. And as we grew up together, I matured as he did.

Off screen I saw him quite often, mostly at my house; he loved tennis and he and Dad had many a Sunday game together, or doubles with whomever happened to drop by for a game. Among the regulars I remember Gilbert Roland, Lionel Belmore, Louis Wolheim and Charlie Farrell. I was "going steady" with Kenneth Hawks—Howard Hawks' younger brother—at the time, and occasionally he played with The Regulars, as they called themselves, but he wasn't warmly welcomed; he was too good for them, having been the tennis champion of Yale.

Kenneth was among several of my beaus who died prematurely; he married Mary Astor and a year or so later went down in a plane over the Pacific.

But back to Charles. He seemed to love those casual, informal Sundays at our house, but Clara, his wife, never accompanied him. She was very social; they gave lots of parties and went to lots of parties, and I gathered that her extravagance worried him sometimes, though he never said anything critical of her, at least not in my hearing. I had the feeling, nonetheless, that he would have preferred less partying, less country-clubbing, a less flamboyant lifestyle. Dear Charles... I liked him very much indeed. But eventually we drifted apart; he had career problems, they sold their house in Beverly Hills, and I didn't see Charles for many years.

Of all the sins I have committed, the sins of omission are those I most regret. One of those sins I committed against Charles.

About twenty years later, during the early 40's, when I was living in Encino, in the San Fernando Valley, I heard that Charles was very ill and had been taken to the hospital in L.A. My first thought was that I should go right down and see him. But downtown Los Angeles is a long drive from the Valley, it was very hot, and I thought perhaps I'd wait until it was cooler. Then I thought that perhaps I would be intruding; his family was probably

Sunday afternoon Miller family tennis matches. Some of the team members, left to right: Charles Ray, (?), Gardener James (?), Lionel Belmore, (?), (?), J. Stuart Blackton, (?), Patsy Ruth Miller, (?), Marion Blackton, Oscar and Winston Miller on far right.

with him. But the real reason I put if off was that I was afraid he might not welcome me, he might even have forgotten me after all those years. It might have been awkward for both of us. So I put it off... and the next day he died... alone.

I've never quite forgiven myself for that. So what if he hardly remembered me? So what if he had family members there who felt I was intruding? It shouldn't have mattered to me because maybe he would have been glad to see me. Maybe he was all alone... I've learned a lesson from that, but I didn't learn it in time to keep me from making the same mistake with F. Scott Fitzgerald only a short time later.

A good rule to live by is this: If there's something you feel you should do, do it right then, because if you wait too long, perhaps only a few hours, it might be too late.

Costume test for "The Girl I Loved".

Ralph Forbes

Carl Laemmle Jr., later the head of Universal Studios.

Charles Ray, far right.

Dorothy, Ray Culley, Winnie, Patsy and Cornwall Jackson

Patsy with Chester Morris.

Malcolm McGregor

John Ford and Winston Miller on location in Wadsworth. Winston played George O'Brien's character as a youngster in "The Iron Horse."

Casting Director Horace Williams, Patsy and Noah Beery, 1921

CHAPTER NINE

Sometimes I've been a bit annoyed by being introduced as Esmeralda. It's always; You remember the *Hunchback* don't you? She played the Gypsy girl in it. Then, if the recipient of this world shaking news is under sixty the response is generally, "Oh really? I thought it was Maureen O'Hara". I knew I was lucky to get the part of Esmeralda but I didn't dream that it was going to be THE picture by which I would be remembered. They politely refrain from mentioning that they'd never have recognized me. (Well 60 years makes a difference in a girl's looks).

It was an epic, the only one that I was ever in. It was known as an epic from its inception. It was ballyhooed as The First Million Dollar picture, which means nothing today, but was a fortune in 1923. The rumor was that Uncle Carl (Carl Laemmle, the head of Universal) had a nurse standing by to take his blood pressure every time another huge set was built or another order went out for a thousand extras.

Today a million dollars doesn't even demand attention; basketball players get it, pro football players sneer at it, and a movie is hardly worth going to see if it cost that little. But way back then it rocked the industry.

Those dollars were real honest to goodness 100 percent dollars. And they were all spent on actual production, not on taxes or labor disputes or politics. Of course our salaries were not included in the cost of production, but I assure you that no one, not even Lon Chaney himself, received enough to make a dent in that million plus. My salary certainly didn't account for much of that sum, but on the other hand, what I received was mine--all mine. No deductions! Cigarettes were 15 cents a pack, two for a Quarter, gasoline was 8 cents a gallon. You could get a good meal in a good restaurant for 2 or 3 dollars, and tips were 5 percent for excellent service.

Still, when I got a call to go to Universal, out in the San Fernando Valley, to test for the lead opposite Lon Chaney, I almost didn't go. For one thing, it was a dreadfully hot September day and I knew the Valley would be like a furnace; remember, this was before the miracle of air conditioning. For another, it seemed that every actress under the age of forty was being tested; I had only been an actress for two years, and although in that short time I had managed to work in seven or eight movies—we knocked 'em out fast in those days! —it

60

seemed unlikely that they would want a virtual beginner for such an important picture.

Well, not to keep you in suspense, I did go, and I got the part.

My memories of the *Hunchback* are good ones. The friendliness of everyone from the grips, the props the cameramen as well as the other members of the cast, of which I'm the only one left! Can you imagine that.

I remember Lon Chaney as being a gentle and kind man. I don't honestly remember much about making the test. It was more for lighting and makeup than acting, I think, I don't recall seeing Wallace Worsley, who was to direct the picture, but I vividly recall meeting Lon Chaney, who came down on the set and explained to me, in a very quiet way, what the role of Esmeralda was all about. He seemed to have been well briefed on my background... a few Tom Mix Westerns, two comedies with a terrific young actor named Cullen Landis, a couple of tear jerkers, and to my delighted surprise he asked me about the picture I had just finished, playing opposite Charles Ray *(The Girl I Loved,)* and I was amazed that Lon Chaney knew about it, as it hadn't been released, but he told me that the word around Hollywood was that Charles had "a sleeper".

The only "sleeper" I knew was a Pullman car on a train, so I rather bristled in defense of Charles Ray, and said, "No, sir, I think the picture is very good."

Chaney gave me a strange look, as though he weren't sure whether he was being kidded; there were to be many such looks throughout the making of *The Hunchback*, my ignorance of theatrical parlance still being colossal, but when he realized that I was quite sincere he managed not to laugh, and kindly explained that a "sleeper" was a movie that no one expected much of, but which turned out to be a box-office smash.

When the part of Esmeralda was offered to me it was with the proviso that I would be available when they were ready to start shooting. If I was tied up in another picture there would be no waiting around for an expendable ingenue; they would simply get themselves another Esmeralda. It wasn't really fair of Universal-it might mean waiting a month, two months, three months, but that was it; I was free when they were ready or I was out.

My parents were still too astonished at having an actress in the family to be able to advise me, so I went again to my dear friend and mentor, Alla Nazimova. I explained the situation to her; it might mean a long wait, with no salary coming in: it might mean missing out on a wonderful part... but, on the other hand, I said, it is going to be a Million Dollar Movie.

Of course you must wait, said Madame, not because it will cost a million dollars, million, billion,... money does not guarantee a good picture... but because it will give you the opportunity of working with Lon Chaney. He was a fine actor, she said, an artist in his way. It would be almost impossible for me not to learn a great deal from him. Providing, she added as I started to leave, that you pay attention, listen carefully, and don't make a nuisance of yourself.

So I waited... How can I resist saying, and the rest is History. By a great show of will power, I merely make the statement that I was free when they were ready.

With Uncle Pat

Many months into the picture, when I got to know Mr. Chaney well enough to call him Lon, I told him all about it, and he was furious. He had personally okayed me, he said, and had taken it for granted that I was immediately signed up and put on the payroll. Had he known the shyster trick they pulled on me (his words, not mine) he would have raised Hell. Whether or not he would really have gone to bat for me, it was nice to hear him say he would, and it made me feel good. And, although he tried to hide it, he was pleased as punch to hear that Madame Nazimova considered him an artist.

Lon Chaney was not an easy man to know; not that he was unfriendly—he simply didn't have the light banter that actors generally amuse themselves with between scenes. For one thing, when he was in his Hunchback makeup it was not only difficult, it was actually painful for him to talk. He usually sat by himself between scenes or retired to his dressing room, so I was surprised when one day, while I was waiting for the lights to be set up, he pulled up a chair and sat down beside me. He wasn't working that day, I remember thinking how nice he looked in slacks and a sleeveless sweater over a rather natty sport shirt... so unlike Quasimodo. He had a pleasant face, although deeply lined for a man of his age.

The scene coming up was of the beggars' camp; I was to run in and do a sort of impromptu Gypsy dance, and my mind was pretty much on that, so I didn't try to make conversation. After a moment's silence he said, "Patsy, I've been watching you, and I'm afraid you're getting known as a soft touch."

To say I was startled is putting it mildly. I wondered frantically whom he had seen touching me, but before I could deny whatever it was I was being accused of, he went on, "You're going to be chalked up like a box car if you're not careful."

As I stared at him in utter confusion that look came over his face that I had seen before when he was talking to me; he shook his head, gave a deep sigh, and patiently explained, or rather, translated what he had just said. When hoboes were riding the rods-the freight trains-if the train crew was tolerant and didn't throw them off, they marked the cars with chalk as a signal for their brother hoboes. The same with housewives; if they found a farm where the lady of the house gave them a hand-out they chalked the fence. That meant, he said slowly and clearly, that the farmer's wife was a soft touch.

Oh, I said, comprehension dawning.

Yes, he said. Exactly.

Then he asked me which story Meg had told me.

Meg was one of the extras who made up the mob scenes. She looked like a scruffy old hag, wearing a filthy sort of sack with a frayed rope around her waist. Her lank gray hair straggled over her face and she seemed to have a front tooth missing.

"Story?" I said. "She didn't tell me any stories..."

"Didn't she tell you the one about being the sole support of her ninety year old invalid mother", he asked; "Or was it the one about the cruel husband who ran off and left her with five children.

No, sir, I said. Nothing like that. All she told me was that she was about to lose her house because she couldn't keep up her payments on the mortgage.

"Bless her inventive heart," he said. "That's a new one." And he actually laughed out loud. When he stopped laughing he smiled at me; he had a very sweet, though rare smile.

"I'm not going to ask you how much you gave her, but I am going to tell you this; Meg is about thirty-five, she lives in an apartment in Hollywood, and she drives a Stutz Bearcat. And I'm not going to ask you what story Skeets told you, he's the one with the eye-patch and the bandage on his leg, I saw you talking to him too. I'll only say this; Skeets isn't blind and he isn't lame."

I don't remember saying a word. I suppose I just gaped at him like a ninny. We sat there for a moment, the two of us looking at each other. Then he said, very gently, "You're probably going to make a lot of money in this business, but remember—you worked for it. You earned it. Being generous, having a soft heart is one thing—being played for a sucker, a soft touch, is something else again, you get it?"

I seem to remember saying, Yes, I got it.

"Okay," he said, and gave me a little pat on the shoulder. "Now run along, Esmeralda, and go into your dance."

Lon Chaney (in foreground) watches a rehearsal for the Gypsy Dance scene. Note: musicians and crew to right. Patsy is in the circle of extras watching Marie dancing.

That was about the longest conversation we ever had together. Anyway, that little lecture made such an impression on me that from then on I was careful never to let him catch me talking to an extra...

How Lon Chaney was about money himself, I've no idea. I never heard that he was a tightwad, as was said about Charles Chaplin. On the other hand, he was known to give generously to The Actors Fund, and things of that sort. The word was that he was very shrewd about contracts, and that he invested heavily in real estate—but that was only hearsay. The truth is that very little was known about his life or his habits, he was thought to live very modestly in an unfashionable part of Hollywood, and although he and his family must have had their circle of friends, as most families have, it did not seem to include members of the motion picture industry.

Chaney's relationship with the other members of the cast was friendly but not chummy. He appeared to have great respect for Ernest Torrence, the brawny Scot who played the King of Beggars, and I daresay he liked him; it was almost impossible not to like Mr. Torrence. With all his impressive size and authority on screen, off screen he was a charming well-bred gentleman with a delightful sense of humor.

Norman Kerry, who played Phoebus, in a curled wig and ornate costume, the rollicking Captain of the Guards was another type altogether, although equally well-educated and of good family background. Norman's real last name was Kayser, of the Kayser Silk family; he had never actually had to work for a living but he liked to pretend otherwise. No two men on the North American Continent could have been as dissimilar in every aspect of living as Lon Chaney and Norman Kerry, yet, in an odd way, they were fond of each other. He also gave me some early-on advice. His was "Don't look at the camera and try not to giggle in the love scenes." And he added, "Don't forget to pick up your check every Friday."

Lon Chaney was a dedicated actor, serious about his work, sensitive to criticism, and unceasingly ambitious. Norman viewed the world and the picture business with whimsical humor and a certain amount of cynicism. He had a take-it-or-leave-it attitude about acting that said clearly," I can stop this nonsense of making faces in front of a camera any time, and never miss it." Mind you, although he took his career lightly, he didn't take his work casually; he was never late on the set and he did his best with whatever the art demanded. His whole approach to his profession was so diametrically opposed to Lon's that it seem to puzzle Chaney, but also to intrigue him. Lon asked him once in my hearing, why he had chosen to become an actor, and Norman replied, Oh, it was that or go to work.

The expression on Lon's face was as clear as though written in letters of fire; he resented that slur on his profession, he wanted to protest—I could almost hear him saying, "What do you mean, acting isn't work!"— but he managed to give a weak grin and say nothing. It

Candid from the Gypsy dance scene

wasn't that Lon didn't have a sense of humor; he did, but it ran more to visual humor and practical jokes than to dry wit or subtleties. As an example:

We were working late one night on a back lot exterior. It was nearly midnight before they got to my scene, just a long shot of me coming home alone after having had a tryst with Captain Phoebus. It had turned quite cold, as California nights often do, so they had fires going in huge metal barrels which gave little heat, but bathed the street scene in an eerie glow. There was no moon, and until they hit the Kliegs the night was black. I wasn't terribly happy waiting in the darkness for my cue. The camera and the crew seemed very far away and I was greatly relieved when the lights went on and I heard, "Okay, Miss Miller... start walking."

On I came, trying to look like a girl in a happy romantic glow, when suddenly, with a horrible yowl, a black figure like a huge bat lunged at me from a doorway. They probably heard my shriek in Beverly Hills, and I didn't stop running until I was tackled and brought to earth by one of the grips.

It was Lon Chaney, of course, wearing a costume from one of the monks in the picture.

I come of sturdy stock so I didn't die of a heart attack. I didn't faint, either, which pleased Lon. That would have spoiled his fun, as well as holding up the shooting. We all had a good laugh and the show went on.

Although he didn't mind scaring the daylights out of me, on the whole he was very considerate of my comfort on the set. He made sure that I got hot coffee whenever he did. He saw to it that I had a director's chair—it's really just a camp chair which folds—and that I had my name put on it. And he didn't play any more practical jokes on me. In fact, there were times when he seemed to take a rather paternal interest in me.

For instance—one day, about three months into the shooting, the scene was a parade of the Guards being led by Norman in full regalia. There was a military band, and it was an impressive sight. I was hauled up on the camera platform to get a good view of it, and Lon, in mufti, joined me there. When Norman spotted me, he raised his lance in salute and called out "Hail, Patricia!" That wasn't in the script, but it didn't matter; with all the shouting no one could hear him and who could read lips? Lon could, that's who!

When the parade passed and we scrambled off the camera platform Lon said something about Norman being an extremely handsome man. I agreed. He then ventured the comment that a man that good-looking must be very attractive to women, to which I also agreed. Then, steering me around a reflector, he said in a painfully casual manner, Norman's married, you know. I know, I said, but I'm partial to blue-eyed blonds!

He gave me that strange, "are you for real?" look, so this time I looked right back with my "Daddy, what is beer?" expression, and no more was said on the subject of tall, dark and handsome Norman Kerry. But I have always treasured that memory of Lon Chaney; it was very sweet of him indeed to be concerned about the moral welfare of his teen-age leading lady.

I have no way of knowing whether Lon Chaney was as protective toward his other young leading ladies as he was of me, or whether he just thought I was too dumb to take care of myself.

I've been told that Lon and Mr. Worsley had been friends for some time and that Lon had convinced Mr. Thalberg, the producer, to hire him based on their three previous pictures, *The Ace of Hearts*, *The Penalty* and *A Blind Bargain* (where he played a similar role of an apeman-hunchback). In the *Penalty*, Lon was a legless man so I guess the combination was a winner in preparing both of them for Uncle Carl's first epic.

It is odd that, as these memories come flooding back, there is so little that I recall about our director, Wallace Worsley. As I try to visualize him, he comes into my mind as rather round and pudgy—but I might not be remembering his looks correctly. He was pleasant looking and, probably was a very pleasant person; I have no recollection of his being otherwise, but that's not very conclusive, as I have hardly any recollection of him at all.

How good he was as a director I'm not qualified to judge. I had not yet had enough experience to recognize the difference between good scripts, good acting, and good direction.

It seems to me, in retrospect, that Lon did as much directing as Mr. Worsley did. Of course, the second unit director would direct flashes or close-ups of extras in the crowd. But for our personal scenes I seem to remember Lon giving advice or suggestions more than Mr. Worsley. Maybe Mr. Worsley knew that Lon had directed many of his earlier films at Universal and some for the Warren Kerrigan company. But the responsibility of spending over a million dollars of Mr. Laemmle's money along with the hundreds of daily problems that came from handling thousands of extras—which by the way was accomplished by the use of a then-modern miracle—an electric voice amplification system now known as a loudspeaker. Although the crowds were handled by assistant directors, Mr. Worsley had complete control by hiding many speakers behind statues and windows, out of camera range and a few hundred feet from where he was stationed. You should have seen the faces of a few of the extras who having been placed way back near the Cathedreal, thought they could goof-off a bit-have an early lunch or take a nap. Just as they settled in for their picnic—Mr. Worsley's voice, calling for action, boomed over the hidden speakers like the voice of God, almost sending the loafers running into the church for confession. As I was saying, with all that responsibility he must have welcomed any help he could get. During the courtroom scene where I, Esmeralda, was being questioned by the judge, it was Lon who made the suggestion that I should underplay the scene, being more exhausted than frightened, and it was Lon who came to me, between set-ups, and told me that I had caught the mood, and to keep it.

As I have mentioned, Lon was at the studio every day, even when he wasn't working; he stood behind the camera and okayed the set-ups, and occasionally even made suggestions about the lighting. In the torture scene-which I believe has been cut from the TV re-runs, and from the tapes-it was Lon who commended me for turning my head from side to side, because, he said, people did that to escape from pain. Incidentally, I hadn't known that; I had just done it instinctively. But I was very happy to get his approval.

Director Wallace Worsley and Cameraman, the first Director to use Western Electric's new public address system

During one of the more emotional scenes, where I was probably over emoting all over the set, Lon came to me and very quietly said "You don't have to cry real tears. I hate these people who brag that they can cry at the drop of a hat. The point is not for you to cry but to make your audience cry. So you must be in control. Don't just throw yourself into it and say 'Oh I felt that scene.' Make your audience feel the scene. Now just remember Patsy dear, you are an actress. You don't have to live the part, you have to act the part!"

Never, to my knowledge, was there any friction between Lon and Mr. Worsley; they often sat together riffling through the pages of the script, or, when Lon was not in make-up, having lunch together in the commissary. A director is supposed to be like the Captain of a ship, who issues orders and does not expect to have to debate them with a member of the crew. I may be quite wrong, of course; it is possible that Mr. Worsley was grateful for Lon's help. A moot question...

One of the assistant directors to the assistant director to Mr. Worsley was a young man just over from Europe. Alsace Lorraine it might have been, I'm not sure now. Anyway, he and his brother Robert were nephews of Uncle Carl. Who wasn't at Universal in those days. Willy was the other brother. Willy took to whatever job was assigned to him with great enthusiasm. I don't remember what Robert did, but he was the one I'd have bet on. He was taller than Willy and quite good looking, although not blonde and blue-eyed. No one could have called Willy good looking but he was very pleasant. I enjoyed chatting with him between scenes in my fractured French and was impressed by how quickly he seemed to catch on to everything, the camerawork, the set-ups and crew preparation.

Willy became completely Americanized, changed his name from Willy to William and became one of our finest directors, William Wyler.

When the last shot was in the can, and the assistant director said, "It's a wrap-up folks" we all went our separate ways without many formal goodbyes. Some of us would work together again—I did a picture with Norman a few years later—some of us would only meet casually here or there—some of us would never see each other at all, unless we happened to belong to the same golf or beach clubs.

It has been my experience that very few lasting friendships are made by working together in a picture. Sometimes the cast is very congenial and you have lots of fun on the set; sometimes little romances develop—but as a general rule, once the last scene has been shot everyone is already halfway out the door.

I remember bits and pieces of my last day on *The Hunchback*. Norman came by my dressing room to say goodbye; he was clad in armor and said he didn't dare give me a hug for fear of breaking my ribs. I offered to run down to the commissary to get a can-opener, he laughed, gave me a pretty good kiss, a quick pat on the fanny, and said, Let's work together again some day when you're grown-up.

Winston and Patsy would not return to this set for over 60 years

Mr. Worsley wished me luck and said politely that he had enjoyed working with me. I suppose I said something about how much I had enjoyed working with him.

The camera crew were darlings, they presented me with a blow-up of one of my closeups, with a very flattering caption which I don't think I'd better repeat.

A girl in the make-up department who claimed to be part Cheyenne gave me an Indian good-luck charm which I wore occasionally, but eventually had to give up as it looked like a swastika.

Then came time to say goodbye to Lon Chaney. Someone told me he was in the projection room, so I put my suitcase in my car—it is amazing how many things you accumulate in a dressing room in six months—and drove over to the building he was in, knocked timidly on the projection room door, and announced that I was leaving. He came out into the hall right away and when I thanked him for his being so patient and so helpful he broke into one of his rare sweet smiles. He wished me luck, said that I looked fine in the rushes, and that he was sure I would do well... and then I had the feeling that he was no longer with me.

Permit me to leap ahead fifty years; it was some time in the Seventies that my husband and I decided to fly from Edinburgh to Glasgow to visit his Aunt Joan. We were to go up on a Sunday, spend the night, and return to Edinburgh on the Monday. Aunt Joan said they would meet us at the airport, she and Uncle George.

We arrived on schedule, but there was no one at the airport to meet us. Worried that there might have been an illness, or an accident, he rushed to a phone. Her number rang and rang before it was answered by an apologetic Aunt Joan.

"Do forgive me, dear boy," she said. We've been watching an old movie on the telly, and we completely forgot about you and Pat. It's *The Hunchback of Notre Dame*... it's still on, as a matter of fact... do, do forgive us..."

My husband said it didn't matter, go back and watch the movie, we'd take a taxi, which we did. It's about a twenty minute drive to Bearsden, the suburb in which they live, and by the time we got there the TV show was over. I couldn't resist asking Aunt Joan whether seeing me on the screen hadn't reminded her that I would be at the airport.

"Not a bit of it, dear," she said. "In my mind I never connected the two of you at all."

That's somewhat the way it was that day in 1923 at the old Universal Studios, when I felt Lon moving away from me. I, Patsy Ruth Miller, was over and done with- she, Esmeralda, was just beginning to live... and in his mind he no longer connected the two of us at all.

Hollywood Boulevard 1920's.

Courtesy Tod Firetag, Poster City

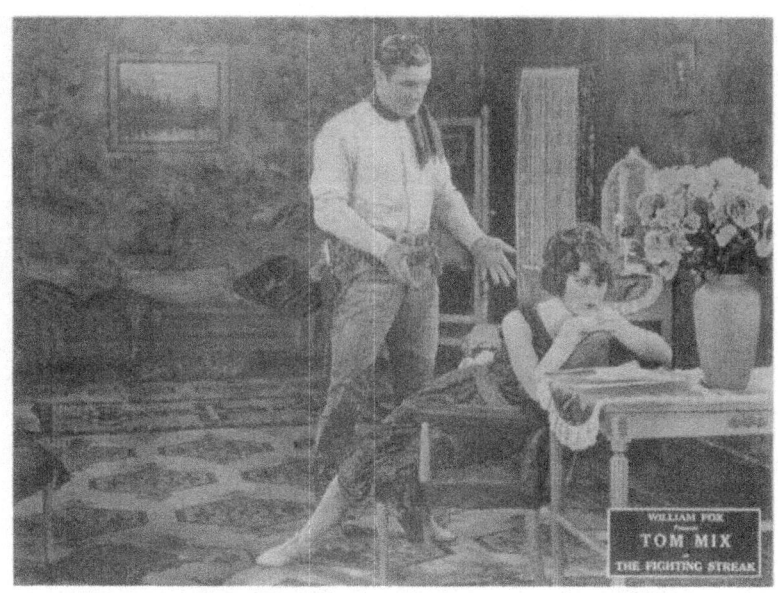

Courtesy Tod Firetag, Poster City

Filming "Hell Bent For Heaven" with Johnny Harron and Director J. Stuart Blackton

Hoot Gibson and Director Jack Conway giving me a ride to "The Hunchback" set, 1923.

Patsy Ruth Miller with Cullen Landis and Clarence Badger in "Where is My Wondering Boy Tonight!"

Ibrihim, Uncle of King Farouk asked me if I wanted a ride while Mr. Ince set up his cameras – to their surprise he drove me through Culver City at 120 mph while the director and crew went into a panic!

Cast and Crew from "Watch Your Step", the man next to Patsy is Bill Beaudine, the Director.

Norman Kerry finds Patsy Ruth Miller in the jungle

CHAPTER TEN

When we parted company on *The Hunchback* Norman had said, "Let's work together again some day when you're grown up." We did that just two years later. It was another picture for Universal, in 1925, called *Lorraine of the Lions*. I was Lorraine.

The story is about a little girl, the sole survivor of a shipwreck, who is washed ashore on an uninhabited island in the South Seas—uninhabited by people, that is. There was every other kind of animal life imaginable: lions, tigers, snakes, big monkeys, little monkeys, and a gorilla. I can't swear that there wasn't an elephant. Quite an assemblage for one little South Sea Island.

Nurtured by the gorilla, I—Lorraine, that is—grew up to romp through the jungle, swing from trees, and generally cavort like a tiny Tarzan, wearing a sort of modest bikini made of fig leaves and bark. It was great fun. Not all fun and games however; In one scene I was to swing from one tree to another, across a wide patch of open space in which lurked a cobra. (Lions were my pals—cobras weren't). A double was standing by, but oh, no, I insisted on doing it myself; all I had to do was grab hold of a thick vine—a rope, actually, with a big knot for me to hold on to—and swing through the air from a limb of one tree to the limb of another. It would have been a breeze had not the camera platform in the second tree jutted out about a foot. Instead of landing on the branch, my leg hit the platform full force, right on the shin bone. The pain was excruciating, but somehow I managed to hang on to the vine, instead of dropping ten or twelve feet to the ground, until I was rescued. Miraculously, the bone wasn't broken, only chipped. The chips were removed in the infirmary, leaving only a small dent in my otherwise flawless leg—a dent which is still there—and I was back at work in a few days. But the double did the swing in the long shot.

There was another incident which livened things up. It was a scene in which I was to swim across a crocodile-infested stream to the other shore. I don't think I was escaping anything, I think it was just to show how frolicsome I was, even among crocodiles. Ed Sedgewick, the director, had no objection to my doing it myself, as he knew I was a good swimmer. For the sake of realism, Ed had a live crocodile basking in the sun on the bank of the stream. I was a bit hesitant when I saw the monstrous ugly creature, but its trainer assured us that the croc was heavily sedated and wouldn't wake up for hours. Thus reassured, the cameras started rolling, I dashed past the supine critter, and plunged into the water. Doing an easy, carefree crawl, I had almost reached midstream when I became aware of frenzied shouts, and looking back over my shoulder I saw the crocodile slithering into the water behind me. Obviously the sedation wasn't strong enough to keep him from going after a good meal.

For one horrible moment I was frozen with terror, then it lent strength to my arms and legs, and I put on a burst of speed that might well have broken all existing Olympic records. I was told afterward that all the frantic crew could see of me was white foam. I reached the far shore still in the lead, but not by much.

The croc didn't follow me out of the water, however. By that time the trainer had waded in up to his waist and managed to hook it with a wire lasso. I crawled out of the water on my hands and knees and just stayed that way until the prop man came over on a raft to take me back. Once I was able to breathe again, I told Ed that he better hope the camera got it all, as I was not about to do it again. Ed, looking surprised, said, "You gotta be kidding. I thought you knew that was only a rehearsal."

That was more or less what I would have expected of Eddie Sedgewick; he had a rather crude sense of humor. Before I could think of a cutting retort, the sardonic smile left his face and in a voice in which I actually detected a quaver, he said, "Jeez, kid, you scared the hell out of us." Then he half patted, half squeezed my wet shoulder turned abruptly, and strode away.

Norman hadn't been working that day. I wonder what his reaction would have been. Oddly enough, that incident was never again referred to by any of us - at least, not to my knowledge. Despite these little *contretemps*, I thoroughly enjoyed making the picture, especially because I loved working with Norman. He played an Englishman who comes ashore from his yacht—maybe he was supposed to be an archeologist or an ichtiologist, or something like that—and to his surprise finds Lorraine romping around with the animals. He takes her back to England to exhibit to his friends, and I loved that part, too. . . getting all dressed up and trying to imitate the manners of high society. Naturally, they fall in love, et cetera and so on. Fadeout on a clinch. . .

Also naturally, since I was now "grown-up", the first week we were working together Norman felt obligated to make a pass at me. It was a half-hearted effort, at best, and I rather suspect that he was relieved when nothing came of it. With that out of the way, we had a ball for the rest of the picture. I hope he like me as much as I liked him.

Director Edward Sedgewick

In Civilization, clairvoyent Kerry behind Patsy.

CHAPTER ELEVEN

Not long ago I received a fan letter from an old-movie buff whose name was Douglas MacLean; he wrote from Australia to tell me that he had seen some posters, or stills, from a film starring an American actor named Douglas MacLean. I was identified as his leading lady, and that is why he was writing to me. The film was *The Yankee Consul* and could I dutifully him anything about Mr. MacLean? He was obviously a Scotsman; did I know where we was born; which country in Scotland did he or his family come from; was he still alive, and if so, where could he be reached?

There are probably a hundred Douglas MacLeans, more or less, in this country, and hundreds more in Scotland; I have my doubts that they were kin, though perhaps from the same sept. But I dutifully replied, telling the Aussie MacLean the actor was the son of a Presbyterian minister, but that's all I knew about him. I think I added that he was completely charming, as most Scots are.

That started the memories flowing with a rush; as vividly as though it were only twenty or thirty years ago instead of more than sixty. I could see Doug MacLean clearly, I could even hear his voice, a very well-bred precise voice. There was no trace of the Scottish intonation, he must have been born in this country. Douglas MacLean was a comedian, but quite unlike the comics of that day. The comedians of the Twenties were slapstick comics— Buster Keaton, Charlie Chaplin, Laurel and Hardy. They took pratfalls, got pie in the face, and were chased by cops.

Doug MacLean broke the mold. He was the first to play for laughs in a smooth, unruffled way, always the well-dressed, well-groomed gentleman. Events swirled around his head; he coped with problems with refined frenzy, sometimes baffled, often frustrated, but never losing an air of not believing that this sort of thing could be happening to *him*. Buffeted by Fate, caught up in a tide of misunderstanding, he remained the well-educated son of a Presbyterian minister, frantic but gentlemanly. It was a different approach, and it was very funny... sometimes hilarious.

He also broke with tradition by always having a romantic love story; in fact generally that involvement triggered the comedy... misunderstandings, wrong phone numbers, lovers' quarrels, and all that. The confused situation was all straightened out in the last reel, and boy got girl... to everyone's great satisfaction.

Harold Lloyd later played comedy without slapstick, but his was not so cerebral as MacLean's. He depended

75

largely on physical effects; it was in a sense, more refined slapstick.

When the name of Harold Lloyd is mentioned, the scene that comes to mind is Harold desperately clinging to the hands of a huge clock on the tower of a skyscraper, a typical scene of visual comedy, as well as wonderful trick camera effects.

Douglas MacLean and Director Thomas Ince. 1921.

When I was still doing extra work I got a call to report to the Thomas Ince Studio in Culver City, to be one of seven stenographers in a Douglas MacLean picture called *One a Minute*. Mother was more thrilled than I was, as MacLean was one of her favorite actors.

The Ince studio was a beautiful white-pillared building, set far back from the road. With it's well-cut lawn and well-trimmed shrubbery, it looked more like a stately colonial home than a studio. There were six other girls already on the set when I arrived, breathless, but rarin' to go.

The seven of us were seated at seven desks in a large office set. Mine was right up front, with an enormous typewriter on it, so I immediately started typing, just to see how it felt. I had never even touched a typewriter key (in those days typewriters were used only in offices), and what came out on the paper was something like 3ifhtpa;vn6g4s, but the sound was right and I must have looked as though I knew what I was doing because the assistant director came over and asked if I used the touch system, whatever that was.

The cameras were set up, the director yelled Quiet! We're rolling! And we seven stenographers started typing.

The director was Thomas Ince himself, I think. He was very nice and didn't object to Mother sitting behind the camera; in fact, he spent a good deal of the between-scene time chatting with her and quite often, as I stood off-camera, watching them set up for the next scene, I could hear her bubbly laugh.

Anyway, we did the one scene in which, as I recall, we all stopped typing and watched Mr. MacLean as he crossed in front of us, looking at him adoringly and sighing as he disappeared into an office. I don't truly think I was outstanding in that scene, and it could have been because of my typing, but whatever the reason, I was selected by Mr. MacLean and the director to do a "bit" as a telephone switchboard operator to whom Mr. MacLean gives several calls.

It was one of those typical MacLean scenes of controlled anxiety in which he was trying to get a very important message to his girl and being baffled by snarled lines, busy signals and wrong numbers. I suppose I automatically reacted to his frantic intensity and played it for comedy myself. Everyone on the set started laughing and when the director yelled "cut!" I thought I was out of a job. But both he and Doug were so amused that they gave me a little scene all to myself and had the camera dolly up for an honest-to-goodness close-up. It was terribly thrilling.

Between chats with the director, Mother had occupied herself by making drawn-work handkerchiefs, daintily hemmed. It was her sole accomplishment in the field of sewing—they were really lovely—and she handed them out lavishly to the crew and to the director when my stint was finally done and we had to say an almost tearful goodbye. She was hesitant about offering one to the star, but Doug, bless his Scottish heart, claimed to be hurt by the omission, so Mother twinkled at him and handed him her finest, one she had intended saving for Daddy.

For months thereafter I hopefully awaited another call from Douglas MacLean Productions. It finally came, four years and fifteen pictures later. It was the lead opposite Doug in a comedy called *The Yankee Consul*.

It was a pleasantly amusing picture, and I seem to recall that it got good notices, but it was hardly a noteworthy picture, not really worth mentioning but for one incident, which I have never forgotten.

The first day on the set, in our first scene together, Doug, with a perfectly straight face, pulled a handkerchief out of his breast pocket, and with a flourish, wiped his brow with it—an action not in the script—and with another flourish, replaced it. I was caught off-guard for a moment, then I recognized it as the one Mother had given him all those years ago. After all, there aren't that many drawn-stitch, hand-hemmed lawn handkerchiefs around.

When I told Mother about it that evening, she got all dewy-eyed and said, "The dear sweet man to have remembered all this time." Daddy was less sentimental. "There's a true Scotsman for you," he said, "using the same handkerchief for four years!"

"The Yankee Consul".

CHAPTER TWELVE

Refreshing my memory of people and events long gone and sometimes forgotten, I have come across some clippings from newspapers and magazine articles that I had thankfully forgotten until now. It seems that I was once called The Most Engaged Girl in Hollywood. Once you get something like that pinned on you by the columnists, all the denials in the world won't change a word of it. Rather like the quote they attributed to Garbo "I vant to be alone." Chances are what she really said was, "I vant to get a loan."

According to one gossip columnist, I was engaged to thirteen men—at different times, of course. It's a nice array of names, I must say—Donald Ogden Stewart, Harry Crocker, Kenneth Hawks, Wilbur May, John Monk Saunders, Patrick Kearney, Richard Barthelmess et al. About Dick Barthelmess, the writer has quite a bit to say.

"When the rumor that Miss Miller was to become Mrs. Barthelmess hit the press, it caused quite a stir on Broadway where a dancer named Mary Hay was appearing in a show with Clifton Webb. Miss Hay, the current Mrs. Barthelmess, was very upset by the rumor, although she and Richard had been separated for some time. In fact, she was so upset that she failed to show up for the evening performance. All eyes are now turned toward Dick himself, to see what he is going to do in the wake of Patsy's bombshell."

Patsy's bombshell indeed! Never, at any time, drunk, sober or in my sleep, did I announce that I was engaged to Richard Barthelmess, or that I was going to marry him.

Richard Barthelmess

The whole thing became very embarrassing; if I so much as had a cherry coke at a soda fountain with an eligible young man it was duly reported as another engagement. It reached its culmination in a crack by George Jessel which reverberated from Coast to Coast.

George Jessel had been starring on Broadway in "The Jazz Singer" and Warner Brothers brought him out to the Coast to make a picture for them. A dinner was given in his honor, to welcome him to Hollywood. Naturally, he gave a speech, saying how delighted he was to be in Hollywood—and then he said that his train ticket West had included a stop-over at the Grand Canyon and an engagement to Patsy Ruth Miller. You can believe I was kidded about that for months.

For the record—if there is one—I was never engaged, which to me means having a ring and the intention of getting married, to anyone but the men I married. So there.

In the second place, also for the record: "going with," or dating, as they now call it, meant just what it said—going to dinner, going to the movies, going to a friend's house or a party. It did not mean going to bed. "Going steady" meant that for a while you didn't have dates with other men, or at least, not often.

That was the way it was done in the Twenties. I gather from the autobiographies of more recent actresses that the custom has changed. While I couldn't swear under oath that none of my girl friends ever had a real love affair—or "had sex", as they now call it—at least it was done with discretion. Some may call that hypocrisy; I call it good taste.

Today, Love never enters into it. Today it goes somewhat like this: Boy, to girl he met an hour ago, "Shall we go to my place and have sex, or to McDonalds for a hamburger? Girl, Oh let's have the hamburger. I can have sex any time.

Ah, well... *autre temps, autre moeurs...*

Patsy with Crown Prince & Princess of Sweden, Lloyd Bacon, Jack Warner, Helene Costello, June Winton, George Jessel, and Ray Black.

CAPITOL
Maryland & Atlantic Ave's
Continuous Performances From 1:30 to 11 P. M.
PHONE—MARINE 271-M

TODAY and TOMORROW

Jazz Mad Youth in a Jazz Mad Age!

A story of youth and its new freedom, boys and girls who sometimes mistake license for liberty and lovers for love.

Daughters of Today

CAST INCLUDES
PATSY RUTH MILLER
RALPH GREAVES   ZASU PITTS
PHILO McCULLOUGH

SPECIAL MUSICAL PROGRAM
"NORMA OVERTURE," by Bellini

Richard Barthelmess had been one of my favorite actors long before we ever met. I thought he was terrific in *Tol'able David* and *Way Down East*, and I had envied his leading ladies, but he was a recent addition to the Hollywood colony, having worked mainly in the East, and our paths had never happened to cross.

Contrary to popular belief, everybody in Hollywood didn't know everybody else. We had our own social groups, just as any small town, and there were many actors who never met unless they happened to work together. That was true even of the big stars, who all knew of each other but didn't necessarily attend the same functions, or have mutual friends.

So I was thrilled to the core to be told that Richard Barthelmess, in person, would be at the cocktail party Charles and Clara Ray were having the following Saturday, and devastated to learn that I would be working that day. Daddy, of course, would be playing golf; no mere cocktail party could keep him off the golf course. But Mother said she would go anyway, so I implored her to meet Barthelmess and do everything possible, short of using undue force, to keep him at the party until I could get there.

That Saturday everything went wrong on the set, with delay after delay, and it was after six when, still in makeup, I burst into the house after a hair-raising drive home, determined to shower, change clothes, and dash over to the party. As I started for the stairs, I heard Mother call to me from the living room.

"You're home early," I called back. "Wasn't he there?"

"Oh yes, he was there," Mother replied. "But he isn't there now."

With a muttered, oh, nuts, I slammed my bag down on the hall table, thinking unkind thoughts about the director, the cameraman, and everyone else who had contributed to depriving me of meeting my screen idol.

"Come in here, dear," Mother was calling in her trilliest voice. "I have an old friend I want you to meet."

There being nothing I wanted less at the moment than to meet an old friend of Mother's, I clumped ungraciously into the room where she was standing arm-in-arm with a man whose face I could not see.

"This is my daughter, Dick dear," said my traitorous parent, and Richard Barthelmess turned and grinned at me.

With a meeting like that, what could we do but become a romantic "item?" So we went around together for a few months, to the great delight of the columnists and gossip writers, but our hearts were never in it. Our "romance" had been born of our sense of theatre. Having met in a sort of screen writer's device of bringing boy and girl together, it would have offended our theatrical instincts to have let it go at that. It might have developed into something real had we anything else in common, but we didn't. On my part, he had so long been my ideal man on the screen that I went on momentum for a while, hating to acknowledge to myself that off screen he was pretty heavy going.

On his part, I suspect that he was using me, in a way, to show his wife that he wasn't eating his heart out in Hollywood.

Before our romantic interlude sank without a trace, I played opposite him in his next picture, *The White Black Sheep*, a rather hackneyed tale laid in the far reaches of the British Empire, replete with fierce desert tribesmen, Oriental Bazaars, and long shots of camels plodding across sand dunes.

The story was that Dick, the Black Sheep of a titled English family, redeems himself by saving a whole battalion of British soldiers from the blood-thirsty Arab tribesmen. I assume they were Arabs, since they wore white sheets and head gear. Despite the trite story, Dick gave a beautiful performance, a diamond in a Woolworth setting. I played Zelie, a Greek dancing girl, wearing costumes that showed my midriff, with bells on my fingers and bells on my toes, so of course I loved the part. (Can you believe that showing a girl's midriff was considered daring then?!)

Actually, I didn't know that I was supposed to be

WOMEN (from left to right) top row: Virginia Fox, Lillian Rich, Lois Wilson, Zazu Pitts, Julanne Johnston, Laura LaPlante, Carmel Myers, Clair Windsor, Gertrude Olmstead, Edna Murphy, Mildred Davis; front row: Helen Ferguson, Ruth Dwyer, Patsy Ruth Miller, Ruth Roland, May McAvoy, Anita Stewart, Billie Dove and Kathleen Key.

MENS (from left to right) Charles Farrell, John Monk Saunders, Tom Gallery, William Asher, Ben Bard, (?), William Seiter, Harold Lloyd, Jerry Miley, Charles Paddock, (?), Robert Z. Leonard, Darryl Zanuck, Mervyn LeRoy, and William Russell.

Greek; I thought I was Arabian, like all the others, not that it would have made any difference to my performance, I daresay. I was made Greek in an explanatory sub-title, so that there could be a happy ending. As an Arab, it would have been unthinkable for Dick, the English officer and gentleman, to have married me and taken me home to meet the mater and the pater. An Anglo-Saxon of high estate marrying other than an American or a European was unacceptable to the average audience of those days. Even making me a Greek was chancing it a bit.

What really held us together that summer was Dick's boat, the Pegasus. I'm always supremely contented when on the water, but it wasn't the boat alone that made me happy to spend weekends sailing with Dick. It was the other guests aboard.

Richard Barthelmess and Patsy Ruth Miller aboard the Pegasus

Dick, Ronald Colman and William Powell, all bachelors at the time, were a Three Musketeer group that year which I was permitted to join for the cruising season, and it was Ronald Colman who kept me devoted to Dick. Or, putting it another way, kept me on good enough terms with him to be invited for weekend sails.

We were quite a free-wheeling foursome... Dick, darkly handsome, inclined to sulk when he didn't get his own way, boyishly extravert when he did, Bill Powell, charming, urbane, seemingly amused by life, and Ronald Colman. Ah, Ronnie... how to describe him?

Not to exaggerate, a tendency I deplore, Ronald Colman was handsome, witty, courteous, and well-mannered. He was outrageously attractive, fairly reeking of Scottish charm. He was a delightful conversationalist and a good listener; he also looked splendid in bathing trunks. To put it quite simply, I thought he was the greatest thing going. He inspired daydreams which, to my regret even now, remained just that.

I would have loved to think that it was only his loyalty to Dick that prevented his taking more than a friendly interest in me, but I looked in vain for some indication that he was being torn asunder by desire versus loyalty. That didn't keep me from enjoying his company, however. I loved to make him laugh, I adored it when he teased me, and I was deeply gratified that he seemed to take pleasure in profound discussions of life and love and all the things that young people discuss profoundly while sitting on a moonlit deck. With that I had to be content; that, and a parting kiss on the brow. Oh well... you can't win 'em all.

Ronald Colman

Most of the men mentioned in the article were really just good friends; a few may have been a wee bit more than that, but not much. They were "mes flirtes" as the French call them. There was one man whom I saw quite often for a while without the gossip columns mentioning it. That's because he wasn't newsworthy; his name was Howard Hughes, but he hadn't become THE Howard Hughes.

I met him through his uncle, Rupert Hughes, who was directing the picture I was working in; REMEMBRANCE, based on one of his own novels. Rupert was a very popular novelist; he had written dozens of books, one of which, THE LIFE OF GEORGE WASHINGTON, was considered the definitive biography of the Father of our Country. I think he was a better writer than he was a director, but the picture turned out to be pretty good anyway.

One day on the set Rupert asked me if I would do him a great favor by joining him, his nephew, and the nephew's wife for dinner the next evening at the Biltmore Hotel, which was where the movie colony loved to dine and dance. He warned me that his nephew was a sort of hillbilly; he hadn't been around much and was rather unworldly, but he was a nice boy and was dying to meet a movie actress.

Howard was not exactly as his uncle had described him; he was no hillbilly, merely unsophisticated and a little awkward conversationally. His sweet little wife seemed just as thrilled as Howard to have the move stars pointed out to her, but she was not easy to chat with. I have been told that I could carry on a a conversation with the Sphinx, but even I had a little trouble getting more than a yes or no from her, and that was only after she had looked to Howard for confirmation.

As everyone knows, Howard took to the Hollywood lifestyle like a fish to water, but his wife was more like a fish out of water, and she soon went back to Texas, never to be heard of again, at least, not in our neck of the woods.

Howard Hughes

That evening stands out in my mind as not one of the most fun times I've ever had.

Rupert tried to keep the ball rolling, but he and his nephew didn't seem to have much in common except the fact that they were related, and family talk wears thin after a while. I don't remember whether Rupert asked either of us girls to dance; I do remember that Howard asked me. Ballroom dancing was then the craze; the big bands played almost without intermission the whole evening, and Howard and I plodded laboriously around the dance floor while all around us couples were exuberantly doing the Charleston and vigorous varieties of same. Also, Howard was very tall and I was - and am - very short, and I felt that we looked ridiculous together. I have heard that he later became an excellent and enthusiastic dancer. It's probably true; nothing is impossible.

One evening, after his wife had returned to Texas, Howard and I and another man - I think it was Harry Crocker - went to a movie together. I don't remember what the picture was about, but I do remember that Howard talked all through it, in a loud whisper, telling me why the scenes were all wrong. It must have been something to do with Texas, or the oil business; whatever the subject, Howard knew all about it and told me so. People all around us were shushing him, but, being rather hard of hearing, he didn't hear the shushes and continued his monologue throughout the picture...which didn't add to my enjoyment of it.

Another time, Rupert had a small gathering at his house to which his brother, Felix, was invited to meet his nephew, Howard. Felix Hughes was a musician, I believe, or a music teacher. One thing he wasn't -- a loving uncle. He hadn't seen his nephew for many years, and apparently he would have been satisfied to leave it that way. I gathered that he and Howard's father had never gotten along, even as children, and the evening sort of degenerated into a rehash of old sibling rivalries.

Chalk up another non-fun evening with H. H.

Another time we went to dinner with two other couples and I lost an earring. I didn't want to make a fuss about it; they were quite nice, but not expensive, and I would have preferred to just take off the other earring and forget about it. But Howard insisted on calling the cab company in which we had come to the restaurant, he insisted on writing all the details to give to the insurance company, and he instructed me in how to present my claim. You'd better say you lost the pair, he told me. They never pay the cost of a pair if you lose only one. He was very concerned and kind, but all I wanted him to do was shut up and forget about it. The other couples were becomeing a bit bored with my earrings, I was becoming embarassed, and on the whole, the dinner party wasn't exactly a success.

So why did I go out with Howard? I don't really know. He was rather sweet, in his way, although lacking my kind of humor. And he was a thoughtful host -- almost too thoughtful at times. I suppose in a way, I liked him.

I think he invited me because he hadn't yet met girls more to his taste. Once he got into the swing of things, I never heard from him which was all right with me.

Perhaps there were one or two dates that I enjoyed very much, and I'm only remembering the others. But I could never have fallen in love with him, not even had I known that one day he would be one of the wealthiest and most eligible men in the world.

Of all the names linked to mine, one and one only meant anything to me: John Monk Saunders. He was indeed my own true love - but not as true as I longed for him to be. Oddly enough, it was through Rupert that I met him. This time, we were having lunch in the commissary when John came in and stopped at the table to say Hello to Rupert, who naturally introduced us, but not very graciously. I sensed a certain tension in the air but was too entranced by John's clear blue eyes and warm smile to give it any thought. When John left us to join friends at another table I did notice that Rupert seemed distracted, but I was wondering if I would hear from Mr. Saunders again, and didn't pay much attention to Rupert's change of mood. I did hear from him - and that was it.

Later, when Rupert realized how serious I was getting about John, he explained why he had been reluctant to introduce us; he not only distrusted John, he actively disliked him, and for what he considered good reason. John had been married to Rupert's daughter, Avis, who had ended the marriage when she and John were on a cruise by throwing herself overboard. John may have been in no way responsible for her suicide; there was no hint of foul play, but Rupert had a strong aversion to the man he believed had caused his daughter to no longer want to live.

Even had I known this from the beginning, it would have made no difference. Nothing that anyone could have told me would have made any difference. By the time John left our table I was already in love.

It was wonderful for almost a year. My own true love was fair of skin but not of soul, but I thought he loved me

John Monk Saunders

as much as I loved him, because he said he did, and I believed anything he told me. Up until then I had shied away from marriage like a horse scenting a mountain lion, which was illogical, as the one marriage I knew about first hand, that of my parents, was as ideal as any human relationship could be. It was proof that marriage need not be the end of love, not even of romance. But until I met Johnny, I wanted no part of it. Possibly I was afraid of missing something...possibly I was frightened by the idea of having to run a household, of being responsible for meals and clean bed linen...I really can't remember now why I was so leary of it.

Even then, it wasn't so much that I wanted to be married to John as it was that I couldn't bear the thought of ever being without him. I knew that he lacked certain qualities which I had once considered important, but they were now less than dust beneath his Packard's wheels.

While I was living in a cloud of love, Johnny was living in a cloud of success. He had written a great picture, Wings, which was the first truly authentic film about the U.S. Airforce during World War I, that great war to end all wars. The story was good and the flying scenes were spectacular for that day and age. If I remember correctly, it won the very first OSCAR for best picture. Johnny had been a wartime pilot, so he knew his subject thoroughly and that, naturally, contributed to its great success. But he was too successful too soon. As so often happens, he never seemed able to top that picture, and he became moody and sometimes very distant. He was a writer without a contract, which is not the best of all possible spots to be in, but all a writer can do then is write, write, write. Eventually you sell something and the doors are open to you. But John didn't try it that way—he tried to get in through the back door, or maybe the bedroom door, by paying court to a producer's wife, by making himself available to a director's unmarried sister, by ingratiating himself into the good graces of another producer's homely daughter. None of this, of course, did anything to further his career. Naturally, I wasn't aware of this at the time. All I knew was that he sometimes broke dates with me at the last minute, pleading a possible business deal, or went away for weekends, explaining that he had been invited by a producer who was interested in one of his ideas, and of course that was more important than just the two of us having dinner together, wasn't it, wee Pat?

He was also insistent that I go out once in a while with other men—friends only, of course—when he was tied up on one of his possible contract deals. I didn't want to go out with anyone else, but occasionally I did. One of those times was when I accepted an invitation from Jesse Lasky, Jr., to go dining and dancing at the Cocoanut Grove. I had known Jesse casually for some time, but he had never asked me for a date before. John had told me that he was going to be the guest of Ben Schulberg that night, an invitation he could hardly turn down, so I accepted Jesse's.

It was a horrendous evening for both of us. The food was delicious, the music was great, and Jesse was a good dancer, but John was at a table just across the dance floor, and he wasn't with Ben Schulberg; he was with Mrs. Schulberg—Ad, I think they called her—and another couple. I couldn't keep from looking at them, wondering what they were laughing about, hating every moment of it. I hardly heard a word poor Jesse was saying. Needless to say, he never invited me out again.

Poor Johnny. He wasted all that time being available to escort Mrs. Producer to social functions when Mr. Producer was busy, filling in at dinner parties, making a fourth at bridge, when he should have been home writing, writing, writing...

Then came the party at Dudley Murphy's house at the beach. A few days before, I had fallen doing an escape scene in a picture, and had pulled a ligament in my ankle. I was still on crutches when Johnny took me to the party, which was a pretty big one. Among the guests was an actress who had been in a picture that Johnny had written before I met him. That they had had an affair while on location was no secret; the actress had seen to that. But it was over and done with. No sophisticated

Michael and William Wellman, 1921.

woman ever brought up a man's past affairs; Johnny told me that. There is nothing so boring to a man as jealousy of the past, he said, and I certainly didn't want to be boring. So I smiled and said "hello" in my pleasantest voice, and wished her red hair wasn't so pretty. Her name was Mary and she looked like a Madonna—the real one, not the one with the frizzy hair who sings.

Everyone made quite a fuss over me at first, as I swung about on my crutches, and showed how I could manipulate stairs. But soon my arms began to ache, and the novelty wore off, and I was glad to have Johnny deposit me tenderly in a comfortable chair and go off to get me a glass of champagne.

He didn't return for over an hour, an hour and seventeen minutes by my wristwatch which I kept trying not to look at. Someone else brought me a drink. Someone else chatted with me for a few minutes... then someone else, and someone else... and then I sat alone in my comfortable chair with a smile on my face that was set in concrete and wished that instead of pulling a ligament I had broken my neck.

They came in from the beach together, Johnny and the actress, then quickly separated. Everyone was very nice about not seeing them come in. Our drive home was a silent one, the good night kiss brief. "I'll call you tomorrow," Johnny said, and I think I said all right, but there was such a pounding in my heart I couldn't hear my own voice.

The next day the studio sent a car for me and I went in to make close-ups for the scenes they had done in long shots with the double. When I hobbled out at five o'clock, Johnny was waiting to drive me home. It was the Fox Studio on Western Avenue, a very crowded street at that time of evening; the traffic roared around us like surf pounding on a beach, but inside the car was an island of silence.

As we turned on Sunset Boulevard toward Beverly Hills, Johnny spoke... at first lightly, making a joke of it, then apologetically, admitting that he had been naughty... Silly little Patricia, to take everything so seriously... than angrily... Okay, if you don't trust me, it isn't as though I hadn't told you about her. So the dame's a nympho, what should I do, hit her with a blunt instrument, fight her off with a golf club? My God, it's not as though anything happened on the beach. I wouldn't touch her now with a ten foot pole... Then, in a voice that had never yet failed to make me melt like butter in the sun, he said, "Wee pat, it's all unknowin' how I love you."

I sat there miserably, huddled in my silence, my foot stuck out awkwardly under the dashboard, and I wanted to say, "I love you too, Johnny, I love you too," because I did. But I couldn't say it. I could feel tears streaming down my face, but I didn't have the sensation of crying.

"What do you want from me?" Johnny finally said, slowing the car. "What is it you want? More apologies? *More meaculpa?*"

"No," I gulped. "No, I don't want that."

"Do you want to get married, little Pat?" he said suddenly. "Is that what you want? If it is, all right. We'll get married."

I could actually feel my heart turning over in my chest. Doctors may say that's impossible. The whole medical world may scoff. I felt it turn. I shifted in my seat to look at him, at his clear blue eyes, the eyelids also faintly blue, almost transparent, like a baby's, at the light brown, almost blond hair which swept so pleasingly from his high, smooth brow, at his mouth, sensitive but wide, generous. His teeth were very white, the two front ones just a tiny bit crooked, which saved him from prettiness. I knew then that I would never, in all my life, forget that face. And, as you can see, I haven't.

There it was, what I had been waiting for, what I had thought I wanted more than anything in life, yet it must have been a full minute before I could say a word, and in that minute, like a newsreel unwinding on the screen of my mind, I saw Johnny with the producer's wife, and I knew, as though it had been written in a sub-title, that

John Monk Saunders

there would be another producer's wife and then another. I saw Johnny with the actress, and I knew there would always be another actress and another beach.

When I heard my voice, from a thousand miles away, saying, "I don't think it would work, Johnny," it was like hearing the order for my execution. But you don't die of a broken heart, as Madame would undoubedly have told me. At least it was broken all at once, driving down Sunset, not nibbled away at over the years.

A year or so later, as I was driving up Sunset on my way home from the studio, I heard someone honking at me. I looked back and saw Johnny motioning to me to pull over, so I drew up to the curb and shut off the motor as John pulled in behind me. He got out of his car and came over to my side, and to my annoyance, my heart skipped a beat as he leaned in the window and smiled. His eyes were so blue, he was so good to look at...

He didn't want me to read it in the paper, he was saying, he wanted to tell me himself. He didn't want me to hear it from some gossip columnist. He was going to marry Fay Wray.

I thanked him for telling me, and then I said—and to my own surprise I meant it—"I really wish you nothing but happiness, John."

"Thank you, wee Pat," he said, and went back to his car.

He married Fay Wray, but apparently didn't find the happiness I had wished him. A few years later he was dead by his own hand.

If you're going to get your heart broken—and who doesn't—it is best to do it when you're young, and get it over with. Young hearts, like young bones, heal quickly, and from then on, the scar tissue protects them.

CHAPTER THIRTEEN

When, after the Douglas MacLean picture was finished, I received an offer to make two pictures at the Whitman Bennet Studio in New York, I accepted without even asking how much they would pay me, or what the movies were about. I found out that the salary was quite good, but I never did find out exactly what the pictures were about. Perhaps I'm exaggerating. I probably knew then, but haven't the faintest idea now.

Mother was as eager as I was to go to New York, which we had never had the chance to visit, and as Daddy didn't mind staying home with my brother, who was in high school by that time, off we went on the good old Sante Fe Chief. It was my first long ride on a train, and I was entralled. I had the upper berth in our stateroom, and I can remember lying there, listening to the rumble of the wheels, hearing the murmurs and shouts when we pulled into a station—and we stopped at many of them—the clank of metal on metal when the train crew went from car to car banging on the wheels, the snorting

Whitman Bennett Studio in New York, 1924

engine as we got up steam to pull out. And that long, lonely wail of the train's whistle as we sped through the sleeping countryside. It was sheer magic.

And the club car! It had big plush chairs that revolved, where the passengers could gather for a drink, or a chat while watching the landscape go by like a huge panorama slowly unfolding. The dining car fairly shone with spotless white napery, glistening silver and sparkling glassware. In addition, the service was perfection and the menu was excellent. The waiters and porters were in a class by themselves: courteous, quick, and pleasant to look at.

When we were passing through Colorado, the conductor came in to ask if we would like fresh trout for dinner; at our next stop we would pick some up, freshly caught from a cold mountain stream. And how would we like it cooked?

When we arrived in New York, we were met at Grand Central Station by someone from the studio, and taken to the Plaza Hotel, on 5th Avenue, which from then on became my headquarters whenever I was in New York. It was love at first sight on my part; I fell madly in love with the Big City (not then called the Big Apple.) It was a love affair that lasted for many years. That I am no longer in love with New York is not because I am fickle, but because it is no longer the clean, beautiful city that won my girlish heart.

I'm pretty sure, when told that I was going to work in Yonkers, I said, fine, but what are Yonkers? I soon found out what it was: a pretty little village about an hour's drive away. I never did find out exactly where it was. The studio car picked me up each morning and drove me back to the hotel each evening, but it was autumn, and the foliage was so spectacular, so blazing with reds and oranges and yellows, so unlike our California greens and browns, that I never really noticed where I was being driven. I'm still not sure *where* Yonkers is—or are?

The Whitman Bennet Studio was almost primitive; functional, I daresay, but so far behind our Hollywood studios that it was hard to believe that East was where it had all started. Clearly the future of the motion picture industry lay out West.

Naturally, I was bowled over by the New York Theatre, real live Theatre, with real live actors playing in wonderful plays by wonderful playwrites. I remember Joseph Schildkraut in *Liliom*, Jeanne Eagels in *Rain*, and Ralph Forbes in *Journey's End*. Our local theatre in L.A. couldn't hold a candle to it, which was an unfair judgement, as we did have many good shows out there. But it didn't have the excitement of Broadway, and really, still doesn't.

Through Constance Bennett, whom I had come to know quite well when we had adjoining dressing rooms at Universal, I met some of Long Island polo playing set—Tommy Hitchcock, Rodman Wanamaker and others of that strata of pretty high society. Connie herself was veddy veddy social... but a darling girl, none the less. Sometimes I felt like a high school kid when I was with her, but I didn't really mind feeling juvenile in her company because she was so ultra sophisticated and soignee. I wondered if I would ever achieve her degree of sophistication and frankly, I don't believe I ever did.

But the real thrill was meeting people of the theatre; I met many of them through Marc Connelly, the playwright, whom I had known in Hollywood, and who took an avuncular interest in me. It was Marc who had the audacity to introduce me to the Algonquin Round Table-ites, where I sat mute and blinded by the brilliance of such as Dorothy Parker, Harold Ross, Robert Benchley, Charles MacArthur, and others of the illustrious literati. They composed a unique little coterie, meeting each day for lunch and the exchange of bon mots and carefully prepared epigrams. I think Marc enjoyed presenting me as an oddity: a movie actress who not only could read, but had read.

For the most part, they accepted me kindly, possibly grateful for a new unjaded audience. In time some of them even became my friends. Alexander Woolcott never did, however. He was the self-appointed Dean of the Round Table, a sort of obese King Arthur holding Court, granting or withholding favors to his Knights and Ladies. I rather suspect he preferred granting favors to his Knights...

Had I not been preoccupied with work, Theatre, parties, and all those amusements which do take up a girl's time, I could have fallen madly in love with Charles MacArthur. He was to be adored; he was a pixie, a Peck's bad boy with talent, who had the good sense to grow up and marry Helen Hayes.

Some years later, when she was on the road with "Coquette," the play Charlie had written for her, she had to leave the show because of the imminent arrival of her "Act of God" baby, and I had the good fortune to replace her in the West Coast production. I felt very honored to be chosen to follow in her dainty footsteps, as Helen Hayes was—and still is—my ideal as actress and as woman.

Of all the plays I was in, eight or nine at least, and some very good ones, *Coquette* is the one I cherish in my memory, partially because of the following letter written by George Ebey, the owner and operator of the Fulton Theatre in San Francisco. I've saved it all these years. If this is boastful, so be it.

> *Dear Miss Miller,*
>
> *I went back to say "hello" after the matinees but you had gone.*
>
> *You are a good actress. Otherwise I would have had a pleasant matinee, maybe. As it was, I shivered and had too many catches in the throat. "Coquette" was too real for my peace of mind... much, much too sad. I am shaking yet, inside of me, old and tough as I am.*
>
> *Truly,*
> *G.E.*

Dear Mr. Ebey. He prided himself on being a tough critic, but he was both sentimental and stage-struck; the perfect audience. His letter was more to me than a flattering critique; it was an assurance that I had done justice to Charlie's beautiful play, and that I had lived up to Miss Hayes' confidence in me. I wonder how *Coquette* would be received today, dealing as it does with such obsolescent precepts as virtue and honor.

Robert Benchley, although regarded as one of the Algonquinites, was with them, but not exactly *of* them. I grew to like him very much in New York, and getting to know him better when he came to Hollywood made me like him even more. He improved upon acquaintance.

About Dorothy Parker the same cannot be said. Perhaps I had never seen her clearly in New York, dazzled as I was by her talent, which seemed to shoot off sparks. But when she was married to Alan Campbell, and lived down the street from me in Beverly Hills, I came to know her too well. The wit which had shone like a jewel in the Algonquin setting was still sharp and able to lacerate, but more as a broken bottle cuts than as a diamond. It was disillusioning to discover that although she spoke with passion of her love for humanity, she didn't like people, and though she wrote of Love with gaiety, with humor, sometimes with desperation, she really didn't know anything about Love at all.

But her poetry still stands, and if you don't read too much of it at one time, it still has magic.

One evening after a show I was taken to the Scott Fitzgerald's by my guide and mentor, Marc. At first I wanted to turn around and go right out, despite my desire to meet my literary idol. It was sheer bedlam. People were standing wall to wall, all seeming to be shouting at each other, with no one listening. A victrola was playing somewhere, and from the bedroom came voices in a sort of off-key barbershop quartet.

While I was looking around for Marc, who had been swallowed up in the crowd, a pretty, thin-faced girl at my elbow said, "I'm Zelda. What do you want to drink?"

Before I could answer, someone grabbed her and she was gone. I said politely to the empty space where she had been, "Nothing, thank you," and suddenly the space was filled by a handsome young man with the clear blue eyes of a child.

"Nothing what?" he asked me.

"Nothing anything," I answered.

"It has to be nothing *something*," said the young man, "or you shouldn't thank me for it."

"I didn't," I said.

"Oh, yes you did. I heard you. Look I don't want to seem insistent, but do try to think. Nothing what? Nothing more? Nothing less? Nothing better? Nothing worse?"

I started to laugh. "Nothing, *please.*"

"Oh, well, in that case," he said. "You're welcome. My name is Scott Fitzgerald."

"I'm Patsy Ruth Miller," I said, "and I've changed my mind about nothing. I'll have some champagne if there is any."

Zelda and Scott

91

So Scott brought me a glass of champagne and took me around to meet some of the guests, and it ended up that Marc, Scott and Zelda and I were finally the only ones left so we went to Child's on Fifth Avenue and had pancakes and ham and eggs and cups and cups of coffee until nearly dawn, talking all the while.

From then on, all the months I was in New York, their apartment was a stopping-off place for me, almost as Madame's had been in Hollywood. I didn't know that "dropping in" is not done in the East as it is on the West Coast; the old Spanish tradition of hospitality still held true in the West, and when people say come by any time, they mean it. Anyway, I was always made welcome, but I never went when they had large groups of people, only when Zelda and Scott were there alone, which they generally were in the late afternoon. Their real day didn't start until after dark, and except on weekends, that was when mine ended.

Sometimes, if there was no party scheduled for that night, the three of us would go to dinner, but more and more often, during those fall months, Zelda would plead fatigue and ask Scott to bring something back for her. Then Scott and I would eat at a nearby restaurant, he would drop me off at the hotel, and would take a pizza or a sandwich back to Zelda.

I accepted her excuses at face value, never for one minute realizing that the "fatigue" from which she so often suffered, was alcoholic.

One night when Zelda was too tired to go out, Scott took me to Luchow's, the world famous restaurant way downtown, and pointed out all the literary and theatrical celebrities to me with the enthusiasm of a small town boy in the big city. It occurred to neither of us that possibly we were being pointed out by the other diners. For some reason which even now I can't explain, I have always felt anonymous, if that's the word I want. I never felt recognizable, and was always surprised when anyone did recognize me. My pictures had played all the New York houses, so I daresay my face was familiar to some of the diners, and Scott, of course, was as much a celebrity as most of those at whom we were covertly staring, but as we weren't feeling famous, we were free to giggle and argue to laugh at our own jokes.

It didn't seem to me that Scott drank more than most of the men I knew. He seemed to become intoxicated on words, and sometimes we would sit, our after-dinner coffee growing cold, while Scott tried to make me see some fine point of writing, or understand why an emotion had been ill or well portrayed. But I often had the feeling that he was unsure of himself as a writer, that he was afraid that one day he'd have nothing left to say, and I also had the impression that Zelda did little to build his confidence, even sometimes, in a perverse way, seemed to enjoy his battle with self-doubt.

On several occasions when Scott brought me back to the hotel, he came up and spent a few minutes chatting with Mother, and he so wooed and won her that she talked for months afterward about the "dear sweet boy" who was so nice to Pat in New York. And that is really what he was—a dear sweet boy, with a great talent which he couldn't quite trust.

I didn't see Scott again for several years, during which time he had to put Zelda in a sanatorium in Switzerland and I had married John Lee Mahin, a charming man and a a brilliant writer himself.

Poor Zelda. What had been a sort of mad-cap sense of fun had become a frenzied seeking of excitement; her changes of mood from hysterical gaiety to deep depression had been symptoms of the mental disease which finally destroyed her.

John often saw Scott at MGM, where they were both working, and told me that Scott seemed very despondent. I said that was only natural, with Zelda in a sanatorium, but John said, No, that wasn't it. He was writing a screen play based on someone else's story and hated his assignment. Then why does he do it? I asked. Money, I suppose, said John, but it's a damn shame.

I finally ran into Scott one day at the studio where I had gone to pick up John. It was true; he did seem to have less sparkle, less animation, than he had had in New York. I remember John saying to him, "Come on, kid. It's all grist to your mill. Some day you're going to write something about Hollywood as good as *The Great Gatsby*."

Scott reacted as though he'd been accused of raping his twin sister. He said that he had never written anything worthwhile, that Gatsby was already dead and best forgotten, that nothing he had ever done would live, and not to give him any of that crap about great literature.

I was too startled by his vehemence, by his whole attitude, to say anything. Then, with a "Nice to have seen you again, Pat," he turned and strode off.

On the way home John said this was all because of the people Scott was surrounded by, all the writers who had suddenly become politically oriented; social-consciousness was the cry, and anyone who merely wrote about people and their everyday problems and emotions, was at least a Fascist or maybe worse. Poor Scott had been tossed into this whirlpool of Liberalism, and without a political credo to cling to, was drowning in it. He had never espoused causes, nor been very interested in politics; as a writer, Humanity had meant little to him, the Individual everything. His work was condemned to total oblivion, they said, and he believed them. He denounced hmself even more harshly than his judges, accusing his work of being trivial and superficial.

"He actually told me he's ashamed of *The Great Gatsby*," John fairly snarled. "Those cursed Do-gooders... they've got him believing his work isn't worth a tinkers damn just because he wasn't waving a banner or marching in a picket line. They've destroyed him, as sure as God made little apples."

"That shouldn't keep him from writing," I protested.

"The Hell it doesn't," John said. "Who can write when you've been told, when you've been *convinced* that anything you have to say is a bunch of crap. He can write rings around every one of those bastards who've done this to him, but he doesn't believe it any more, and if you don't believe it, you can't do it."

"Maybe we ought to ask him out to the farm," I said after a while. "Maybe it would be good for him to be with someone he knew in the old days, with people who still think he's great."

But we got to thinking about it; he was living with Sheila Graham, a gossip columnist, whom we didn't know. We'd have to invite her too; maybe she wouldn't want to come. Maybe she'd resent his seeing a friend from the past. Maybe being with me would bring back too many memories, reminders of the honeyed days when he and Zelda had been a golden couple, trailing banners of youth and fame and fun across the New York sky.

So we didn't invite him out to the farm. He was living nearby in the Valley, but for one reason and another, we didn't invite him. It might have changed nothing, but I should have tried. So what if he had turned us down? So what if Miss Graham had snubbed me? I should have tried.

And then he was dead. I had not learned that lesson in time. . .

Scott and Richard Barthelmess on the set.

Nazimova's home became 'The Garden of Allah', a haven for writers and home for Scott when he first came to Hollywood.

Arriving home from our New York trip, 1924.

CHAPTER FOURTEEN

Several years ago there was a movie on Television which was well publicized as telling the real true-life story of William Randolph Hearst and his long-time mistress, Marion Davies, as well as scenes of San Simeon, that legendary estate, in which famous people from all over the world had been entertained.

Having been a guest there many times, nothing would have kept me from watching it and wallowing in nostalgia.

My husband had to attend a St. Andrews Society dinner in New York that night, which was probably just as well, I thought: I could shed a few sentimental tears better alone.

The tears I shed were of annoyance—and boredom. It was utter tripe; a dull story, about dull people, aided and abetted by dull acting. Robert Mitchum, whose work I generally admire, played the role of Hearst as though he had been given a shot of novocaine in his lips, and with a dead pan expression that would have done credit to Buster Keaton. If Hearst had been as uninteresting as he was in that movie, I can assure you, from what I knew of Marion, she wouldn't have given him the time of day, much less lived with him all those years—not for all the wealth and power in the world.

As for the actress—I don't remember her name—who was supposed to be Marion, she had blonde hair, done somewhat as Marion did hers, but there the similarity ended. If Marion had been the nit-wit she was portrayed as, Mr. Hearst would have enjoyed and forgotten her in a matter of days, not loved and cherished her all those years. After all, bubblehead blondes are a dime a dozen.

Marion was a doll, but far from being a nit-wit. She was a lively, intelligent woman, with a delightful sense of humor. Everyone who knew her, liked her. So much for my evening of nostalgia.

I almost never made it to San Simeon in the Twenties.

When the phone rang one evening and a voice said it was speaking for Marion Davies, who would like to know whether I would care to spend the weekend at San Simeon, I thought it was a gag, probably perpetrated by Donald Ogden Stewart, a writer friend, who was scornful of tycoons like William Randolph Hearst and such establishments as San Simeon. Having in mind Don's jibes about roughing it in castles, I replied flippantly, and the voice coolly said that my regrets would be conveyed to Miss Davies.

"You mean Mr. Stewart, don't you?" I said, to show that I had not been taken in.

That was how close I came to never being a guest at that fabulous gathering place of celebrities. Fortunately, Marion's secretary was smarter than I was, and instead of hanging up, she assured me that it really was an invitation from Miss Davies, that no Mr. Stewart was involved, and that if I was free to accept, a car would pick me up Friday afternoon to take me to the railroad station. Then came the tricky part: I had to get permission from my parents. There was I, a young woman, not a child, and an actress to boot, and I had to get permission to go away for a weekend. But so did all the girls I knew, and we accepted it as perfectly natural... which it was, in those days.

The secretary dutifully waited while I found Mother and, almost incoherent with excitement, asked if I could go. Permission was granted doubtfully, Mother asking who else would be there, me saying, Heavens, I can't very well ask that, Mother saying, You really should wait until your father comes home. He's next door playing pinochle with Don Marquis, me saying, Please, Mother, it's an honor to be asked, Mother saying, Really, Pat, I should like to know a little more about it. Me wailing, But I do know about it. Everyone knows about it! I may never be invited again.

Just as I told the secretary I would love to accept, came the dreadful realization that I might have to work Friday, but this was waived aside. You're working at Miss Davies' studio, the secretary stated rather than asked. I said, Yes, at MGM, and she assured me that I would be free Friday noon at the latest. And I was.

Friday afternoon a limousine came for me and I was driven to the railroad station downtown where a private Pullman car was waiting on a siding. There were already about twenty people aboard, some of whom I knew by sight, some I had met. Among the latter was Carmelita Geraghty, an actress about my own age. Feeling terribly ill at ease, I clung to Carmelita, who appeared to be poised and unruffled, as though this were an everyday occurence. And why shouldn't it be, I thought. Her father, Tom Geraghty, was Douglas Fairbanks' favorite writer and intimate friend, so she must have been used to hob-nobbing with famous people.

Carmelita, who became one of my dearest friends, later confessed that her enviable aplomb had been a sham. After all, she said, being a house guest of William Randolph Hearst was hardly comparable to knowing movie stars; there are dozens of famous actors, only one Mr. Hearst.

By the time we got rolling, I had lost a good deal of my shyness in the festive air of the club car, where all the guests were assembled, and when I finally went to my compartment about midnight, I felt that I was part of the most delightful group of people in Southern California.

We pulled into San Luis Obispo very early in the morning, which is not my best time. As some of the others had not retired until much later—if at all—it was a silent group who entered the waiting limousines and started the long drive to the ranch, but by the time we turned off the main road and entered the San Simeon estate, we were all wide awake. It was like going on safari through South Africa; animals of all kinds were browsing along the side of the road, or crossing fearlessly in front of us. Once a llama, meditatively chewing his cud, stood and stared at us, refusing to cede right of way, and the driver just sat patiently until the llama decided to go somewhere else. It was strictly forbidden to blow the horn, or to frighten the animals in any way, even by saying "shoo."

Huge crates lined the road, scattered as though having fallen off a truck. I was told they contained parts of European castles, carved doors from cathedrals, pediments, pillars, all sorts of architectural treasures from all over the world which Mr. Hearst intended to use some day. They were there unopened on my first visit, and they were still there on my last, some three or four years later.

The normal procedure was for the guests to be taken first to their quarters, which in my case was always one of the bungalows, rather like miniature villas, which were grouped on terraces below the Casa Grande, as they called the castle. There were some guest rooms in the Big House, but they were reserved for very important couples. Our luggage having preceded us, by the time we arrived our clothes were hung up, our toilet articles neatly laid out, and all we had to do was freshen up and walk to the Big House for breakfast. There Marion and Mr. Hearst waited to greet us. I had often glimpsed Mr. Hearst at the studio, but as he stood at the top of the broad flight of marble stairs, it was though I were seeing him for the first time. Here his massive bulk fitted in with the background; he was the seigneur of the demesne. His small blue eyes twinkled, his voice, although rather high-pitched for a man of his size, had warmth and friendliness, and his hand-clasp was firm and welcoming.

I have read strange tales of San Simeon. I have read even stranger tales of Mr. Hearst, none of which fits in with my memories. Mr. Hearst appeared to me to be a man of gentleness in his personal contacts; what he was in the world of business I have no way of knowing. He seemed to enjoy playing the role of genial host, and I admired him very much, from a respectful distance, of course.

We had no heart-to-heart talks and although he finally, to my pleased surprise, called me Patsy, I always called him Mr. Hearst, although most of Marion's friends called him W.R.

Charles Chaplin was there one weekend, and as usual, gave an after-dinner show. I can't recall a party at which he was present that he didn't give us all the privilege of listening to his operatic arias in double talk, or his imitations of other actors, but that night at San Simeon he ran through his repertoire as though being paid for it. Mr. Hearst had obviously never heard his act before, and was a most appreciative audience, but the rest of his captive audience became restive and Marion finally had to spill a drink in her lap so that she could jump up and apologetically excuse herself, which caused enough diversion for the rest of us to beat a strategic retreat. Not that Chaplin wasn't good, you understand. . . but enough is enough already!

In addition to being a show-off, he was a tightwad. Listen to this: One afternoon, during the Second World War, my cousin, Jack MacFadyen, and the comedian, Jack Oakie, went to Chaplin's house to collect money for the Veteran's Hospital in the valley. It was to provide recreational facilities for the marines who had been wounded in the Pacific.

Well, Chaplin greeted them cordially and said he whole-heartedly agreed with their project; he excused himself to go into the other room to write a check, returned with the check in an envelope, and with many thanks the two Jacks left. As they reached their car, Jack Oakie opened the envelope and took out the check expecting at least $1,000. It was for Ten Dollars! Oakie took the check delicately between his thumb and forefingers and tore it into as many pieces as he could, tossing them up in the air like confetti. . . all the while calling Chaplin every name he could think of.

Do you get the impression that I wasn't all that crazy about Mr. Chaplin? You must have E.S.P.

The Great Hall at San Simeon, where we all congregated before luncheon and dinner, was two stories high and nearly one hundred feet long, and filled with priceless antiques, as well as being pretty crowded with furniture. Somehow, despite its size, it was possible to have comfortable friendly groupings, and when there was a fire in the Gargantuan fireplace casting a warm glow on the dark polished oak, it had almost a homey feeling.

The rules of San Simeon were few, but not to be ignored. The principal rule was that when the bell pealed from the Tower, everyone was to assemble in the Great Hall for luncheon or for dinner. Loiterers were frowned upon. Breakfast you could have served in your room, but all must be present and accounted for at noon and at dinner time. That seemed fair enough; serving thirty or forty people in odd lots would put a strain on even the finest staff.

Another rule which I thought fair, although not everyone did, was that no guest should bring his own liquor. There were those who felt that it impinged upon their unconstitutional right, one of them being Eddie Sutherland, a young director who was on the train with me.

He had been to San Simeon once before, he told me, and had had a quart of Scotch in the pocket of his raincoat. The first evening, when he reached in the closet to fortify himself before the dinner bell rang, the bottle was gone. He thought the help had snitched it, but was hardly in a position to complain, so he bore his loss as philosophically as possible. But lo and behold, when he was packing for the return trip, there was the bottle back in his raincoat pocket.

It seemed to me the message was pretty clear, and I told him so. But Eddie apparently regarded it as a challenge and this time, he said, he had it where they wouldn't find it—in his briefcase with a script he intended to read over the weekend. Unfortunately for Eddie, the briefcase was taken on ahead with the rest of the luggage.

The next thing we knew, Eddie was on his way back to Hollywood. The reason for his abrupt departure, we were informed, was a sudden call from the studio. We who had been on the train with him looked at each other, raised an eyebrow, and said nothing. It was rather high-handed behavior on the part of our host, I admit. But on the other hand, Don't Bring Your Own Liquor seemed a small enough request to honor in return for the lavish hospitality and congenial surroundings. After all, anyone should be able to survive for three days on cocktails before lunch and dinner, wine with the meal, and liqueurs with the coffee. There was also a sort of after-hours club, when Mr. Hearst had retired, presided over by Marion, who was not one to go without another drink if she wanted one.

That was perhaps the only flaw in their relationship; Marion liked to drink a little more than Mr. Hearst wanted her to. She was certainly not an alcoholic; she just enjoyed having that extra drink. So after W. R. was presumably safely tucked in for the night Marion would reappear, and for those who had waited, the bar was open for as long as anyone would stay up and keep her company.

The dining room was on the same scale as the Great Hall. I think the table could accommodate about fifty people—but maybe it just looked that way to me. The service was perfection, the food was good but simple. Apparently Mr. Hearst did not have gourmet tastes, which was fine with me, as I had not yet been exposed to the French or Italian culinary arts and thoroughly enjoyed the typical American fare.

My place was generally above amidships, somewhere about the salt, but never beside my host. It never occurred to me to care about where I was seated; just to be present was exciting enough. I was not aware of the rivalry which I was later told existed, and which actually erupted into feuds, over how far up or down the table you were seated.

Tapestries covered three of the four walls, at least two of them being Gobelins. They were, of course, magnificent, but not exactly conducive to an air of coziness.

Often, during lunch, Mr. Hearst would launch into one of his favorite games, which was to ask a new guest to look at one of the tapestries carefully, then stand and deliver a speech on it, the speech to run precisely two minutes by his watch. Two minutes is a long impromptu monologue, the equivalent of two typed pages, and presented quite a challenge. I remember Jimmie Walker as one who met that challenge magnificently. Walker was then the Mayor of New York—the Beau Brummel Mayor, he was called.

His Honor Mayor Jimmy Walker

97

He was quick witted and articulate, and from that conventional moyen-age scene, ladies leading greyhounds, men at arms running down wilde beasties, he drew a political parallel of such sharp satire that even I, who knew nothing of the New York political scene, understood and laughed at the humor.

The mention of Jimmie Walker reminds me of my first meeting with him, before seeing him at the castle. I was in New York for some reason—perhaps the opening of a picture I was in—and again was staying at the Plaza Hotel. A dear friend of mine, Lois Wilson, had an apartment right across the street.

To appreciate this story, you must know that Lois was a lovely person, who never forgot she was a Southern gentlewoman, and no one in her presence better forget it either. She was proper to the point of primness. There was never a breath of scandal about Lois; indeed, she was seldom even mentioned in the gossip columns, although she did have various male friends—she was no wallflower. But she was definitely not thought of as glamorous or sexy. Pretty, popular and proper, now you have the picture.

May McAvoy, Patsy Ruth Miller and Lois Wilson.

Anyway, one afternoon on my way back to the hotel I decided to drop in on her, as I often did. A split second after I pushed the buzzer on her door, it opened just a crack and Lois peered out, recognized me, and slipped out into the hall, pulling the door almost closed behind her.

"There's a newspaperwoman in there", she said. "I'm being interviewed." Okay, I said, I'll come back later. "No, wait," she whispered. "I'm expecting a visitor. . . be a dear, Pat. Go down and stop him." I said of course I would, but how would I know who to stop? "It's Jimmie Walker," she whispered. I think I just gawked at her for a moment, trying to place the name. . . I couldn't believe it. "The Mayor," she hissed. Then she gave me a little push. "Please, Pat, please. . . keep him in your room until I call you."

Without giving me time to reply, she opened the door, raised her voice, and said, "I'm sorry but no, I really don't want any." Then she went inside, closing the door loudly behind her.

So I went downstairs and sure enough, in a few minutes up came a cab and out stepped His Honor the Mayor, the Beau Brummel of New York. I waited until he had paid off the cab, then, feeling idiotic, I stopped him as he was entering the building by saying, of all the corny things to say, "Wait! Lois sent me." That got his attention, all right. He cocked his head and looked at me with such quizzical expression I thought for a horrible moment that Lois had been playing a joke on me. But when I stammered out the explanation, he grinned. . . he really had a charming grin. . . and said, "All right. Now what?" Well, I told him, Lois wants you to wait in my room until she calls. He looked at me doubtfully, for which I don't blame him—then suddenly his face cleared.

"You're Patsy Ruth Miller, aren't you?" he said. I nodded.

"I've seen and admired you on the screen. I'm that delighted to meet you in person."

"Me, too," I said idiotically. Then we both laughed, and with no further ado we crossed the street and went into the hotel through the 58th street back entrance. There was no one in the elevator, which was lucky and most unusual. I was still a bit flurried, but his quiet humor put me at ease, and we were soon chatting away like old friends. When the phone rang and I heard Lois' voice, I was really sorry to say good-bye to him. After he left, thanking me for my hospitality, I was bemused by the thought of our Lois and a married man, and a Mayor. But of course, they could have been discussing politics. . .

The next day I was called back to the Coast and didn't have a chance to see Lois again.

It was a few months later that Jimmie Walker was a guest at San Simeon when I was there. He entered the Great Hall the first evening looking wonderfully debonair. He looked around the impressive room, his gaze passing right over me, then Marion took him by the arm and led him around, introducing him to everyone. When they stopped in front of where I was seated, she said, "And this is Patsy Ruth Miller."

With a twinkle in his eye, he said, "I've seen and admired you on the screen. I'm that delighted to meet you in person."

"Me, too," I said.

As Marion led him to another group he turned, looked at me over his shoulder, and winked.

During the weekend we were often in the same group of people, but only once, down by the swimming pool, were we alone together. We talked of this and that and the other thing, but the New York episode was not mentioned. I thought of assuring him that I had never mentioned it to anyone—but I didn't. Somehow I knew he did not need that assurance.

When he left he gave me a light good-bye kiss.

He was a darlin' man.

Well, back to the tapestry. Max Aitken, a Canadian publisher who later became Lord Beaverbrook, head of a British newspaper empire which rivaled Hearst's, was also very witty in a wry restrained manner. He likened the various characters in the tapestry to British historical figures, as seen through the eyes of a Canadian. He also injected some political comments which were undoubtedly clever but way over my head. I was fascinated by his Canadian accent, the first I had ever heard.

Another time there was a publisher of a French newspaper—I don't remember his name—who interpreted the scene quite differently. As seen through the eyes of a Frenchman, it had to do with "l'amour" and even though I didn't understand all the references, I understood enough to make me giggle into my napkin. Marion roared with laughter, but it appeared to me that Mr. Hearst, although amused, was not entirely approving.

Once a Hollywood writer, in an effort to be funny, resorted to some rather crude language, and Mr. Hearst said abruptly, "Time's up" although we were all aware that no more than a minute could have elapsed. The writer was also aware of it; he sat down and never uttered another word for the rest of the meal.

It's a pity that I didn't keep a record of the many famous and fascinating people I met at the ranch, at least none that I can find.

I do remember Elinor Glyn, the author who made the word "It" synonymous with Sex Appeal through her novel *Three Weeks*, which was being filmed at my studio. The word around the lot was that it was very Hot Stuff! Hot stuff, in those days, was just a teeny bit more racy than Sesame Street. Madame Glyn looked like the cover of one of her sensational novels, with a few years added. She had a fine firm Valkyrien figure which she adorned with drapes and floating scarfs. Her hair was an incredible mahogany color, her eyelids matched the green of her eyes, and her eyebrows were fiercely black and horizontal, which was not the fashion at the time.

Not one to suffer young girls gladly, she was coolly civil to me at the studio; she had the dressing room next to mine, so we sometimes passed each other on the balcony. Writers don't generally rate dressing rooms, but she insisted upon having one as she was on the set every day (to the great delight of the director, I'm sure) and had to have somewhere to relax and re-furbish her geisha girl makeup.

Meeting me as a fellow guest at San Simeon was a surprise to her, I think. I detected a warmer note in her voice when she greeted me at noon, and later that day she actually asked me to join her under her parasol down by the pool. It was that conversation, more than anything else, which has fixed her firmly in my memory. With perhaps more naivete than necessary, I had asked her whether she ever suffered the shyness of us ordinary mortals when meeting persons of great importance, such as royalty.

"Not at all, dear child," she said. "I never think of them as being important, merely as people who have to go the bathroom just as everyone else does. I visualize them sitting in the Loo—and who can be in awe if anyone in that position?"

I hope this profound bit of wisdom will be as helpful to you as it has been to me.

I also met Arthur Brisbane there; he was a very famous newspaperman, although I didn't know it at the time. Boy, the things I didn't know astound me! Anyway, we went for a stroll one afternoon, and Mr. Brisbane talked. Then we sat on a bench in the shade of a tree, and he continued to talk. All I ever said was, Oh, really? How interesting! How true, how true. Oh, Mr. Brisbane, how fascinating!

That evening Mr. Hearst came up to me, gave me a little pat on the cheek, and said, "Arthur tells me you are a most delightful conversationalist. He thoroughly enjoyed his little chat with you today. That's very nice, Patsy, very nice."

How to be known as a brilliant conversationalist in one easy lesson just listen—or pretend to listen!

That I remained on the guest list so long was not so much because Marion was mildly fond of me—or because of my conversational abilities—as because I was a comely lass and never became troublesome. There being so many world figures there, often without their wives, the latter attribute was possibly the more important.

Put like that it sounds faintly immoral, as though we were call girls, but nothing could be less true. All that was expected of me, of any of us, was to be agreeable. If we were also amusing, so much the better, but I was not obligatory. Marion and Mr. Hearst were simply being good hosts. They knew that even the most world-famous men would enjoy the weekend more if there were pretty young girls around with whom to safely ride or swim or just chat. And if those girls were also well-known movie actresses, it added a little spice.

One of the famous people I met at San Simeon was Norma Talmadge, one of my very favorite dramatic actresses. She was seated on a couch between Marion and her sister Constance, also an actress, but more on the light comedy side. When Marion introduced us I was so overcome at seeing Norma Talmadge in person that I sank to a cushion on the floor, never taking my eyes off the beautiful Miss Talmadge, happily unaware that I was making her very self-conscious. After a few minutes, she gave me an odd glance, turned to Marion, and with a nod in my direction, said something under her breath. Marion gave a burst of laughter and said, "No, no... not at all... just a member of your fan club," and then in a whisper, "she's really awfully young."

Pretending not to have heard her, I murmured something about getting a coke, rose to my feet and drifted away. Awfully young indeed! A few minutes alone with Miss Talmadge would disabuse her mind of that image of me. We would chat casually in a very adult fashion; I would express an opinion on current affairs, maybe drop a few French phrases—but I never had a few minutes alone with her, not even one moment. I think she still had a few doubts about me and was taking no chances. I still loved her on the screen.

On another occasion I met the tiny writing tornado, Anita Loos, whose book, *Gentlemen Prefer Blondes*, caused a run on peroxide in pharmacies all over the country, and didn't do Marilyn Monroe's career any harm when it was made into a movie.

Anita was also a member of the famous Algonquin Round-Table-ites, but like Robert Benchley, she was *with* them, but not really *of* them. She was more real; you didn't have to talk to her in epigrams or quotable *bon mots*.

Mother was thrilled to hear of all the celebrities I had met, and thought Marion Davies sounded like a dear sweet girl, but was a little distressed that I was accepting so much hospitality without reciprocating in kind. Of course I sent an occasional posy to Marion along with my thank-you note, but to Mother, having been brought up to believe in the sanctity of repaying social obligations, that was not enough, and I was beginning to fear she'd take a hard stand and not allow me to accept any more invitations.

One day while driving home, I was brooding on this and on a sudden impulse, stopped by Marion's house in Beverly Hills. I wasn't sure what I was going to say to her if she was home, and after I rang the doorbell I was hoping she was out, but not only was she there, she opened the door herself and greeted me as though my unheralded visit was an everyday occurrence, though it must have puzzled her. We went up to her bedroom—really a suite of rooms—and it took me some time to get to the reason for my dropping in. I finally blurted it out. Marion must have been amused, but she listened in all seriousness, then assured me that she understood perfectly, which she probably did. She said that she and W.R. would hate to lose me as a friend just because I couldn't return their hospitality; what I must understand was that it wasn't expected of me. She even offered to call and talk to Mother, but I said that wasn't necessary, I could explain it myself.

I could have felt like a fool had not Marion been so tactful; she led the conversation on to other topics, and soon we were gossiping away like any two girl friends. It never occurred to me then, as it does now, that there may have been many like myself who were hesitant about inviting her to anything less than a big social function, and that she might have enjoyed a simple lunch with a girl friend, or a small informal family dinner.

Anyway, that day our talk turned to speculation about the future of an actress who had just made headlines for her latest indiscretion. It must be remembered that in those days promiscuity was frowned upon, and having a child without benefit of clergy was not a subject on which to give boastful interviews. I felt sorry for the actress, I said, but I also thought she was stupid. It was apparent to all who knew her that her way of life wasn't making her happy, and since happiness is the whole point of living, why go on doing those things that make you unhappy?

Marion's big china blue eyes stared at me reflectively then, her little stammer much in evidence, said, "The thing is, you d-don't often know in which d-direction you're headed. You've got a long way to go, Patsy. L'look out for that first step. It's a sonuvabitch."

I duly reported the pertinent portions of my talk with Marion, and there were no further objections to my accepting invitations to San Simeon, although toward the end of the decade there were fewer and fewer weekends there, Mr. Hearst seeming to prefer the lodge at Wintoon which was more rustic, I was told, though the Hearstian definition of "rustic" might not be Webster's. Twice I was invited for a weekend at Wintoon, and twice I had to refuse for one reason or another. . . very likely a masculine reason, or maybe a football reason.

One non-acceptance was permissable; two, apparently, were not. I was never invited again. To parties, yes—in Beverly Hills and at the Beach House—but not for weekends at San Simeon or Wintoon.

Ah, well. . . it was great fun while it lasted.

CHAPTER FIFTEEN

It is a truism—or if it isn't, it should be—that the busier you are, the more things you can find time to do. During the delirious decade of the Twenties, I not only made seventy point three pictures, I also took singing lessons, dancing lessons, flying lessons and made a crazy quilt. I even squeezed in two trips to Europe, one with a friend and her father, the other, alone on invitation from a French film company.

Unfortunately, I didn't make the picture in France; there were script problems and money problems and before they were solved I had to return to Hollywood because of a picture commitment. It was disappointing because I would have been one of the very first Hollywood actresses to have made a movie in Europe.

Your first trip to Europe should be made by boat. Of course, in those days there was no other way to get across the ocean. But even now it's the best way, if you can find a ship; they're getting fewer and fewer, more's the pity. By air is too abrupt, too impersonal. There's no one to wave goodbye to as you take off, no band playing, no confetti tossed over the rail, no deep-throated siren announcing your departure. And no one at the other end, either, except the customs inspectors.

And, oh, those midnight sailings: stateroom filled with flowers, magnums of champagne, friends down to wish you *bon voyage* with all the corney jokes and warnings. Going by plane is merely leaving one place for another. I still get a sort of school-girl thrill when landing at a foreign airport, but it's not comparable to the thrill of leaning over a rail as the pilot boat comes alongside, and hearing shouts in a foreign language. Ah, well. . . nothing stays the same, as I have observed many's the time and oft.

Remembering my first trip to Europe brings me in a roundabout way to thinking of Rita Hayworth. When I read of her death, I felt a sense of loss, although I didn't know her personally. She was so lovely to look at, so radiant; it didn't seem fair that she had to die with less grace than she had lived. She must have been a loving and lovable mother to have had such a loving daughter. After the flood of books by unloving children, it was heartwarming to hear of the tender care and warm solicitude with which her daughter, Princess Jasmin, cherished her through all that dreadful illness.

As I said, I never met Rita Hayworth, but I did at one time know her husband, Aly Khan, the father of the Princess. It was in London that I met him and such was my ignorance of the world at that time that I didn't know he was a prince. I never heard anyone call him Prince, or Highness, so how could I know? He looked and behaved like a nice young college student, not like someone whose father, in addition to being literally worth his weight in gold, was the supreme ruler of an entire nation. Or, rather, the religious ruler, which amounted to the same thing.

He and a young Englishman whom I knew had just "come down" from Oxford—or maybe it was Cambridge—and were sharing a flat in London and we three frequently had tea there together. It was all quite proper and frightfully British. Then somehow I was recruited into acting as a cover-up for Aly and his lady love which, of course, appealed to me tremendously.

While awaiting his lady's phone call, Aly would pace restlessly, playing and re-playing Lucienne boyer's recording of "Parlez-Moi d'Amour," obviously *their* song. When the call came, they would arrange where to have a stolen moment together, I would be hustled into my wraps with hardly time to powder my nose, and Aly and I would saunter out to some nearby cafe, always followed by one or more of his father's spies. Apparently Papa Khan had no objection to Sonny escorting li'l ol' me about.

After a few moments, my English friend would show up, as if by accident, and after a "fancy meeting you here" routine, he would join us at our table. Eventually, Aly would excuse himself, presumably to go to the men's room. My friend and I would stay put until Aly returned, sometimes an hour or more later. How he managed to elude his father's spies I never found out, perhaps he slipped through a window or sneaked out the kitchen door. However, he did it, and they never caught on, although they must have worried about his kidney condition.

The reason for all this romantic skullduggery was that Aly's lady love was not only a good bit older than he, and married, she was the wife of a man so high in the British Government that a scandal might have rocked the Empire, let alone making relations between His Majesty's Government and the Aga Khan's very strained.

My role in this exciting drama ended when I had to go to Paris to talk business, leaving Aly to his own devices, which I'm sure were successful as no scandal broke. I never saw my accomplice, the charming Englishman who became Lord Something-or Other, again. Or perhaps I did and didn't recognize him. The fair-skinned, fine-boned, well-bred Englishman of that class all tend to look alike.

Some years later I heard that the lady's husband had, with the Crown's permission, divorced her, but by that time, Aly had wandered down other primrose paths and plucked fairer and younger blossoms.

Whatever else you might say about Prince Aly Khan, he had a daughter to be proud of...

A year or so later, on my next trip to Europe, I met Papa Khan. I was in Paris and was presented to His Highness at the home of the Count and Countess de Baubigny, nee Madeline Bamburger from Philadelphia. I wondered whether the Aga Khan would know me by name as a friend of his son, but apparently his spies hadn't reported it, as he had shown no sign of recognition when Madeline gave him the guest list which, of course, had to be approved in advance.

Just before I was to be presented, the butler came through with a tray of hors d'oeuvres and I took a few steps backward to make room for him. I didn't realize there was a tea table behind me, and I backed right into it and a dish of chocolate mousse. It made a spot—a big spot—on the back of my beautiful turquoise gown, which I had bought especially for the occasion. I grabbed my hostess and headed for the powder room. We tried to wash it off, but it only smeared and looked even worse.

"I'll have to leave," I said frantically.

"But no one is permitted to leave as long as His Highness is here," my hostess told me. "It is a rule of etiquette that cannot be broken."

"But I can't meet the Aga Khan like this! Maybe if I faint..."

"Illness is no excuse," the countess said.

Finally, we did arrive at a solution, and I was introduced to His Highness wearing my knee-length mink coat. He looked at me with a puzzled expression and asked if I was not warm wearing a heavy coat indoors, but I smiled and managed to calmly reply that I had only recently recovered from influenza, but still had the chills.

When the Aga Khan finally left, over an hour later, I was the first one out the door by a good three minutes.

CHAPTER SIXTEEN

Once while I was in Paris (I don't remember which trip), I got talking to an Apache. Not an American Indian A-pach-ee, a French Apache, Aposh.

Guy Rennie, an American night club entertainer, had taken me to a late night spot in the Apache quarter; it was pretty much for the tourists, but not entirely. The dancers were probably professionals, but the men sitting around the tables were the real thing. What they did for a living was anything but honest work—a little stealing, some cheating at cards, pimping, of course, and dope and white slavery on the side. A delightfully disreputable lot, quite attractive to tourists.

Guy thought the whole set-up pretty theatrical, but figured we might as well go along with the gag, so he invited one of them to join us. He said his name was Pierre, but that we could call him Pepe. He was darkly handsome in a pinched sort of way, despite a few pockmarks, and rather fun to listen to, although his accent was unfamiliar to me and I didn't understand everything he said. As it turned out, I think I misunderstood quite a bit of what he said; I suspect that several times when I smiled and said, Ah, oui, I should have frowned and said, Oh, non!

On our way back to the Elysee Parc, the small hotel at which I was staying, I had the strong feeling that we were being followed, but Guy laughed and accused me of trying to make a movie scenario out of what had actually been a pretty tame evening.

Late the next day I had a caller, a gentleman from the French Surete. He asked most politely to see my passport and my *carte d'identite*, which all foreigners were required to have if they resided in France for longer than one month, I believe it was. After assuring me that the photograph did not do me justice, but all was in order, he asked me if I had visited a certain boite the evening before, had I spoken with a certain Pepe, had I seen or heard from him since, and what were my plans regarding my future stay in France. All this in the perfect English that could only have been learned in a boys' English Public School. (In England, a Public School is really a *Private School*. Typically British, isn't it?)

102

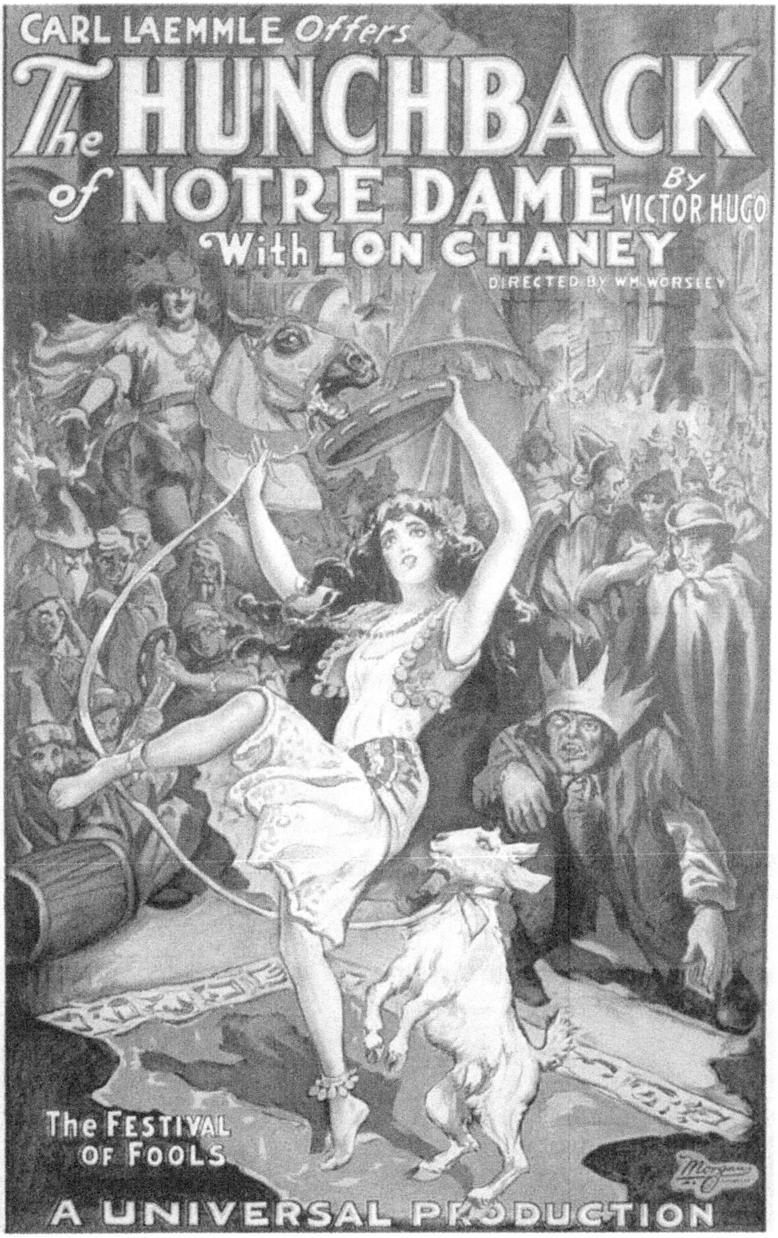

Courtesy Wes Shank

PATSY
RUTH
MILLER
in
South Sea Love
FBO

If You Were Mine
AL. BRYAN
GEO. W. MEYER
THEME SONG
from
FIRST NATIONAL'S
VITAPHONE PICTURE
Twin
Beds
WITH
JACK MULHALL
VITAPHONE

When The Right One Comes Along
Theme Song
"MARRIAGE BY
CONTRACT"
A TIFFANY
TONE
SOUND PICTURE
MABEL WAYNE
NEW YORK

Anyway, I managed to reply, quite calmly, although I had a queasy feeling inside that, yes, I had spoken with such a man, No, I had not seen or heard from him again, and I intended to remain in Paris for another week or so, after which I hoped to visit friends on the Riviera. And, in my grandest manner, might I be permitted to ask why this was of importance to the police?

"It is a delicate situation," said the Inspector. "Through our informant, our 'plant,' as I believe your police call it, we have learned of a plan hatched only a few hours ago to kidnap you, for ransom, you understand, Mamselle. We were given the impression from our informant that perhaps you would not resist so strenuously."

Well, really! I said, and the Inspector said quickly that now that he had met me, he felt that perhaps their informant had jumped to the wrong conclusion. After all, he said apologetically, you *are* an artiste of the cinema. Meaning, of course, what can you expect of a movie actress! None the less, the officer said, the kidnap plot existed; their informant, who was the wine waiter, had overheard enough to be sure of that. Crime was commonplace in that district and of little concern to the police, provided it was confined to that quarter. Once outsiders were involved, particularly foreigners, it became an affair for the Bureau. And the Bureau did not welcome international incidents.

I assured him I quite understood his concern, but it really wasn't my fault, was it? (I didn't mention that I just might have smiled and said, Ah, oui, when I should have frowned and said, Oh, non!) He assured me that there was no blame attached, but the Bureau would take it as a favor if I would promise never to visit the quarter again—I swear it, I said hastily—and would further suggest that I leave Paris for the time being. Otherwise, with regret, but inevitably, my *carte d'identite* would be revoked, and without it I could not remain in France.

I said I understood perfectly. I said I was sorry to have caused the Bureau such trouble. I said I would immediately visit my friends in Nice. He asked what I meant my immediatly. I said, well, as soon as possible. He said, How about tomorrow? I said, Do I have a choice? He said, Not really. I said, This dialogue sounds like a John Wayne western. He said, John Wayne is a great horseman. I enjoy his pictures. Can you catch the noon train? I said I would give it the old college try. He looked puzzled for a moment, then actually smiled. Do so, he said. Then we parted with mutual expressions of good will and the next day I caught the noon train to Nice.

Mildred Knopf, my hostess, was surprised to see me so soon, but expressed herself as being delighted and I made up some story as to why I had come ahead of time. Somehow I didn't want to tell her about Pepe and the plot; it sounded too corny.

A week or two later we all went to Monte Carlo where my pal Guy Rennie was entertaining. He joined us after the show and was very reproachful that I had left Paris without even telling him I was going.

"You missed the excitement," he said. "You remember that fella you made eyes at the night I took you slumming, that Pepe character?"

"What about him?" I felt I had to ask.

"He knifed the wine steward at his joint, claimed the fella ratted on him. Seems he was a police stoolie."

"What will happen to Pepe, do you think?"

"Devil's Island if he's lucky," Guy said. "They throw the book at anyone who kills a cop."

Poor Pepe. . . if only he had spoken Mary Institute French.

105

When I came back from Europe, I stopped off in New York for a few days, shopping and re-newing Eastern acquaintances. Late one afternoon, on my return from a day in the country, I was standing in Grand Central Station trying to remember where the taxi stand was, a young man asked if he could be of help. I told him I was disoriented; I had forgotten which direction to go for a cab so, quite naturally, he led me to the right exit, but there wasn't a single cab parked there. The young man offered to find one for me. I said never mind, I'll walk over to Madison; you can always pick one up there.

Somehow we fell into step and found ourselves casually strolling toward Madison Avenue together. There I saw several cruising cabs, but it was such a balmy twilight that it seemed a shame not to walk a bit further...

Eventually, we walked all the way to the Plaza Hotel, fifteen blocks or more, chatting all the way. He was Irish, the black-haired, blue-eyed Irish with the soft speech of Dublin which falls kindly on the ear. He had such a pleasing way about him I was sorry to reach the doors of the hotel. I told him I thought he had kissed the Blarney stone, and he smiled, showing fine, strong white teeth, and denied that anything complimentary he had happened to say was Blarney.

No names were exchanged, no mention made of meeting again, but in the back of my mind was the thought that he might have recognized me, that he might call me one day... perhaps it was more than a thought. It might have been a hope.

He didn't call that evening. The next day I knew that he never would.

His picture was on the front page of the morning paper. His bullet-riddled body had been found not fifty yards from where he had left me. There was a lengthy story about the gang war going on of which he was the latest victim. He was one of Dion O'Banion's lieutenants, O'Banlon being one of the biggest mobsters in Chicago, second only to Al Capone. The theory was that O'Banion had sent his young lieutenant to explore the possibilities of moving into New York. Apparently the possibilities were nil.

We must have been followed all the way from Grand Central Station, I realized. At least they had waited until I had gone into the hotel before opening fire. They weren't shooting innocent bystanders in those days, only their own people.

I looked again at the picture; he was getting into a car, smiling at the camera, and I thought of that soft-voiced, well-spoken Irishman who had kissed the Blarney Stone, and I could have wept for the terrible waste. That's what crime is, a terrible waste... a terrible, stupid waste.

CHAPTER SEVENTEEN

I hate waste. I hate to see things thrown away that could be used by someone. The waste of time, as well as money, to me is wicked. The waste of talent is the most wicked of all—with the exception, of course, of human life. Frequently they go hand in hand.

A prime example of tragic waste was John Barrymore. I only knew him to say "hello" to, but I saw him frequently at the Brown Derby in Beverly Hills. On Thursday nights—maid's day off—it was almost like a club. All we Beverly Hillites, mostly of the film colony, assembled there for dinner, table-hopping, and local gossip. John Barrymore was one of the regulars, always at the same table with his drinking buddies.

What a gorgeous man he was, as well as a magnificent actor, before he became a sodden wreck. It was heartbreaking to watch the gradual disintegration, almost before our very eyes, of a once great man. Week after week, seated always at his favorite table, surrounded by his same drinking pals, he would go from jocular greetings to boisterous conviviality, to crude obscenitities, ending in just plain sloppy, incoherent drunkenness.

Why? He seemed to have everything. Born with a great theatrical name, he had added luster to the name; he was admired and respected by audiences all over America, his talent was not only recognized, it was well rewarded. What was it he lacked?

I have finally figured out what it was. It was gratitude.

It's simple when you know the answer, isn't it? All these people, rich and famous, beautiful and successful, you name it, they have it—they go around killing themselves with drugs and booze and sometimes with guns, because they have no gratitude to God for the lovely gift of Life. It doesn't matter to which God they're grateful, it's the gratitude that matters.

To those who are grateful for what they have, and don't waste a thought on what they don't have; for those who are grateful that there are friends and family who care for them, and don't give a hoot for those who don't; for those who are grateful for being alive in a truly wonderful world, Life is great fun. In fact, it's terrific.

But what about misfortunes, you ask. What about such things as losing your job, or losing your money, or losing someone you love? Are you supposed to be grateful for those?

That's pretty much to ask of any mere human being. But what you can do is operate on the law of physics—or some such law. To wit: a container cannot contain more than 100 percent of its capacity. If you begin to fill yourself with gratitude for what you still have, little by little the sorrow for what you have lost will be forced out; there's simply not room for both. It really works. I know from experience. I wouldn't recommend a remedy I hadn't tried myself.

Then once more you can awaken in the morning with that Glad-to-be-Alive feeling. Maybe not instantly—but after coffee and orange juice. And you can sort of murmur to yourself, Thanks, dear Lord—thank you for giving me another day in which something wonderful might happen.

And it's the darndest thing—how many times, when you least expect it, something wonderful does happen.

Of course, if you go killing yourself with drugs or booze or a gun, you're not around for that wonderful thing when it happens.

It seems that every evening on the news, I hear of more young athletes dying of drugs. One young basketball player had signed a contract for *one million dollars*, and he didn't live to collect one millionth of it. Drugs—crack, coke, I don't know all the names it goes by—but its one sure name is Death. And actors, too. You'd think they have enough of the world of fantasy, that they wouldn't need more...

When I hear, as I do nearly every day, of drug dealers standing openly outside the schools not only selling dope to the school children, but enlisting them as pushers, I get so upset I can hardly finish my coffee.

If I were the President, the first thing I would do is make drug selling a capital offense. Anyone caught—and they can very easily be caught, as they don't seem to make any effort to hide—should be shot. Shooting's actually too good for them, but I'd settle for that.

Someone to whom I expressed that opinion protested that even a drug pusher must be given a fair trial, to which I agreed. That's the American way. Give them a fair trial, by all means—and then shoot 'em!

Lest I seem too righteous, let me confess that I have had a bit of experience in that field myself. This is how it happened:

On one of my trips to Paris, I met a most delightful French Government official, actually he was a Basque, named Jean Debove. Jean had served his country in French Indo-China, not less happily known as Vietnam, where he had picked up many customs of the Chinese there, among them the smoking of opium, considered fairly commonplace as less of a vice than drinking. As Jean later described it, smoking an opium pipe was something like having a Martini after a hard day's work, relaxing and soothing. I'm not sure that I entirely agree with that, but then I'm hardly qualified to judge, as I hate Martinis.

Let it not be thought that Jean was trying to make me a drug addict. The subject would never have been mentioned but for the fact that one day, when we were going to the races at Longchamps, I had such a cold in my chest that I wheezed as though I had run the quarter mile, and Jean said that instead of going to the races, he would take me somewhere to cure my "bronchite." He didn't say at the time where, or what the cure was. So, being careful not to breathe deeply lest I go into a fit of coughing, I got into a taxi with him and heard him give an address in the Auteuil district. I think I assumed that he was taking me to a hospital, or to a clinic.

We pulled up before a stately house on a quiet, residential street; a gardner was trimming a hedge, another was pulling weeds from a flower bed, and the whole thing couldn't have looked more suburban and respectable. Still, I felt a certain reluctance to go in; it was obviously a private residence, and not the same as having tea with two young men in their flat in the heart of London. Jean sensed my feeling and assured me, before dismissing the cab, that this was not his house, in fact, it wasn't really a private residence at all, but a sort of *pied-a-terre* for members of the Government, a place where they could come to relax, to be free of the prying eyes of the press and the public. What he didn't say, in front of the cab driver, was that it was also where a number of them, including M. Herriot, who was then Minister of Affairs, came to smoke opium.

The downstairs were elegantly furnished, in typical French style: a good deal of gilt and brocade, many little *bibelots*, and everything placed with great precision as though seldom used and never moved. When Jean started up the long curved stairway I hesitated again. He smiled, and said, "There's nothing to be afraid of. If I were going to seduce you, this is not the way I would do it. I would be more subtle."

"I sincerely hope so," I said.

"Well then, believe that I only want to cure your cold."

"I believe," I said, and followed him up the stairs.

The landing, as large as a room, had doors on all sides, all of them closed. Jean opened one of the doors and I followed him into what was certainly intended as a bedroom, but not furnished as such. I don't think there was any furniture, nothing but beautiful cushions scattered on the floor, and two long mattresses covered with yards of exquisite yellow material. Between the mattresses was a very complicated looking object, something like a spirit lamp, but of finely etched silver. On either side of the lamp lay two long pipes, seeming to be of ivory and some black substance, possibly onyx, most beautifully carved. The whole thing looked straight out of a movie set.

"An opium den?" I said in English, not knowing the word for den in French.

"C'est ca," he said with a grin. Then he lay down on one of the matresses, so I brazenly stretched out on the other. In for a penny, in for a pound, I thought. I might as well enjoy whatever is going to happen.

But nothing much happened, except that Jean advised me to loosen any wearing apparel which was tight. So I untied the belt of my dress and kicked off my shoes, and Jean, with an apology, discarded his jacket and loosened his tie.

Then started the ritual of opium smoking. He ceremoniously lighted the spirit lamp and, with elegantly embossed silver tongs, dipped into a little ivory pot and took out some gummy substance which I took to be the raw opium. This he held over a flame, twisting and turning it until it was malleable. When the consistency was to his liking, he scooped a bit of the almost liquid opium into the tiny bowl of one of the pipes, put it between his lips, and gulped in a deep breath of smoke. I waited for something dramatic to happen, but nothing did. He just let the smoke out slowly, smiled at me, and said, "Now you try it. Don't inhale too deeply at first. It might make you dizzy."

I took the other pipe, held it as he did, and put it gingerly between my lips, intending to puff very warily. But without intending to, I drew the smoke in as though it were a cigarette. The effect was something like taking a strong sedative; first there was a numbness in my legs, then it slowly rose and engulfed my arms, making the pipe too heavy to hold up. The sensation was rather pleasant, but certainly not exciting.

After a few moments, Jean said it was all right to take another puff, which caused more drowsiness, but not the state of euphoria I had been expecting. Relaxed is more the word. I was allowed one more inhalation, and I think after that I dozed for a while. Jean already had his eyes closed, looking very peaceful and contented. Maybe he was having sweet dreams of being in a Sultan's harem, or whatever a Basque would dream. No dreams came to me, possibly because I was too aware, too interested in my own reaction.

Then Jean said it was time to leave, before anyone from the Ministry arrived, so I put my shoes on, tied my belt, and out we went, through the still silent house. Outside, Jean told me to take a deep breath, which I did doubtfully. For the first time in three days, there were no rales, no cracklings, no cough.

"You see?" he said. "La bronchite est parti."

And it was. The air was flowing sweetly through my lungs, my chest was no longer confined in a tight iron band, and aside from a slight drowsiness and a weakness behind my knees, I felt fine.

From that one experience I can hardly claim to be an expert on drugs, nor do I recommend that smoking opium be taken up by the medical profession as a cure-all. But this I can say, if one must depend on something, opium smoking would be the least harmful, I should think. If one must temporarily escape from this world, opium seems the entry into a world of placidity and peace. It does not induce violence; no one full of opium is going to rush out and hold up a gas station; no one full of opium is going on a rampage of rape and murder; no one full of opium is going to do *anything*.

Maybe our drug-infested cities should stop trying to shut down the "shooting galeries"—they just re-open the next day—and turn them into opium dens; at least the addicts wouldn't be a menace to innocent bystanders, they'd just lie around and sleep.

It's no wonder that the Chinese Emporers, back in the Nineteenth Century banned opium smoking under penalty of death. It must have been very frustrating to try to run a country in which everyone wanted to lie around and dream sweet dreams, instead of getting out and hustling. It can't be very good for the economy, can it?

I also wonder about M. Herriot and his Cabinet. If they all took their coffee break smoking opium at that house in the suburbs, who was running *la belle France*.

If anyone is curious, I never had the urge to try it again. There's not enough time as it is; why spend more than you have to sleeping.

CHAPTER EIGHTEEN

I make it a point not to read the Tell-All, Oh-What-They-Did-To-Me, And-Then-I-Slept-With books that are spewed out of Hollywood annually. However, when I heard that Leatrice Gilbert, the daughter of Leatrice Joy and John Gilbert, had written a book about her father, I was eager to read it. Knowing Leatrice, her mother, I was confident that her mind would not have been poisoned against her father, no matter what had happened to cause her parents' divorce.

I was correct in my assumption; she did not portray John Gilbert as a monster — but neither did she show him as the man he was — part *enfant terrible*, part Sir Galahad. The Jack Gilbert who made feminine hearts flutter — including Greta Garbo's — didn't come through at all. I don't like to criticize a fellow author, but I think young Leatrice dealt too much with facts and figures; contract disputes; the running feud with L.B. Mayer. The personality that made John Gilbert a star didn't take shape.

After all, how could she describe a man she hardly knew, a man seen only through the eyes of a child? The child whose father has "visitation rights" only sees him on specific occasions, and for a limited length of time. Through the years young Leatrice had undoubtedly read, or heard of Jack's amorous exploits, of his charisma, of his appeal to women — but that's not the same as seeing him through grown-up eyes. Seeing him in action, you might say.

How could little Leatrice Gilbert see her father as anything but her father? Very probably, when with his daughter, Jack was the epitome of devoted fatherhood. Not that he was putting on an act; I'm sure he did really adore her, but I'm equally sure that he relished the role of loving parent, and played it to the hilt, as he played everything to the hilt.

The flamboyant gesture, the delight with himself when he knew he was behaving outrageously, the intensity with which he attacked new ideas, all combined to make him personally charming, as well as good company.

So what was John Gilbert really like? He was half child, half Lothario, with a little Mercutio thrown in, and a smattering of Peter Pan. One day he would be the knight errant dashing to the rescue of some fair damsel, the next day he was a little boy sulking in a corner because someone had hurt his feelings. Mercurial, I suppose, is the word that best describes him.

But how could little Leatrice see that?

No one understood why Leatrice and Jack broke up. They appeared to be the perfect couple; she, so poised, so gracious, with old-fashioned Southern courtesy, and Jack so... well, what he was. They seemed to complement each other. Of course, outsiders seldom know the true reason for the breakup of a marriage unless the man has a tendency to use his wife as a punching bag, or the wife takes out her annoyance by filling her husband full of lead.

I was saddened to learn of their divorce, as I had been the first person to learn of their marriage, and felt a sort of proprietary interest in it. Leatrice had invited me to what she said was going to be a little get-together; she mentioned Charlie Chaplin and Max Linder, a French comedian newly arrived in Hollywood—I think Govvie and Ruth Morris—Bella and Sam Spewack—I don't remember who else.

I happened to get there early, before anyone else had arrived, and it was obvious that something was up. Leatrice appeared to be rather flustered, very unusual for her, and Jack was beaming from ear to ear, and prancing around like a circus pony. I finally asked what the occasion was, and Jack couldn't contain himself any longer; they had been very privately married that very morning! I wasn't greatly surprised, as they had been an "item" in the gossip columns for some time. They looked so happy it brought tears to my eyes. As the other guests started arriving, Leatrice asked me not to say anything; they wanted to wait until everyone was there, and then have a big, formal announcement.

About twenty guests eventually arrived, and it ended up anything but a *formal* announcement... at about two or three the next morning.

Whenever anyone hears that I knew Jack Gilbert they invariably say "Oh, then you must have known Greta Garbo." Their names are still linked in the public mind.

I did meet her, but I didn't know her. Our original meeting was way back in 1925, I believe.

Lars Hansen, Garbo and Sjöström

She had just come to Hollywood. An MGM writer, whose name I can't recall, was giving a Sunday brunch at his house on the beach, and he told us that we were about to meet an actress from Sweden who had just been signed by MGM. He wasn't sure of her name, Greta something, he thought.

Sure enough, she arrived a little later with her mentor, Mauritz Stiller, also a Swede, who was fairly well known as a director, at least in Sweden if not yet in America.

Garbo and Mauritz Stiller, 1925

Garbo was not very impressive at first sight. She didn't radiate that glamour that later shone from the screen; in fact, she was almost drab in appearance, sort of mousy light brown hair, and very little make-up. Naturally, she was rather quiet. Who wouldn't be, thrust in among famous strangers, and probably with a language barrier as well.

I venture to say that if a vote had been taken that day as to whether she would one day be Hollywood's greatest star, there wouldn't have been one Aye—except possibly Mauritz Stiller's.

She certainly fooled us all. On screen she sparkled like a diamond. There's never been another quite like her, more's the pity.

The only other times I saw her in person were when she and Jack were going together, after his divorce from Leatrice. That was during his boating phase. Many of us had boats, and would often drop anchor in Catalina Harbor or down at the Isthmus over weekends, and once in a while we'd see her on Jack's boat. Most of us boating people would visit back and forth, but I don't think she ever did. I don't recall that she ever entered into that cameraderie that generally exists among sailors. Especially those who know each other on shore.

I caught a glimpse of her now and then, but it seemed that when we were in port, she generally stayed below. I do recall that once Jack did come aboard and had a few drinks with us—maybe more than a few—and had a little problem rowing back to his own boat. From a distance it looked as though she was a bit annoyed as he missed the ladder several times, but he finally made it on deck, and we were

Gilbert Photo: Ruth Harriet Louise

Garbo

too far to hear what she said to him.

It was said that Jack's voice ruined his career as an actor. There was nothing wrong with his voice. The early sound recording method was dreadful and many an actor's voice registered higher than it really was.

I remember him being nervous about the director's lack of experience in sound films and that the script had him saying, "I love you, I love you, I love you". He thought it sounded ridiculous. Which it did.

I once overheard Clark Gable talking to Jack. He complained that his voice sounded two octaves higher than normal. His first talking picture scared him. He thought he was ruined. He had been in the theatre and knew how to speak correctly, but he couldn't control how his voice sounded on screen.

Had Jack gotten good parts in good pictures his career would have continued. Punching his boss, L.B. Mayer in the nose was not, however, conducive to furthering his career. The reason for the sock in the nose has as many versions as there were gossip columnists.

But his voice was fine. Clark's voice was high but it didn't distract from that wonderful all-man charm of his. The same goes today for Tom Selleck, the star of the popular TV show Magnum and that wonderful film, *Three Men And A Baby*. I've never had the pleasure of meeting Mr. Selleck—but on screen he has the same quality of clean-cut maleness. He also has the quizzical raised eyebrow, which say's "I don't take myself too seriously". And he seems to have humor, plus just plain good looks. In addition, he has a rather high-pitched voice; high, that is, for a man his size, as did Clark and John Gilbert before him—which somehow did not detract at all from their masculinity.

Broken Hearts of Hollywood, the picture I did with Doug Fairbanks Jr., was directed by Lloyd Bacon, who directed me in several pictures. Lloyd was an excellent light comedy director, and I think most of the pictures he directed turned out to be pretty good, but *Broken Hearts* was outstanding; not because of his direction or my acting, but of what happened during the making of it.

We were working late one night and everyone was pretty tired. The scene we were shooting had been besieged with problems; every time we thought it was a take a camera malfunctioned, or a light flickered, and we were all getting pretty edgy and drinking too much black coffee. Finally Lloyd said, "Okay, folks, one more time, and I promise this will be a wrap-up", and we all dutifully took our positions but just as he started to say, "Quiet, we're rolling", Jack Warner came tearing out on the set, yelling, "Hold it! Hold it!" Before Lloyd could say what he obviously had in mind, Jack threw his arms in the air and shouted, "Harry just called from New York. . . we're in! We're in like Flynn!"

Then he calmed down enough to tell us that *Don Juan* had opened, it was a hit, and Warner Brothers had the first synchronized sound motion picture. Their investment in the Vitaphone had paid off. When the shouts and cheers had died down, Jack said expansively, "Okay, boys and girls, you can all go home. . . and to hell with expense!"

Without waiting for Lloyd to protest, we all made a dash for the exit, some of us, probably, wondering what this would mean to the industry; others, possibly, what it would mean to the future of Warner Brothers stock.

Oddly enough—and contrary to what many film historians have written, very few well-known actors wondered what it would mean to their futures. For one thing, many of us had had stage experience so we weren't nervous about reading our lines. For another, we learned our dialogue for the silents just as though it could be heard.

"BROKEN HEARTS OF HOLLYWOOD"   WARNER BROS. PRODUCTION

The dialogue was written in the script, and we spoke it. Sometimes, in the cutting room or in the editing, subtitles were put in which didn't match our spoken lines, and then we would hear from the lip readers in the audience. Of course, there was a certain adjustment to make to the microphone, which in the beginning was apt to be awkward, but as the sound control improved, so did the ease of the actors.

It was the producers who panicked. They immediately started sending for actors and actresses from the New York stage, some of whom did well on the screen, some of whom didn't. Helen Hayes adapted beautifully, Catherine Dale Owen didn't. Lunt and Fontaine were magnificent on stage; on camera they appeared stiff and stylized. It is perhaps more a matter of personality than of ability; over the footlights is one thing, the eye of the camera is something else. There is no real explanation for it. Some very fine actors and actresses have never become movie stars because they lacked that certain something, that charisma; some mediocre actors have achieved stardom and a world-wide following because they had it. When the dust settled, and most of the Easterners had gone back East, it was pretty much business as usual.

Al Jolson and Director Lloyd Bacon on the Warner's lot.

Ernst Lubitsch, Louella Parsons, Monte Blue, Lilyan Tashman and Patsy Ruth Miller in "So this is Paris."

CHAPTER NINETEEN

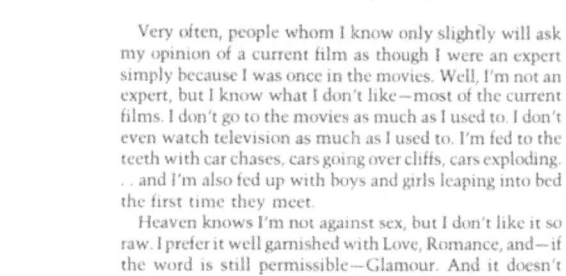

Very often, people whom I know only slightly will ask my opinion of a current film as though I were an expert simply because I was once in the movies. Well, I'm not an expert, but I know what I don't like—most of the current films. I don't go to the movies as much as I used to. I don't even watch television as much as I used to. I'm fed to the teeth with car chases, cars going over cliffs, cars exploding. . . and I'm also fed up with boys and girls leaping into bed the first time they meet.

Heaven knows I'm not against sex, but I don't like it so raw. I prefer it well garnished with Love, Romance, and—if the word is still permissible—Glamour. And it doesn't hurt to occasionally spice it up with a bit of humor. Personally, I have always considered making love an intimate, private thing; watching what goes on in the movies today makes me feel like a "voyeur." I don't like the feeling.

How I yearn for another Lubitsch. Ernst Lubitsch, the chubby little director who was a master of inference, sublety and naughtiness. The famous Lubitsch Touch! Sex with a twinkle in the eye. Dalliance with gaiety. It was fun. Everything was implied—not shown. The silk stocking thrown over a chair, a bedroom door opening and closing, a breakfast tray for two left in the hall. . .

I made a picture for Lubitsch in 1926 called *So This is Paris*, and I thoroughly enjoyed working with him. I had already known Ernst for quite a while; I spent many pleasant evenings in his Beverly Hills home when he was married to his first wife, Helene, who was a close friend, and I thought I knew him quite well. But on the set, Lubitsch was a different man than the pixie I knew and adored off it. On the set it was always Miss Miller and Mr. Lubitsch, although Monte Blue, my leading man, who had been in several of his pictures, called him Ernst. Lubitsch had a very sane outlook on life, and didn't take his fame too-seriously, but there was no doubt as to who was the captain of his ship, and neither crew nor passengers were expected to offer suggestions.

At home, he was a different personality—mischevious, impish, utterly delightful. He loved to tease me about my boy friends. "Bring the one and only man in your life over for dinner Saturday night," he would say, "whoever he is this week."

Of course he had a wonderful sense of humor, but he didn't believe in humor for humor's sake; it had to be based on something solid. I remember him saying, "when a clown trips, it's funny. But when a sedate businessman wearing a high hat trips, it's funnier."

Ernst, like many of our best directors, worked on every script with the screenwriter, and knew to a comma what he wanted in each scene. I felt at times that I was restricted in my acting because of his adherence to the script. For instance, there was one scene early in the picture in which I was standing by the window staring, as if in trance, at my would-be lover (played by Andre de Berenger) who was standing, apparently nude, in a window across the street. All I could see was his torso from the waist up; actually he was clad from the waist down. I wasn't happy with the way Ernst had me play the scene; I felt that it was forced. But the reviews were so good I had to admit that, as usual, Papa knew best.

Lilyan Tashman, playing de Berenger's wife who was also having a little fling with my husband, Monte Blue, told me that she had the same feeling occasionally. Ernst was so definite about how he wanted each scene played that she wondered if she didn't look stilted at times. But she, too, got great reviews. QED.

In addition to being popular with critics the world over, the Lubitsch pictures made money. Wouldn't you think some of the big shots in the industry would take the hint?

Here's a further observation on something I just said; that Lubitsch, like many of our best directors, worked on every script with the screenwriter. I should have said, like *most* of our best directors. Many of them not only worked on the screenplay, they wrote most of it, John Huston as one example.

In the old movie-buff world of today, there seems to be something akin to adulation for the directors of well made pictures. While I agree that direction is important, in many cases it is mistaken for the writing; what the director puts on the screen was already clearly written in the script. Many so-called "directorial touches" are right there in black and white for him to read. In my opinion, the screenwriter is being short-changed.

Another director who seems to have a cult following is

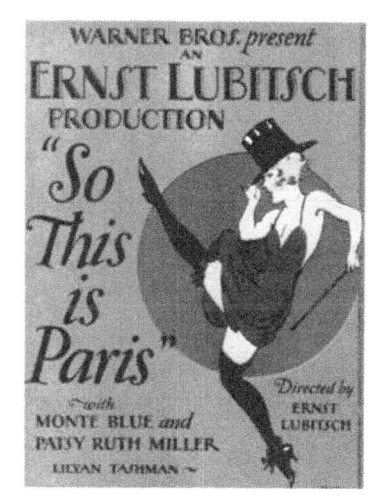

Victor Seastrom. I'm told that he is highly regarded by film scholars as the Father of Swedish Films, which I accept on faith. He didn't make many pictures in Hollywood: *He Who Gets Slapped*, which I seem to remember having liked, *The Scarlet Letter*, which I don't remember at all, and *The Wind*, which I didn't see, but I'll bet I know what it was about... the wind... the wind... it's driving me mad... Can't you just see all those wind machines off-camera blowing their little propellors off?

Victor Seastrom and Crew

on the set, where he generally sat very quietly, offering few, if any, suggestions. I played Conrad Nagel's wife, wore some quite attractive outfits, and as far as I know, gave the impression of being an English gentlewoman, suffering her husband's infidelity in a ladylike manner.

Above: With Joseph Schildkraut.
Below: Replaced by Conrad Nagel.

And, of course, there was the one I was in. It was the very first movie he made in America: *Name the Man*. It didn't start out very auspiciously. Due to the stupidity of someone — the casting director, L.B. Mayer, or Seastrom himself — Joseph Schildkraut was cast in the leading role, that of an upperclass Englishman. Schildkraut — Pepe, as he was called — had just had a stupendous success on Broadway as "Liliom" in Molnar's play. He had been wonderful as a strange character in that strange play set in a Budapest amusement park. To cast him as a titled Englishman made as much sense as casting Sylvester Stallone as Peter Pan.

While we were in San Francisco on location, Pepe was notified that he was being replaced. The train ride home was not a happy one. Pepe took it very hard, being not only very emotional but also very sensitive and easily offended. He felt that aspersions had been cast on his acting ability, and I felt it my duty to make him understand that it was only because of his dark good looks and his dramatic intensity that he had been replaced by a more stolid, Anglo-Saxon type, which turned out to be Conrad Nagel. In addition to his hurt feelings, he also had a new and rather jealous wife: Elise Bartlett, a lovely red-headed non-professional, unaccustomed to the informality of show biz. To her, it appeared that I oversympathized a bit, and there were a few sticky moments in the compartment as our train rolled toward Los Angeles. However, by the time we reached Pasadena it was all straightened out, and we almost became friends.

Seastrom is rather vague in my memory. One thing I do recall: he had a glass of Aquavit (a Swedish whiskey) every morning on the set, sometimes in the afternoon, too. Whether he also had one at lunchtime I do not know — we never had lunch together. In fact, I never saw him except

The kudos given to John Huston as a director are well-deserved, but, of course, he was one of those whose writing and direction went hand in hand. I didn't know him professionally, only as a friend. Back in the Thirties, when both of us were spouseless, he took me out once in a while to dinner, but mostly to the prize fights or wrestling matches. I didn't really like fighting or wrestling, but I liked John, so I went. On one of those evenings, he made a remark which has forever endeared him to me.

To put it in its proper context, I must go back a bit: I met George Raft only once, but that one meeting so impressed me that I tried to immortalize it in a short story which was published in Vanity Fair Magazine. I didn't use his real name, but the character was so thinly disguised that everyone knew who it was supposed to be, certainly everyone in Hollywood.

Herewith the story:

JACKIE CARTER AT HOME

We were at the the Anderson's tea, in Hollywood, wishing people we didn't know very well a Merry Christmas and asking people we didn't like very well to give us a ring sometime, when Ken said, Let's get out of here.

I didn't want to go... at least I didn't want to go home. I was on my second eggnog and felt like seeing people and talking to old acquaintances about the good old days and all that. So I said, "to where?"

Well, it seemed that Jackie Carter, that darkly glowing star in the cinema firmament, was giving a tea. He had never entertained before, to anyone's knowledge, and it was sure to be good. Certainly everyone would be there. Jackie was sitting pretty... his background of hinted gangster connections, as well as his former night club activities, appealed to the public imagination.

I objected at first, because I had never met Jackie. His name was really just Jack, but somehow everyone referred to him as Jackie... it seemed to suit him better, but I don't know why. Anyway, his meteoric rise had begun after I left the country, and in the short time I had been back I had only had occasional glimpses of him here and there... at the Mayfair, at the Vendome... always dining or dancing with some screen beauty. He was sleek and well-groomed. His cabachon sapphire cuff-links were at least five carats apiece.

"He wouldn't know me," I insisted. "I hate people who drop in with other people."

But Ken assured me that he would be delighted to have me. Everyone I knew would be there, anyway. And Jackie had told him to bring someone.

He lived in one of those big, Barker Bros. furnished apartments in a nice section of town. Not Hollywood, not Beverly, but very nice. It smelled a little of damp stucco, and as you walked down the hall you could tell that some of the families did their own cooking, but it was all right. We knocked on his door. I was surprised that we didn't hear the hum of voices that generally floats like a tangible cloud around cocktail parties. It was seven o'clock by that time.

We knocked again. The little iron grilled gate in the door suddenly opened, and an eye peered out at us. I plucked at Ken's sleeve. "This is the wrong place," I whispered. "This is a speakeasy."

Then the door was opened wide, and a man said, "Hyah, folks! Come on in." I went into the hallway, and then I turned and looked at the man. I know it was rude, but I couldn't help it. He was tall and thin, and the blue of his chin, oddly enough, seemed to match his suit. He also wore what was either a red silk shirt or the top of his pajamas. And blue felt carpet slippers. I was sure it was the wrong place, but I followed Ken.

We were in the right place, all right. Jackie Carter was stretched out in an armchair, with his feet up on an ottoman. His attire was definitely pajamas... red ones, with a black silk dressing-gown over them and his feet were encased in really beautiful red morocco slippers.

I was terribly embarrassed. I thought it must be the wrong day, or too late, or something, because he obviously wasn't expecting company. But as I turned to make an unobtrusive exit, I saw that the party was on. At least, there were other guests there.

Seated around three sides of the room, primly, on straight-backed chairs, were girls. They all had their hats on, and glasses in their hands, and at the first quick glance they all seemed to be very blonde and to look alike.

Ken said, "Jackie, this is Miss Montgomery."

I said, "I hope you will forgive my coming uninvited, Mr. Carter."

Mr. Carter rose, waved an iridescently manicured hand at me, and said, "Oh, don't be that way."

I couldn't seem to find the exact answer to that. I believe I murmured, "Thank you," but I'm not sure. Then I found myself seated on a couch, and a girl next to me was saying, "What'll you have, dear? Me, I'm sticking to straight Scotch."

"Scotch and soda, please," I said.

"Sammy!" she yelled to no one I could see. "Bring Miss Montgomery some Scotch and... what'd you say, dear?"

"White Rock," I said.

"Oke. Hey, Sammy... she want White Rock." Then, turning to me, "I been drinking like this for three days," she confided.

All I could think of for that was, "Have you?" But she had lost interest in the subject.

The radio was very loud, and mostly advertising. I kept wishing someone would change the station, but no one else seemed to mind it. The girls—there were eight of them, actually, although it seemed like more—just sat. Occasionally one would say something to another in a low tone. The girl next to me got up, and very carefully took the three steps necessary to get her to the ottoman where Jackie's feet were. She sank down, spilling her drink but not noticing it, and placed her hand on Jackie's bare ankle.

"Cut it out," he said, without looking at her.

I looked around the apartment. It was what is known as a double, furnished. There were two pictures on the buff-colored walls—one a pastel print of Notre Dame, and the other of two girls with bouffant skirts and a Russian wolfhound, in the Nell Brinkley style. There were two floor lamps, but only the harsh overhead light was burning. Even with all those people in it the room looked unoccupied.

On my right was a kitchenette, from which suddenly appeared a little man in white flannel pants, a yellow sweater, and red suspenders over the sweater. He apparently was Sammy, as he bore a drink in his hand which he presented to me. And he was shod in carpet slippers.

"Want anything else?" he asked. "Some crackers?" he leaned over to me and held out a box.

"No, thank you," I said. I looked around for Ken, but he had disappeared. So I sat there, holding my drink which seemed to be much more Scotch than soda.

The bedroom door opened and a grey-haired man, with a cigar clenched tightly between his teeth, came out. I didn't dare look to see if he had on carpet slippers too.

"Arnold's in town," he announced to no one in particular.

"That so-and-so," said Jackie. "He's the world's prize." Then he used some initials. Not S.O.B. or anything like that, but some that I had never heard before. I don't know what they stood for, but it must have been funny, because they both laughed.

The girl on the ottoman got up, and leaned over me. "I'm psychic," she said. "Honest, it scares me, I'm so psychic. Jackie got a telegram, and I told him who it was from before he opened it. Didn't I, Jackie?"

"As though you didn't know," he said.

A girl on the other side of me, not quite so blonde, said, "She guessed a girl's birthday once, and ever since she's been psychic."

"How interesting," I said. I meant to do better, but I just couldn't. The not-so-blonde girl said, "I met you once before—at the Gordon's party. You remember?"

There had been two hundred people at the Gordon's party, but I said, "Oh, yes, of course. How are you?"

"I'm fine," she said. "I shouldn't be here. My friend would kill me if he knew I was here. He won't go places except like the Gordon's. He took me there. He'd die if he thought I was here. I don't know why I came."

"Why don't you leave?" I asked.

"I think I will," she replied, "as soon as I have a drink. Sammy, another of the same."

Sammy touched me on the elbow. "How you doin'?"

"Fine, thank you."

"Freshen it up for you?"

"No, thanks, it's fine."

"That's Sammy," the girl who shouldn't have been there whispered. "Bodyguard, you know."

The man who had opened the door yelled from the kitchen: "Who wants to stay for dinner? Come on, speak up... we're goin' to phone downstairs and get some food."

None of the girls said anything. Jackie said, without turning his head, "You better make it dinner for fourteen."

I counted up quickly. There were eight girls, and four men.

"I'm afraid we have to go, Mr. Carter."

"That's all right," he said. He didn't change the order. The gray-haired man spoke around his cigar. "That guy Arnold hands me a laugh."

"Me too," said Jackie.

Ken came in. "Ken, we've got to go."

"Don't you want to finish your drink?"

"No thanks. We'd better go." I rose and Ken helped me on with my coat. I walked to the door. The radio was louder, and the announcer was saying something about Walter Winchell.

"That guy hands me a laugh," said Jackie.

"Me too," said the man with the cigar.

"Good-bye, Mr. Carter," I said. "And thank you for your hospitality." Mr. Carter was pinching the flesh above his abdomen to show the man with the cigar how much weight he had gained. He let go of the roll of fat he held to wave a languid hand at me.

"Oh, that's all right," he said.

The End

One night, shortly after the issue with my story in it came out, John and I were sitting at the bar in Ciro's having a nightcap after having been to the Friday night fights, when one of Raft's plug-uglies came up to me and said, out of the side of his mouth, "Ain't you Patsy Ruth Miller?"

I admitted that I was, and he said, "Georgie ain't happy about that story you wrote!" and he gave me a threatening scowl right out of a gangster B movie.

"Oh?" said John, swinging around to look down at the goon. "Who read it to him?"

John Huston

Gibson Gowland, Patsy, and Charles Emmett Mack taken the day before his tragic death.

CHAPTER TWENTY

I've had so many near misses, close calls, or whatever you want to call them, that sometimes I wonder if I've been spared for a particular reason.

Musing on this brings to mind a picture I made in 1927 called *The First Auto*, directed by Roy Del Ruth. That I could have been part of the tragedy that occurred during the making of the picture stands out in my memory more than the picture itself.

I do remember that it was about the development of the automobile in America and that it was to end in a spectacular racing scene. Barney Oldfield, a world reknowned racing driver of the day was the technical director and he had seen to it that everything was authentic, except for having put new, more reliable engines in the old autos. Most of the really old cars wouldn't go more than forty miles an hour at best, but with the new motors they could get up to sixty.

I was enjoying working on the picture, partly because I loved wearing the costumes of that period, it was a pleasant atmosphere. Roy Del Ruth had directed several comedies I was in so we hit it off well, and I liked my leading man, Charles Emmet Mack. He was a D.W. Griffith discovery and there were high hopes for his future in Hollywood. The weather had cooperated, we were shooting right on schedule, and everything was going along beautifully... until tragedy struck.

Charles Emmet Mack was killed. He had insisted on doing some of the racing driving himself, but the irony was that he wasn't killed while racing. He met his death on a country lane driving out to the track.

How the near-miss came into it was this: we were on location in Riverside, which had an old race track nearby. One morning I didn't have to work until noon so Clara, my studio maid, decided that I should stay in bed until then, but Charles called to ask if I wanted to drive out with him to watch the race which was being shot that morning

Roy Del Ruth

121

Barney Oldfield was going to do some of the driving, he said, and it would be very exciting to watch. I assented eagerly, but Clara took the phone away from me and said, "No, Mr. Mack, Miss Miller ain't goin' with you. She's lookin' tired and needs to rest up a bit." When Clara said I was going to rest, I rested.

His wife didn't go with him because she had an appointment at the beauty parlor, so Charles drove out alone. On the way to the race track, a farm truck pulled out of a side lane and struck Charles' car broadside, knocking it clear across the road. He was killed instantly, they said.

I was so shocked when told about it that it didn't hit me for a while that had I been in the car, I would probably have been killed too. It was Clara who reminded me of it. "I practically saved your life," she said, "If I'd a let you go with Mr. Mack," she said, "you could a been squashed flat as a fritter." She was right. I could a been at that!

The worst of it was having to break the news to his wife, who was still in the beauty parlor. It was up to me, they said, I being a woman. The director implored me, the assistant director begged me, I really had no choice. Imagine telling a woman who is sitting under a hair-dryer that her husband has just been killed!

I got her up to her room on some pretext before breaking it to her as gently as I could—but how gently can you tell a wife that she is now a widow? It was ghastly.

They sent her home, of course, and it was agreed that I should go with her. Thankfully, I don't remember the details of that ride. There were no broad freeways in those days, just a one-lane road from San Bernardino to Los Angeles. I think it took about four hours, but sitting in the back seat with that poor woman, it seemed like an eternity. She was completely destroyed, one minute in shock, the next in hysterics. All I could do was let her cry on my shoulder. I never saw her again after the funeral. I do hope she found someone else and lived happily ever after.

The picture was finished without him. The show must go on, you know, but it certainly put a damper on the whole production. They used what footage they had, used close-ups of Charles, got a double for the long shots, but I think a few sequences that would have been too hard to fake were left out. So I suppose the picture wasn't as good as it might have been. I had grown to like Charles very much. He was a fine actor and a gentleman. Such a waste...

"THE FIRST AUTO" with BARNEY OLDFIELD — A Warner Bros. Production

While we're on the subject of close calls, have I mentioned that I took flying lessons while I was working at MGM? The flying field was just ten minutes from the studio in Culver City, and I used to rush down at lunch time, have my 45-minute instruction, and rush back to the set. Clover Field was really just a vacant lot; the planes were left-overs from the war. It was no big deal, several other actors and actresses were learning to fly, to the dismay of the studios where they were under contract.

With one exception, the planes were all open cockpit jobs, the exception being a Monocoupe; the cockpit was enclosed, much better for me as I didn't have to wear a helmet and muss my hair. It was a tricky little thing to handle, but as I didn't know the difference, I happily climbed into the cockpit with my instructor, yelled "switch on," waited until the ground crew had cranked the propeller, yelled "contact," then gave her the gun and took to the skies with never a thought of catastrophe.

There was often another student there, a young man who, when he wasn't flying, sat in a little shack they called an office and fooled around with charts and diagrams, constantly making notes on a big pad and drawing sketches. I never asked him why he was interested in dynamics and warp and all that sort of thing, but I later found out. His name was Donald Douglas. The skies are now filled with aircrafts bearing his name.

There was also another young student with whom I became friendly, chatting of this and that and comparing our progress, and when he asked me to accompany him as his passenger, after he had passed his solo flights, I accepted with pleasure. He said it would probably be the following Friday and I said, Great, I'll be here at noon.

On Thursday evening the studio called and said there had been a change in the shooting schedule, and I wouldn't have to work the next day, Friday. I thought all the better, I can get there earlier and have a longer flight, but Mother wouldn't hear of it.

"You're going to stay home and straighten out your closet," she said, "and answer some mail, and autograph a few stills. You always say you'll do it over the weekend, but you never do, you're always out. So you just stay home today and get a few things done."

I called the airport the next morning and left word that I couldn't make it, and dutifully stayed home that Friday to straighten out my closets and answer mail.

So the young man took off without me. He didn't go very far—he never even got off the ground. The plane blew a tire, veered off the dirt runway and crashed into a concrete piling. The pilot was killed. . .

Patsy's love for flying continued through the years. These pictures were taken 13 years later in 1938

Front row: Virginia Valli, Laura LaPlante, Gloria Hope, Virginia Fox, Mary Pickford, Pauline Garon, Mildred Davis, May McAvoy, Clara Horton, Edna Murphy. Back row: Julanne Johnston, Zazu Pitts, Billie Dove, Ruth Roland, Claire Windsor, Gertrude Olmsted, Carmel Myers, Carmelita Geraghty, Helen Ferguson, Patsy Ruth Miller, Lois Wilson.

CHAPTER TWENTY ONE

Reminiscence brings back such clear pictures to the mind; they are as vivid as the scene before me now. It is like a tape being run past my mental eyes, a sort of video film complete with sound and color. I used to be sceptical about memoirs written by men and women in their older years. How could they recall past conversations, past events, so clearly? But now I understand it; it seems that very few experiences are really forgotten, they are just stored away in the safe deposit of the brain, readily available at any time. It only takes the right key to open the safe and withdraw the memory. Unless, of course, it is something you can't bear to recall. Then, it seem, the eraser tape wipes it out.

Perhaps that is why I remember so little of *The First Auto*, other than Charles Emmet Mack's death. Returning to the location and finishing the picture must have been a grim experience for cast and crew. I don't remember what the story was all about, but I would bet a pretty penny it had to do with a young man who had wonderful ideas as to how to improve automobiles, no one would listen to him, but his girl encouraged him and in the end he was acclaimed, the big companies sought him out, he married the girl, and they drove off into the sunset in the car he had invented.

Maybe I'm doing the writer, Darryl F. Zanuck, an injustice. Darryl was a pretty good writer, and perhaps he had a better storyline than that. But the old cars were the stars, and it's too bad that there seems to be no prints of the picture in existence today. It would be historically interesting, as well as a bonanza for the "Classic" car enthusiasts of whom there seem to be hundreds.

Darryl Zanuck was not one of my favorite people. When I first met him, he was walking along a street at the studio—I think it was First National—going toward the office building, which is where I was headed. He looked very out of place, somehow; he was wearing an ugly brown suit and carrying a briefcase which was shiny new and larger than average.

I stopped the car and called to him, asking if he wanted a ride as it was a long way to the office building and the sun was hot. He said he certainly did, he was looking for the writers' building but seemed to be lost. I felt sorry for the little man with the buck teeth in his heavy brown suit, so inappropriate for sunny California, so I asked him where he was from. Iowa, I think he said, or maybe Nebraska. He told me that the briefcase contained a novel which he had written, and naturally I said, That's great, has it been published, and he said, Yes, in a way. He had paid to have it published himself and he was hoping to sell it for a movie. I wished him luck, thinking, the poor little guy, he'll be on his way back to Nebraska, or wherever he came from, within a week. But as everyone of reading age knows, I could hardly have been more wrong. Darryl Zanuck went to the top in an extraordinarily short time, and when I was

124

later under contract at Warner Brothers, he became my boss.

Our strained relationship didn't come about because of the passes he made at me; he made passes at all the girls on the lot, and it was no great problem dodging them which, to the best of my knowledge, all of us did. We used to giggle about it in our dressing rooms, comparing notes on what the latest pitch was. What destroyed any feeling of friendship I might have had was how he treated me professionally.

Michael Curtiz, Alan Crosland, John Adolfi, Robert Milton, Darryl F. Zanuck, Roy Del Ruth, Ray Enright, Al Green, Lloyd Bacon, Warner Brothers Directors, 1928.

Patsy, Edward Everett Horton and Laura La Plante

After I had made three pictures with Edward Everett Horton I wanted to do something different. Not that I didn't like Eddie; he was a doll, and delightful to work with, but playing a straight to a comedian, even one as nice as Eddie, can get to be a bore. The two of us were a big box office draw, and that's always the bottom line, so I kept being cast as his leading lady... his foil, actually.

The studio had bought a story which has a wonderful part for an actress... for me, I thought, when I read it. I asked Darryl abut it, and he said very kindly that if I would make just one more picture with Eddie, the part would be mine. He said he understood exactly how I felt, sympathized and all that, but the upcoming Horton picture was already being written with me in mind, we were what the exhibitors wanted. "So just do this one like a good girl, and the next picture will be on the story you're sold on."

So I made the picture with Eddie, and when it was finished I went in to ask Zanuck when the movie I was so keen about would start. You can imagine what a shock it was to be told that the role had been given to another actress on the lot—one who probably has been friendlier to him. At first I couldn't believe it, then I became so furious I actually trembled with rage.

"But you promised!" I fairly shouted. "You gave me your word. You promised!"

He leaned back in his leather upholstered chair, took a long puff on his cigar, and said coolly, "So I'm a liar."

I never spoke to him again if I could help it, but for the sake of my good friend, Virginia Fox, whom he married, I was never less than civil when I couldn't avoid it. Nor did I ever tell Virginia why I didn't go into rhapsodies when she told me she was marrying him.

She broke the news at a meeting of Our Girls' Club, showed us her ring, and told us we were all invited to the wedding. All the girls oohed and aahed, and made all the remarks girls make at a time like that. It was all I could do to congratulate her, but I forced myself to make the appropriate comments. Inside I was thinking, how could she? Virginia was petite, pretty and good-natured. How could she fall for a guy like that? He'll lie to her, I just bet he will. And I bet he did. I don't think Virginia had the happiest of marriages.

Our Girls' Club was truly unique, in that it had no rules, no membership fee, not even a list of members. We met at alternate houses on Friday nights, sometimes two Fridays in a row, sometimes not for two or three weeks, depending on the schedules of the members. Some of us were stars, some leading ladies, some only bit players, but we were all actresses. Our status in the industry didn't matter; all that mattered was that were were all congenial, and that we liked to get together once in a while with other girls. One thing we did not do—we didn't talk shop. We gossiped about everything and everyone, we discussed the foibles of the famous, we told funny stories about the goings-on at the studios, but we never talked about what picture we were making or were going to make... unless, of course, there was an amusing story connected with it.

I daresay the reason we didn't talk shop was that we felt it would be tacky for those of us who were under contract, and always working, to talk about what we were doing in front of those who weren't doing anything. Or, as we put it, were between jobs. Two of my closest friends were May McAvoy and Lois Wilson, both Paramount stars. Lois is best remembered for her role in *The Covered Wagon*. She complained that she had been criticized for always looking so immaculate, even out on the prairie for presumably many weeks; I was anything but immaculate, she said; I was a mess... my clothes were filthy, I hadn't had a real bath for Heaven knows how long, my hair was full of sand and dust, but there wasn't enough water to shampoo it—could I help it if the camera didn't pick that up! I sympathized with her, because I had the same experience once. I fell out of an overturned buggy in one of the Westerns I did, rolled down a gully, was full of burrs and tumbleweed, and was lambasted by the critics for looking so immaculate in a closeup, leading them to the conclusion that a double had taken the fall for me. All those aching bones for nothing!

Another close friend was Laura LaPlante, a beautiful

blonde, and one of Universal's stars. I also remember Julanne Johnston, who played opposite Douglas Fairbanks in The Thief of Bagdad and was gorgeous in her harem costumes. And there was Billie Dove, one of Howard Hughes' loves; Lillian Rich, and Claire Windsor, who always acted the typical beautiful but dumb blonde. (Some said it wasn't acting); and Gertrude Olmsted, pretty as a picture, who retired when she married Robert Z. Leonard, the director, and devoted herself to learning to cook and fattening up her husband—fattening herself in the process. It was said that when the two of them went out to dinner they required a table for four.

And I remember Helen Ferguson; she became an agent and Edna Murphy, who became Mervyn LeRoy's first wife; Mildred Davis, who married Harold Lloyd.

We had older members, too; Ruth Roland, who succeeded Pearl White as the Serial Queen, back in the days when the movie theatres played serials every Saturday afternoon, which always left the heroine hanging from a cliff, or tied to a railroad track by the villain, with the train roaring toward her. Then came the "to be continued next week" on the screen, and we kids trooped out; the heroine always escaped, but I don't recall ever seeing the happy ending. Serials were already on the way out, but Ruth wasn't worried. She had invested all her money in real estate, and simply changed her title from Serial Queen to Real Estate Queen, and boy, was she loaded!

Another older star was Anita Stewart, one of my favorites when I was in school. There was a time when she wished devoutly that I was back in school. It was because of her younger brother, George, who was spied by a neighbor climbing up a balcony of our house to pay me a visit through the window. My kid brother had come down with measles or mumps, I forget which, but at first it was feared to be small pox, and we were quarantined, so I couldn't let George in the front door, and he chose that way of entering. Encouraged, I may add, by me, as the quarantine had played hob with my social life. Anita had to go to the police station to explain and bail him out. Not the sort of publicity a movie star relished.

I remember the name Vola Vale—at least I think that was her name, but all I can see in my mind is a pretty round face and big round eyes. I wonder whatever happened to her?

And Virginia Valli... Virginia was a bit older than most of us, but one of the most charming of all. She married Charles Farrell, who later gave up acting and founded the famous Tennis Club in Palm Springs.

And how could I forget Colleen Moore, one of our best-known members. Colleen, of the Dutch Bob—the epitome of Flaming Youth—the gal who helped bring the Charleston into every home and on to every dance floor. Colleen was lively and great fun to be with, but she also had a very practical side, and often she and Ruth would be over in a corner discussing business deals and such, while we others were talking fashion, or exchanging the latest bit of gossip. As a matter of fact, Colleen was so busy that she didn't come to as many meetings as most of us did.

One of our members was a cute redhead named Gloria Hope, who wasn't much of an actress—or rather, wasn't devoted to an acting career—but remains in my memory because she was married to one of the best-looking men I have ever seen; Lloyd Hughes. Like Robert Taylor, Lloyd was handsome almost, but not quite, to the point of prettiness. Also, like Robert Taylor, he was all man. Occasionally Lloyd came to pick Gloria up, and on those evenings none of the girls left early even if they did have to work the next day.

We were quite a bunch of gals.

Never having been privy to the conversation in a locker room, or at the nineteenth hole, I don't really know whether men discuss women as much as I've been told they do, but I can tell you we girls gave each other the low-down on men. We didn't use the terms in use today, but were quite explicit in our own restrained fashion. For instance, Walter Pigeon, then a handsome hulk of a man, was one to avoid in the clinches, like Frederic March, whom no gal would willingly accompany to the kitchen for more ice cubes. We classified them as feelers, pinchers, and gropers; many a leading man would have been shaken to the heels of his Cordovan brogans if he had ever heard our giggled exchanges. We all agreed that the ones to beware of were the shy non-gropers, and that those who bragged the most had the least to brag about. I repeat: we were quite a bunch of gals.

Once a year Mary Pickford gave a party for us at Pickfair, for which she was unanimously elected Honorary President, the only office holder of the club. Once a year we threw a big formal bash for ourselves at the Biltmore Hotel downtown, to which we brought our boy friends, fiances, and/or husbands, and for which we dressed to the teeth.

Our Girls Club never came to a formal end; it just faded away as more of us got married and had babies. (We did it in that order in those days). Some, less successful, quit the business and moved away, some became too involved in other interests to come to meetings.

It was great fun while it lasted. I doubt there will ever be another Club quite like it.

May McAvoy, was a lovely actress, *Sentimental Tommy* and *Ben Hur* (the silent version), being just two of her many pictures, but she was also very charming and a lot of fun to be with. She lived near us in Beverly Hills and spent a lot of time at our house simply because it was larger than hers. I remember her very well because she taught me how to smoke a cigarette. We were just teenagers—I was anyway, she might have been twenty or so—and we would take the cigarettes into the bathroom and blow smoke out the window. I turned 18 about that time, and after my birthday dinner was finished, my father took out a cigarette to smoke, which was his custom. But before he lit it, he looked at me and said in all seriousness, "Would you like one too?" I think I managed to get out a polite no, thank you, but he only grinned. "If you're going to smoke, you might as well smoke with me instead of hiding in the bathroom." So I smoked with him... Let me give you some advice: never try to hide anything from your father. It's no use!

CHAPTER TWENTY TWO

The difference between then and now is incredible; there have been more changes in my brief life span—well, not brief in the sense of years I have lived, but brief in the over-all span of mankind—than in any other century. Some are improvements: medicine, science, automation and that sort of thing. Others are what Jack Smith, a Los Angeles columnist, calls "DEprovements." Among the latter are architecture (practical but ugly), women's fashions (ugly and impractical) and moral values.

An example of the progress in medicine is an experience I had while making a movie in 1928 called *Red Riders of Canada*, the Red referring not to their politics but to the red coats worn by the Canadian Mounted Police.

We went to the mountains of Big Bear Lake to shoot snow scenes. There was more snow than we needed, and it was also exceptionally cold. We were quartered in small cabins which were strickly for summer occupancy; some had small fireplaces, others, like mine, had portable electric heaters which were suposed to keep the cabin warmer. That was true until a blizzard hit and knocked out all the power and telephone lines. And that was also the day I couldn't get out of bed. I ached in every achable place and had such a fever I fairly sizzled. Someone in the company got down to the nearest village on snow shoes, phoned my home, and arranged for the one doctor in the village to come up in a sleigh. He examined me and announced that I had pneumonia. There was nothing to do but stay in bed, he told me—as though I could have gotten up! However, he was nice enough to stay with me until my father arrived, which he did the next day—also by horse-drawn sleigh—bringing with him a priest, which was comforting in a way, but in another way, not terribly reassuring. Father O'Reilly had heard about me in the village, and when Daddy asked directions as to how to get to me, he offered to come along. I think my father was glad to have his company.

Vaguely, through my fever, I heard the doctor explaining that there was nothing to be done other than keeping me warm. (There was no known cure for pneumonia then. Bed rest and heat, that was it.) My illness would come to a crisis, he said, after which I would either get better or, to put it bluntly, I would die. The only thing he could really do for me was to insist on more heat in my room. So a stove was brought in and a hole was cut in the wall for the flue, which didn't make the cabin's owner very happy, but quite possibly saved my life.

Father O'Reilly stayed on, praying for me and playing double solitaire with Daddy while I lay there and sweated it out. And, as you may have surmised, I passed the crisis and fully recovered. But that's doing it the hard way. Just think of the difference today, with all the antibiotics, penicillin and its derivitives. There wasn't anything like that then, not even the sulfa drugs which came in during the Second World War. I'm aware that people still sometimes die of pneumonia, but at least they have a fighting chance, and generally they're very old folks, not youngsters. That is certainly a plus in the discovery area, as they are clearly Twentieth Century miracles.

However primitive the treatment for pneumonia may have been in 1928, I soon went back to work and we finished the picture, although a little behind schedule, and I think it turned out pretty well, with handsome Canadian Mounties, deep eyed villains, and more snow scenes than Nanook of the North. But a strange thing happened to me: I completely lost my taste for snow. Even today, if it snows where I am, I go somewhere else...

Medical Science and medical treatment have gone a long way in my lifetime, and so have doctors—but in a different direction. They are no longer just men of medicine, they are now men of finance, forced to deal with the intricacies of Medicare, Medicaid, and the skyrocketing cost of malpractice insurance. That means extra accountants and extra bookkeeping; they can't afford to give those extra moments of personal attention to a patient, nor can they afford to waste time on house calls. Time is money—their time, that is not yours.

Also, today they're all specialists. If you have a pain in your right ear, you go to a right ear specialist; he doesn't do left ears. Nor windows.

Does anyone but me remember family doctors—like William E. Branch, for instance, who became Hollywood's favorite physician, but who came to the house when you called, sat by your bed, listened attentively to your symptoms, and answered your questions in terms you could understand? No matter how much in demand he became, Bill Branch always had time for that word of reassurance, that bit of comfort, that means so much when you're ill. Does anyone reading this have a doctor like that? If so, hang on to him for dear life—literally.

Another example of the difference between Then and Now -the Twenties and the Eighties—is a picture I made called, *Tragedy of Youth*. It is the public's reaction to that picture which point out the vast difference in moral standards.

The story was fairly sophisticated—not just boy-meets-girl stuff. It showed what happens to young couples who are not ready for the responsibilities of marriage. A splendid young actor named Buster Collier, who left movies after talkies, became my husband. There was a scene in our apartment after a rather rowdy party, in which we had a bitter argument, and as we were arguing, he followed me into the bedroom. Still talking, I turned my back to him and he casually unzipped my dress for me. I let it fall, stepped out of it, and went into the bathroom, slamming the door after me.

Under the dress I was wearing a satin slip, the kind we all wore in those days. It covered me from arm-pit to mid calf. Even without my dress on, I was more fully clothed than the average girl of today walking down the street in warm weather. Yet that scene elicited outcries from the critics, more than one sermon from the pulpit, and several editorials decrying the lack of modesty of certain actresses, especially me. One critic said it was all right for C.B. DeMille to show half-nude girls in his extravaganzas, but it was hardly the thing for family entertainment. Another wrote that Miss Miller did not have to resort to nudity—nudity indeed!—to attract an audience, and a columnist claimed that I was cheapening my talent by disrobing on the screen. I think the picture got good reviews otherwise...

I hardly need point out the difference in reactions of yesteryear and today.

Not entirely in the then and now category but close enough to be worth recording was *Marriage by Contract*, a picture I made in 1928 which was based on a book written by Judge Ben Lindsay. The book's title was *Companionate Marriage*, which today is referred to as a "live in relationship." It dealt with the pros and cons—mostly cons—of couples living together without benefit of clergy. The Judge took a dim view of it, as did most Americans of that day, believe it or not. It was really just a compilation of case histories, but the studio bought the book because of its popularity and wide publicity, and with the help of a couple of good screen writers, made a fine scenario out of it. Why they then changed the title, as that was really what they had paid for, is a mystery known only to studio heads.

The story line was simple: a young girl takes marriage too lightly, going from husband to husband, then from man to man, until she ends up with a gigolo half her age.

I did the aging, from a young girl in her twenties, to a woman in her late fifties, not with wrinkles and gray hair, but by thickening my waist, putting cotton in my cheeks to make them chubby, using too much make-up, and wearing an elaborately coiffed blonde wig. The effect was that of a middle-aged woman pathetically trying to retain her youthful looks, and when she learns that her young lover, on whom she has lavished wealth and gifts, intends to leave her for a younger woman, she shoots him.

The movie moguls, in their wisdom decided that an ending like that was too grim for the public to accept. It might have been acceptable had I been protecting my honor, but as it was pretty clear by then that I didn't have any honor left to protect, a new ending was tacked on showing that it had all been a dream.

Oddly enough, the "happy ending" didn't hurt the picture, which opened to rave reviews and was one of the big hits of the year. Modesty forbids my mentioning what they said about my performance. I will only say that upon reading some of the notices, my father remarked to my mother, "Well, well, it seems we have an actress in the family."

To emphasize the difference in outlook during the Twenties, I quote from an advertisement: "Greatest picture ever made on the subject of companionate marriage. Is contract marriage destroying the family? Is it tearing down everything that is sacred, holy and good? A warning to the womanhood of America. The most daring picture of all time."

Can't you just see the young people of today reading that ad? They would be rolling in the aisles, laughing themselves into hysterics. But not so back then; the public flocked to the box office in droves... and no one laughed.

Sermons were preached about the picture, one pastor telling his congregation to see *Marriage by Contract*, heed it well, and benefit from the lesson therein.

Twenty-five years later *Sunset Boulevard* was made, starring Gloria Swanson and William Holden. The plot was not unlike that of *Marriage by Contract*: a once-famous movie star, clinging to the memory of greatness and youthful beauty, takes a young lover and, when she discovers that he wants to leave her, shoots him dead.

Gloria gave a magnificent performance—possibly the best of her career—and it goes without saying that William Holden was terrific. (I never saw him give less than a great performance.) All in all, it was a memorable picture, and it is the difference in the way it was accepted that makes me mention it.

The public accepted *Sunset Boulevard* all right, in fact, they loved it. It didn't bother anyone that Gloria murdered her lover. But, of course, in the end she went stark raving mad, which might be considered atonement of a sort.

An unwritten rule was that it was all right for the star to be somewhat less than saintly, if she saw the error of her ways and repented before the final fade-out. All things considered, not such a bad rule to follow...

Sunset Boulevard, one of the last pictures Gloria Swanson starred in, gave her a great exit. The only trouble was that the audience seemed to believe it was the true story of her life; that it was Swanson's real swan song. It was shown not long ago to a class of students studying old movies, and the concensus of opinion was that she was great in the part because she was Norma Desmond, the character in the movie, in real life... clinging to fame and faded glory, unable to accept the loss of youth and beauty.

Gloria was as much like that pathetic character as I'm like Greta Garbo.

For one thing, Gloria never lost her beauty. It didn't fade, as prettiness does; the bone structure and the gorgeous eyes defied age. For another thing, she had a sublime sense of the ridiculous, and no one with that gift can become a Norma Desmond. But she did not make of herself an open book, that all who run may read. Only close friends were privileged to know the real Gloria—the impish child behind the veneer of sophistication and poise. She was one of the most glamorous beauties of her day—of any day—and she protected her image in public, and rightly so, in my opinion, but behind that beautiful face was a keen mind and good sound Swedish common sense, plus a delightful sense of humor. She loved playing practical jokes, never mean ones, just funny ones. As an example, here's one that she played on Jane Grey, a mutual friend. I'll tell it in Jane's words.

"A group of us had taken a boat trip up a river one day; don't ask me which river, I don't remember... We were going to a little island to have a picnic, of all things, but the water became so shallow that the men couldn't row, so we pulled up on the bank to find a shady place to have our lunch, and I had to help drag the boat up! I felt like a Volga Boatman.

"I was wearing an old pair of shorts that were a mile too big, and a horrible blouse that I should have thrown away; it was torn in several places from briars, and so was I. I was also soaking wet and tired, so I slumped down on a stump and spread out my long skinny legs, panting like a dog, my mouth open and my tongue hanging out. Gloria was her usual perky self, making wise-cracks and wandering around snapping pictures of birds and trees and whatever.

"Well, we eventually had our picnic lunch, turned the boat around, and went back, thank God. And that was that.

"A few weeks later Gloria invited me to the unveiling of a new portrait by some well-known painter whose name I don't recall. There were a dozen or more guests already there when I arrived at her apartment, having champagne and *hors d'ouevres*. A red velvet drape at the end of the room covered the large portrait. Gloria announced that the unveiling was about to take place. The lights were dimmed, a spotlight was aimed at the wall, Gloria pulled a cord, the drapes parted... and there I was, larger than life, sitting on that stump, legs spread out, stringy hair hanging down in my face, tongue sticking out... I could have died. But not before killing her!"

That was my Gloria.

When I was living with Ruth Chatterton, who was directing *Windy Hill*, a play I had written, I nearly lost my mind. Ruth was a brilliant actress, and, it turned out, a good director, but she was one of those people who knew everything, and would brook no contradiction. It was during the War; hotels were so crowded I couldn't get a reservation for love or bribery, so I stayed with Ruth and went slowly mad. To give you an example, she made a pronouncement about our 94 senators being hopelessly archaic. At that time, before Alaska and Hawaii joined us, there were 48 states, therefore 96 senators.

When I pointed this out to her, she replied firmly, No, dear, there are 94 senators. I happen to know.

I was telling Gloria about it one day, and she said, Why don't you stay with me before you blow your top, and I took her up on the invitation before she had time to say another word.

The point is that Gloria and I were good friends before I stayed with her, and we were even better friends when I left, some two months later. How could I possibly have lived happily with her all that time if she had been anything like Norma Desmond? Or how could she have put up with me had she been that kind of woman? That answers that question once and for all.

On the maid's day out we used to sit in the kitchen over our breakfast coffee and carry on like a couple of school girls. She was no more a cook than I am, so the breakfasts were sketchy, to put it kindly. But I didn't mind. In fact, we were always so busy talking and laughing that I hardly noticed the burnt toast or the watery eggs.

John Lee Mahin, Patsy, Gloria Swanson and Bart Marshall

Once in a while I would answer the phone and hear a voice that I came to recognize—that of Joseph Kennedy. I would sing out, It's for you, Gloria, and tactfully leave the room. I believe it was understood that their little fling had been flung, but from the purr in Gloria's voice when she answered the phone, I wouldn't bet on it.

When rehearsals of my show, *Windy Hill*, were over and it was to open in Philadelphia, we parted with a quick hug. I had no words to express my gratitude, but she knew how I felt... and will always feel. Norma Desmond indeed!

She did have one eccentricity in later years, she went in for health foods like Jane Fonda goes for exercise—with fanaticism.

Once she came out to visit us in Connecticut with her new husband, Bill something-or-other and a weekend supply of health food. It startled my husband, no end, he being a brawny Scot and a hearty eater. However, he went along with the gag until the day she offered to fix him a very special dish—a salad, he understood her to say—and he took a mouthful of it. "My God!" he exclaimed in horror. "It's grass!" And so it was—dried grass. Even Gloria's persuasive powers couldn't get him to take another bite of it—if you can bite dried grass.

Windy Hill had a wonderful cast: Kay Francis, Roger Pryor, and Judy Holliday, before she had that big hit with *Born Yesterday*. I couldn't have asked for better actors, and, as I said, Ruth turned out to be a damn good director, so the opening in Philadelphia was very satisfactory. It was decided to take it out on the road for a while before bringing it into New York, and we stayed on the road for nearly a year. That was largely due to Kay, who was a very shrewd business-woman. We did a knockout business, mainly due to Kay's name, and, not one to turn down a fast buck (she was getting, not only her salary, but a cut of the box-office). Kay preferred the sure thing of the Road to the uncertainty of a New York opening.

We finally had to close due to Kay's contract with the Monogram Studios, who had a picture ready for her, and threatened a breach of contract suit if she didn't return. That effectively closed our show, as the producer wouldn't hear of putting anyone else in Kay's part. To my regret, *Windy Hill* never did get to New York. By the time Kay was again free the producer had died, his estate was involved in a legal battle, and I got tired of the whole thing and went back to California, which was probably stupid of me. But it had been a great experience, and I had come to love Kay.

One of the endearing things about Kay—although she didn't think so—was her difficulty with the letter "R". One evening as we were sitting chatting after a long rehearsal, she said plaintively, "Why did you have to pick that poem... 'Bweathless we flung us on a windy hill, laughed in the sun and kissed the lovely gwass'—by Wupert Bwooke. Why couldn't you have chosen 'Now I lay me down to sleep' by anonymous?"

CHAPTER TWENTY THREE

Much has been written about the Nineteen Twenties, generally with emphasis upon gangster and the "Flapper" generation with its bobbed hair and jazz bands—and who could forget the Charleston?!—but little is said about the true quality of life as it was lived by people like my parents and their friends.

Peace had laid it soothing hand upon the fevered brow of Europe. The War to end all Wars was over; Europe was once more available to American tourists. Crime was not a matter of great concern. Theft existed, as it always has, but there were no drug-crazed rapists and murderers roaming the streets; you could stroll after dark in almost any big city without fear of being mugged. Aside from the vendettas of the bootleggers and the gangsters spawned by Prohibition, there was very little violence in the average city. And as they only killed each other, who cared?

We of the younger generation thought ourselves very sophisticated, what with our discovery of Freud and Jung. Some of us were of two minds about God, although almost all of us went to church. Of one thing we were certain: War would be eliminated as soon as we took over. It is amusing, in a sad way, to recall our earnestness, our certainty that our generation would accomplish that which no generation before us had been able to do.

We loved discussing Life in capital letters, but we also loved ballroom dancing, parlor games, and necking in rumble seats. Dancing was at the top of our list; we danced at hotels, to big name bands; we danced at roadhouses, where there were soft lights and soft music; we danced at each other's homes to the music of a victrola or, later in the Twenties, to the radio. We waltzed, we tangoed, we did the fox-trot and the Charleston.

Next in popularity were parlor games. Many a Sunday afternoon, after tennis or swimming or whatever, a group of us would get together at my house and play what we called The Game.

We chose up teams, one of which we had to act out, in pantomime, the title of a book or movie, a quotation, a phrase, the name of a person, or something like that; the other team had to guess it. We were fiercely competitive, and some of the subjects really demanded inventiveness and a certain amount of histrionic ability. For instance-Nietzsche's "Thus Spake Zarathustra". Try doing that in pantomime! Sometimes a little naughtiness crept in, and we often exploded into gales of laughter at our own witticisms. This may sound to most of you like a very dull form of entertainment, but to us it was fun.

Judging by today's mores, our amusements were of an innocence hardly to be found in any present day kindergarten, except in the matter of juvenile drinking. As the sale of anything alcoholic was against the law, a law forbidding the sale to minors would have seemed redundant, so the hotels and restaurants looked the other way as the contents of pocket flasks were poured into set-ups, without questioning the age of the customer. The result was that many young men imbibed before they were of an age to handle the liquor.

Most of us girls—or young women, if you prefer—only took a drink when we were out on a date because it was the thing to do. We generally disguised the taste with various fruit concoctions until they looked more like fruit cocktails than alcoholic beverages. The Maraschino Cherry stocks must have hit a new high.

Women didn't work unless they had to, except for those in the arts and sciences. When they had to earn a living, they went mostly into office work, as secretaries or switchboard operators. Men were the bread winners of the family; that was understood. Women were the home-makers. They did volunteer work for hospitals and charity organizations, of course, that was part of their lives, but they looked to the man of the house for financial security, and didn't mind at all being supported by their husbands. It was taken for granted that women should be protected from the seamy side of life; even the Courts protected them, and in any legal dispute, the women had the advantage.

I strongly doubt that any woman, in those days, would have opted for the right to dig ditches, work in a coal mine, or become a member of a man's club which didn't want her, in exchange for the countless privileges she enjoyed. Chivalry was still in fashion and male courtesy was as natural as breathing.

It is my observation that American men are beginning to behave more like the Japanese in respect to their attitude toward women. In my many years of visiting Japan, on my way to Hong Kong, I have yet to see a Japanese man stand aside for a woman, open a door for her, or lend his arm to help her out of a chair. They are apparently sending us not only TV sets, cars, and a myriad of electronic devices, but their manners as well. But I suppose it's only natural that, as the supply of gentlewomen in this country diminishes, so will the supply of gentlemen.

Since Europe was at peace, or so it seemed, our world was safe. Who knew what was going on in Asia, Africa, and the Far East—and what did it matter? Who cared what some despot in such an unlikely place as Ethiopia was up to? Who was disturbed by goings on in the mountain kingdom of Sikkim? Quite a lot was going on all over that far-off world, but it didn't affect us because we didn't know about it. We had no modern marvel of radio and television to bring plague, pestilence and violence to our breakfast tables with our orange juice.

Our newspapers gave us more local news than international, so few Americans knew and fewer cared that Arabs were busily engaged in killing French Legionnaires and vice versa, that African tribes were industriously trying to decimate—and possible eat—neighboring tribes, that Latin American governments were rising and falling with the tide to the staccato accompaniment of gunfire. Beirut, Bahrain, the Persian Gulf . . . merely romantic names in novels by Kipling and Maugham.

The invasion, annexation, and final obliteration of Armenia by the Turkish Empire went largely unnoticed until a novel about it was published: *The Forty Days of Musa Dagh* by Talbot Mundy. That stirred some sympathetic public reaction, but by that time the siege of the fortress of Musa Dagh, the eventual surrender of its stareved defenders, and their ultimate slaughter to a man, was merely history, something that had happened to a country on the other side of the world, a country from which rug merchants came.

Such a short time ago, as Time goes in this Universe of ours, there was no strife-torn Iraq at war with its neighbor, Iran. There was only sprawling Mesopotamia and gentle Persia, where Omar Khayam sat under a bough and sang of love and life.

There was no Thailand, where students demonstrated in front of the Palace, demanding the resignation of the Prime Minister, and when he did resign, were so stupified that, unable to think of a better one, they all just went home. There was only Siam, from whence came Siamese cats, and where Anna, the English Governess, tamed a proud and haughty King.

There was no North or South Vietnam, no Cambodia or Laos, only a vast area known as Indo-China, the setting of many a romantic novel. Few people had ever heard of Hanoi, but Saigon was known as the Paris of the East . . . to those who knew of it at all.

Today, whether we are concerned or not, we at least know about the war in Beirut, and many of us even have a fairly accurate idea of where Beirut is located, mostly due to jet travel.

If hatred and violence now rule the world, as certainly seems the case, I hold the airplane largely responsible, not only for the obvious reason that bombing an enemy is a neat and efficient way of disposing of him, but because air travel has brought together people who would have been better off staying far apart. Despite pious pronouncements from politicians and preachers that to know one another is to love one another, anyone with the brain of a gnat knows that quite the opposite is true. Familiarity often breeds not only contempt but loathing.

Traits in other nations unlike our own seem amusing in books; when lived with they can become irksome to the point of frenzy. Customs that are quaint at a distance often seems disgusting at close range. Some national characteristics, delightful to read about, can be as irritating as a skin rash when encountered.

Aye, tis a sair fact, but a fact nonetheless—we were all better off when we kept our distance. But I daresay the airplane is here to stay, and we must make the best of it.

So the pleasant, zany Twenties drifted by, more slowly than the years do today—a phenomenon readily recognized by anyone over fifty. It was a good time for the country and a wonderful time for me, despite my unhappy love affair from which I made a great discovery—you don't die of a broken heart unless you really want to. Except for the idiocy of Prohibition, it was a most satisfying decade almost to the very end.

But it ended bleakly. The stock market crashed, my Mother died, and I got married.

Sadie Miller

133

CHAPTER TWENTY FOUR

The stock market crash didn't seem to affect our family, at least I never heard my father say anything to that effect. Maybe he wasn't heavily in the market, or maybe he just never bought on margin, I don't know. But I do remember when it happened, and for a rather odd reason.

It may have been a dark day on Wall Street, but it was sunny in Beverly Hills. On that afternoon, my father was playing tennis with Townsend Netcher, commonly called "T". It was about three o'clock when the phone rang and the operator's voice said, "This is Chicago calling for a Mr. Townsend Netcher. Is he there?" I said yes, he was, and went to call him to the phone. I knew that he owned a big department store in Chicago—The Fair, I think it was—so I said, "Hey, T, someone's calling you from Chicago. Maybe your store's on fire. Or maybe someone passed a bad check!"

"Very funny," he said as he came in to answer the call.

He was on the phone for quite a long time, and when he came out he looked sort of dazed.

"What's the matter?" Daddy asked. "Bad news?"

"In a way", T replied. "My broker has been trying to reach me all day, ever since the market opened."

Daddy looked at his watch. "Well, it's after six in New York. It's closed now."

"I know. That's what he told me. Too late to do anything about it now."

"About what? For God's sake, man, what are you talking about?"

"That the market has taken a dive... It seems I've been pretty well wiped out."

"Jeez, fella," Daddy said, putting down his racket. "That's tough. What do you want to do, have a drink? Or maybe you'd rather go home?"

"What do you mean, go home?" T said. "The score's five-four, my favor. Do you think I'm going to quit while I'm ahead? No way. Come on back to the court and watch me beat you."

So back to the court they went, and finally won, seven-five. *Then* he had a drink.

Now that's what I call the ultimate in *sang froid*.

The stock market crash was devastating to our country but my life experienced *its* crushing blow several months later.

On the evening of November 27, 1928, my mother and father drove me downtown to the theatre where I was appearing in the play, "Nightstick." Generally I drove myself, but a new beau of mine, Tay Garnett, had offered to pick me up after the show, so I didn't need my car. Mother was her usual vivacious self, but when Daddy suggested taking in a movie, Mother said she had a long day and was feeling tired, so they dropped me off and went straight home.

I never eat much before a performance, usually having a snack when I get home, so Tay took me to a nearby restaurant after the show, and we had sandwiches or something, and sat over our coffee for a while. It must have been well after midnight before he drove me home.

When we pulled up in front of the house, I knew something was wrong. They always left the porch and downstairs lights on for me, but that night there were other lights, and a car parked in the drive, a beat up old car which I thought I recognized as belonging to Dr. William Branch, our family doctor ever since we had lived in California.

I don't really remember much about the next few hours. Mother was lying in bed, looking serene and beautiful. Dr. Branch was sitting on the bed, holding her hand, saying over and over, but in his soft Southern voice, "You've got to pull through, dahlin. You've got to do it, you heah me?" He turned when I came in and said, "Damn it! I feel so damn helpless. It's her heart, and there's nothin' I can do. Damn it all!"

I knew Mother had always had a little heart problem. She carried pills with her, but I had never thought of it as being really *heart* trouble. Not really, not the kind anyone actually dies from. I stood and listened to Dr. Branch damning the medical profession, but I didn't really take it in. He was right, of course. In those days there was nothing to do, no by-pass, no pace-maker, no real heart medication.

You won't believe what I found myself doing; I wouldn't believe it myself, except that I can see it clearly in my mind as I write this. I walked over to Mother's dressing table, picked up a comb, and started combing my hair.

"Maybe you'd better go to your Daddy," the doctor said, and I realized for the first time that Daddy wasn't there. I could hear faint sounds from the next room, but I didn't go to him.

Mother gave a deep sigh and I went over to her. She opened her eyes, smiled at me, and said so softly I could barely hear her "Take care of your father, dear." Then she looked at Dr. Branch, gave his hand a little pat, as though to say, I know you did your best, and died.

I have no recollection of what I did then. I don't even remember the funeral very well. Somehow I feel that I wasn't much comfort to my father, or to my brother who came home from Princeton although, when I mentioned this to him not long ago, he assured me that I had helped him a great deal. I was so immersed in my own grief—no really, my own rage, my fury—that I don't think I even tried to understand what my father was going through. I daresay no one can truly understand what it means to lose a dearly beloved husband or a wife, until it happens to them. The loneliness, after all those years of togetherness, is indescribable.

Someone must have taken over and notified the theatre; the show went on the next night with my understudy, and for a week longer. I didn't want to go to the theatre at all, but the owner called me and said that the box-office was falling off, and if I didn't return the show would have to close.

Well, what could I do? You can't let the side down!

134

"All the News That's Fit to Print."

The New York Times.

THE WEATHER

NEW YORK, WEDNESDAY, OCTOBER 30, 1929

STOCKS COLLAPSE IN 16,410,030-SHARE DAY, BUT RALLY AT CLOSE CHEERS BROKERS; BANKERS OPTIMISTIC, TO CONTINUE AID

GRUNDY FOR CURBING 'BACKWARD STATES' ON THE TARIFF BILL

KAHN REFUSES POST IN SENATE CAMPAIGN; CALLS CHOICE UNWISE

WAS RELUCTANT, HE SAYS

LEADERS SEE FEAR WANING

Point to 'Lifting Spells' in Trading as Sign of Buying Activity.

240 Issues Lose $15,894,818,894 in Month; Slump in Full Exchange List Vastly Larger

CLOSING RALLY VIGOROUS

Leading Issues Regain From 4 to 14 Points in 15 Minutes.

INVESTMENT TRUSTS BUY

BIG TRADERS HARDEST HIT

U. S. STEEL TO PAY $1 EXTRA DIVIDEND

RESERVE BOARD FINDS ACTION UNNECESSARY

Robert Armstrong, George Green, Lois Wilson, Winston Miller, Virginia Zanuck, Paul, The Bride, The Groom, Helen Ferguson, Kenneth, Lila Lee, John Farrow, James Gleason, Tom Buckingham

Tay Garnett at Pathe Studio, 1929

Courtesy The Museum of Modern Art, New York City

BING CROSBY
RHONDA FLEMING
WILLIAM BENDIX
SIR CEDRIC HARDWICKE
With New Bing Song Hits!
A Connecticut Yankee in King Arthur's Court
COLOR BY TECHNICOLOR
From the Famous Classic by Mark Twain
A Paramount Picture with MURVYN VYE · VIRGINIA FIELD · HENRY WILCOXON
Produced by ROBERT FELLOWS · Directed by TAY GARNETT
Screenplay by Edmund Beloin

Where's the old team spirit? Get in there and pitch! Laugh! Clown, laugh!

So I went back and finished the run of the play. The show must go on... and all that sort of thing.

Mr & Mrs Tay Garnett

CHAPTER TWENTY FIVE

Since I had been with Tay, laughing and enjoying myself, while my mother was dying, it seemed only right that I should marry him. I don't quite understand my reasoning, but perhaps a psychiatrist can explain it.

My marriage to Tay Garnett (before John Lee Mahin) comes under the "Had I But Known" heading.

It seems that Tay was cherishing a secret love for years before he met me, and he went on cherishing it, on and off, all the while. It started during the First World War when Tay was a Navy flyer stationed in Brooklyn. There he fell in love with the wife of a superior officer. Although Joan, the officer's wife, returned Tay's love, she could not, in all honor, divorce her husband as a scandal would ruin his career. In those days, the Navy was stuffy about such things.

Tay undoubtedly loved her all the more for putting honor first, so when the war was over he left Brooklyn and his true love, and came to Hollywood where he became a screen writer, and eventually a very good director. Then, some ten years later, he married me. A trite tale, you might say, of a man caught on the rebound, although a ten-year lapse might be something of a record in rebounds, but there's more to come.

Shortly after we were married, Tay learned somehow that Joan's husband had died. At last she was free! But, alas, he wasn't. He was saddled with me. By the time he was once more free, tragedy struck. He had somehow lost Joan's address!

Unable to get in touch with her, he did the next best thing; he married again. This time it was to a girl named Helga. Shortly after he and Helga were joined in holy wedlock, a letter arrived from Joan (who had probably found his address in the L.A. phone book) telling her that she had married a Frenchman and was living in Paris.

So there they were again, each tied to the wrong mate, and with an ocean between them.

In due time Tay was again free. He got an offer to direct a picture in England, and as England is only a short hop from Paris, he accepted the offer. This time he had been careful to keep Joan's address, and the first weekend he could get away he flew to Paris. There he called on Joan, who was living in a beautiful apartment on the Rue Hauptmam. It must have been a touching reunion, for he persuaded her to ask her husband for a divorce.

They both agreed that this would not be dishonorable as her husband was not an officer, nor a highly-placed government official, but merely a wealthy—an *extremely* wealthy—business man. I'll bet you'd never guess what happened—or maybe you would. The very night that Joan plans to tell her very wealthy husband that she loves another, her extremely wealthy husband has a heart attack! A shock such as that could be fatal!

No woman of honor could desert a wealthy invalid husband whose days might be numbered, and as we know, if there's one thing Joan is, it's a woman of honor.

So once more Tay returned to Hollywood alone where, faithfully following his formula, he got married again.

In due course that marriage ended in divorce, and also in due course Tay wrote to Joan to tell her that he is free, and to inquire as to the health of her invalid husband, if indeed, he is still alive.

Well, imagine Tay's surprise to have the husband answer the letter; he is not only alive, he is quite well. He thanks M. Garnett for his inquiry, and he regrets having to tell M'sieur that his dear Joan has been dead for three years.

How's that for star-crossed lovers! Doesn't that belong right in there with Pelleas and Melisande, Romeo and Juliet, Bonnie and Clyde?

I think it is a very sad story, and it was none too happy for us three—or four?—wives, either.

Lon Chaney and Lila Lee in "The Unholy Three", MGM, 1930.

CHAPTER TWENTY SIX

If I have thus far given the impression that I danced through life on my tippy toes, with never a care other than what fun thing shall I do next, allow me to correct that impression. It was not all beer and skittles, by any means. I had my share of sorrows, disappointments, and self-doubt; there were bleak times as well as laughing ones, but I have been blessed—and I do mean blessed—with a sort of automatic turn-off which effectively shuts off the bad memories.

There was one period, though, when I was so despondent that I seriously considered suicide. My brother was back East in college, my father was visiting relatives in Illinois—he still couldn't face living in our house without Mother in it—and I felt too alone to live. I remember quite distinctly lying in the guest room because my bedroom was too cheery, and I didn't want to feel cheerful, and considering how to go about disposing of myself. Poison would have been my first choice, except that we didn't have any in the house; all I could find were vitamins and a bottle of aspirin. I didn't think I could swallow enough aspirin to kill me without gagging on it, maybe even throwing up, and I couldn't quite see myself driving down to our local drugstore and asking the pharmacist to kindly give me a few dollars worth of poison and charge it, please.

Cutting my wrists was out; there would be too much blood, and the sight of blood made me queasy. I had my trusty revolver in the house, but, alas, I didn't know where to find the bullets, and I didn't feel like rummaging through tool closets and storage bins. There was a shot gun in the hall closet, and I gave that some serious thought. There were drawbacks, however; my arms were too short to reach the trigger if I pointed it at my head. I would have to hold it upright and pull the trigger with my toe, but I'd be damned if I would let myself be found stretched out on the floor with my toe on the trigger. It would be undignified, to say the least. And besides, it would splatter me.

I lay there for quite a while, brooding; it hadn't occurred to me that it would be so difficult to make a stately exit, leaving everyone sorry they had been so mean. I would lie there, beautiful in death... and suddenly I started to giggle. "You know what, Patricia?" I said out loud. "You're suffering from the 'You'll be Sorry when I'm Dead' syndrome, and wouldn't it be a joke on you if he wasn't sorry!"

The more I thought about it, the funnier it struck me,

140

and I began writing lines of dialogue in my head. He'd come home with his pal, Tom Buckingham, who always brought him home after a three-day binge, and he would say, Who's that lady lying dead on the bed? And Tom would say, That's no lady, that's your former wife. Then he'd say, I'll drink to that, and they'd have a drink. Then Tom would say, Better dead than wed, and she didn't even muss the spread! And then they'd drink to that.

I got to giggling over a few rather bawdy rhymes I thought of, then I came up with:

> They found a young girl in their bed
> Who claimed she was not really dead
> So they gave her a whack
> In the small of her back
> And another on top of her head.

I broke myself up with that one, and when I stopped laughing, I decided not to kill myself after all, but to go to Tahiti instead.

A week before, John Farrow had called and asked me if I could go to Tahiti with Lila Lee, his lady love. They had been invited by Gouverneur Morris and his wife to stay with them on the island, where they had a coconut plantation, and John thought it would be wonderful for Lila, who had just returned from a sanitarium in Tucson where she had put up a courageous battle against T.B. The problem was that John couldn't get away. He was in the middle of writing a script at Paramount and wouldn't be free in time. He didn't feel that Lila should travel alone, so if I couldn't go with her, the trip would have to be cancelled. I had told him that I would think it over, but hadn't actually given it much thought until that moment of decision on the guest-room bed.

Gouverneur Morris was a very popular novelist, as well as being a direct descendent of the G.M. who signed our Declaration of Independence. He was also a delightful man, and I knew he would be a wonderful host, so with no further ado, I called Johnny and said, Okay, I will go with Lila. When do we leave?

"Next Friday," he said. "A good thing I didn't cancel the tickets. See you on the boat." Then he hung up before I could explain that next Friday was only five days away and I could never be ready in time. But somehow I was. Not an early riser except when working, for the next four days I was off and running at daybreak. I got my French Visa, bought a new bathing suit, paid all current bills, bought our clothes home from the cleaners, left a note to Tay who was on location in Florida, and was on the pier in San Francisco with John and Lila with an hour to spare, slightly winded but otherwise fine.

Going to Tahiti today is no big deal, with jet planes criss-crossing the skies over the Society Islands every day, with thousands of tourists over-nighting there in transit from some Pacific island to another. Marlon Brando has a home there, probably on Bora Bora or Moorea, and I have read that Raymond Burr also lives on one of the islands and practically commutes to Hollywood for his television movies.

It was not so in 1931. Tahiti was way off the beaten track. No planes crossed the Pacific then, nor the Atlantic. It was all they could do to cross the country in short hops. Tahiti could only be reached from the United States by one line, the Union New Zealand, which sailed once a month from San Francisco, stayed in port for three days in Papeete, then went on to New Zealand and Australia. A month later it came back, stopped in Papeete, and sailed back to San Francisco. Except for an occasional tramp freighter, there was no other transportation to the States, so like it or not, once in Tahiti, you were there for a month.

From the moment Lila and I sailed through the Golden Gate, we were in a different world. For the next two weeks there was nothing to look at but sea, sky and the other passengers. Most of them were Australians returning home from England—which they professed to dislike but secretly admired—or from Canada, which they praised fulsomely as being very like Australia. The few Canadians on board did not appear to regard that as an unqualified compliment.

The Australian contingent seemed to me rather like overgrown puppies, playful and eager to be liked, quite delightful companions once the language barrier was overcome. The differences in the meaning of American words and Australian words can produce some awkward moments; for instance, one day a very nice Aussie, openly enamoured of Lila, asked if he could come to her cabin next morning and knock her up. The poor man was visibly shaken at her indignant reaction, blushing to the roots of his hair and beating a hasty retreat. Lila was equally shaken when informed that all he had meant was that he would rap on her door to awaken her.

Another time, while sitting in the lounge after dinner, we started discussing the various customs of our countries. In Australia, we were told, most girls went to work as soon as they left school, a way of life not then prevalent in the States.

"Sometimes they don't even wait until they've finished their schooling to try to get office jobs," one of the Australians said.

"Why do you suppose that is?" Lila asked.

"Simple," was the answer. "They like their weekly screw."

After one startled gasp, Lila let out a whoop of laughter, finally managing to say, "I do admire their frankness."

The men looked at her, then at each other, in complete bewilderment. What had been so funny about the statement that a girl liked to receive a weekly salary?

Lila was getting stronger and healthier by the day and except for the rare days when the Pacific belied its name, held sway from her deck chair, using her pansy eyes and throaty voice to such good advantage that she never lacked companionship. Such was her charm, even the other women passengers liked her and forgave her her beauty.

As for me, what with shuffle board, deck tennis, and the other games the Australians insisted on playing, the time passed too quickly. It's strange how one becomes submerged in shipboard life, enjoying the rhythmic monotony of each uneventful day. It becomes a life style, no longer merely the means of reaching a destination.

Our first sight of land was a coral atoll rising slowly from the sea, feathery palm trees waving languidly in the offshore breeze which brought us our first fragrance of the tropics. It is an indescribable aroma, a blending of flowers and coconut and vanilla and lush steaming jungle. The island seemed to float by us; we could hear the pounding of the surf, dashing itself against the coral reef which enclosed a clear, calm lagoon lazily reflecting the sunrise. It was even more beautiful than I had imagined it.

An hour later we had entered Papeete Harbor and lay at anchor facing the misty mountains that lie behind the town. When the few of us who disembarked looked back from the tender and saw the rail lined with waving handkerchiefs, we had the feeling that we were leaving a cherished home filled with old friends.

At first glimpse there was little charm in the town itself. It was a seaport, and like most seaports, seemed dingy and squalid; the buildings, tin-roofed, were drab. The natives, mostly half-castes, were not as I had imagined they would be, dressed as they were in cheap imitations of European clothes. But still there was something, an indefinable feeling in the air, a pleasantness in all the faces, that made me glad I was there.

Govvie and Ruth Morris were at the pier to meet us and we were rather formally introduced to Teri, their driver, and to Lee Wong, the houseboy, who was to follow us home in a taxi with our bags. Teri immediately enchanted me. He wore a pair of chino pants, a wild shirt, a chauffeur's cap and a flower behind his ear.

As soon as we left the seaport activity of Papeete the spell was cast; I was enslaved by my first South Sea Island. On all sides were colors so strong you could feel them, flaming hydrangeas, scarlet flamboyants, greens of every shade, from golden to almost black. On our right, as we drove, lay the cobalt water. Above, a pure Madonna-blue sky was saved from monotony by the misty clouds swathing the mountain tops. Along the road strolled men and women in red and white flowered pareaus, waving, laughing, calling to us. On grassy plots beside the road lay others peacefully sleeping. It was pure Gauguin.

The Morris plantation was in Paea, about twelve miles from town. The two-storied house was set in a clearing, coconut palms all around it, the beach across the road. The house was large and cool, with no actual doors or windows, just apetures. Screens weren't necessary, as there were no flying insects that bit, though an occasional powdery-winged moth fluttered around the candles and oil lamps, and tiny lizards sometimes scampered up the walls or across the ceiling. No one minded them; they kept the insect population under control, minded their own business, and were quietly efficient at zapping up the stray spider or gnat that was so foolhardy as to enter the house.

Only once did a lizard cause a certain amount of confusion, and that was at a dinner party at the Governor's mansion. As the dessert was brought out and placed on the table—a magnificent piece of French pastry, ornamented with scrolls of whipped cream—a lizard lost his grip and fell from the ceiling, sploshing right into the center. Whipped cream flew in all directions, and the poor little fellow disappeared in a froth of mousse. With never a change of expression, Madame, the Governor's wife, probed with a beringed hand, fished the lizard out by his tail, dropped him gently on the floor, and said, "You may serve now," to the butler standing by. He served the dessert and we all ate it.

The Morris Manage was considerable; in addition to another house-guest, Marcella Gump, member of the fabulous Gump's of San Francisco, there was a Chinese cook, who allowed no one, but NO ONE, in his kitchen except his assistant, of whom we never caught more than a glimpse, an upstairs maid, a downstairs maid, and Trower, the manager of the plantation. He presumably had no first name, or perhaps no last name. He was just Trower, a wiry sandy-haired little Australian, dry and hard as a coconut shell.

Except when we were invited out to tea, or went into town to do some shopping, we wore nothing but shirts and shorts if we had guests, a pareu when we didn't. We wore it in lieu of bathing suits, which is chancy until you learn to twist it over your bosom in just the right way. Once, before I learned the trick, I swam right out of my pareu, to the great edification of a passing canoe load of French sailors.

The pareu is a wonderful invention. Actually it is nothing but a length of cheap cotton cloth of a brilliant uncompromising red, splashed with huge white floral designs. The cloth came from France, where it was manufactured only for the Islands; no French woman would have used it for a dust rag. I think today it is made in other countries; I have seen it, or something similar, in Hawaii and the West Indies. But in those days it was confined to the South Seas, and was fascinatingly new to me.

In addition to being used as wearing apparel, pareu cloth took the place of doors, windows, and lamp shades. It was hung as window curtains, to partition rooms, to cover chairs, to sit on, to lie on, and as a tote bag. It seemed as indigenous to the Island as the Tiare Tahiti, an incredibly fragrant white flower which grows nowhere else in the world, and which, when worn behind the ear allows you to float in your own sea of fragrance.

Tucking the Tiare Tahiti behind the ear was not only ornamental, it had a special significance. Behind the right ear meant that you were available, behind the left ear meant that you were taken. A flower behind both ears— Aha! That meant that you had a lover but were open to offers.

Govvie and Ruth returned to the States on the next boat from New Zealand, leaving the three of us no longer house guests, but mistresses of the manor, but we ruled our domain something like the Queen of England; we had nothing to say about anything. The cook decided what we would eat and did all the ordering, and I couldn't help noticing that when Trower brought us the food bills they always ran about the same, whether we had had twenty guests that week for dinner, or none. We didn't dare question them, and Marcella explained that it was just "cumshaw," the Chinese version of "totin'".

Trower also decided when we could use the car, and Teri more often than not decided where he would take us in it. I didn't really mind. It was rather pleasant having no responsibilities and no decisions to make.

One day in Papeete I ran into an actor named Barry Norton, who had done an outstanding role as the young dying soldier in *What Price Glory?*. We had never happened to meet in Hollywood but naturally, meeting in far-off Tahiti, we fell into each other's arms like long lost lovers, and celebrated by going to the Bouganville Club, a waterfront cafe famous throughout the Society Islands for its Rainbow Cocktail, a lovely concoction of fruit juices and varicolored liquors, beautiful to look at, beautiful to drink, and lethal. Barry was from Argentina and looked very much like Ramon Navarro, which was a wonderful way to look, I thought—and so did Marcella.

We were joined by two Englishmen whom we had met at the Governor's Ball a few nights before, Victor Conventry, grandson of the Earl of Coventry, and a British naval

Barry Norton, Lila and Patsy

officer named Cousins.

Cousins was tall, trim and unemotional, and while not much of a conversationalist, he was an excellent listener. Victor, on the other hand, never stopped talking unless out-shouted. He was darling, slight of build, with babyfine blond hair and baby blue eyes that gazed upon the world with an innocence he hadn't had for years; the epitome of the almost-bred-out English aristocrat.

By the end of lunch it was decided that we would all go island-hopping on the next trip of the France Astrale, a trading vessel that sailed from a nearby dock; all, that is, but Lila, who abstained on the grounds that she was alergic to anything smaller than an ocean liner, and just thinking about a boat the size of the France Astrale made her seasick.

Barry dashed off to make arrangements and before any of us could have a second thoughts was back with the announcement that the France Astrale was sailing the next morning and he had booked passage for us. Thanks largely to the Rainbow Cocktails we all agreed enthusiastically to meet on the pier by eight the next morning. I seem to remember Marcella kissing Barry a rather tearful good-bye before Terri packed the three of us into the car.

By the dawn's early light I got my first look at what was to be our floating home for the next week or so. A luxury liner she wasn't. About fifty feet long and broad in the beam, her decks were already cluttered with gear, boxes and cartons, and uncoiled ropes lay in wait to trip the unwary. A faint aroma of bilge and copra surrounded her like a cloud.

My instant instinct was to say, "Well, bon voyage, youall," and scurry back to Paea. But there we were with our sleeping mats, our Cognac and bottled Perrier water, our straw baskets stuffed with shirts, shorts, and bathing suits, so what could I do but pretend it looked like great fun. Cousins suggested that we go below to stow our gear and grab the best accommodations before the rest of the passengers arrived, which was a sound idea except that there were no accomodations. Below deck was just one big cabin already filled to overflowing with natives of both sexes and all ages. What with their bedrolls, their baskets, their children and pets, there wasn't a square foot in which to sit down without having a baby or a puppy in your lap.

143

So back up on deck we went, where the rest of our fellow passengers were still coming aboard, a good many of them live-stock. There were goats, live chickens, piglets, and even a mynah bird giving everyone hell at the top of his voice. Noting that the animals were being herded to the forward deck, we decided on the after-deck on which to settle. Although we were thus to windward of the goats, we had some space in which to spread out, we also had our own private head, and wouldn't have to go below to use whatever the facility was down there. Since there was no running water aboard, only drinking water in big drums, I think we had the best of it, even though what we had was about as primitive as you can get, as I learned before we had been many hours out to sea.

It was what might be truly called outdoor plumbing. You could hardly get more outdoors: the ladies'—and gentlemen's—room was a plank with a hole in it jutting over the stern. Someone with a nice sense of delicacy had erected a rod on the deck from which hung a length of pareu cloth, giving at least an illusion of privacy—from the front, at any rate. From the back and both sides it was completely open to the ocean breeze and to the view of anyone sailing by. Happily, we were not in a shipping lane.

The Captain was straight out of a B movie, a huge barrel-chested man, obviously a mixture of Polynesian and something, probably Portuguese. His belly bulged over the rope he used as a belt; his voice was either a roar or a mumble, and he hadn't acquired English in Eton or Oxford. Between oaths it was understandable, however, and while not unfriendly he did nothing to encourage idle conversation, the Portuguese side of him dominating the Polynesian in that respect.

Our early morning departure finally took place well after noon, as we should have known it would. Our destination was Bora Bora, an island about 80 miles due west, another twenty-five up and down, which due to our late start we could not make that day. We chugged along at what Cousins estimated as about 5 knots, dropping anchor once off a tiny island whose name I don't remember, where we unloaded some Chinese families and took on some copra. As they all had boxes and bundles and livestock to take ashore, the canoes plied back and forth for several hours like an assembly line, the difference being that it was done to the accompaniment of shouts, laughter, and song.

I spent most of that night at sea trying to figure out how to be comfortable in a sleeping bag on a heaving deck, but before I had it figured out it was daylight, and Bora Bora lay dead ahead. I was very keen to see Bora Bora because of a picture, Tabu, which had been made there by a German director named F.W. Murnau. I think it was his last "Hollywood" picture, although shot almost entirely on location on the island. Murnau had acheived recognition as a fine director for a film made in Germany called *The Last Laugh*, with Emil Jannings, and he had come to Hollywood with great fanfare. Before he could take his place among the Greats, he was killed driving off a cliff in Santa Monica.

We pulled up to a rickety pier about twenty hours after leaving Papeete, and fell in love with Bora Bora at first sight. To add to the sheer enchantment, we seemed to have a welcoming committee; scores of natives were gathered on what appeared to be the village green; drums were throbbing, soft voices were chanting, lovely Tahitian maidens clad in grass skirts and flower leis were swaying sinuously. It was altogether too perfect, a Hollywood version of a South Sea Island.

"Nothing like traveling with a movie star," Marcella said. "Did you send your press agent on ahead?"

As no one gave me a second glance, it was obvious the activities were not in my honor; we were just fortunate to have arrived on the day of the island's annual dance contest. If there was a guest of honor at all, it would be William K. Vanderbilt, whose ocean-going yacht lay half a mile off shore and who, we were told by the Captain, was coming in with his party to photograph the dancing.

We all felt pretty grubby, and much as we wanted to watch, we wanted even more a place to freshen up, but we looked around in vain for something like a hotel. Cousins strode purposefully off and in no time returned with a pretty Tahitian girl in tow. "Her family has rooms," he told us. "They have two we can rent."

Marcella in her fluent Tahitian French explained that we only wanted some place for a few hours; there'd be no time to move in to a rooming house as we were scheduled to leave that evening, and certainly didn't want to miss the boat.

The girl giggled. "Oh, no," she said. "The boat will be here several days. The Captain has two girls here in Bora Bora."

She had underestimated the Captain. We were there four days.

Matari's home was a sprawling compound of thatch-roofed buildings, seemingly all fitted with members of her family, who greeted us with such warmth and laughter that we felt more like guests than lodgers. After a wonderful meal which they insisted we share with them, the five of us ambled back to the village where everything was still going on at fever pitch. Suddenly a man bedecked in flowers and feathers, who seemed the master of ceremonies, shouted something, at which silence fell and all heads turned toward the sea.

The Vanderbilts were coming ashore.

The landing party was impressive. Pulling up on the beach was an Admiral's gig complete with fringed awning and sailors in starched white uniforms, two of whom leaped briskly ashore, put down a landing ramp, and stood smartly at attention. I thought I heard a fanfare of trumpets as William K. and Mrs. Vanderbilt trod down the ramp. They were followed by their guest—a famous ichthyologist, we later learned—who seemed slightly ill at ease. Mr. Vanderbilt was very nautical in blue blazer and snow white slacks, a yachting cap four-square upon his head.

Mrs. Vanderbilt was not to be believed. From head to foot she was protected from the sun; not only with sun glasses and a big straw hat; she was also swathed in veils, wore long white cotton gloves and carried a parasol.

Two more sailors hurried ahead of them carrying canvas folding chairs, and by the time the Vanderbilts had reached the green the chairs were unfolded and set up, with another parasol over Mrs. Vanderbilt's. It was quite a spectacle.

The contest then started in earnest, to the beating of drums and gasoline tins, which is more musical than you'd think, and to beautiful harmonizing of male and female voices. Each group danced with perfect precision, but also with gaiety, which kept it from looking like just a well-trained chorus line. We five, lolling on the grass in our

The Vanderbilts

rumpled shorts and shirts, beat time, applauded, and shouted our approval in unconstrained exhilaration. The musicians grinned at us, and the girls, giggling, gave us little waves of recognition as they ran off-stage.

I glanced over at the Vanderbilt group to see their reaction—but there was none to see. Sitting erect in their canvas chairs they might have been watching a high school play in which none of their children were taking part.

When they first came ashore Marcella and I, standing within arm's length, had smiled and said, "Good morning." The Vanderbilts had graciously inclined their heads without breaking stride, and the ichthyologist had given us a tentative smile. "I guess being together on a South Sea Island doesn't constitute and introduction," I whispered.

Suddenly it struck me as terribly funny; here we were, seated not twenty feet apart, the only white people within a radius of eighty miles, scrupulously ignoring each other's presence. During a break in the dancing we began to devise ways to scrape up an acquaintance and perhaps get invited aboard the yacht. Marcella said Victor should break the ice—"You won't have to touch your forelock," she assured him—"by strolling by nonchalantly and remarking when in earshot, 'Oh, how I wish my grandfather, the Earl of Coventry, were here.'" I thought it a brilliant idea, but Victor flatly refused. "I'd feel like a bloody fool," he said. "Besides, I don't want to go on their bloody boat."

The next idea was that Cousins should get chatting with one of the crew, and let drop the information that he was in the Royal Navy, here on a secret mission for the King.

"You might as well be an Admiral," Marcella said. "Or are you too young?"

"Come off it," said Cousins. "Do I look like an Admiral?"

He dropped that in favor of having Marcella go over and ask if they would consider selling her their boat for a million dollars cash, as hers was getting dirty. Marcella liked the idea but reluctantly vetoed it; she didn't happen to have that much cash with her, she said, and doubted that they would take a check.

Barry debated for some time, before turning down our next suggestion, which was that he take off his shirt and walk slowly past Mrs. Vanderbilt flexing his muscles. He countered with the proposal that one of us go catch a fish, as an excuse to talk to the ichthyologist, and then let him in on the big secret that I was a movie star.

"They'd just move their chairs further away," I said, which annoyed Barry, who was very sensitive about any slur cast on his religion, nationality, or profession.

What with this and that and a few rum drinks, offered us by one of the drummers, our hilarity had mounted until frankly, I could hardly blame my fellow Americans for keeping their distance.

When the competition ended and the Vanderbilts had returned to their yacht, the real festivities started. The Tahitians insisted that we join in their dancing, which was no longer the set routine, but joyous and uninhibited. They even tried to teach us some songs and we earnestly roared out the strange words, accompanied by squeals of laughter from the girls.

The moon was high overhead before we wended our rather uncertain way homeward still singing little snatches of native songs, quieting down as we approached the compound, then giggling as we bade each other good night.

As I undressed in the moonlight I thought that probably never again would I know such pure gaiety, such wholehearted innocent joy, and I remember murmuring drowsily to Marcella, "Isn't it wonderful to be some place where you just know nothing bad could ever happen?", and hearing her grunt, "Don't be silly. There's no such place."

As it happened, she was right.

As none of the others seemed interested in Murnau—or in anything but lots of hot coffee and maybe an aspirin—I went off alone with Matari's brother to see the island on which Murnau had lived while shooting his South Sea idyll. It was barely an island, just an atoll a mile or so offshore; there on a slight rise of ground stood the windowless hut which Murnau had occupied.

The inside was only one room with a cot against one wall, a table and a chair against the other. On the table was a pipe and a large manilla envelope covered with shreds of tobacco; on the floor were some crumpled papers and one canvas sneaker. A German newspaper lay on the cot, a striped shirt hung from a nail on the wall.

"It is as he left it," said Matari's brother. "We like Murnau. We keep it this way in his memory." He won't be coming back, you know," I said. He nodded. "We are very sad when we learn that he is no more."

"How did you learn of his death?" I asked. "Did someone come over from Papeete to tell you?"

He looked at me oddly, then smiled and shook his head. "We go," he said, tapping his chest. "We go to Papeete to tell *them*. Because we like Murnau, we know as soon as he goes away."

It was true. They had known in Bora Bora the moment Murnau died and had sailed to Papeete to tell his friends there. The boat carrying the newspaper reports of the accident didn't arrive until two weeks later.

It may have been my imagination, but suddenly the hut seemed dark and cold. I shivered, and hurried out into the warm sunlight.

They were waiting for me when I returned, and Marcella informed me that the Captain was nowhere to be found, so we were all going stone fishing with the villagers. The women had gone on ahead to start weaving their nets, but the men waited to take us; Matari's mother gave us all sandwiches of a sort, wrapped in tapa cloth, and to Marcella and me she gave hats which she had made herself, woven of palm fiber. They had very wide brims and were so light that if you tossed them in the air they floated down like bubbles.

We were each assigned to a different canoe as passengers, and Marcella yelled over to me, "I forgot to tell you the good news. The Vanderbilts will be there."

"Goody goody," I said.

"I thought that would make your day," she shouted. "Adios. Vaya con Dios."

Then her outrigger shot ahead and ours followed. My crew had put me up on the very bow of our canoe; a leg dangling over each side, and what with my lunch clutched in one hand, my box camera in the other, I had to grip my knees to keep my balance, rather like riding an English saddle.

Now everyone knows that outriggers are as safe as any water craft can be. They will not sink, and due to the weight of the outrigger extending several feet from the side of the canoe, they never tip over. In all Polynesian folklore there is not one tale of an outrigger canoe being capsized... at least, there wasn't until that day. It doesn't sound possible, but it happened. I capsized the canoe.

When I surfaced, still clutching my sandwiches and camera, I was in the air pocket under the overturned boat, so I went down again, and this time when I came up I was between the canoe and the outrigger. The men were all about me in the water, shouting at me, I assumed telling me to go down and try again, so I did. This time I came up near the stern, but still inside the outrigger. Obviously, they couldn't right the boat until I was disentangled without fear of beheading me.

I was still wearing my hat, the brim drooping over my face, and I must have looked like a sea anemone as my head broke water. By this time we were laughing so hard it's a wonder we didn't all drown. Finally one of the men ducked under the outrigger, came up beside me, put his hand firmly on top of my head, and pushed. As I went down for the fourth time he gently steered me away from the canoe, swimming underwater with me for about ten feet, and this time when I came up the outrigger was safely behind me, and a coral reef was at hand. My mentor pointed to the reef with a gesture that said more clearly than words (especially as he spoke only Tahitian): Get up there and stay there until we get this God-damn boat turned over! So I did.

They had it righted in no time, but of course it was full of water up to the gunwales. This they emptied by pushing it vigorously back and forth, the water sloshing out the ends at each shove.

When the canoe was emptied, they paddled close to the reef and hoisted me back to my figurehead position on the bow. I was pretty soggy but otherwise all right, aside from a tiny scratch on my knee from the coral. I had even managed to hang on to my sandwiches and camera. After a while I noticed a tiny trickle of blood from the scratch, but it was not enough to bother about and after an occasional wave slapping the bow rinsed it off anyway.

By the time we pulled up on the beach, the last to arrive, everyone had gone to the other side of the island where the fishing was to take place. I started walking down the beach to find them, turning as I rounded the curve to wave another farewell to the men. Four of them waved in return; the fifth and youngest stared at me with a strange expression, then started coming slowly toward me. It gave me an uncomfortable feeling, and I involuntarily backed away a few steps. Then he called something to me, made a beckoning gesture, and quickened his steps.

The young man said something and when I tried to smile and shake my head, indicating that I didn't understand, he broke into a trot. My heart began to pound and I could feel my legs beginning to shake; I turned and began to walk away, trying to break into a run, not to show my fear. The beach was so empty, never had I felt such emptiness, such aloneness, only unfeeling sky, uncaring water. This can't be happening, I thought, it can't be really happening...

Maybe he's given up, I thought; maybe it was only a joke—but a quick glance over my shoulder showed him just a few yards behind me, and seized by blind unreasoning panic, gasping in deep quivering sobs, I started to run. I was outclassed from the start, and I dare say the whole race didn't last thirty seconds, but they were among the worst thirty seconds I've ever experienced.

As I sensed him closing in, a group of women strolled around the curve of the beach, stopping in wonderment as they saw us. Before I could get my breath to cry for help the man called something to them. They called back, then started to laugh.

"My God," I thought, "They're going to stand there and watch me being raped."

At that instant I was tackled from behind and went down on my face; in the next instant I was grabbed by the ankles and flipped over like a pancake on a hot griddle. All the fight knocked out of me, I looked up in mute appeal as my attacker squatter on his haunches, seized my left leg, lifted it to his lips—and started sucking the coral out of the cut. He sucked and spat—sucked and spat—until the wound was clean, while the women looked on approvingly and I lay there feeling like eighteen kinds of a fool.

My pursuer, the darlin' man, had spotted the blood on my knee, realized immediately what had caused it, and unable to explain to me, had taken the only means he could think of to save me from a fate, if not worse than death, certainly very unpleasant. Coral is an animal, a living sort of polyp; when it dies, the skeleton becomes like rock and, combined with millions of other skeleton forms reefs and atolls. If a piece of live coral enters the body through an abrasion it will continue to grow and spread almost indefinitely, causing severe infection and sometimes death.

During this emergency treatment more and more women had gathered to watch and to enjoy the description of my flight, as rendered by the first women on the scene, their graphic gestures leaving no doubt that they knew exactly what I thought I was fleeing. When I was finally able to join in their laughter, albeit weakly, they became warmly solicitous, one of them even tearing a strip from her pareu to be used as a bandage. I later exchanged it for one of Cousins' clean handkerchiefs, but I appreciated the thought.

Stone fishing is not done for sport, strictly for food. There's no nonsense about pitting one's skill against a monster of the deep. Enough fish can be caught in one day to feed many villages for weeks. Eating a week-old fish which has not been frozen is evidently their idea of a tasty meal.

Holding their nets waist high, the women wade out into the shallow water while the men paddle out into the deep water, lining their canoes bow to stern across the mouth of the cove. They have large rocks encased in fiber and attached to ropes. On signal, they hurl the rocks into the water, pull them back into the canoe, and hurl them into the water again. And they do it in rhythm—in the water-out-in the water-out. It looks like a Billy Rose Water Carnival.

But it's no carnival to the fish. The underwater concussion drives the fish to dash erratically in all directions, hundreds of them trying to escape by swimming into the shallow water. The women then scoop them up in their hands, toss them on the beach, or, if they are small, stuff them down their bosoms, having tied ropes around their waists to keep them from sliding down.

Some of the fish I saw on the beach were so weird looking it was hard to believe they were really fish. Some had come from such depths that when they hit the air they exploded.

Sure enough, the Vanderbilts brought their ichthyologist ashore. He was in a perfect frenzy of scientific disbelief; there were not only fish he had never seen before, there were species he had never heard of. He had to share his excitement with someone, I suppose, and as Mr. and Mrs. Vanderbilt had retreated to the shade of a tree, he turned to the nearest non-Tahitian, which happened to be me. It was then that he noticed my bandaged knee, and asked me about it. Though I assured him the poison had been sucked out—not going into the details of its extraction—he insisted that I have the ship's doctor look at it. (Oh yes indeed, the yacht carried its own doctor) and he went straight off to tell Mr. Vanderbilt, who was very concerned and immediately sent the gig out to bring the doctor ashore.

The doctor gave me little lecture on the perils of Polynesian life and put some iodine on the cut. I assured him that Cousins' handkerchief had been thoroughly boiled and sterilized, so he tied it back on my knee. I think the parting pat on my bottom indicated relief rather than romantic interest.

When all the fish had been distributed, we returned to Bora Bora without further incident, although Marcella swore she had seen the men throwing dice to determine who would take me back, the losers getting me as a passenger. I don't believe that for a moment. Where would they have gotten the dice?

The third day was spent lolling and swimming and loving the island more and more. Matari's family set a lavish table, and I ate everything offered, even the raw fish, which isn't really raw, having been marinated in lemon or lime juice. Smothered in coconut cream—not milk, but cream—it is delicious.

Those members of the family living in the outskirts of the compound never joined us at meals, which seemed odd as they supplied much of the food, always to be seen working in their little vegetable gardens or feeding their chickens and pigs. They seemed very friendly, greeting me with a smile and a cheery "Iorana" whenever I walked by; I assumed that there was some sort of caste barrier. Perhaps they were the poor relations.

When the Captain had dried out sufficiently to make it up the gangplank, we were summoned back to the boat. Matari and her brother accompanied us to the dock; never would a true Polynesian let a friend depart without being on hand to wave and weep. After teary farewell speeches I mentioned that I was sorry not to have gone down to the garden and said goodbye to her family there.

"Oh, it is better not," said Matari airily. "They will understand. They are lepers."

I decided not to think of all their food I had eaten...

Our next port of call was Raiatea, a rocky island, unlike Bora Bora in appearance and first impression. Dominated by a rugged mountain, its harsh foothills rolled down to the sea in partial shadow cast by the heavy clouds around its peak. Even the foliage seemed to lack color. I was not surprised to learn that in the old pre-missionary days, Raiatea had been the burial place of the gods.

We would leave the next afternoon, the Captain told us, presumably having only one lady friend on the island. We must have shown our dismay at the thought of a day in this cheerless place, for the Captain, with unaccustomed solicitude, offered to get someone to take us sight-seeing. There was the sacred *Marae*, he told us, a wonderful temple constructed of huge stones skillfully fitted together, built in the old days before they had cement or mortar. In it were the bleached skulls of all the warriors killed in battle. He waxed enthusiastic as he described how they were stacked, piles and piles of them, higher than a man's head; surely something that anyone would want to see.

Maybe tomorrow morning, we said.

Plainly disappointed in us, the Captain went ashore where he was greeted by a young man with whom he got into a lengthy discussion. From the way they both looked at us, we were sure that we were the subject of the conversation. Finally the Captain signalled to us to join them. "It is the sorcerer," he told us. "He says you may watch fire-walking this afternoon. If you want to, you must say so now, as it takes a few hours to heat the stones."

I had to admit that the young man didn't look like my idea of a sorcerer. He just looked like a nice young Polynesian wearing frayed khaki shorts.

"I bet it's a phoney," said Barry. "It's one of those shows they put on for tourists."

"It could be the gen," Cousins said. "I've heard about it. They really do walk on fire, on red hot stones, anyway. Let's have a bash, what? If they'll do it at the right price," he added hastily.

It was decided that we might as well have a bash at it, so after some haggling, a price was agreed on and the young sorcerer left.

"Someone will come for you" said the Captain, and hurried off, leaving his first and only mate to oversee the rest of the unloading.

How we filled the next few hours I don't recall; probably by having lunch somewhere. There were some French merchants and Government officials on the island, so there must have been at least one good restaurant. The French in those days had a far-flung Empire, but it was never flung too far to have good food.

In due time a native appeared, and telling us in fractured French to follow him, led us on a ten minute walk down a narrow dusty road to an open glade where the ceremony was to take place. There was an open pit, about fifteen feet long and six feet wide, filled with smooth stones varying in size from a grapefruit to a cantaloupe; they rested on a bed of red hot coals from which the heat rose in shimmering waves, melting even Barry's skepticism.

Somewhat to my surprise, there was no sign of our young sorcerer, but we were greeted by a gray-haired native wearing a grass skirt over Levi's, a khaki shirt, and an ornate headdress. He was obviously another sorcerer, even more obviously in an advanced stage of elephantiasis, his left arm and leg being twice the size of the right ones. After some preliminary waving of palm leaves and muttered incantations, he crossed the fiery pit, followed closely by his disciples, young girls and boys also dressed in grass skirts and carrying huge palm leaves. They stepped off on the far side quite unharmed, and as they started back toward us Cousins yelled, "Clear the decks!" ran to the far side, and leaped on the rocks behind the procession. Once in the pit he had to slow up because the footing was uncertain, but as nonchalantly as though strolling down Bond Street, he walked the length and stepped off in front of us.

"Come on," he said. "It's a piece of cake."

"Should we?" said Marcella.

149

"Why not?" I said.

"I know why not," said Victor. "We'll get the hell burned out of us."

I turned to Barry. "What do you think?"

After a long pause he said slowly, Well... if he can do it.

The old sorcerer now came over nodding his head happily. "Tu viens avec moi?" he asked me. "Okay," I said, "We're all coming with you." Then, with a great deal of palm leaf waving and chanting from his followers, he asked each of us in turn, "A tu fois?"—have you faith—and in turn we answered, "Oui, J'ai fois" although at the moment my faith was a little shaky, and judging by Barry's expression, his was smaller than the proverbial mustard seed.

However, when the old man said "Suivez-moi" we all followed; Marcella first, then Victor and I side by side, then Cousins, and Barry last. I had to look down to watch my footing, and the heat seared my face, but I felt none at all on my feet, nor on my legs up to the waist. It was an odd sensation. Ahead of me Marcella was nearing the end. Beyond her I saw our young sorcerer from the boat; he was in a heated argument with the old man who had already stepped off the pit. Suddenly the old man flung his arms in the air, uttered a cry which sounded like Aite, aite (no, no) and fell to the ground as though he had been pole-axed.

At that moment Victor put his hand against my shoulder and pushed, propelling himself off to the side, and almost causing me to fall. Then, with an oath, Cousins brushed by me, scrambling in great strides toward the grass and nearly colliding with Victor. I was so astonished by their behavior that I forgot to watch my step, and one foot slipped between two stones. A little spurt of flame licked my ankle, but I felt no pain, quickly recovered my balance, and continued on my course.

(The next day I noticed a huge blister on that ankle; it looked awful, but it never hurt me, although it left a scar which I bear to this day.)

Marcella, meanwhile, had stepped off at the end, and turned to me with a broad smile and an out-stretched hand. Before I could grab it she stared at something over my shoulder, he smile changed to a look of horror, and she ran past me without a word. Taking my last step off the stones, I turned to see what had caused her sudden panic—and I, too, froze in horror.

Surrounded by strangely silent natives, Victor and Cousins were lying flat on the grass, their legs stretched out before them, their faces ashen. Even from where I stood I could see that the soles of their feet were horribly burned. Horribly.

Barry, who seemed unharmed, took charge; somehow, someone got an automobile, somehow we got them to the only doctor in town, a Frenchman. He could do little but give them sedation and wrap their blistered feet in oiled bandages, with the suggestion that we get them to Papeete as soon as possible, and into the hospital there. The doctor's wife, a pretty woman of mixed blood, helped with the ministrations and I noticed that when Marcella indignantly demanded to know how this could happen, who was responsible, how they could permit such fakery, she cast furtive glances at her husband but said nothing. Why were *they* burned and *we* weren't, Marcella kept asking, but the doctor just shrugged, as though to say, why were you such fools as to believe in the native voodoo.

His wife caught my eye and nodded imperceptibly toward the door so, claiming to need air or to be sick—which was not far from the truth—I went outside.

In a few moments the doctor's wife joined me.

"I do not like to say in front of my husband," she said in a whisper. "He prefers that I do not talk of such things. But I know why this has happened."

This is what she told me: it was the doing of the young sorcerer. It was he who had made the arrangements, so it should have been he who took us across the fire. When he arrived and found the old sorcerer making magic, he was very angry. There was a feud between them anyway, the young one thinking the old one should retire, the old one refusing to. So in his anger the young one, to prove his power, broke the spell of the old man, allowing the fire to burn us. Not all of us however; in a spirit of chivalry he had spared the women. (Lest that might seem to cast a slur on Barry, I think his lack of enthusiasm for the venture had caused him to hesitate just long enough.)

The Captain was wonderfully cooperative. He put everyone ashore who wasn't going to Papette—I suppose promising to pick them up later—gathered up his crew by walking up and down the main street of the village shouting for them—and within an hour or so we were under way. As we were backing away from the pier Marcella thought she saw the young sorcerer standing at a distance watching us leave. Cupping her hands like a megaphone she shouted, "Sale espece de cochon! Fils d'une greu!"

The man, whoever he was, turned and walked away. "I hope he understood me," Marcella said.

I rather hoped he hadn't. After all, we weren't home yet.

It was a ghastly trip back. The Captain pushed the France Astrale to the limit, but the night seemed endless; if it seemed that way to me, I can imagine what it must have been for Victor and Cousins. Their sedation soon wore off and we had no pain killer to give them, but fortunately there was plenty of wine aboard so we got them drunk. Barry, Marcella, and I slept in shifts, one of us always on hand to soak their bandages with oil or pour more wine into them, if they showed signs of sobering up enough to feel anything.

It was dawn when we finally chugged into the harbor and pulled up alongside the mole looming high over our heads. While we were wondering how to hoist our casualties up, a face peered down at us and a familiar voice said, "Iorana, Parti. Est-ce que je peux vous aider avec les pauvres brules?" Do you need help with the poor burned ones? It was Teri, waiting for us with the car.

When we knew that everything possible was being done for Victor and Cousins at the hospital, and that the best doctor on the island would take care of them, the three of us lurched out into the daylight, too exhausted for protracted farewells. Barry went off to wherever he was staying. Marcella, with a muttered "Home, James, and don't spare the horses," crept into the back seat of the car and promptly fell asleep.

Sitting in front beside Teri, the warm morning breeze refreshing me, the beauty of sky and sea soothing away the tension, I fell into a half doze. The horror of the past twelve hours became unreal. It couldn't have happened, not in this placid Paradise, not in this gentle land of gentle people. Glancing at Teri's pleasant, flat Polynesian profile, the flower as always tucked behind his ear, I thought how lucky it was that he had happened to be at the dock to help us.

Then I sat bolt upright as though I had had an electric shock. How *had* he happened to be there? I had accepted his presence—we all had—without question... but what was he doing in Papeete at that hour of the morning? Why had he been right there when we pulled in? Why... unless he knew in advance that we were coming. But we weren't expected back for days—how many depending on the mood of the Captain, or that of his light o'live of the moment; how could he have known our sudden change of plan? The France Astrale had no wireless; there was no communication from Riaitea except by boat, and none could have passed us in the night...

Above all, I wondered, thinking back to his greeting, how had he known we had "poor burned ones" aboard?

He glanced at me out of the corner of his eye. "I knew," he said.

"Well, how? How did you know we'd be there? How did you know about the accident?"

He gave me the same look Matari's brother had given me when I asked how they had known of Murnau's death. "I knew, Parti," He said, and that was the last word spoken on the subject then, or ever.

From our beach we could see Moorea across the water on which it seemed to float, constantly changing color, shimmering in the morning light, touched with flame at sunset. It was said to be the loveliest of all the islands, and I longed to see it, to bathe in its sparkling pools, to look at the sky through the great round hole in one of its highest peaks made, so legend has it, by a giant God who had hurled his spear through the solid rock, but no one would go with me. Marcella's attitude was if you've seen one

151

island, you've seen them all, and Lila had heard too much about our France Astrale trip to set foot aboard an island steamer.

Then one day Lila and I were invited to go sailing with a pleasant man named Wainright, who owned one of the few hotels in Papeete, and who went to Moorea every few weeks on business. He would take us to the island for the day, he said; if business detained him, we could stay overnight. On his solemn assurance that sailboats, while they might occasionally dip a wee bit up and down, never went from side to side, Lila stocked up on dramamine and off we went.

The crossing was pure joy. It was a perfect sailing day, with a brisk wind over our starboard quarter allowing us to make the island in a straight run, and even the groundswell as we approached the pass through the reef didn't upset Lila's equilibrium. Once inside the lagoon, which surrounds the whole island, it was like gliding over a sea of glass all the way to the wharf at Faatoai, the only town then on Moorea.

I think Moorea must be one of the most beautiful islands in the world, but I remember it for another reason. It was there that the chance encounter took place which was to effect many lives—perhaps my own included; of that I shall never be sure. It was as though the wake of the little sloop which carries us there spread and spread until it touched shores half a world away.

But sitting at lunch in the sprawling bungalow which served as Faatoai's only hotel we felt no finger of Fate pointing at us, no premonition; we simply felt exhilarated by our sail, and pleasantly hungry. When two young Frenchmen entered and greeted Wainwright, he invited them to join us, which they seemed delighted to do. Nor were Lila and I displeased. The first to be presented, Count Jean de St. Perrier, was tall and handsome in a lean way, sunbleached hair topping a somewhat sardonic face. The other, Count Noel de Ville Neuve, was shorter and broader with straight black hair and dark eyes shielded by thick black lashes that any woman should have envied.

Quelle bonne chance, they said, that had bought them to town on this day, for the first time in weeks. Generally they were too lazy to change from pareus to shorts and shirts, a minimum requirement, they felt, for dining out. Did they live here?, we asked. Oh, yes, they had lived here for months, they told us, in a little shack a few miles down the beach. With such desultory conversation we lingered over the delicious native meal—I still remember the heavenly taste of the dessert, a sort of poi made of mango and pineapple, baked in some wonderful way, and smothered in coconut cream—until finally Wainright announced that he had to go to the other end of the island on business and suggested that we wait for him here. He would try to be back before dark but, if by any chance he was delayed we could stay overnight at the hotel, and he would pick us up in the morning. That was perfectly agreeable to us, especially as Messieurs les Comtes promptly offered their service as guides for the afternoon.

Count Jean de St. Perrier

To no one's great surprise, Wainright did not return that evening. Nor the next evening. Nor the next. He returned to pick us up three days later, which according to Jean, was punctuality itself by Moorea reckoning.

Lila and I didn't spend those three days down at the wharf, anxiously peering out to sea. We spent them seeing the island with Jean and Noel. We visited pineapple plantations, picnicked beside fresh water pools, and watched Tahitian boys clamber up the coconut trees like little brown monkeys, to cut down the coconuts for us. We learned how to punch a hole in the end of the nut through which to drink the sweet milk, and how to munch the tender meat, when laid open by one stroke of a machete like a watermelon. We visited their shack on the beach; i was literally on the water's edge, the gentle surf lapping us a dinner they had prepared themselves.

Lila and I were naturally curious as to why such intelligent, cultured men were isolating themselves from the world. It was not merely to have a *maison a deux*, as they were quite definitely not homosexual; innocent as I may have been by today's standards, I had been around the theatre too long not to recognize that when I saw it. Besides, there are things a woman just *knows*. Little by little we drew the story from them.

They had known each other in Paris, being of the same background, and had much in common; both were children during the war, growing up in its aftermath, seeing their families affected by "la crise", the French equivalent of our later Great Depression. They were both ill-equipped for the new order of things, for being expected to make their own way in the world, for being forced into competition with those better qualified than they.

It had so happened that the year before, at some soiree in Paris, the talk had turned to world conditions, the chaotic political picture in France, and the devaluation of the franc which was playing havoc with those who, like Jean and Noel, were living on fixed family incomes. They found that they were in agreement that their familiar world was crumbling. "We felt like leftovers from the age of the dinosaur," Jean told me, and didn't even smile when I said that he was better looking than any dinosaur I had ever seen. Whenever they met, after that, they talked of escaping to some tropical island; at the point they were like all men who have dreamed of the South Seas, of beautiful native girls, of living on fruit from the trees, fish from the sea. But one day they read an article about the Society Islands in French Oceania, and their desire crystalized. Arrangements were made, their families' disapproval was more or less overcome, they left that familiar world no longer familiar to them, et voila... here they were. Never once, Jean assured me, had either one regretted his decision.

They weren't hermits, Jean said; they went to Papeete occasionally to pick up mail, perhaps attend a Government function or drop in on an acquaintance—but they were always glad to get back to their fishing and swimming and Polynesian indolence. So, after nearly a year, their experiment could truly be called a success. They were both content. Or so Jean said.

Lila and I had no hesitance about accepting their hospitality and their companionship, having made it quite clear that I was not interested in acquiring a lover, and Lila already had one. With that understanding, we had a wonderful time touring the island, canoeing, and just generally enjoying one another's company.

It was inevitable that, although always a foursome, we should pair off in a way. Logically it would have been Jean, who was tall and spoke fluent English, with Lila, who was tall and spoke no French. Noel's English was limited to about ten words, but it was clear from the start that he preferred Lila, so that's the way it was, and I must say there seemed no lack of communication between them.

When Wainright finally showed up, with the laconic remark that it had taken a little longer than he had expected, Jean and Noel decided to return to Papeete with us. The return trip was not the same as the one going over. We were bucking head winds and heavy seas the whole way, and Lila lay moaning in the gunwales, green water breaking over her, while Noel tenderly mopped her face with a sodden handkerchief as each wave receded. Despite her misery, and in between prayers that the boat would sink, she managed to ask me to invite the boys to be our house guests for a while, in return for their hospitality, which I thought an excellent idea, as did they.

Our house had four bedrooms, two on each side of the upstairs hall which was entered from outside steps. At the end of the hall was a large storeroom, filled mostly with luggage. Lila and Marcella had the bedrooms on the right, as you came in; I used one of those on the left. We gave the two on the left to Jean and Noel, and I moved in with Lila, who had the largest room, with a more than king-sized bed which she shared with a German Shepherd named Fritz and a Schnauzer named Gretchen. The dogs fancied themselves as part-owners of the plantation, and guarded it ferociously, even barking furiously at people as far away as the road. Of course, they had never bitten anyone, but if a trespasser with evil in his heart had ever happened on the place he would have been scared out of his wits.

The first night the boys were there we sat up pretty late. Lila undressed first, and by the time I was ready for bed she lay all curled up on her side, apparently asleep. I eased carefully into my side, arranged the dogs around and over my legs, and was just about to doze off when I heard a faint sound, not exactly a footstep, more a soft shuffle, as though someone wearing shoes with rope soles were ascending the outside stairs. The sound got closer, then there was silence. The moon was full that night; it flooded the hall and I stared at the door on the landing. But there was no shadow. I was just about to call out, "Who's there?" when both dogs who had been snoring peacefully, awakened abruptly, growling low in their throats, their heads turned toward the hall.

Now the faint shuffling resumed, it went past our door toward the storage room at the end of the hall. Still I had seen nothing. The dogs were standing on the bed, stiff-legged, staring as I was at the moonlit hall.

Suddenly, Fritz gave a little whimper, quite unlike him,

leaped from the bed, and scurried down the steps, his nails clacking on the concrete. Gretchen followed as fast as her shorter legs would carry emitting terrified yipes as she ran. I could hear the crackling of the palm leaves on the ground outside as they headed for the beach.

Strangely, I wasn't frightened. "It's a tupaupau," I thought and glanced over at Lila, who hadn't moved. Lucky she's asleep, I thought; she'd have been scared to death. Then the shuffling steps came back, and this time, as they passed our doorway, I heard a chuckle, a warm friendly chuckle. The kind of chuckle that makes you want to join in. It was telling me quite clearly that there was nothing to be afraid of. I could feel myself smiling, and I almost said aloud, "That's all right, you didn't frighten me."

Then I closed my eyes peacefully, still smiling, and the next thing I knew the sun was bright on my eyelids and Lila was already up.

All through breakfast I held back, but by the second cup of coffee I had to talk about it. Just as I started with "Guess what happened. . ." Lila burst out with, "You'll never believe what I heard. . ." We both stopped and stared at each other. "Go ahead," she said. "What were you going to say?"

I tried to be casual. "I saw. . . rather, I heard. . . a tupaupau last night.'

"You heard it too?" she said. "I thought you were asleep. Or else I was dreaming."

'I thought you were asleep," I said. "We couldn't both have had the same dream, could we?"

"I don't think so," she said after a moment's reflection, "unless Fritz and Gretchen had it too. They weren't there when I woke up this morning."

By this time everyone's curiosity was aroused, and it was suggested that we each tell our version of what we had heard—or thought we had heard—separately. So I waited outside while Lila told her story, then I came in and told mine. We couldn't have agreed more in every detail if we had been reading from the same cue card. As further proof that we hadn't been dreaming, the dogs were still missing. (They didn't come back until the next day and even then, although ravenously hungry, they gave anxious looks over their shoulders as they ate.)

Anyone who has been in Tahiti more than a few days has heard about tupaupaus. They aren't ghosts in the strict sense of the word; not the spine-tingling chain-clanking kind. Though unnerving when encountered for the first time, as disembodied spirits are apt to be, tupaupas were considered harmless. Lila and I agreed that there had been nothing sinister about our night visitor; no spirit with such a warm chuckle could be anything but friendly.

"In fact," Lila said thoughtfully, "It was almost more than friendliness. . . sort of reassuring, if you know what I mean."

I nodded, but suddenly I wondered—reassuring about what? Why did we need assurance?—and I felt that quick tightening in the chest that comes with unexpected bad news. I carried a slight malaise for days, but no bad news arrived from home and I forgot all about it when Lila received a cable from Johnny Farrow telling her that he was on his way to Tahiti on the next boat.

Lila and Johnny had been going together for several years. They had met at the Paramount Studio; she was one of their stars, and though not in the same firmament as Gloria Swanson or Pola Negri, she shone in her own orbit. John Villier Farrow was an Australian writer, newly come to Hollywood. It was spontaneous combustion.

They were a striking couple. Farrow was lean and wiry, quick-moving, with the controlled power of a coiled spring; Lila was soft, yielding, languidly graceful. Farrow's chiselled face, ice blue eyes, close-cropped white-blond hair was perfect foil for Lila's dark beauty. It should have been the perfect romance; it might have been, but for one flaw. Lila was married.

She had been seventeen when she married James Kirkwood, then in his fifties, and still a handsome man. The leonine head, proud high-bridged nose, and mellifluous voice all proclaimed him the matinee idol he had been for years. Like many another man who, in his youth, has succumbed happily to the temptations of life and with age finds them less tempting, Kirkwood, when he married Lila, decided to foreswear the fleshpots. He bought a small ranch where he could play the new role of devoted husband and country gentleman, and to protect this young bride from the follies he had committed, kept her there in virtual seclusion. Except when she was making a picture, she saw no one but Jim and his friends, all much older than she, and even when she was working she was driven to the studio in the morning and driven straight home at night, with no dalliance along the way.

When Lila was swept off her feet by the sophisticated, worldly actor she had envisioned quite a different married life. The birth of her son kept her contented for a while but in a way made her more than ever a prisoner. It was inevitable that sooner or later she would meet a Johnny Farrow.

Jim Kirkwood was outraged. That a chit of a girl could walk out on him—in the middle of a performance, as it were—was intolerable. For a long time he refused to give her a divorce; for her own good, he said, and to give her a chance to come to her senses. Finally, realizing that there would be no third act curtain coming down on a repentant Lila imploring him to take her back, he did the gentlemanly thing—he divorced her on the grounds of adultery.

Everyone thought that John and Lila would get married right away, but they didn't. Instead they fought and made up. . . and fought and made up. . . fought. . .

But now Johnny was coming to Tahiti to be with her. It could mean only one thing; he wanted her to marry him. Marcella, although she had never met Farrow, agreed that he would hardly come all the way just to fight.

I sounded Lila out by asking what color Mother Hubbards she'd like her attendants to wear, but her reaction was unsatisfactory. At first she pretended not to know what I meant, then, when I said, "I'm going to be your matron of honor, Marcella will be a bridesmaid, and Trower will be the page boy carrying the ring on a cushion," she laughed at the thought of Trower as a page boy, but other than that seemed unresponsive. I was getting more and more annoyed with her, partly because her attitude was making me feel ridiculous, the way you feel when you've planned a surprise party and your guest of honor doesn't show up.

"What makes you think Farrow has wedding bells in mind?" she said.

"Don't be ridiculous," I snapped. "Why else is he coming here?"

"Maybe he's on his way to Australia," she said. "Anyway, I think he was carrying on with someone before I left. I never did believe that story about having to finish a script."

I gave her a stern lecture on the evils of jealousy, how awful it was to have such a suspicious nature, how love should be founded on faith, and more of the same, in the middle of which she shrugged and turned away, saying over her shoulder, "I don't know why you're so determined to make an honest woman out of me."

I didn't know myself. Possibly it was my Mid-Western respectability, combined with the belief that all women have, whether or not they will admit it, that true love should end in marriage. Perhaps I had dim forebodings; perhaps I sensed what her future would be if she didn't marry the man for whom she had left her husband and child; aimless drifting, hapless love affairs, rootless marriages...

But as the days went by, each one bringing a radiogram from the approaching ship—none of which Lila let us read—her attitude changed, and I began to believe that there'd be a happy ending after all. Marcella seemed to have been in a strange mood ever since we came back from Moorea with Jean and Noel, alternating between vivacity and morose silences. I dismissed it as being Marcella. After all, I hardly knew her well enough to judge usual behavior from unusual.

One evening, while seated next to the Tahitian Prince at a dinner party, I told him, in confidence, that Lila's "fiance" was due in a few days, and I thought it would be wonderful to give them a real Tahitian wedding. He agreed enthusiastically, and insisted that his mother be told, as he knew she would be delighted.

The Prince was really princely. He had been educated in England and received at Court by Queen Victoria who, so the story went, patted him on the cheek and told him that, though a bit dark for her tastes, he was a pretty boy. When we met him he must have been in his late forties, a handsome man, tending toward corpulence, his Polynesian charm shining through the superimposed British manner. He cherished the tradition of four o'clock tea, always wore a blazer and Old School tie in public, and was very keen on cricket.

So the next day Marcella and I called on the Queen, who lived in a small house on the outskirts of Papeete, and told her our idea. Not only did she approve—she suggested that the wedding take place in her garden, and offered to have a reception for the bride and groom as well, the only stipulaiton being that she could remain seated throughout... not because of royal privilege, but because of royal poundage.

Some time during the week of waiting for Farrow, Noel and Jean returned to Moorea. The leave-taking was casual to the point of off-handedness; Teri was driving them to town to catch an early boat, and none of us felt like prolonged farewells at that hour of the morning. Noel looked rather pathetic, I thought, as Lila, stifling a yawn, said, "Adios—I mean, au revoir, cheri," which was about all the French he had managed to teach her. Jean said if it would please me, he would return to see me off when I sailed for home, and I said it would please me very much, we were leaving on the next boat from Australia. See you then, au revoir, a bientot... and they were gone.

Johnny Farrow

The arrival of any liner from anywhere was a festive occasion, the European and American residents flocking in from the country to watch the passengers disembark, whether or not they knew any of them. And of course the arrival of a friend, or the friend of a friend, called for a celebration at the Bougainville Club which naturally included an introduction to its famous Rainbow cocktail. John Farrow's reception was an exceptionally lively one, all of our acquaintances being on hand, so by the time we all piled in the car and started back to Paea any constraint Lila or John might have felt had been liquidated.

Their happiness at being together again was evident. For the first few days there were no quarrels, not even a minor disagreement, but neither was there any clue as to why Johnny had suddenly decided to come to Tahiti, nor any hint as to future plans. As Lila and I had our reservations to return home on the next boat, sailing in less than a week, I thought that someone had better bring up the subject pretty soon, and since Lila seemed to be drifting along in a state of euphoria and Marcella had apparently lost interest in their romance—or had possibly found one of her own elsewhere—it seemed to devolve upon me.

The opportunity arose on the fourth day, a Friday; we three were alone together in the house and it seemed quite natural to mention our impending departure, how time flew, how much I would miss Tahiti, and other such banalities. I remember saying, "There's an old adage that goes, a week in the islands is too long, a year is too short"; My subtle approach achieved nothing and in sheer frustration I finally blurted out, "We're sailing next Wednesday, for Heaven's sake, so what about it?"

"What about what?" John asked politely, and I dried up. What I had intended to say, in a lightly bantering tone, was what are your plans? Did you come down here to get married or just to see the frangi-pani trees in bloom? Is Lila

155

returning with me, or isn't she? All good logical questions, asked in the spirit of friendship—or so it had seemed just a moment before. But as John's ice blue eyes rested on me I saw myself as he probably saw me, not a concerned and devoted friend but an interfering busybody who should be told to mind her own business. I turned in appeal to Lila, but she was gazing off into space, her hands folded placidly in her lap.

"What about what?" John repeated implacably. Drymouthed, I heard myself mumbling about Prince Arthur and the Queen, what fun it would be to have *himenes* instead of organ music, how wearing Mother Hubbards might set a new trend in bridal fashions. Finally my voice trailed off into an earsplitting silence. After what seemed hours, John said softly, "Lila, would you mind telling me what she's been talking about?"

"Us," Lila said, still gazing into space. "She thinks we ought to get married."

"Oh," said Johnny, and stared at me thoughtfully. I stared back, feeling idiotic. Then his face broke into a warm smile and he said, "I think so too."

"Really?" Lila said, and as she turned to look at him I thought she had never looked so pretty.

"Yes, really." Then with a grin, "Hey, Pat, isn't there an old adage that goes, better late than never?"

I could feel my eyes filling up. I've always been a pushover for a happy ending.

Trower chose that moment to barge in with some fool question about something or other, and before he left Jasper Moore, a neighbor, dropped in to invite us to dinner that night. Then John and Lila wandered off to the beach, Marcella came back from wherever she had been, and the cook wanted to know how many for "suppah." By the time I had summoned all my pidgin English to explain that only Trower would be home for dinner it was too late to pursue the subject further.

That didn't keep me from thinking about it, however, and all the while I was showering and dressing I was making mental notes. Call on the Queen tomorrow—use Jasper's phone to invite guests, sending chits would take too long—a Sunday ceremony would be nice, too soon, though, better try to Monday, there are probably lots of papers to be signed tomorrow. . . .

It was dusk when we walked down the road to Jasper's bungalow; not the lingering twilight of more Northern countries, but the sharp, quick sunset of the tropics, an abrupt transition from soft golden light to velvety blackness. We were all quietly happy, even Marcella seeming at peace with life and herself. Of the party itself I remember little. It was the usual assemblage of French and English residents, a Swede or two, some Americans on their way to somewhere else; mostly the same faces we had seen at the last such gathering. Lila and John left early and when I was ready to leave Marcella wasn't, so I said a quiet goodbye to Jasper, assured him that I didn't mind walking back alone, which was quite true, and started home.

Walking down the road in Paea was as safe for a woman in the middle of the night as it was in the middle of the day, and at no time was I really alone. Couples strolled by, hand in hand; family groups passed me, calling a cheery "orana"; from the bushes beside the road came snatches of song, girlish giggles, hearty male laughter. An occasional car chugged by, generally with one headlight and six to eight passengers. It was night life of a kind I had learned to love.

When I turned into our driveway I saw lights downstairs, which meant that Lila and John were still up, so thinking this would be a good opportunity to discuss the details of the wedding, I made for the front entrance, being careful to scuff my feet on the gravel in due warning. I needn't have bothered. It was no love scene I walked in on, it was a full scale battle; the very air seemed acrid with gunpowder as I stepped into a crossfire of charges and counter-charges that were being hurled like hand grenades. Lila's face was flushed with anger and tears, Johnny's was white with rage, and they both looked at me as though I were an unwelcome stranger, which threw me into such a state of shock that it was some moments before I understood that he was accusing her of having had an affair with Noel, and she was counter-attacking with accusations of his infidelity with an unnamed Hollywood actress. I gathered that the row had been triggered by remarks made at the party—by Marcella, according to Lila, by scores of people, according to Johnny—these remarks being to the effect that our recent house guests had been something more than mere guests.

I was outraged, and said so, but my vehement protests and passionate defense of Lila merely served to turn Johnny's suspicions toward me. When he virtually accused me of not only being a party to Lila's betrayal of him, but probably encouraging it, the unfairness was too much for me, and I fled in tears leaving them to tear each other apart with their jealousy.

Had I been able to talk to Johnny without the fluttering pulse and pounding heart that always assail me when faced with hostility or open disbelief, I felt sure that I could have made him understand what had really happened; there had been no infidelity, actual or contemplated. It had been a flirtation, true, but nothing more. Under such idyllic conditions how could there not have been some lighthearted banter, some pretense that—ah, who knows what might have happened had things been different. . . But things were not different; Lila had a lover, I didn't want one and with that clearly understood there had been no dalliance beyond the gay persiflage and the kiss on the hand. Noel had perhaps exceeded the rules of the game in his devotion, but it had been merely a game, nonetheless, a game that was played not to win, only to enjoy.

All this I felt I could make clear if given the chance, but when I awakened the next morning Johnny had already taken a bus in to Papeete, and didn't return all day. Lila stayed in her room and although there was no door to close and lock, the drawn curtains kept me out as effectively as though there had been. Just as I was leaving the breakfast table Marcella came down, all smiles and good humor, asking where was everybody, and when I told her she said, "My goodness—sounds like a lovers' quarrel. I hope it wasn't anything I said—you know I wouldn't for the world—"

"Why don't you shut up," I said and wandered morosely

down to the beach, my lovely Saturday, that was to have been so full of plans and preparations, just an empty day.

It was very late that night, way past midnight, when Johnny came home. I had just blown out my candle when I heard him. Our rooms adjoined, his being nearest the outside entrance; our beds were headboard to headboard against the thin partition separating the rooms. If either of us sat down heavily or got up quickly the bed bumped against the wall, keeping the occupant of the other room well informed of his neighbor's movements. So I knew that he had lain down, and I was dropping off to sleep when a slight tremor of the wall told me that he had risen. That was not alarming in itself, but the silence that followed was. Why was he standing in silence in his dark room? I began to feel uneasy, as though I were getting thought waves, unpleasant ones; I sat up very carefully to keep the bed from moving, and strained to hear some movement, but all I heard was a pounding in my ears. Then it came—a slight sound, as of someone moving stealthily in the hall. I knew I had only to call out, "Is that you, Johnny?" to dispell the ridiculous panic that was seizing me, but I couldn't force myself to break the silence, which in the pitch blackness of the room seemed to be smothering me.

I fumbled on the bedside table for matches, remembering too late that I had used the last one on my candle to read by, so slithering to the floor like a snake, I crawled toward the dressing table. But all my groping hands could feel were a comb and brush and some lipsticks. There was no moon; no faintest gleam of light to help my eyes become accustomed to the dark. The square outline of the open window was only a shade less black but I crawled to it, afraid to stand lest he see my silhouette. There was no reason for me to be so sure that Johnny was coming to my room, nor that he meant me harm, but my terror was beyond reason; it was as though, projected against the blackness, there was an inner vision, bright and clear, in which I saw him coming, quiet step by quiet step—with a knife in his hand.

In his unreasoning jealousy could he have let his emotional state reach a point where he held me responsible for his imaginary beliefs of Lila's infidelity? I had no answer to these questions. I only knew that he meant to harm me.

In my terror I managed to crawl over the window sill and let myself down onto the narrow slanting roof of the porch below, where I lay, my head below the casing, my fingers desperately clutching the sill, my feet dangling in space. Holding my breath, I thought I heard a long indrawn breath, followed by a deep sigh; then there was the faint rap that my bed made when it touched the wall. The faintest breath of air stirred the palm trees, making their leaves tremble with a soft shushing sound, but over that I seemed to hear an even fainter shuffle of footsteps. Then again there was a silence that pressed upon me like a vise.

Somehow I pulled myself back into my room. With my eyes closed, because I could no longer bear looking into the darkness, I groped my way across the floor to where I thought a chair should be on which I might have tossed my shorts, all the while praying soundlessly, Please, God, just let me have light...please...light...then my fingers found what they were searching for, the shorts I had been wearing, and in the hip pocket a package of cigarettes and a match folder. From there to the candle on the table beside the bed—and there was light, changing the world into one in which I could breathe and function.

Shielding the precious flame, I tiptoed across the hall and edged my way along the wall toward Lila's room, all the time keeping my eyes on the curtain hanging limply in the doorway of Johnny's room. Once I thought I heard a sound, like a low moan, and froze into immobility, but it was not repeated and I continued my cautious progress. The terror dissipated by the light had been replaced by fear of another kind, by a sense of desperate urgency.

I had to shake Lila to awaken her, and when she opened startled eyes and muttered, "What is it? What's the matter?" I whispered with absolute certainty, "Something's happened to Johnny." Then I began to tremble and the hot wax from the candle splattered my hand and fell on Lila's bare arm. Without a word she swung her long legs onto the floor, took the candle from my shaking hand, and holding it high, without bothering to put on a robe she walked ahead of me to his room.

The flickering light disclosed Johnny lying peacefully in bed, his eyes closed, a look of utter serenity on his face. The covers were pulled up to his chin, but one arm lay, palm up, on the outside and from that arm slow globules of blood were dropping rhythmically to the floor, landing with little clinking sounds on the knife with which he had slashed both his wrists.

There is a blurred memory of tearing something in strips—a towel, a shirt, something—and binding his wrists; of Lila, expressionless, wiping his clammy face and repeating like a litany, "the damn fool, oh, the damn fool." Then I was running down to the beach house to get Trower, stumbling and tripping, blundering into tree trunks despite the hands stretched before me like those of a blind person; unseen roots grabbed my bare ankles, palm fronds gave me malicious little cuts, unseen creatures scurried out of my way in a rustle of dry leaves. When I crossed the road I started calling Trower's name and by the time I felt the sand under my feet he was in his doorway, shirtless but trousered, with a flashlight in his hand.

Aside from some ripe Australian oaths on the way back to the house, Trower offered no comments, merely gave orders in the manner of a top sergeant. First, showing us the area of the arm on which to apply pressure in order to stop the bleeding, he stationed us, one on each side of the bed, with the stern injunction to keep our thumbs on the pressure points until a doctor arrived; then he got Teri out of bed and sent him for the nearest doctor; then he appeared with a bottle of Govvie's finest brandy, a few drops of which he forced down Johnny's throat before pouring drinks for Lila and me, and a larger one for himself.

The sky was showing the faintest hint of coming daylight when Teri got back with the doctor, who had an air of distinct disapproval; whether of attempted suicide, or suicide attempted at that hour of the morning, wasn't clear. However, he stitched Johnny up very neatly, said it was lucky he had been found before he bled to death, accepted a drink, and bowed himself out with the suggestion that Lila and I get some sleep, as we looked worse than the patient.

Possibly Lila or Trower sat up with Johnny for the rest of that horrible night. I couldn't have had I wanted to. Fatigue lay so heavy on me I was asleep an instant before my body sprawled on the bed.

It was long past noon when I awakened, and as soon as I was dressed, I went in to see Johnny. All evidence of the night before had been removed. He was propped up in bed, a spotless sheet pulled up to his chest, but both arms were resting outside the covers, almost as though he were presenting the bandaged wrists defiantly. Other than a slight pallor beneath the tan, and a drawn look around the eyes, he seemed his usual self.

What do you say to a man who has tried to kill himself? How do you ask him whether he had tried to kill you first?

How do you look into the clear blue eyes of someone you have known and ask him if he is a potential murderer.

Besides, as I stood there, the sun sliding over my shoulder to brighten his yellow hair, the familiar quizzical smile daring me to say anything unkind, the events of the night became more and more unreal. One side of my mind said, "Do you doubt the evidence of your own senses?" The other said, "What evidence? What senses? I didn't see anything. I only thought I heard something." So I stood looking at him, and he looked back at me, and for a moment the cocky confident Farrow was a very young, very vulnerable boy, and I knew it had all been a waking nightmare.

"How are you feeling?" I asked.

"Pretty good," he said. "In fact, I'm feeling fine."

"That's good," I said. "Well, better luck next time."

"Thanks," he said, and laughed out loud as I went downstairs for breakfast.

He stayed in bed all the next day, Monday. Lila spent most of the day with him and I could hear them chatting and sometimes laughing, but when she joined us at dinner we talked about everything else, mostly the gossip of the island, which was always plentiful.

On Tuesday, our last day there, he got up and he and Lila went in to Papeete. I assumed they had gone in to make reservations for Johnny for the return trip. It was a busy day for me; people dropped in to say good-bye, I did all my packing, tipped the servants, and straightened out my account with Trower (and sure enough, the food bill was the same for when we were in Moorea as for when we were home) so I had no time to wonder when Lila was coming home to do her packing.

Jean came to say farewell as he had promised, and I asked him to stay for dinner, although with some qualms, as I wasn't too sure of Johnny's reaction when he met one of the Frenchmen who had caused so much trouble. Jean had heard rumors, and asked me what had really happened to call the doctor out in the middle of the night, but I answered evasively with no mention of what I was now convinced had been self-induced terror.

I needn't have worried about a confrontation; there wasn't one, because John and Lila didn't come home.

I sat up the whole night waiting for her. About one in the morning Marcella said, Nuts to this, and went off to bed. About two hours later Jean fell asleep on the couch. At five I went upstairs to pack the final little bits and pieces, and at seven I awakened Jean and he drove me to Papeete in his borrowed car.

So I sailed home alone, hoping that wherever Lila was, she was happy.

The trip home was not as much fun without Lila, and I re-lived that awful night several times in my dreams. However by the time we docked in San Francisco, I had come to the conclusion that I had only heard sounds from Johnny's room and thought they were from mine. So I dismissed it from my mind and I had no more nightmares.

A month later Lila returned to Hollywood alone. Farrow, she told me, had gone to Europe on a French freighter. When I asked where they had been the day I sailed, she replied vaguely, "Oh, on a little island somewhere." Never, in all the years we continued to be friends, did she ever again mention that little island somewhere.

When next heard of, Farrow was in Rumania, from which unruly land he eventually returned to marry Maureen O'Sullivan and beget several children, among them Mia Farrow.

Had Lila not taken her dramamine, that day in Tahiti, and bravely sailed to Moorea, there to meet Noel de Villeneuve, there might never been a Mia Farrow; Frank Sinatra would be short one wife, Andre Previn, might never have had twins, and Woody Allen would have to find himself another leading lady... and another mother for his child. How far the ripples from Moorea have spread...

There is a sequel to the story of Tahiti; some ten years later, after an exhausting day of rehearsals on a show I had written, I dropped by Lila's apartment for a chat, a cold drink, and a place to put my feet up, and there was Johnny Farrow.

He was passing through New York on his way to Europe to direct a picture, he told me, and had dropped in for a farewell chat with Lila before catching his night flight. We both expressed our delight at seeing each other again, and with the amenities duly established we all sat down, had our cool drinks, and started chatting. Eventually the conversation turned to Tahiti-with no mention, of course, of that agonizing night.

"Remember the hymanes going on all night during a death vigil, and how they sent us an invitation to join them at three in the morning?"

"We might as well have. We couldn't sleep anyway. I also remember the barrels of wine we used to buy for the plantation workers."

"We used to set them out by the road, remember?" Lila said, "So that anyone passing by could have some—and that night everyone who went by stopped and had some wine and joined in the singing and dancing..."

"They really knew how to enjoy a funeral," John re-

158

marked.

"They enjoyed everything," Lila said. "Oh, and remember when you danced the wedding dance with Teri's brother, not knowing how it was supposed to end? Honestly, Pat, if you could have seen the look on your face..." She burst out laughing, and I said to John, "He wasn't really my type."

"I remember you telling me some things that weren't so funny," John said. "Didn't that Raratongan foreman spin some weird tales about Raratonga?"

He had indeed. He told us how they disposed of their old people when they became useless; how delicious a newborn baby was, much better even then suckling pig. Lila remembered how hurt he was by our disapproval, explaining that on such a small-island as Raratonga it was necessary to keep the population down at the same level so that all might survive-a form of early ecology. Anyway, he said sadly, such customs no longer existed, not since he was a little boy, when the missionaries came.

"Nothing stays the same," John murmured. "A pity..."

As we were fondly recalling Captain Wainright, who married our friend Turea and all her lovely sisters, the phone rang in the other room and Lila went to answer it. I got up to leave, and John followed me to the door, we stood for a moment in silence.

Abruptly, without the usual mockery in his voice, he said, "Do you remember that night?"

I didn't pretend not to know which night he meant. "Yes, I remember it."

He lowered his voice and spoke with an intensity quite unlike him. "I wouldn't have harmed you, I want you to know that. I just came to your room to talk to you, that's all. I just wanted to talk-I wouldn't have hurt you, I swear it. On my honor-I swear it. You do believe me, don't you?"

The full implication of what he was saying didn't register at once; I didn't imagine it-it hadn't been a dream-I was still taking it in when Lila reappeared. With a hasty good-bye I got out without having to give him an answer.

To this day I'm not sure what that answer would have been.

Lila, Carmelita Geraghty and Patsy

159

CHAPTER TWENTY SEVEN

Seeing David Niven in an old movie the other night made me realize how few men of his caliber we have on the screen today. They're a vanishing breed—David, Cary Grant and Ronald Colman—only Douglas Fairbanks Jr. is left.

It brought to mind the first time I met David Niven. It was on my trip to Europe to meet Tay for our divorce, on board a Cunard liner going to London, a stopover on my way to Berlin where Tay was directing a picture with Rod LaRoque. A charming young actress name Constance Cummings was also on board. Though we had only known each other slightly ashore, afloat we became the Bobbsey Twins. Another passenger was a nice, well-bred Scotsman returning to his regiment after having spent his leave in the States. He became our constant companion, regaling us with his wit and infectious high spirits; it was my impression that he would have relished regaling Constance even more, had she given him the opportunity.

This delightful young Scot had been the house guest of various members of the cafe society set, shuffling back and forth between their homes in New York and Palm Beach, and the tales of his adventures, larded with spicy comments on his hosts, were hilarious. Even funnier was his saga of Army life as shared with an unbelievable character named Trubshaw. Connie and I agreed we had never met a more skilled raconteur.

A couple of years later he left the Army and turned up in Hollywood, where we met again by chance. That brief shipboard acquaintance might have flowered into something beautiful but the Fates decreed otherwise. One night, several years later, I was having dinner with some friends at Romanoff's when a tall, slim young man came over to our table, squatted down on his haunches beside my chair, and said, boyishly, "I say, you remember me, don't you?"

A few nights before, I had been to a costume party down at Marion Davies' beach house and had had a bit of a problem with a young Brithish actor who was definitely in his cups. It was the British accent that did it. I mistook David Niven for the other actor and instead of saying, with pleased recognition, "Why, hello there, David," I replied coolly, "I'm afraid I do remember you, Tony."

When he recovered, David reminded me of our transatlantic trip together, and we remained firm acquaintances

160

throughout the years.

That trip to England, in the Spring of 1933, couldn't have been planned at a worse time had I stayed up all night working on it. The London weather alternated between pretty bad and awful, and most of the friends I had looked forward to seeing were somewhere else trying to get warm. I caught a nasty cold, and to top it off, our new President, Mr. Roosevelt, declared a Bank Holiday.

The term, Bank Holiday, has a certain ring to it, bringing to mind cashiers tossing bank notes in the air, tellers frolicking in their cages, and red, white, and blue bunting decorating the mortgage and loan offices, but it's not as festive as it sounds. All it meant was that the banks in the United States were closed, and no one could get any money out of them.

I don't recall the exact date, but I well remember the event. I was still in bed when the room waiter brought me my morning tea and a folded copy of the London Times. After lighting the little gas fire he drew back the window curtains, revealing what looked like another curtain outside, a yellowish grey one.

"A bit foggy, I'm afraid," he said with true British under-statement.

"Not a very cheerful morning," I replied.

"Not aw'fly cheery for Americans, I should say" was his cryptic remark.

While I was still trying to figure out why a pea-soup fog should be worse for Americans, he unfolded the newspaper and handed it to me with the sympathetic manner of the chief mourner at a funeral. "It's all in here, Modom," he said—and there indeed it was; in as much of a headline as the London Times permitted itself: (Moratorium on Banking in U.S. American Funds Frozen for Indefinite Period. Confusion on Wall Street.) There were abatements from the Bank of England, Members of Parliament, and various and assorted financial experts, all expressing confidence in the United States, but with what seemed to me a slight tinge of satisfaction.

I took my purse from the drawer of my bedside table; it was deplorably light, and I remember that I had intended to cash a check the day before—but hadn't. the waiter, pretending not to, listened attentively as I counted my cash aloud; it amounted to six pounds and a few shillings. With the Pound at $4.80, my total wealth was about thirty dollars.

"Not much to live on in London," I said.

"Not to worry," he said kindly. "No doubt your banks will reopen one of these days." And with a "Thank you, Modom," he bowed himself out.

One of these days, indeed! And what about now, I wondered. I soon found out. Would the cable office send a cable, collect, to my father to ask what to do? They wouldn't. Could I charge a cable to the hotel? I couldn't. The management was very decent about the whole thing; as a captive guest, I would still have my morning tea, but kindly not to charge anything to my room. And of course I could remain until this little temporary embarrassment was resolved—as it soon would be, they assured me; they had the greatest confidence in the financial stability of my country—but meanwhile. . . morning tea only. It was comforting to know that I wouldn't starve.

I would have spent some of my precious Pounds to cable Tay for help but I didn't know where he was exactly, I only knew that he was somewhere in the Alps, shooting S.O.S. Iceberg, a picture he was directing for Universal. We were to meet later in Berlin to discuss a divorce. It may seem rather a roundabout way—from Hollywood to London to Berlin, to discuss a divorce, but we wanted to avoid all publicity if possible, and figured we could separate more quietly in some far-off country that didn't have Hollywood gossip columns. Anyway, that avenue of escape was closed.

Tay filming "S.O.S. Iceberg"

The next day I received a long cable from my Father—apparently the American cable company had faith in the future—telling me that he and my brother were doing fine; he couldn't send me any money, but not to worry. Then came a cable from Rex Cole, my business manager, assuring me that there was enough cash on hand to take care of any emergency and so forth; he couldn't send me any money, but I was not to worry.

So who worries? I'm six thousand miles away from home, with no money, with no credit and with a nasty cold—but is that any reason for a girl to worry?

You can bet your sweet life it is.

Despite the constant reassurances—or perhaps because of them, I was beginning to suspect that the United States was really dead broke, and I was the only one who didn't know it, when out of the fog came my hero—or heroine, in this case—to the rescue. My savior was Charlotte Greenwood, who was playing on the Strand, and had heard somehow that I was in town. Charlotte was an extremely popular comedienne of both stage and screen; better known for her stage performances, however. I had been in one of her few pictures in Hollywood a year or more ago, and had found her to be a warm, throughly delightful person. She was fun just to look at—tall, blonde, with long legs that came right up to her chin; she could kick straight up, well over her head, and that long lanky body did amazing feats of limberness. She had a wonderful flair for comedy and she even had a good singing voice. All in all, she was quite an unusual performer.

Charlotte was even more popular in London than she had been in New York, and had been playing to full houses for over a year; when Londoners take a performer to their hearts they never let go. That wonderful woman, when she heard my rasping voice on the phone, came right over to see me, bringing flowers and a prayer book with her. No kid by any means, doing eight strenuous performances a week, she filled my room with sunshine for the next three days; she also told the manager that she would be good for anything charged to my room, and ordered hot chicken soup for me. She was a devout Christian Scientist; she didn't believe in doctors, but she did believe in hot chicken soup, and the power of prayer—which I do now, but wasn't so sure of then.

As Charlotte naturally was paid in Sterling, the Bank Holiday hadn't affected her, but her offer of money wasn't what mattered; it was the time out of her busy life which she gave me that mattered. And when she promised me that I would soon be well and strong and healthy, I believed her—and by golly, I was! In no time I was up and walking the streets of London, becoming more familiar with that fascinating city than I ever had in previous visits. I threaded my way through the maze of lanes and mews and side streets, visited Muesums and Art Galleries, and took in everything that was free. It was actually fun.

Then came a letter from my father which put everything in its proper perspective; he made it all sound like a lark. He said that after the inital shock everyone was taking it with good humor; the barter system was being used and was working so well that some politicians were advocating it on a permanent basis. The movies were still crowded, the Friday night fights were well attended. He had paid for his ticket with a bag of avocados from our backyard tree, and had seen other foodstuffs in the box office, as well as a Mickey Mouse watch and a tennis racquet. He said there was a certain camaraderie such as one finds during war times. After all, when no one has money, no one feels broke. He said that when I returned he'd tell me some of the jokes that were going around—although there were some he wouldn't tell me.

I was so proud of my fellow Americans, so uplifted by Daddy's letter, that with lavish disregard for the future I ordered a champagne cocktail before dinner and paid for it with one of my few remaining Pounds. It was a sublime pleasure not to order from the right side of the menu—especially after having had all my lunches in a fish and chips shop, stuffing myself so that I could do without dinner.

One beautiful day—the sun had almost appeared, and it was merely drizzling—I decided to walk to Harrod's, to browse, not to buy. I stood on a corner trying unsuccessfully to light a cigarette, and I noticed a cab driver parked nearby who was watching me with amusement. After my third try, he called to me: "'ere, Miss, let me give you a hand."

Rather doubtfully I walked over and handed him the book of matches. He struck one with a flourish, deftly cupping the flame in his hands, and gave me a light. "Thanks," I said, "that was great, the way you did that."

"Nothing to it," he said, "It's all in knowin' 'ow."

I offered him one of my preciously hoarded cigarettes, which he took with a flourish and stuck behind his ear, giving me a casual "Ta." I asked if it was much further to Harrods, and he said, yes, it was quite a bit for a lidy to walk. "'ere, 'op in, and I'll have you there in two shakes."

"Thank you," I said, "But I think I'll walk—I, uh—I need the exercise."

"You're a Yank, ain't you?" I nodded. "A bit short of the old fox and hounds, right?" I stared blankly; it was the first time I had heard the Cockney rhyming jargon. "Pounds," he translated with a grin.

"Oh, I said. "Yes—a bit short."

"Op in," he said firmly. "Come on now, 'op in. It's on the house."

So I 'opped in and he drove me to Harrod's, making comments all the while on Life, Politics, the bloody traffic, and other subjects which I never quite caught, although I got the gist of it. Cockney is like English played on a defective disc; most of the words sound familiar but you can't quite place them.

At Harrod's, when I got out he asked me how long I'd be, and I said that, as I wasn't buying, only looking, it wouldn't be more than an hour... "Give a look-see when you come out," he said. "I just might be 'ere." I thanked him very much for the lift and his little ferret face split in a wide grin. "Alfred's the name, Miss." So I said, "Thank you very *very* much, Alfred."

"Not to worry" he said, and was off with a clash of gears.

When I came out of the store about an hour later I had a look-see and sure enough, there was Alfred, hunched down in his seat, smoking my cigarette.

"Blimey, if it ain't you again. Where to now, lidy?"

Back to the hotel, I said, and back we went, Alfred talking non-stop.

He asked me where I was from, and when I told him California, he said he had a cousin who emigrated to Canada; was that anywhere near California? I said it was a bit north. He asked me did I live near Hollywood where all movie actors lived, and when I said I did, he wanted to know if I had ever seen any of them up close. When I admitted that I had, upon occasion, seen one or two of them, he shook his head in wonderment. "'and 'ere you are ridin' in my cab!"

When we got caught in a traffic jam he wanted to know if the traffic was this bad in New York, and when I said that it was even worse, he said, "Too many bleedin' private cars, that's what's the trouble. The city weren't meant for so many private cars." It appeared to me that London had more cabs than private cars, but I didn't say so. As I got out at the hotel I said, "Thanks again, Alfred."

"Not to worry," he replied. "'and across the sea, and all that." And with another grin, he added; "Me chums call me Alf."

"Thanks again, Alf," I said, and with a wave of the hand he was off, calling over his shoulder, "Next time you go for a walk, don't forget your brolly."

A telegram from Tay awaited me at the desk: he was now back at the Adlon Hotel in Berlin; he had sent some Reichmarks to my account in Barclay's Bank; I was to buy a ticket on Luthansa's noon flight Saturday; he would meet me at the airport. Love, Tay.

There was also a message from Irving Asher, an old friend from Hollywood, now managing the Warner Bros. Studio in England. I had tried to reach him as soon as I arrived, but had been informed that he was out of town on business. His message said to call him not only immediately, but at once. When I got him on the phone I told him what a louse he was to be off somewhere lolling in the sun while I was shivering and starving in London, and he apologized profusely, saying that had he but known, while he was indeed lolling on the beach in Cannes, that I was in such desperate straits, he would have done without the olive in his second Martini. And how about having dinner with him tomorrow night? I said I would attempt to overcome my aversion to men with a deep tan, and he told me to get all gussied up and be ready by five-thirty, as the French Restaurant he was taking me to was quite a way from London. Indeed it was. It was in Paris, France.

Irving Asher

How can you not love a guy that crazy? He picked me up in a Rolls Royce Limousine, had a small chartered plane waiting at Heathrow airport, a car awaiting us at Orly airport, and on we drove, in great style, to the restaurant in Paris. I can't remember the name of the restaurant, but I'll never forget the food, the champagne, and the laughter. Then we flew back to London, and I was in my hotel by two in the morning, still laughing. And still full. That was a date to remember!

The next day when I started to walk to the bank to get my money and airline ticket, a cab rolled slowly by and there was—you guessed it—none other than Alf. "Just 'appened to be in the vicinty?" he said. "Op in. . . eh where's your brolly?" I had to admit that I didn't have an umbrella, and he shook his head dolefully. "You need lookin' after, you do—no brolly in London!" On the way to the bank I heard about the ten bob he had on a horse that would have romped home if the bleedin' jockey hadn't pulled him—about the tanner he'd won on a soccer match but the punt took a bunko, and about the barmaid at the Cock and Bull who was sweet on him and always slipped him an extra helping of chips.

When I came out of the bank there was Alf, cigarette dangling from his lip, parked in front of a NO STANDING sign. "Just happened to be in the vicinity?" I said, and he gave me his one-sided grin. On the way home we discussed the relative merits of football and soccer—wondered if they called Frenchmen Frogs because they ate frogs' legs—and agreed that politicians, for the most part, were a poor lot. The trip from the bank seemed to take longer than the trip to the bank, and I thought we passed the World War Monument twice, but the byways and lanes of London are hard for a foreigner to keep track of, and I wasn't really sure.

When we pulled up in front of the hotel I handed Alf a few pound notes, saying I had enough for my hotel bill, with a bit left over, but he refused to accept them. "I told you it was on the 'ouse," he said firmly. I told him I was leaving Saturday, and he said so was he. "Because of the storm and strife," he added.

"Because of the weather?"

"The wife," he explained. "She 'as it in 'er'ead to go to Brighton for a 'oliday, so off we go tomorrow." He leaned out to open the door for me, and I stepped gracefully down into a pool of water. Alf looked at my Dorsay pumps, and muttered, "Blime, no boots neither?" "No boots," I confessed. He shook his head in disbelief. "No brolly, no boots—how about a mac?"

I promised to wear my raincoat from then on, and handed him my pack of cigarettes, which he accepted with a grin and a "Ta." "I'll never forget you, Alf," I said. "Same ere," he mumbled. "And thank you again," I said fervently," from the bottom of my heart."

"Ere, now-no need to go on about it." He put the cab in gear, and as it started slowly moving, called back, "'ave a nice oliday—and mind you take care of yourself."

"You, too," I called out—and he was gone from view—but not from memory.

By the time I got home no one was interested in my penniless adventures in a foreign land. The Bank Holiday was ancient history; the comics had dropped it from their night club routines, and wry jokes were no longer going the rounds. What everyone, including my father *was* interested in was the repeal of Prohibition after thirteen long, semi-dry years. Compared to that the closing and re-opening of banks was hardly worth mentioning.

Many 'appy 'olidays, Alf.

Saturday, as ordered, I took off for Berlin. The flight must have been uneventful, as I don't remember it. (Uneventful flights are the best kind.) Sure enough, Tay was at the airport to meet me.

Except for the noticeable number of soldiers in brown shirts, it looked no different than when I had been there the first time, several years before. But as we started our drive to the Adlon Hotel, I seemed to sense, as well as see, a difference.

It was dusk as we drove down Unter den Linden; the lights of the evening were coming on, but there were no young boys roaming the streets, made up with cheek and lip rouge. Tanks now rolled where prostitutes had paraded, wearing black leather boots, and flourishing whips.

Berlin, when I was there before, had been as wide open as a city can be. Anything went. There were topless bars and bottomless bars, and what we now call "gay" bars. Nudity was commonplace in the theatre, and pornography was accepted in the guise of "Art."

(If anyone wishes to find an analogy between Berlin then, and New York now, feel free to do so.)

All that was over. Hitler had come. He was not yet in full power, but he was making his presence felt. He promised Berliners a return to the days of bourgeois respectability and Gemutlichkeit, and though most of them didn't like the bombastic little Austrian with his dreadful accent, they accepted him as the lesser of two evils.

There were no longer brothels openly displaying their wares, and families could stroll with their children without fear of being accosted, or subjected to indecencies before the eyes of their little ones. For this return to decency one must take a little bombast and saber-rattling; was the general attitude.

I recalled quite clearly my former sojourn in Berlin. Innocent Babe from the Holly Woods that I was, it took me a while to understand what I was seeing and hearing, which was sheer, deliberate decadence, something few of us encounter in a lifetime, Heaven be praised.

That first visit to Berlin was with an old friend of mine, Kay Morse, and her father, after having spent a week in Holland, and the contrast was startling. Amsterdam, in those days, at any rate, was a neat, respectable city, filled with neat, respectable burghers, plus wonderful restaurants. Mr. Morse was a diamond buyer for Tiffany, and we met many Dutch diamond merchants, among them a Mr. Van Dam. I remember him because he bet me a diamond that I couldn't eat a whole full-course luncheon at a restaurant called Dykkis Thys (I'm not sure of the spelling, but that's the way it sounded.) Even for a diamond I couldn't get more than half-way through, but Mr. Van Dam gave me a D for effort; not a huge one, but not tiny, either. What trenchermen those Dutch men are! And what beautiful diamonds they cut and polish.

Constance Cummings o' Patsy

Visiting Mr. Van Dam's diamond cutters

Anyway, as I said, when we got to Berlin the difference became all too apparent. Our second evening there I ran into a writer whom I had known in Hollywood, Lars something-or-other. He was with a Russian friend, and they invited us girls to have dinner with them. Kay had a headache, but I didn't, so I went with them. We had a good German dinner, heard Jan Kiepira sing, and ended up in an after-supper night spot, with which the boys seemed familiar.

I think it was called The Paradise, a vast place hung with much gold and red brocade, gleaming with crystal chandeliers, altogether too ornate in the worse possible taste. It was crowded, however, seemingly hundreds of tables jammed together around a dance floor on which men and women, most of them in evening clothes, were swaying to the music of a five-piece band.

As I sipped my Creme de Menthe frappe, the only thing I ever drank after dinner, I looked around, much impressed by the beautifully gowned and be-jeweled women, and caught the eye of a man sitting alone at a table nearby. He smiled and raised his glass to me. Rather uncertainly I smiled back, then quickly looked away, but not before Lars had noticed.

"She has an admirer," he said to Kyrill, and they both grinned. I tried not to look at the man again, but I couldn't help seeing him out of the corner of my eye, and he was always staring at me. Kyrill suggested that we invite him to join us, and Lars assured me that it would be perfectly proper, since they were with me, and even as I was protesting they beckoned to him and he was at my side, bowing over the hand I reluctantly extended.

Lars moved over so that he could sit beside me, and he chatted pleasantly, in a low husky voice, asking how I liked Berlin, saying what a privilege it was to meet foreigners. I asked him where he had learned to speak such good English, and he said he had spent some time in London. After a few moments of such desultory conversation he rose abruptly, bowed, and asked me to dance with him, with, of course, the gentlemen's permission. They both said, why not, so we moved out to the crowded dance floor. Once there, he was quite different. He held me too close, and he whispered compliments in my ear which became much too personal and finally his ardor was so embarrassing that I pushed him away from me. Then and then only did I realize that he wasn't a man. He was a woman!

I was never so startled in my life. I muttered something about being tired, sort of pried myself loose, and almost ran back to the table where my two false friends were beside themselves with glee. They had known it all the time, of course. We were in the most notorious homosexual club in all Germany; the beautifully gowned and jeweled women were all men, the few men who weren't with the lovely creatures weren't men, they were women.

I didn't think it was funny; in fact, I was trembling with rage and embarrassment, and demanded that we leave at once. Lars and Kyrill rather shamefacedly agreed and called for the check. But meanwhile my dancing partner had followed me, and stood there, his—I find it hard to say "her"—his hands clasped in entreaty. Nein, nein... I must not leave... a million pardons if I was offended... Then, as I rose, he—she—grasped my arm and Kyrill, who spoke fluent German, told her to get lost or something even ruder, judging by the tone of his voice. Heads were turning and a few couples had stopped dancing to look when, from across the room came a blonde fury, screaming curses as she came. She was so young, so delicately pretty, it didn't seem possible that she could be using such language. As she appeared to be heading for me, I took refuge behind Lars, but it wasn't at me she was hurling her invective, it was at my erst-while dancing partner.

As Kyrill threw some money on the table and Lars pushed me ahead toward the exit, I glanced over my shoulder in time to see the fragile little beauty take a swipe at my suitor with what looked like a steak knife. I think she

missed, but I didn't stay to make sure.

It seems funnier to me now in retrospect than it did then, but it's still not one of the memories I cherish.

Going to Berlin from California may seem a rather long way to go to discuss a divorce, but neither Tay nor I wanted any publicity and that seemed a good way to avoid it; they didn't have a Hollywood gossip column in the Berlin papers. Both Riga, in Latvia, and Budapest, in Hungary, were suggested as having the simplest divorce laws, since I didn't wan't anything from Tay, no settlement, no alimony or anything like that. There wasn't even any property to split up; I owned my own car, and we had been living in my family's house in Beverly Hills all the time we were married, so it should be just a matter of signing a few papers, blowing a kiss to the judge, and skipping out of the courtroom a single woman again.

My few weeks in Berlin were unusual to say the least; Tay had taken a suite for us, consisting of two bedrooms separated by a drawing room, and we occasionally had Rod Laroque who was starring in Tay's picture, and his lovely wife, actress Vilma Banky, join us for cocktails before dinner. Once or twice we dined together, but I don't believe they were ever entirely at ease with us, no matter how we strove to keep the conversation going on a light, impersonal note. The miasma of the impending divorce hung in the air like a cloud, though it was carefully never mentioned. It was all very Noel Cowardish.

Tay and Patsy meet in Berlin.

I had just about decided on Riga for the divorce because no one I knew had ever been there, when Paul Kohner, the picture's production manager, remembered that Universal had a man in the Budapest office—Joseph Pasternak, a Hungarian—who might be of help to me if I chose to go there. Mr. Pasternak, when contacted, assured Mr. Kohner that he would be more than happy to do anything in his power to be of help; he would make hotel arrangements, get the right lawyer, anything at all to accommodate a friend of Mr. Kohner. So the decision was made, I would go to Budapest, and the distinction of being the first movie actress to go to Riga for a divorce went to Laura la Plante a year later. Laura told me some time ago that Riga had been pretty dull; Budpest was anything but, so I owe Mr. Pasternak a debt of gratitude, just for having been the reason for my going there. Incidently, Universal later brought him to Hollywood where he produced those wonderful Deanna Durbin pictures and a dozen others, and Laura married Irving Asher.

I've no doubt that everyone gave a sigh of relief when I was finally put on the train, and sent on my way.

Joseph Pasternak

The train ride was pleasant and almost uneventful, but one tiny little incident kept it from being dull. I shared a compartment with a very nice young Hungarian, the fair-haired, blue-eyed type—actually, his eyes were more grey than blue—and we managed to converse in a bit of English, German and pantomine, with a French phrase thrown in now and then.

Suddenly he looked apprehensive; I followed his gaze out the window and saw that we were coming to the Czeckoslovakian border. We had to cross it twice, both coming in and going out, and as Anschluss was very evident in the many guards everywhere, all in German uniforms, I gathered that he was nervous about that. Which indeed he was. With sign language and a little bit of this and that, he made me understand that he was carrying something that possibly the Nazis would disapprove of. From his expression I gathered that they would disapprove strongly.

"A present?" I asked. "Un cadeau, ein Gescenck?"

"Igan," he said quickly. "Ja, ja... Ein Gescenck."

"Fur seine mutter," I suggested helpfully. He looked surprised, then quickly agreed.

"Igan. Ja. Fur meine Mutter... and auch Documenten." When I gazed at him inquiringly, he pointed to some papers lying on the seat.

"Oh, documents... ja, ja," I said. It came to me in a flash: those nasty Nazis would take away the lovely gift he was bringing to his little gray-haired mother, as well as confiscating some love letters from his sweetheart who was far far away... I could not let that happen to such a nice handsome young man, could I? Quick, I said, Geben Sie mir.

His face lit up like a torch, and with no further ado, he handed me a tubular package and a wad of papers, one with what seemed to be an official seal on it. I tucked the package deep down in my new Vuitton Shoe Bag, turning the shoes so that the sharp heels stuck up, and the papers I jammed into my purse, poking them down to the bottom and putting my lipstick, compact and handkerchief on top of them.

The train was stopped at the border, and I just had time to sit back and look like a bored traveller when the compartment doors slid open and there stood two uniformed German customs inspectors. The young man said, "Magyar," and handed his passport to one of them. I said "Americanish," and handed my passport to the other. He looked at it briefly, said anything to declare, I smiled, pointed to my luggage, made a grimace, and said, "clothes, shoes," then I made a pretense of opening my handbag, and said, "Lipstick, powder... Oh, my goodness, what a mess..." The Nazi allowed himself a faint smile and said, "Bitte, bitte.... okay." I giggled and said, "Okay. Americanish, nicht? Thank you... Bitte shon, Herr Officer."

Taken by my Hungarian travelling companion just moments before the Nazi agents arrived.

While this was going on, the other Border Guard was giving my friend a thorough going over, opening his bags, making him turn out his pockets, the works. Finally, both satisfied, they left. My companion and I didn't say a word until the train had pulled out of the station, then he gave me a lovely smile and said, "Danke, Danke shon. Bitte Shon." I said, "Anytime, as long as it doesn't tick."

"Tick? he asked. "Oh, Ich verstehe. . . tick tock, tick tock, eh?" Then we both laughed heartily.

Crossing the border into Hungary presented no problem. Once across, I gave him back his litte gift to his Mutter and the love letters. He kissed my hand, we both said, "Auf Weidersehn," and that was that. Mr. Pasternak was waiting for me at the station; he took care of my luggage, drove me to the hotel, The Gellert, saw me to me room, a lovely big one overlooking the Danube, and left me to unpack and think.

I wonder what would have happened if they had found "the little present." Would it have meant a prison camp? A firing squad? Well, it *wasn't* ticking. . . and they might really have been love letters that just happened to be written on paper that carried an official government seal.

I fell in love with Budapest from the very first moment I saw it. The hotel was on the Buda side of the river; on the Pest side were the business offices, the markets and shops. The hotel had a huge swimming pool, a Wellenbad, in which, every half hour, there were waves. It was a delightful place to sunbathe, full of friendly Hungarians, many of them tall, fair and blue-eyed like my train companion, or grey-eyed. Whatever their coloring, they were all eager to make a foreigner feel at home, which I greatly appreciated, as I might well have felt very lonely and out of place otherwise.

While waiting for the lawyer to make out the proper papers, I was kept so busy seeing the country, taking moonlight boat rides and doing a little shopping, that I became very remiss in my correspondence. One day I received a letter from a very dear close friend of mine, Corney Jackson—Cornwell, really—who wrote plaintively that he had had no word from me and was beginning to worry; Was I all right, how were things going, and why the Hell didn't I keep in touch with a friend?

Instead of writing him a letter, I borrowed a typewriter from the hotel and wrote a short story about how it was to be an American in Hungary. I called it, "Oh Say Can You See."

Once I mailed the short story to Corney, I more or less forgot about it. It must have been several weeks later (I was graciously allowing my lawyer to take his time) that I received a bulky envelope in the mail from, of all people, the editors of *Vanity Fair*. They informed me that my story had been accepted, a check would follow shortly, and if I had any other stories they would be pleased to read them. I couldn't believe it! My very first short story accepted by that prestigious magazine! Corney had sent it in, of course. I sent him an ecstatic wire, offering to marry him, but he wired back sending his regrets; he had already promised to marry Gail Patrick, which he did, in due time. My story, "Oh, Say Can You See," which I had sent just for fun, really, ended up in the O. Henry Collection of Best Short Stories that year, so I always held Corney to blame for entering the gruelling, grinding world of writing.

Cornwell Jackson went on to fame and fortune as the producer of the Perry Mason television series, but he told me once that seeing them on the screen never gave him as much of a kick as seeing my first story in print, due to him. I don't think he meant it, but it was sweet of him to say it.

Buda and Pest

168

There were two young men, brothers, who came to the hotel nearly every day to swim and sun-bathe; Csepreghy Jeno (they put the last name first in Hungary) and Csepreghy Bela. When I got to know them I called them Jeno (pronounced Yenur) Johnny; it's easier for the American tongue. His brother Bela—pronounced Bay-la—I called Benny. Gabi, a friend of theirs who often joined us, remained Gabi. How can you simplify that?

The second week another American girl arrived at the hotel. Oddly enough her name was also Kay—Kay Von Gontard. All her folks did was sit by the pool and read, so Kay soon joined our foursome, and we became a fivesome, though it soon became apparent, to me, at any rate, that Kay would have preferred a twosome, with Gabi the twoth. (If there wasn't such a word, there is now.)

A long, lovely island—Margueritén Island—lay in the middle of the Danube River, with a bridge connecting it to both shores. On it was a beautiful restaurant, serving wonderful food; it also had a large outdoor dance floor, strung with colorful lights, and an orchestra that played American popular music, as well as lively Hungarian Csardas dances. We five spent many an evening there. It truly had a fairy tale beauty.

Our young men also took us on drives into the country, through villages in which the peasants, in their colorful costumes, looked like the chorus of a Rogers and Hart musical. You expected them to come down to the footlights and go into their number.

Once we visited a horse breeding ranch, in the middle of a vast plain, at round-up time. The cowboys resembled Argentine gauchos, with their wide pants and big black hats; they rode like Comanches and roped like Tom Mix, and John Ford couldn't have staged it better.

We went to Lake Balaton, high in the mountains. We stopped at a nearby village, nestled in the foothills, where they were having a fair, and of course Kay and I bought embroidery of all sorts which we had no use for. As twilight settled over the village, a three piece band appeared from somewhere, two violins and what I think was a balalaida, and soon couples were dancing on the village green, skirts swirling, boots stamping; it was an operatta from the 1950's. All at once I found myself dancing wildly with a sturdy young peasant, to the encouraging shouts of Johnny, Benny, and Gabi. It had the Charleston beat to a frazzle. Kay later told me she was asked to dance, but declined. She was afraid, she explained, that the locals might have fleas. If my partner had them, he kept them to himself.

Thus the weeks of waiting passed pleasantly. My attorney, Dr. Daicovitch—a doctor of law, not medicine—had warned me that if there was no urgency, legal cases moved slowly, and I was not to worry. (Where had I heard that before?) I assured him there was no urgency, and managed not to worry. Joe Pasternak called to tell me that Dr. Daicovitch had everything in hand, and to ask if I was concerned about the delay, and I assured him that I was not concerned, and he was not to worry.

Then, two days before the case was to come up in Court, Tay arrived in Budapest. His picture, S.O.S. Iceberg, was in the can; Rod and Vilma had already returned to Hollywood, and he had just come to see what was going on, and why he hadn't heard from me lately. I explained about the sight-seeing, introduced him to my friends, and checked with the hotel manager to be sure he had a nice room, with a good view, on another floor.

The day of the divorce dawned bright and beautiful. Properly clad, with hat and gloves, I met Dr. Daicovitch outside the courthouse, and was escorted in, somewhat in the manner of a Duchess being presented to the Queen. It was all pretty much as I was told it would be—a formality. Tay wasn't asked to testify, not even to appear, and there wasn't a journalist to be seen.

Tay stayed on for three days, which he seemed to enjoy. Then he had to go to London for some technical stuff on the picture, after which he was sailing for New York, he told me—and I was sailing with him. He had already made reservations on... whatever boat it was. I cannot for the life of me remember the name of the liner. I couldn't think of any reason to stay on in Hungary, except that I wanted to, so I said Okay, I'd meet him on board. Which I did.

Another odd thing—I don't remember whether I boarded at Southampton or Bremerhaven; probably the latter, or else why would I have gone to meet him via Vienna?

Kay left before I did, and the farewells were tearful. She took me aside to tell me that she was in love with Gabi, and was heart-broken that he hadn't begged her not to go, but had only kissed her hand, said "Auf Wiedersehn" and taken his leave. Furthermore, she was seriously considering suicide, and nothing I could say would make her change her mind—and when I said nothing, she demanded to know how I could be so heartless as to not try to make her reconsider. My advice would have been to go to Tahiti, but I suggested instead that she continue the tour. "You'll have a good time in Italy" I told her. "The Italians love blond American girls." As far as I know, she went to Italy. I do know she didn't kill herself, as I met her for lunch a few years later in New York.

Dear romantic Kay—she had broken one of the basic rules of tourism; after *don't drink the water* comes *don't fall in love with a native.*

One person's heartbreak can be another person's idea for a short story; I wrote one, disguising Kay enough so that she wouldn't be embarrassed is she happened to read it. I called it *Csardas*, sent it in, had it published, and received another little kudo.

I raised my arm high above my head, calling out loudly "HI".

When I finally reluctantly left Budapest just in time to catch the boat, Johnny kindly escorted me as far as Vienna, and was very helpful with luggage, tickets, travel papers, and all that. With time to spare, we were strolling through St. Stefans Platz, the big square in front of the Cathedral, and somehow we became separated. After an anxious moment I spotted him through the crowd of shoppers and strollers, and raised my arm high above my head, calling out loudly as I did so, "HI!"

Suddenly I was in the center of a ring of silence. Even the swallows circling the buildings seemed to have ceased their twittering. It was eerie. I lowered my arm, looking around to see the cause of the silence, but all I saw was a circle of unfriendly faces. I felt—or thought I felt—the circle closing in on me, the stony impassive faces coming closer. My God, I thought, it's a lynch mob...

Then Johnny came breaking through the silent crowd; he took it in at a glance, and, standing beside me, speaking very calmly, he explained in his best German that Americans say, "Hi!" to call to someone. It was Hi—not Heil. Raising my arm was only to show where I was—it was *not* the Nazi salute. Fortunately, they believed him. The crowd broke up, some of them laughing. One or two even patted me on the shoulder, and said, "Welkonnen su Wien, Fraulein." I smiled back and said "Danke" but my legs were still trembling. It was probably laughed about in the coffee houses for many a day.

Now comes the strange part: I know that I joined Tay on board ship—but what ship? I know that we sailed home together—in separate staterooms—and that Tay's sweet mother, Rachel, met us in New York—but I don't really remember any of it. It's as if my computer memory bank was swept clean by a power outage, and everything after Vienna was erased. It's probably just as well.

CODA TO MY HUNGARIAN RHAPSODY:

When Csepreghy Jeno came to Hollywood to see for himself the wonderful country I had told him about, I was married to John Lee Mahin and living in the Valley. We suggested the use of the name John Shepridge as more spelleable and pronounceable, and it suited him very well. He got a job with Frank Morgan, that unforgettable Wizard of Oz, and learned a great deal about making movies. Then he went to New York, where he got a job with an independent producer, and learned more about the movie business.

Later he stopped over in England on his way back to Hungary, but he never got to Hungary. In London he met Orson Welles, who was making a picture there; he became not only his production manager, but his friend and companion, and through Welles met many members of the gentry as well as of the theatre. He liked England so much that he became a British subject. In due time he married a lovely English girl, and lived long and happily as an English gentleman of means.

What would have been his life had I chosen Riga? As Csepreghy Jeno he would undoubtedly have remained in Budapest with his brother Bela—and perhaps, like his brother, been slain on the Field of Mars.

The Field of Mars was one of the first places I was taken to see by my unofficial tour guides, Johnny and Benny. It was a large area on the outskirts of town, rather like a football field, and was reserved as a Memorial to the battle which had been fought there—a battle in which a youthful army of volunteers met and defeated the trained forces of Bela Kuhn, the Communist traitor.

A huge banner, in the brilliant colors of the Hungarian flag, floated high over the field, and there were many

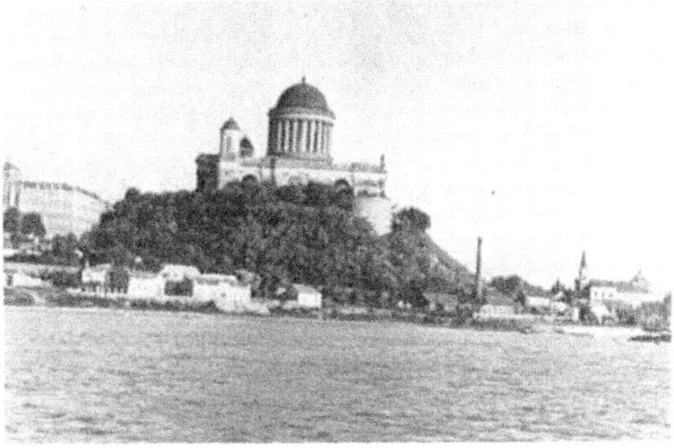

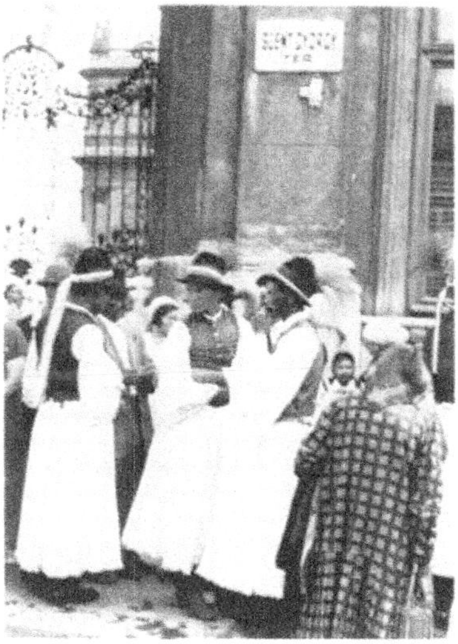

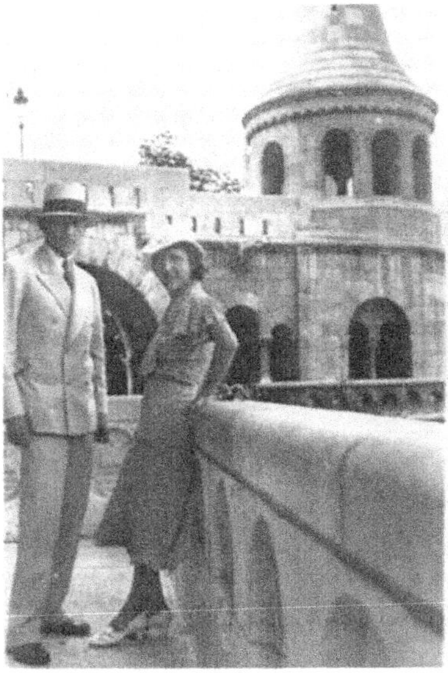

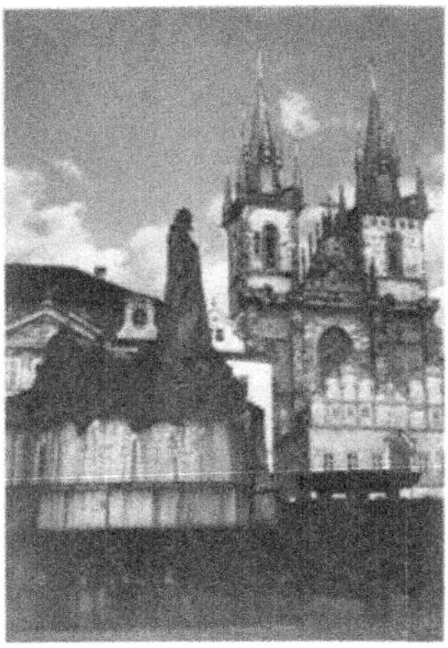

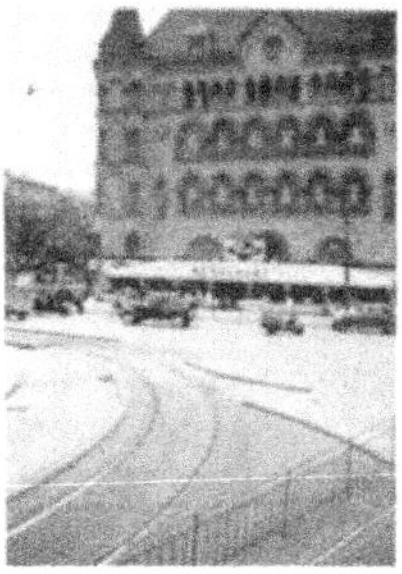

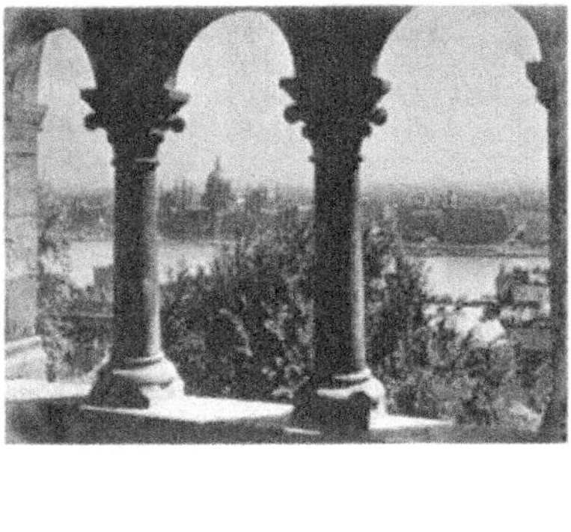

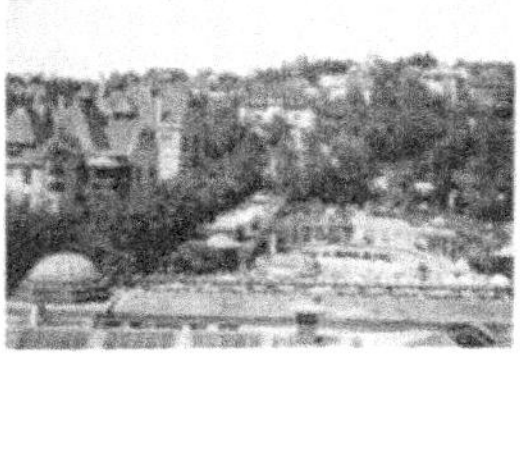

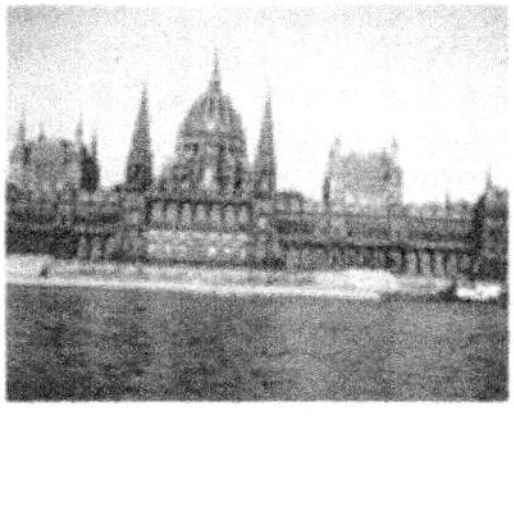

smaller ones on buildings throughout the city. Nem Nem soha! the banners proclaimed. Nem Nem soha—never never again.

It was a short Never.

Not long after the War, when Russia was supposedly on the side of the Allies, Bela Kuhn and his Russian masters held out the olive branch of friendship to Hungary. The Kremlin demanded nothing; it wanted only peace and friendship with its esteemed neighbor. There was nothing to fear. If they could meet with the leaders of the Resistance on the Field of Mars, a treaty would be drawn up guaranteeing Peace between the two countries for a hundred years.

The young Hungarian leaders went trustingly—unarmed—to the Peace Conference—and were mowed down by machine guns... slaughtered to a man. And the Russian Army moved in.

I shall probably never see Budapest again, but I shall always remember it as it was, and I pray that it has recovered from the blight of Communism, and is once more a city of gaiety and charm and music, of beautiful women and fair-haired friendly young men.

Johnny Shepridge.

While I was in New York, before Johnny Shepridge went to England, he introduced me to the most fabulous Hungarian of them all Zsa Zsa Gabor. In fact, I spent a weekend at her house. I doubt that Miss Gabor remembers that weekend—or me—but I shall never forget it. It is written in my memory in letters of fire.

Johnny and a friend had been invited to a Sunday supper and Zsa Zsa had been kind enough to tell Johnny he could bring me along. We drove to her house, somewhere on Long Island, in the late afternoon; when we arrived there were already a number of other guests, mostly Hungarian, none of whom I knew. It was the first and only time I ever met Zsa Zsa Gabor; I have never seen her since, except on television. But I remember her as being a charming hostess, and looking as young and pretty then as she does now.

During supper a storm came up, and by the time we were ready to leave it was almost a hurricane; there were warnings on the radio that driving was hazardous, and that it would get worse before it got better, so Miss Gabor hospitably invited us all to spend the night there. As I remember, everyone agreed with great relief, and we were all assigned rooms. A Hungarian woman and I were asked to share a large room in the attic, which seemed to have been used as a child's playroom. There were two cots, one in a corner against the wall, one beside a window. My Hungarian roommate made a beeline for the one by the wall, so I sat down on the other, took off my shoes and my dress, and, keeping my slip on, lay down for a good night's sleep.

Just outside my window was a huge tree, and hanging from one of its limbs, attached by a heavy metal chain, was a child's swing. As I started to doze off, a flash of lightning lit up the room; there was a thunderous crash as it struck the tree, traveled down the chain, and knocked me out of bed. I lay on the floor, blinded and deafened for a moment, then I became aware of screams. Lifting my head, I saw my roommate, stark naked, flattened against the wall and yelling at the top of her lungs in Hungarian. Suddenly she made a bolt for the door; I scrambled to my feet, saying, "It's all right, it's all right" but she continued her headlong dash.

With the feeling that I shouldn't let her run down those steep stairs—especially with no clothes on—as she dashed

172

past my bed, I tackled her. It was a neat tackle, around the waist; the next thing I knew I was rolling around on the floor with a naked woman in my arms, and a stranger, at that. It was an odd sensation, to say the least.

Suddenly she snapped out of it; she went limp in my arms, looked around in a dazed way, became aware of me sitting astride her rump, and in a shaky voice said, "It's all right, It's all right now." I threw a blanket over her shoulders, and she murmured, "Danke. Thank you. Ja, thank you very much."

When I got her back to bed she explained to me, in German and English, what had happened. She had been dreaming; when the thunder and lightning awakened her, she thought she was back in Budapest, under bombardment from the Russians. She had lived through that agonizing period and still often dreamed about it.

I sat beside her, holding her hand, until she drifted off to sleep, then I returned to my own cot, a bit shaken, but otherwise okay. It wasn't until then that it occurred to me what a sight that would have been to anyone entering the room; me, in my slip, rolling around on the floor with a naked woman in my arms. It would have been a scandal to rock Hollywood! That's back *then* I'm talking about.

Today I daresay anyone entering by accident would merely murmur, "Oops-sorry... wrong room," and back out. Or possibly, "Mind if I join you?"

Hollywood Boulevard, 1936.

Some the the Encino residents included Al Jolson, Edward Everett Horton, Don Ameche and Chill Wills.

CHAPTER TWENTY EIGHT

A few years ago when I was in Beverly Hills visiting my brother and his wife a friend, Norma Churchill, asked me if I'd like to drive out to the Valley and see where she, Mrs. Ernest then Pagano, and I, then Mrs. John Lee Mahin, had once lived. Foolishly, breaking my own rule of "never go back" I said Yes. Norma and I have known each other for at least umpteen years; all the way out, through the pass and down into San Fernando Valley, we reminisced about the past, the fun the four of us had had, the gags and the jokes, the evenings of good talk and laughter. Ernie Pagano was a comedy writer, and one of the best; he had written several of the pictures I made with Glenn Tryon, and working on those, with Ernie generally on the set, had been a ball, from nine to five... and on.

It was in that wonderful sentimental mood of nostalgia that we turned on to Ventura Boulevard—and there went the nostalgia. What had been an ambling two lane highway was now a four lane speedway; the roadside, once lined with trees and dotted with small family stores was now packed, cheek to jowl, with office buildings and shops of all kinds. When Norma cried, "There's Zelzah"-the street John and I had lived on, I didn't believe her. But it was Zelzah... She turned off, past the service station and there ahead of me stretched a broad road going on and on as far as the eye could see. Zelzah had been a dead-end street, ending in a vast alfalfa farm belonging to the Adohr Dairy; it hadn't been more than three blocks long, with a sprinkling of small houses on each side. Now, standing shoulder to shoulder, were tall apartment buildings. What had once been our Farm, at the end of the street, was buried under tons of concrete. I could have cried... maybe I did.

There were lots of picture people living in the valley back then; I wonder if there still are. Jimmie Gleason-Clark Gable-Stan Laurel-Mischa Auer-Barbara Stanwyck and Robert Taylor... Now there was one of the best looking men I've ever known—and I've known some good-looking men in my time. And just as nice as he was handsome. We weren't palsy-walsy, or anything like that, but I felt a bond between us; we were sort of in-laws, in a sense. My mare, Brown Bawd, was serviced by Bob's Arabian stallion, and dropped a filly which I named Michelle. She had a touch of her sire; the rather Arabian nose, but she also had the bawdiness of her Mommy. She was a darling. Bob was very pleased at how well she turned out, proving that it wasn't a mistake letting his pure-bred Arabian marry out of his class.

Jimmie and Lucille Gleason became very good friends of ours. He was such a delightful comedian, with his dry, quick humor, his acerbic comments delivered with machine-gun accuracy. They had a son, Russell Gleason, who was the delight of their lives. Russell was about my brother's age; he was a good young actor but not what I would call a dedicated one. He married a lovely girl named Cynthia, then, before his child was born, went off to war. It must have been at least a year before he returned; I recall it only too well. Jimmie and Lucille were ecstatic when he landed in New York, safe and sound; he hadn't been wounded, not physically, at least. What had happened to him while he was overseas no one will ever know. Russ didn't come home from New York; he threw himself out the window of his hotel room, many stories up. Lucille and Jimmie were never the same after that. They lived on for quite a while—Jimmie even told jokes sometimes—but they were never the same. How can a son be so cruel to his parents!

Thinking back on those pre-war days in the Valley, on what we euphorically called The Farm, brings memories of a dear friend and neighbor, that English-mangling zany, Mischa Auer. He seems to be remembered mainly for his imitation of an ape, in My Man Godfrey, a hilarious picture with Carole Lombard and William Powell. It's just as funny now as when it was first released; the laughs still come, good old-fashioned belly laughs. It's nice to hear that kind of laughter in a theatre.

He was just as funny, in a different way, in Destry Rides Again, a delightful comedy with James Stewart and Marlene Dietrich. Casting Mischa in a Western was an inspiration.

Then there was You Can't Take It With You, also with Jimmy Stewart, in which was again outstanding. I can't remember all the pictures Mischa made, I only remember that he always gave a great comedy performance. He had perfect timing, and knew how to take a scene to the edge of burlesque without falling over the edge. He could get a bigger laugh with a roll of his expressive eyes than many comedians could with a pratt fall.

To see Mischa offscreen, always immaculate, always well-groomed (he even looked well-groomed in Levis and cowboy boots), and with a certain air, one would assume that his childhood had been spent in an atmosphere of gentility and good schools.

Such was not exactly the case. . .

The first time I ever saw Misha was before he had become a movie actor. He was playing piano—he played great piano—in a little band at a night club in Pasadena. My escort, who had been there before, invited Mischa to join us between numbers, and I was immediately charmed by his easy manner and his humor, but had no idea that some day we would become close friends.

That came about when I was married to John and living in the Valley. Mischa and his beautiful wife, Joyce, lived less than a rifle shot away, in Encino; we had stables, they had stables, so the three of us (Joyce didn't care much for riding) rode through the hills almost every day the men weren't working. Soon we were in and out of each other's houses almost daily. When Mischa didn't have an early call, and could stay up late, we spent hilarious evenings together.

Both Mischa and Joyce loved having company; on weekends there were always a few Russian emigres at their house, having one of Mischa's fantastic meals which he concocted out of God knows what kind of a cook book. . . or more likely, his imagination. In the feeding of Russian compatriots, it reminded me of Madame's house.

There were other guests, too, of course. I met Lucille Ball and Desi Arnaz there several times, and thought they were delightful. I'll never forget the two of them, Mischa and Desi, doing duets together, hamming it up, and having us all in gales of laughter. What was even nicer was when Desi played his guitar to Mischa's piano accompaniment and sang his throbbing Cuban songs.

Those care-free days in the valley didn't last forever—as what does? To finish the story of Mischa Auer, I must take you ten or more years into the future.

176

Mischa is on the far right.

I was in New York for rehearsals of a musical, "Music in My Heart," for which I had written the libretto, and because my son, Timothy, [Mahin] was with me, I had sublet an apartment on 99th and Riverside Drive, in one of those once-gracious old buildings still retaining an air of elegance, though with some effort.

Mischa was doing summer stock on Long Island, so I invited him to spend the weekend with me, which he said he would be delighted to do. When I heard the bell and answered the door, instead of the bear hug I expected, I got a strange, puzzled look. He stood stock still in the doorway, then with a casual, "hello dolling," he stepped past me and paused again on the threshold of the living room. That room was the apartment's greatest asset; it had obviously been two rooms at one time, but with the dividing wall down it stretched thirty feet or more, all the windows on that long wall looking out over the Hudson River.

Mischa, still in his strange silence, walked to a window, turned his back to the view, and gazed from one end of the room to the other as if mesmerized.

I can remember how uncomfortable I felt; I wasn't sure whether he was ill, or planning some kind of joke, or what. I finally made some inane comment about the view which he ignored.

At the far end of the room was a grand piano, left there by my landlord because it was too expensive to move it out. Mischa broke the spell by going to the piano, running a arpeggio up and down it, and then crossing himself... backwards, in the Greek Orthodox manner.

"The other piano used to be in that corner," he said, pointing down the length of the room.

What other piano?

"Grandfather's. He always had two. That's why he took down the wall... it was two rooms... to make room for the two pianos."

"Your grandfather used to live here?" I asked stupidly, not sure whether or not he was teasing me.

"This is it," Mischa said. "I thought the address sounded familiar. This is it, the very first place I lived in, my very first home in America."

"Are you sure?" I said. "The people I rented it from were named Strauss."

"I went to school from here every morning for two years," he went on as though I hadn't spoken. "My room was the second bedroom down the hall." He crossed the room, went down the hall, and stopped at what was now my son's room. "This is it. It looks smaller now. It seemed enormous to me then. This was my room, my very own room."

Just then Frederee, my big warm, chocolate brown housekeeper, nursemaid, and general consultant came barging down the hall, arms outstretched. "I thought I heard your voice, Mr. Auer. My, you're looking fine, but thin. Mighty thin. You need some of my cooking."

Mischa embraced all 180 pounds of her. "I can't say the same for you, Free-Free. New York must agree with you."

"I takes some gettin' used to, but I'm gettin' used. How about a drink and a snack before dinner?"

Mischa grinned at her."Fine. Now you just follow me to the kitchen. I can find it with my eyes closed." And to her open-mouthed amazement he strode unerringly through the labyrinth of rooms, talking all the while. "The big bedroom is on the left, that's a small library on the right, here's the dining room—et voila, the kitchen. And the refrigerator—that used to be an icebox—should be right in that corner... How's that for ESP?"

Frederee shook her head in wonder. "You sure got it, Mr. Auer."

"He's teasing you, Free-Free. Mr Auer used to live in this apartment with his grandfather."

"Nearly thirty years ago," Mischa said. "Nearly thirty years ago."

"Ain't that one for the book," Frederee said. "A million apartments in this here city, and we're in the same one you lived in. It don't hardly seem possible."

"One chance in a million, wouldn't you say?"

"I would indeed."

Incroyable. Etonnant. Epouvantable.

"All of that."

"You want to know how I got here, to this apartment?"

"Of course," I said. "How did you get here? By taxi?"

"Oh, funny," he said. "Very funny. I got here from Harbin, China... it was China then, anyway. God knows what it is now. From Moscow to Harbin to 99th street and Riverside Drive. Quite a parley..."

I wisely said nothing. Then, in bits and pieces, Mischa told me this story...

His father was a White Russian, a General in the Tzar's army. When he saw the trouble coming he sent his family to their summer Dacha somewhere near the border of Finland, and he joined his friend, Count Tolstoi, in the White Army putting up a pathetic resistance to the overwhelming horde of Revolutionaries. The General thought his wife and children would be safe in the little village where everyone knew them and where they were well-liked, but he was wrong. The long arm of the Revolution reached into the village and they were forced to flee for their lives.

The older brother was put in the care of two faithful servants who swore they would smuggle him into Finland as one of them. The last Mischa saw of his brother was the wave of a mittened hand as he was drawn on a sleigh out of sight.

Mischa, his mother, and his sister, were passed along from villager to villager, and managed to elude the Bolsheviks for a while, but, the penalty for helping an aristocrat being death, his mother felt that it was asking too much of the peasants to risk their lives for her and her children, so she decided to try to get to St. Petersburg, where she might find refuge with friends.

Disguised as peasants, they tried to reach the city on foot. They passed through scenes of such carnage and destruction, in the confusion they might well have been safe, but typhoid was taking a higher toll than guns, and in the outskirts of the city his sister fell ill and died.

Mischa told me all this in a flat unemotional voice. Only when he described his mother cradling the thin little body, crooning to it, refusing to believe that life had left it, did his voice break for a moment, and he took a deep slug of brandy.

They never found their friends. Mischa didn't remember clearly where they found shelter, but he did remember a soldier who came in the dead of night with a message for his mother. The soldier was a Revolutionary, but he had served under Mischa's father, had been his orderly at one time, and risked his life to bring news of the General. It was a message of hope; the British were with them, all would be settled soon, he would see her in Moscow before the year was up. He had been slightly wounded, but it was nothing, a mere scratch, the young soldier assured Mischa's mother. It would take twenty such scratches, thirty, forty, to have any effect on a man such as the General. Then the soldier faded away into the night. A deserter, undoubtedly.

Since his father had said he would meet them in Moscow, off they started for Moscow, Mischa and his mother. They got as far as a town called Klin, about 20 kilometers from Moscow, and there his mother died. So many were dying that there was no proper burial for anyone. Horse drawn carts patrolled the streets, picking up corpses, which were stacked like firewood and taken out of town to an open pit into which they were dumped.

Mischa walked behind the cart as the plow horses drew it over the bumpy dirt road. His mother's body slid back until her head hung over the tail gate of the cart, bobbing with the uneven gait of the horses. He couldn't bear to see her looking so uncomfortable, so he held her head up, cupped in his hands, until they reached the funeral pit, then he turned and ran...

I just ran," Mischa said. "I just ran and ran..."

His voice trailed off. He took a sip of brandy. Then, without looking at me, he said, "It's all right, Petrushka. The worst is over."

After another few moments of silence, he said in a very matter-of-fact tone, "And so I went on to Moscow..."

He didn't find his father; he found other boys his age and younger, orphans like himself...

So Mischa became one of the Wolf Children of Moscow, one of a pack of children left homeless by the Revolution. They roamed the streets, living like animals on what they could steal or salvage from garbage piles. The government, what there was of it, paid no attention to these children whose parents had been killed by the Bolshiviks, leaving them to forage for food, or to starve to death. If one of them, by mistake, stole from a Party Member, he was shot for his insolence. Other than that, no notice was taken of them, even by the shopkeepers from whom they filched a bit of bread or a piece of clothing. Everyone was too concerned with staying alive to care about a pack of scrawny, filthy, lice-infested kids.

"We were all from good respectable bourgeois homes," he said, "but hunger strips away the veneer of civilization, and we became a savage wolf pack... willing to do anything to survive. Anything."

He gave a little start, as though coming out of a deep sleep, and finished his brandy.

"But here," I said. "How did you get here?" I refilled his glass, poured a little for myself, and sat down again, waiting. "How did you end up here in this apartment?" I think I spoke loudly. I may even have stamped my foot.

"Ah, yes," he said, "The Odyssey. Gulliver's Travels. Well, one day I left Moscow..."

He was very vague about when he left. He only remembered that it was still summer, the nights were short. Why he made the decision, he wasn't sure.

"I knew I had to go," he said. "I knew I had to be somewhere else."

"With no idea where you were going?" I said. "You just went off by yourself... into nowhere..."

"The longest journey begins with one step," he said, and gave me his first grin of the evening. "Confucius. Or maybe Dostoevski."

Whatever his reason for leaving the Wolf Pack, that fourteen year old boy started on what must be one of the most incredible journeys ever attempted. On foot, except for rare occasions when a sympathetic farmer gave him a ride, he crossed that vast expanse of harsh, inhospitable land; he crossed mountains, forded rivers, evaded wolves, eluded roaming cadres of Red Soldiers... just look at an Atlas and you will get an idea of how incredible his journey really was.

How he survived is a mystery—but he did. He ate what he could find. Often he would stop in a small village, do a few chores for the storekeeper or a friendly kulak, and be fed for a few days. Sometimes for days he didn't eat at all.

At one time, somewhere East of Moscow, he was picked up by a British sentry and taken to the White Army Headquarters. When he told the officers, in his schoolboy English, where he had come from they looked at him in obvious disbelief. Whether or not they ever completely believed his story, the officers were genuinely concerned and insisted that he stay with them, at least long enough to be fed and clothed and made to look human again. He must have looked more like a scarecrow than a teen-age boy.

There was no news of his father in this British camp, nor

did anyone know where Count Tolstoi and his army were. However, the men were all kindness itself to Mischa, and outfitted in a British uniform, bathed and well-nourished, willing to try anything, he became a sort of unofficial mascot, running errands, learning to shoot, picking up barracks-room English, and in general living a good life. There were moments, Mischa said, when he was actually happy.

But then the word came that they were moving forward, toward battle, toward Moscow. Battle he would have welcomed—but not Moscow. He could not go back there so, taking only the ill fitting uniform he was wearing, and a canteen kit, he crept away in the night, without even a farewell to the men who had called him "chum" and had shared their rations with him.

Mischa couldn't say how long he traveled—days, weeks, months, he only knew that when the cold became a worse enemy than hunger, the farmers who befriended him occasionally told him to go South, always South, and so one day he crossed the border into what was then Manchuria, a part of China. A Mongolian farmer for whom he did a few days work drove him to the market place in Harbin, where he left him. It so happened that he noticed a European lady struggling to carry two heavy baskets of food, and offered to help her. "She wasn't European," Mischa said. "She was American, but in Asia all non-Asians are considered European. And anyway, I wasn't quite sure what an American would look like, never having seen one."

This American lady was amazed to hear him speak English, and explained that she was a Missionary, and that there were many refugees being taken care of at the Mission, and that he would be welcome there. He could be of help with little odd jobs now and then in return for his food and shelter.

So he went to the Mission, where he met other Russians and from one of them he learned that his father, the General, was reported killed in action. (I don't remember Mischa's father's name... Auer was his mother's name.) When the Missionary Lady heard of this she was very sympathetic, and offered to try to find whatever family he had in Russia. No one, he told her, he had no family left. Only a grandfather, his mother's father, whom he had never known.

The Missionary Lady said that the Red Cross might find his grandfather if her Mission couldn't, but Mischa said no, not possible, because he had gone to America a long long time and who could find him in such a big country? All he knew was that his grandfather's name was Auer—Leopold Auer.

When she heard that name, Mischa told me, the Missionary Lady really flipped. Leopold Auer—the great violinist, the Maestro of Maestros... of course she knew who he was. She had once studied violin herself, but alas, no real talent...

Anyway, in a matter of days she had contacted Leopold Auer in New York through the Red Cross, and sent him a telegram saying, "Do you have a grandson named Mikhail?"

The message she received in reply said simply, Send my grandson to me. So, with the aid of the Red Cross and the Missionary Lady's mission, he was sent.

Mischa couldn't remember from what harbor he sailed. He said it might have been on the Yellow Sea, but he wasn't well, and it was all telescoped in his memory. He had a fever, which blurred everything, but he didn't dare tell anyone for fear they wouldn't let him go. Which they probably wouldn't have.

There was a train ride, there were kindly people giving him food, there were written instructions and papers to be signed and more papers that he had to show time after time... and finally there was another boat—and the day came that he arrived in New York.

His grandfather was on the pier to meet him. Then his grandfather brought him home... to this apartment... 3B. 270 Riverside Drive...

"Welcome," I said. "I'm glad you made it."

"Me too," he said.

"God works in wondrous ways," I said.

Then I got up, kissed him on the forehead, and went to my room, leaving him sipping his brandy and gazing at the corner where the other piano used to stand.

There is no sequel to this story. It was never referred to again.

Mr. & Mrs. John Lee Mahin.

With Peter Ustinov.

Sailing with Spencer Tracy and Howard Hawks   Michelle

Richard Rodgers   Cotney Jackson     Robert Taylor

Charlie Chaplin

With our neighbor Victor Flemming

CHAPTER TWENTY NINE

The War years brought out the best in what was still my Hollywood. Everyone has heard, or read, about the movie people who went overseas to entertain the troops, but not much has been written about the off-stage unpublicized activities; for instance, the Hospitality House that a group of us set up in the Valley. We women—actresses, daughters of actors, writers, script girls, and just pretty young girls—got together, rented a big old vacant house standing in the middle of an orchard, spruced it up a bit, brought in odds and ends of furniture, and made it a pleasant place for G.I.'s to spend their off time. We cajoled various companies into putting in coke and candy machines—for which the boys used tokens—and as a crowning glory, a juke box was donated.

There were hundreds, possibly thousands, of soldiers stationed in the Valley. It was considered a very vulnerable area, what with the air bases and factories and lots of hush-hush activities. There were few places that the boys could go for entertainment in their free time, and the Hospitality House was welcomed with enthusiasm and the blessings of the Brass. It was open from noon until exhaustion. We women took turns in being hostesses, the younger ones chatting and joking and dancing with the boys, we older ones (!) seeing to it that there was always enough coke, a few snacks, and that the kitchen and bathrooms were kept clean. Some of us even jitter-bugged ocassionally with a beardless G.I., to the great delight of the rest of them.

No liquor was permitted on the premises and no one seemed to miss it. I suspect that an occasional beer was drunk out in the orchard—and possibly a flirtation or two took place—but we never had one unpleasant incident, which speaks well, I think, for the young people of that generation. The M.P.s dropped in from time to time, looked around, had a coke, sometimes exchanged a few pleasantries, and that was it; we had their stamp of approval.

And I'll tell you who else dropped in—twice-with no fanfare, no publicity, no cameras clicking—Bing Crosby. He just dropped in, in that informal way of his; chatted with the boys, sang a few songs with them, kidded around, and left, first getting our promise that we'd never mention his visit to the Press. Probably the boys told their comrades in arms; we women never breathed a word of it. You can be sure it made an evening to remember for those boys who happened to be there.

What a nice guy Bing was. Now I'm going to tell you another nice thing he did—something that I have remembered all these years. It goes way back to the Beverly Hills days when we young movie people used to play parlor games in my parlor. Bing was not yet a famous actor; he was singing with a group called The Rhythm Boys, at the Ambassador Hotel; I don't really remember how I met him, or who brought him to my house the first time. He didn't become what you'd call a steady customer—he came out perhaps five or six Sundays, generally with a mutual friend named Ray Kress. Ray played terrific piano, and of course it would end up with Bing singing, giving his little Boo-Boos, and The Game would be forgotten. He always signed off with "Sweet Leilani," the orchestra's theme song.

We now skip a few years later, when my brother was back at Princeton and Bing was a big star. He was making a personal appearance with his latest picture at a New York theatre, and my brother and his Princeton pals went to New York to see him.

During the intermission, between shows, Brother incautiously remarked that Bing used to come to his house sometimes, that Bing and his sister were friends. That led to much scoffing—yeh, any time, if you really know him why don't you go say Hello to him—so Brother reluctantly sent a note to Bing, telling him how much they were enjoying the show, and mentioning that he was my brother.

In a few minutes the usher returned with an invitation from Mr. Crosby to come around to his dressing room and bring his friends. Now Bing hadn't seen my brother since he was a kid—if, indeed, he had noticed him at all. But he greeted him like a long-lost pal, sent his love to me, had drinks for everybody, and kept them there, laughing and chatting all through the intermission. My brother was a big man on campus for a while.

I claim that was a very nice thing to do—over and above the call of duty. And I think it showed what a damn nice guy Bing Crosby was.

Now back to War Time in the Valley.

John was overseas. Gray, who took care of the farm and the live stock—Daisy, the cow—some chickens, some pigs, and a pigeon cote—was working in an airplane factory; Ky, who took care of the horses, had enlisted in the calvary. I'll bet you didn't know we still had calvary; I didn't either, until Ky enlisted in it. Thank God, I still had Frederee, who took care of Timothy, my son—but that left l'il ole me to do everything else, which kept me fairly busy. I let the Army use our back half-acre; they installed an

183

anti-aircraft battery, and there was always at least one farm boy in the cadre who was only too happy to milk Daisy and clean out the stalls. Going overnight from the princely sum a top screen writer gets to the $166.66 a month Uncle Sam paid its lieutenants necessitated a dramatic change in life style; I took on odd jobs of writing—additional dialogue, cutting over-long scripts, bits and pieces like that. It brought me no credits, but it brought in a little cash, which was more important. It also kept me in touch with people, which was equally important.

War widows, as well as the other kind, can become very lonely. At first everyone makes a point of including you in gatherings, but after a while even your best friends tend to forget about you. The invitations fall off and the nights become longer and longer. They are not to be blamed; after all, there were so many of us.

Why I never tried to get a job acting, I don't know. It simply never occurred to me. Of course, I may not have been able to get one even if I had tried. On the other hand, some producer might have hired me for old times' sake, had I asked prettily. Or a good agent might have been able to wangle me a part at some studio where I still had friends I'll never know, because I didn't try. My acting life, much as I had enjoyed it, seemed so far away as to never have happened. It had sort of dissolved, the way our Girls Club had. What with marriage, writing, traveling. . . I can't explain it, so I won't bother to try.

What I did do, to help fill in the dark lonely hours, was volunteer for Aircraft Warning duty, together with my friend Norma Pagano, whose husband was away, in Washington, I think, doing some sort of propaganda work for the Army. We took the night shift. The Army built a wooden platform up the hill, facing down into the Valley; they put a roof of sorts over it, gave us a telephone with direct connection to the airbase snuggled below us across valley, and even gave us enough electricity to plug in an electric heater which kept our feet warm if not the rest of us, on those cold California nights. All we had to do was pick up the phone and report any movement in the air; as I remember, it went like this; Hi Bi—over head—heading east. . . I don't remember the rest of the jargon.

Naturally, we had to be checked out by the FBI before being accepted by the Air Force. The nicest young man came to see me; kind of a real-life Elliot Ness, only taller. Over a cup of coffee I told him that Mrs. Pagano and I were looking forward to starting our vigil and we weren't a bit concerned about being up there on the hill alone all night; the platform was too high for the stray hyena or coyote to bother us and there had never been prowlers or anyone like that in the Valley. He found that very admirable, he said. He was glad to hear that we had nothing to fear.

Well, there's one thing, I told him; we had to drive past the truck farm of a Japanese—or maybe he was a Nisei—to get to our observation post, and we did sometimes wonder. . . in the event of an attack by air, or something. . . I mean, if he wasn't on our side—I know it sounds absurd—but wouldn't our warning post be the first thing he'd knock out? That's a silly idea, isn't it. . .

Not silly, the FBI man said, but very unlikely. The Bureau had run a pretty thorough check on the 20,000 or so Japs and Nisei in the area and along the immediate Coast, and were quite confident that ninety-seven, maybe ninety-eight percent of them were completely trustworthy.

That's comforting, I said–then, with the speed of lightning my keen mathematical mind went to work. Say 98 percent are okay—that leaves two percent unaccounted for two percent of 20,000—let's see; one percent is 200—2 times 200 is—Hey, I exclaimed—that leaves 400 possible spies and sabotiers running around loose.

"That occurred to us," he said gravely. "The Bureau is also very good at mathematics."

For a split second I considered telling him about the Japanese house-boy, but stories about Japanese house-boys who turned out to be officers in the Japanese Army or Navy or Air force had proliferated like wire coat hangers in a closet; they had become apocryphal, so I only asked if he would like another cup of coffee. He declined with thanks, started to leave, then, taking a card out of his pocket, he scribbled a number on it and handed it to me. If anything comes up that you want to talk to me about," he said, then, after a long pause, "Anything–just call this number. It's a direct line. . . well, thank you for your hospitality, I've enjoyed meeting you. . . good luck" and he was out the door and away. Then I did a very melodramatic thing; I repeated the number over and over—it was a very easy number to remember—and I tore up his card!

At least I didn't chew it up and swallow it.

Perhaps I should tell my Japanese house-boy story. Why not? If there's anyone still alive who has a similar story to tell, I'd love to hear from them; we can compare notes. So here it is.

An acquaintance of ours, a film editor name Bob Abrams—or maybe it was Abrahamson—who lived near us in Tarzana, had a Japanese houseboy whom he called Mr. Moto—not his real name, of course. Mr. Moto was excellent at serving hors d'oeuvres and drinks at parties, and Bob's neighbors often borrowed him for that purpose. We used him two or three times ourselves, for pool parties and the like. He was a nice little man-efficient, courteous, and self-effacing.

In November of 1941, as historians will confirm, a Japanese delegation visited Washington to confer with President Roosevelt. Their well-publicized mission was to promote Peace and Friendship between our two countries. The Press carried daily reports, with many pictures of President Roosevelt and the Japanese envoys laughing and chatting, toasting the friendship of our two great countries, causing a run on Japanese kimonos and Saki. It was all very heart-warming.

As further evidence of their love and good will, a Japanese battleship pulled in to San Diego Harbor; all the local dignitaries were invited aboard for a tour of inspection, and to top it off, a reception was announced, to be held on Sunday before they raised anchor and sailed for home. The guest list included all the Navy brass, a few Hollywood stars, and of course, several Mayors and politi-

184

cal big shots.

We were not on the original guest list, I'm sure. Our being invited was a fluke; it so happened that the Lt. Commander in charge of entertainment was a Harvard classmate of John's, Roger something. He had spent a weekend with us when he was first stationed in San Diego which turned into a sort of class re-union. Two other classmates joined us; Tommy Wheelock-later married to Mary Astor for a brief time-and Charles (Chuck) Adams; I remember his name because it was the same as John's brother-in-law. Apparently Roger took it upon himself to send us engraved invitations to the big bash, including one for Chuck if he hadn't gone back to Chicago. He hadn't—so the four of us drove down to San Diego on a glorious sunny Sunday.

The battleship looked magnificent. She was in full dress, pennons flying, flags whipping in the breeze, the whole deal. We joined the line of guests going up the gangplank, stepped aboard, and were greeted by the first in a welcoming party of about six or seven very gold-braided Japanese officers. As I approached the fourth officer in the receiving line I got a shock. "My God," I said to John, "It's Mr. Moto!"

"Don't be ridic—" he started to say—and at that precise moment the officer saw us. Our eyes met for an instant, and the shock and surprise on his face gave him away. I truly believe that if he had managed to maintain that famous Oriental inscrutability, we would not have been sure it was he. With all due respect to the children of the Rising Sun, one Oriental does look pretty much like another to our untutored Western eyes... that is, until we get to know them well. But Mr. Moto blew it.

Nothing was said, however. He greeted us formally, thanked us for coming, and passed us on to the next officer. We were swept along with the crowd, and didn't see Mr. Moto again. Later, on the quarter deck where they were serving Japanese tid bits, saki, and champagne, Tommy and Chuck re-joined us, and Tommy said, "didn't one of those officers remind you of that Jap you had bartending a week or so ago? Funny thing—had the same kind of worried expression."

John and I sort of passed it off, and it wasn't until we were on the way home, a few hours later, that we told Tommy it had, indeed, been Mr. Moto, who had made it pretty clear that he didn't want to be greeted as such. That led, naturally, to a long discussion of why he had been masquerading as a house boy, and various opinions were offered; he was earning extra money while on leave—he had an American girl friend living in the Valley—the Navy trained cadets by having them do menial work... I don't think the word "spy" was ever mentioned, except, perhaps, laughingly, as something too far-fetched to be taken seriously.

Besides, why would the Japanese have spies in our country? They were our friends. Weren't some of their top men at this very moment wining and dining and chatting happily with our President?

Chuck, who had never met Mr. Moto, doubted the whole thing. Before leaving on Tuesday he suggested that I call Bob. Ten to one, he said, your Mr. Moto is back on the job, if he ever was away. I took his bet and called, asking Bob if he could spare Mr. Moto for the next Sunday.

He wasn't there, Bob told me. He had taken the weekend off, as he often did-but he had always been home Sunday night by midnight, at the latest. Bob was getting a bit worried, he said; he was afraid something might have happened to the poor little guy.

"Oh, he's probably just staying with friends," I said. "Well, let me know if he gets back." I hung up and took my ten dollars from Chuck.

Two Sundays later Pearl Harbor was bombed.

One day, a few months after Norma and I had started our nightly vigil, I stopped at Tarzana Post Office to mail a package, and the Post Mistress called me aside, looking around to see if we were alone. Almost whispering, she said that she was very upset, she needed my advice, but I mustn't mention it in case there was nothing to it, she wouldn't want anyone to get in trouble. Upon my promise of secrecy this is what she told me: her grandson, age eight, often brought a schoolmate home for lunch, a little Jap boy, the son of a man who owned the truck farm—did I know the one she meant? When I assured her I did, she went on to tell me that yesterday her grandson was bragging to the little Jap boy about his father's collection of guns... he had a rifle with an engraved stock and a six shooter, that a real cowboy used to own, and a pearl handled revolver, and the little Japanese kid said, aw, that's nothing... he said his father had pretty near a hundred guns and some big ones on wheels, and her grandson, Tommy said, aw, you're fibbing, and the Japanese boy said he was not, they're all there, right in the cellar where they grow mushrooms and keep the bulbs. So what did I think? Was it just children bragging, or what...?

So I told her she should call this number, and I wrote the number I had memorized on the back of a torn envelope. "Tell whoever answers that I gave you this number. Then tell your story just as you told it to me. Then tear up this envelope and throw it away."

The guns were there, all right. There was reported to be two anti-aircraft guns, not yet completely assembled; they must have been brought in in sections, buried under garden produce. Rumor had it that incendiary bombs were also found. The whole FBI operation was carried out so quickly and quietly not many people even knew about it until it was all over and there was a "For Rent" sign on the gate leading into the property. The local newspaper carried the story after it was a *fait accompli* but I don't remember that it made headlines in the national Press. The postmistress told me that her grandson missed his little Japanese friend—he had gone away without even saying "goodbye"—but that was all.

Well, not quite all. Norma and I enjoyed our ride up to our observation post more than we had. We even tooted our horn the first few evenings as we drove past the closed gate. And you could almost hear the collective sigh of relief from all of us on the West Coast when we heard that the Japanese, including the Nisei, were being moved inland. (The truck gardener was a Nisei) They weren't moved very far, only to a Santa Anita race track, a beautiful spot with comfortable accommodations and plenty of bathrooms.

This is something that people seem to have forgotten; the internees were free to leave, if they wanted to-but not to return to the coastal area. They could go inland, as many of them did, to Arizona and Colorado, and even as far East as Minnesota and Michigan. Some returned to California, some settled down in their new homes after the war.

There was surprisingly little animosity on either side. Only when food rationing became more stringent was there some grumbling by the Californians. Dairy products were in short supply, and fresh meat became a rarity; even liquor was not always available. We understood that the food was for our troops—but the liquor? Were they giving the soldiers cocktails before sending them into battle?

The reason for the grumbling was not so much the rationing as the fact that there were no ration cards needed in the internment camp. The Government supplied the internees with their food, just as it did the troops. To some people it didn't seem fair, that the "enemy" was being better fed than they were, and a few meetings of protest were held, a few housewives wrote indignant letters To the Editor, and there were typically American jokes going around—but that was about all that happened. I don't recall hearing of any dangerous outbursts, or any acts of violence.

I do remember one sign a truck driver had on the side of his truck: "Beat the ration rap—make friends with a Jap."

The rationing didn't affect us at the farm; we had plenty of eggs, butter, and milk—even some vegetables. I gave all the surplus to friends and neighbors. And when no meat was available, we ate one of our chickens. But not everyone had a farm; tiny as ours was, it fed Frederee and Timothy and me and a few friends, for which we were all duly grateful, and didn't begrudge the Japanese their three meals a day in exchange for their freedom.

My brother Winston still thinks that putting people in an internment camp just because they were Japanese was a disgraceful, cruel, inhumane thing for our Government to do. He was not in California during the war; he was in the Marines, in the Pacific, but he heard all about it. He says that just because other countries do that sort of thing is no excuse for our country to do it, and that we never should have. I agree with that statement, with the addition of one word: We never should *have to*.

I think everyone felt a certain amount of sympathy for the innocent victims of a war not of their making—but what about that two—or maybe three percent who were not so innocent?

One moonless night a Japanese plane, presumably launched from a Carrier, dropped an incendiary bomb in the Coachella Valley. Undoubtedly intended for the new Air Field there, it missed its target by a mile or more, landing in a foothill of the Santa Rosa Mountain range. Other than starting a brush fire, it did no damage.

But what if there had been someone on the ground to signal to the pilot—to pinpoint the target?

One day, in the wee small hours of the morning, a Japanese sub-marine surfaced off the coast of Santa Barbara and lobbed a shell into its waterfront. The target could have been the drydock or the Navy's oil tankers. It missed both and hit an old warehouse. Before the sub could readjust its sights and fire again, one of our surveillance planes spotted it and sank it. It still lies, many fathoms down on the bed of the ocean, off the coast of Santa Barbara.

Aside from a burned-out warehouse, the damage was minimal. But what if there had been someone on shore to signal the submarine, to direct its fire?

There were other such stories circulating in our part of the world, but I am only telling these two because I got them at first hand, from actual witnesses. Other than a brief mention in a small local paper, few of these incidents were carried by the Press. The War Board of Censorship kept a tight curb on all the news media, as it did on all overseas correspondence. When I was stupid enough to write and tell John about our friends in Santa Barbara finding debris from the sunken sub on the beach, the letter John received looked like a jigsaw puzzle. The censors didn't cross out the offending sentences, they cut them out; when you have written on both sides of a page, it leaves a lot of guess work for the reader.

Censorship in wartime is certainly justifiable, if it is to keep from giving information, aid, or comfort to the enemy. If, as some people believe, they kept these incidents quiet for fear of creating a panic among the citizens of the West Coast, they badly misjudged their fellow Americans, but Government officials often do that, don't they?

Just to be sure I didn't have an idle moment I joined the Women's Ambulance and Defense Corps. We were taught what to do in case of a bombing attack; how to care for the wounded, how to stop bleeding, how to splint broken bones. Our instructor was a Sergeant in the Nurses Corps, who took her duties very seriously.

There were six of us in our group, or unit, or whatever it was called, one of them being Irene Rich, a beautiful woman and a lovely actress. Our lesson for the day was how to handle broken bones. One of us always pretended to be the victim, and this time it was Irene's turn. She lay down gracefully on the stretcher as our instructor said, "She has a broken leg. Now, remember—splint 'em where they lay. Don't move 'em—splint 'em where they lay!"

On the signal, we rushed to Irene, who began to groan and writhe in pain. In fact, she got so carried away in the part that she began to gasp for breath. Our instructor, unaware of Irene's histrionic ability, lost her cool and shouted, "Get an ambulance, somebody! This woman's having a heart attack!"

"I am not," Irene said indignantly, sitting up in the stretcher. "I have a broken leg, and it hurts."

Norma Pagano signing photographs from her Laurel and Hardy film 1988

Now, on the more serious side, I must tell the strange story of what happened to Norma and me one evening on our lonely observation post, Norma and I think of ourselves as survivors. We have outlived almost everybody we ever knew in our youth. For instance—I am the sole surviving member, counting star, director, cast and most of the crew, of that movie epic, The Hunchback of Notre Dame. Pretty awesome isn't it? And Norma, so far as we know, is the lone survivor of the silent Laurel and Hardy comedies. At one time, before she got married, she thought she wanted to be an actress; as Norma Drew, she was the leading lady in one of their pictures. That's the reason we like to think of ourselves as survivors—but we almost didn't survive as aircraft observers...

One evening, just at twilight as the sun was sinking behind us, out of the West, silhouetted against the rosy sky, came what appeared to be a full squadron of planes, flying in perfect V formation. Although visible to the naked eye, they were so small they must have been flying at a very high altitude. Norma had the phone, I had the binoculars. I trained my glasses on the flight as Norma, trying to speak calmly, reported: Bi-High-Heading east-overhead-heading east—I tried to count the planes; there must have been fifteen, maybe twenty... I swung my glasses around to the base, and saw the P38's trundling across the airstrip—then I quickly looked back at the flight now nearly overhead. We still couldn't hear their motors, but the leading plane seemed almost close enough to reach up and touch.

Suddenly the air was filled with a vibration that shook our flimsy platform to its foundation, and I realized with horror that the leader not only seemed close—he *was* close. But he wasn't an airplane—he was a goose! And the thunderous throbbing noise that was assailing our ears wasn't the sound of motors—it was the sound of wings... thirty or forty huge wings flapping in unison. We had alerted our defense system to repel an attack by geese.

"Good grief," I yelled, "It's not planes, it's birds."

This Norma had seen for herself, as they weren't more than ten feet over our heads. With great presence of mind, only dropping the phone once, she shouted "Cancel previous report. Cancel previous report!"

In a matter of seconds the flock had passed over us and was disappearing into the dusk below. Not a light anywhere had come on; it was a total blackout. Only at the distant airfield could we see some moving lights... With a desperate sense of urgency I yelled into the phone which Norma still held, "Hey, down there... Hey... somebody cancel that report—*please* cancel it—they aren't enemy planes—they're geese. We reported a flight of geese.

Silence enveloped us like an eiderdown quilt. There was no sound of wings, no sound of motors, no sound of traffic. .. no sound at all.

Then, from the interceptor base nearly five miles away Norma and I could swear we heard the sound of laughter.

That's what we almost didn't survive—the kidding we got from the United States Air Force for the next few weeks...

So what with this and that, and one thing and another, I filled my days. Little by little I created a new life—and little by little I stopped missing John.

On the other side of the world much the same thing was happening to him. John was living a different life in England, with new duties, new friends, new interests. And, it stands to reason, missing me less and less.

When he was mustered out of the service, a Captain, we had both become different people; sadly, we failed to recapture the rapport we once had. Our marriage became just another of the casualties of War.

Of John Lee Mahin I can only say this; he was a fine man, as well as a fine writer—he was sensitive, humourous, and generous. I know he would have given me anything I asked for—and he did give me the only thing I wanted; he gave me my son.

So I left the Farm and everything in it and on it, and in doing so I left Hollywood. Not the geographical Hollywood; the Hollywood of studios, friends in the business, the movies... MY Hollywood, that I had fallen in love with when I was sixteen. Life doesn't stop because it changes; with Timothy, Frederee and some wearing apparel I went to New York, rented an apartment on Riverside Drive, took a holiday in Bermuda... and tripped over the sun-tanned legs of a braw Scotsman, of whom more anon.

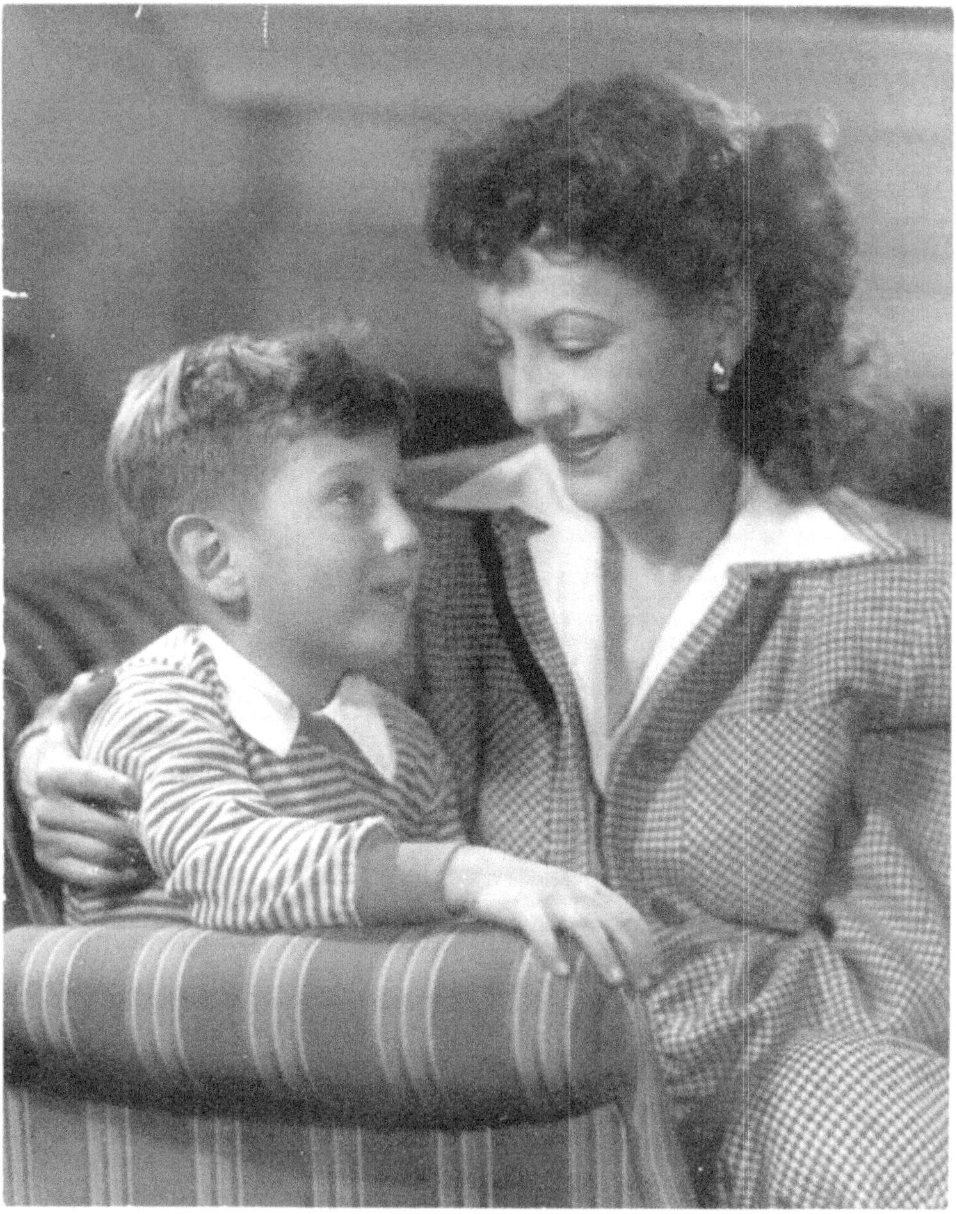

CHAPTER THIRTY

There's a lot of hoop-la about Marilyn Monroe as I write this. It's the twenty-fifth anniversary of her death. We were in Torremolinos, on the coast of Spain, when she died. I saw the headline in a London newspaper which an Englishman at the next table was reading, and involuntarily exclaimed, "Oh, what a pity!" The Englishman turned, said, "Yes, isn't it?" and offered me his paper. The story didn't give many details; it covered her career briefly, and the implication was that she had committed suicide.

"A compatriot of yours, wasn't she?" the Englishman asked. "Did you know her?" I told him No, I had never met her, that I had never even seen her in person, which he seemed to think rather odd since we were both from the same country.

Mentioning that I was in Torremolinos, Spain, when I first learned of Marilyn Monroe's untimely death was not just place dropping. It was my sneaky way of working in the story of the dogs of Torremolinos.

The dogs have nothing to do with Hollywood. I've just always wanted to write about them. If you're a dog lover, I think you'll forgive their intrusion. If you only like dogs well enough to pat them on the head, say, Good doggie, and look anxiously around for their owner, you still might enjoy reading about the Torremolinos ones.

If, however, you're just not all that interested in dogs, you can skip the next few pages and no harm done.

Fair enough?

Torremolinos, back in the 1950's and 60's, was not much more than a fishing village about a twenty minute bus ride from Malaga. The town consisted of a *carneria*, a *farmacia*, a *bodega*, several *cantinas*, and a few shops, their wares displayed in dusty stalls along the roadside. Facing the sea, on the edge of the beach which ran for mile after golden mile, sat El Remo, which might loosely be called a hotel, and its bungalows.

The beach in front of the bungalows was populated mostly by foreign visitors, which made it no different from any other beach on the Mediterranean; what made it distinctive was its canine population. I venture to say, in that respect, it was unlike any other beach in Europe.

The dogs of Torremolinos cannot be classified, at least not in generic terms, as one can classify Boxers, or Dachshunds, or Setters. They can hardly even be described as one can describe a certain breed. After all, except to those near and dear, one Dalmatian looks very much like another Dalmatian, one St. Bernard closely resembles another St. Bernard. Not so the dogs of Torremolinos! Numerous as they were, there were no two-of-a-kind, no two who looked enough alike that one could say with certainty, somewhere in their ancestry were a mother and father of the same breed.

It is strange that no true Torremolinos type ever developed, sequestered as they were with a certain amount of inbreeding, to say the least. I suppose there was just enough foreign blood, due to tourists who *would* let their pets run loose, to avoid such stereotyping. Thus we guests at El Remo had the unique privilege of becoming ac-

189

quainted with Wolfhound types with short legs, Dachshund types with curly tails, and a variety of equally startling combinations which were hard to believe even as you were looking at them. There was one kind of dog, however, which we never encountered—an undernourished dog.

Though no two looked alike, in behavior they were very similar. Different as they were in looks, character and personality, in one respect they resembled each other like peas in a pod; they were both the laziest and the busiest dogs in Spain, if not the world. They were much too lazy to learn tricks, or even commands, but incredibly active in the pursuit of food, shade and comfort. They operated on a very rigid schedule: on the beach in the morning, at their favorite *cantina* at noon, back to the beach for a siesta in the shade of someone's umbrella in the afternoon, and under the table of their chosen sponsor-of-the-week that evening.

The dining was al fresco, and meals were for all. Most of the El Remo dogs visited practically every table in the course of a dinner, and as it is the custom in Spain to straggle in to the dining room any time from ten to midnight, you can see that the dogs had to cover a lot of territory in order to check the progress of the meal at each table. This, in my opinion, accounted for their excellent physical condition; they were outrageously overfed, but they walked it off between courses.

The Andalusian waiters and waitresses apparently had an extra-sensory perception which enabled them to step over or around both dogs and the occasional cat without even glancing down, somewhat in the manner of an experienced actor finding the chalk mark, stage center, without lowering his gaze from the balcony. To give credit where credit is due, the dogs had an uncanny ability to avoid being trodden upon, wending their way through a crowded dance floor like an all-American broken field runner.

Although some of the hotel guests complained that the dogs were difficult to please, I had no problem; it was simply a matter of remembering their tastes. Manolo, for instance, who was very fond of fish, wouldn't eat a sardine on a bet. Whiskey (black and white, of course), cared only for meat, medium rare, whereas Quisquillosos liked almost all vegetables, except carrots, and was particularly keen on fried potatoes. Quisquillosos was very low slung, had trouble going down steep stairs, and actively disliked all tall dogs, hence his name, meaning "touchy."

Then there was little Carinoso, the loving one, who would eat anything offered rather than hurt your feelings, but would look at you reproachfully if it was veal, which she disliked. And Tony, a huge black Newfoundland-cum-Labrador type, who looked as though he could consume a six-course dinner in one gulp, but would sometimes visit four or five tables before finding what appealed to him. Even then, he would only nibble at it daintily from a lady's hand.

In his nightly pilgrimage from table to table, Miguel, my hero, led all the rest. Knowing that you could hardly slip him a piece of soup, he never patronized you before the fish course. In the event that you were so *gauche* as to order a fish with bones in it, instead of a fillet, he waited for the entree before honoring you with his patronage.

And then came the day when my husband received a cable from Scotland requesting his immediate presence for an important business meeting, and off he flew that very afternoon. Until that time, I must confess that although Miguel had always greeted me very politely each morning on the beach (he was always the very soul of courtesy), I had no idea that he had anything in mind but a friendly acquaintanceship. I had wanted to believe that he favored me a bit over the Englishwoman who talked baby-talk to him (Imagine! Baby-talk to Miguel!) but I was not prepared for the eventful moment when he suggested spending the night with me. Although, like any red-blooded woman, I had had many such suggestions, none ever thrilled me more. His timing was so perfect, I sometimes wondered if he had anything to do with sending that cable. . .

From then on, until my husband returned, almost a month later, having to go to England, Ireland, and back to Scotland, we were a *menage a trois*, Miguel, my ten-year-old son, Timothy, and me. Miguel came in every night to sleep, sometimes at the foot of the bed, sometimes on it. As doors were never locked—except when gypsies were in town—and even if shut could be easily pushed open, I didn't have to wait up for him. My only chore as his hostess was to keep the bidet in the bathroom filled with water so that he could get a drink any time he was thirsty without having to ask permission.

Living with me didn't intefere with his regular schedule: patrolling the beach in the morning, dropping in for a handout at his favorite bar, taking his siesta, and cadging dinner as usual. He didn't object to my staying out late on occasion, so long as I came in quietly. Sometimes, if he had had an exceptionally busy day, he slept in Timothy's room, and often in Timothy's bed, which was much narrower than mine, but adequate, at least for Miguel, if not for Timothy, who occasionaly ended up sleeping on the floor.

Not many of my fellow guest were aware that my friendship with Miguel had become a "meaningful relationship," as he maintained his casual attitude toward me in public. I did notice, however, that whenever one of his conferees came strolling over when Miguel and I were lolling in the shade of our beach umbrella, he would slowly get up, yawn, and amble over to the stand between me and the visitor. As all I could see was his rear end, I don't know what his expression said, but I think it must have been something like "Private Property," "Trespassers will be Prosecuted," or "Get Lost!" because invariably the visiting dog would give a little toss of his head and with an air of nonchalance stroll off in the other direction.

We guests who had served our apprenticeship had great fun watching the newcomers, especially the English, as they oohed and aahed and said, I say, what a beastly shame, the poor little buggers; no owners, you say? A bad show; just what we've always heard, they would tell each other in their well-bred, high pitched voices. Spaniards have no feeling for animals, but what can you expect from people who love bull fights! Who feeds the poor beasties?

Of course, they soon found out about the poor wee

homeless orphans... then they would sit back, with the smug smile of the novitiate, and eavesdrop on the next crop of newcomers...

Where are the dogs of Torremolinos today? Where are the snows of yesteryear? You won't find them in the lobby of the Madrid Hilton, nor the dining room of the Iberian Sheraton, not even in the Kentucky Fried Chicken shack. There are no more casitas on the beach, only huge buildings of concrete and steel, with many, many rooms, but no room for Manolo, or Carinoso, or Miguel...

Lest any reader get the impression that I dislike the English because of my jibes about some of their customs and mannerisms, let me assure you that they are meant as the affectionate teasing of someone you like. I share the British admiration for their Queen, I share the belief in keeping a stiff upper lip, and I strongly approve their respect for tradition, being inclined that way myself.

With that cleared up, let's get back to Marilyn Monroe.

All I knew about Marilyn Monroe that bewildered child-woman, other than what I had read in fan magazines, was that Kay Gable, Clark's widow, resented her bitterly. It was not jealously—far from it. She felt that working with Monroe in *The Misfits*, the picture she and Clark had made together just beofre his death, had been partially responsible for bringing on his heart attack. The picture was shot largely in the desert, and added to the problems of any outdoor location was Monroe's behavior.

Clark was a pro. Despite being one of the most famous men in the civilized world, and a star of the first magnitude, he never threw his weight around. He was first and last a professional actor. If the call was nine o'clock, he was ready to go. He always knew his lines, and he expected his fellow actors to know theirs. He was cooperative, didn't gripe about tough working conditions, and was well liked by everyone he worked with, from the director down to the gaffers and prop men.

Marilyn Monroe was the exact opposite. She was never ready on time, she rarely knew her lines, and she behaved like an old-fashioned prima donna. It was very galling for Clark to have to wait around on the set until Miss Monroe condescended to leave her dressing room and play a scene with him. Often, after waiting an hour or more, the scene would have to be re-shot four or five times before she got it right. This was particularly exasperating to Clark, who was known as a one-take man.

At the end of a day's work, Kay said, Clark was so tense, so exhausted from having to wait around for Monroe to get in the mood that he would often just fall into bed, too tired to even eat any dinner. Kay wanted him to have it out with Monroe, but Clark was afraid that a confrontation would only make it tougher for the director, John Huston, who was having enough problems as it was.

Perhaps it would have been better if he had had it out with her. It might have eased the tension that was building up inside. Whether or not he would have lived longer had he not made *The Misfits* with Monroe is, of course, an unanswerable question. I suppose the point is, he *might* have.

I didn't know Clark until I married John and moved out to Encino, where Clark also lived. John had written many of the pictures Clark starred in: *Red Dust, Wife versus Secretary, Boom Town* — and they were very close friends. We all became even more friendly when he married Carole Lombard, whom I had known since she was a kid named Jane Peters. I was fond of Carole—it was impossible not to like her—but she used to love to shock me by using language that no nice girl should use, and every time she did, I would react just as she knew I would. I'm a real fuddy-duddy about pretty girls using ugly words. In retrospect, I think she often threw in a four-letter one just to see the expression on my face.

Clark loved hunting and fishing, which John liked mildly; but they shared a common love of horses. I don't remember Carole ever riding with us. In fact, I'm not sure that she rode at all. Clark also loved motorcycles, which John most definitely did not. Almost every Sunday, Clark and Victor Fleming and a couple of friends who were stunt men, would go tearing up Ventura Boulevard, which wasn't the crowded thoroughfare it is today, and would stop for a few minutes at our house before heading up into the hills.

Aside from motorcycles, John and Clark saw eye to eye on pretty much everything, and when we got into the Second World War, they joined the Air Force together.

On their "delay en route" leave, just before being sent overseas, John and Clark and I, along with other officers

John overseas writing and producing films

and their wives, spent two weeks in Colorado Springs. Carole had died in that terrible plane crash, so Clark sort of borrowed me as a shield to fend off the onslaught of feminine fans. I would cling possessively to his arm as we strolled the streets, acting as a kind of buffer, or at least a deterrent... although my presence didn't deter many of them. There were screaming women everywhere. I was appalled at the way some of them behaved when they saw Clark, who was admittedly quite magnificent in uniform. Their frenzy was almost frightening.

John and Clark.

John with Clark and Victor Fleming

A few women became quite rude when Clark declined—politely—their offers of God knows what. There were moments when I felt ashamed of my own sex, but Clark handled it all with charm, with patience, with just the right amount of gratitude for being recognized and sorrow that he could not accept their invitation.

It was a lesson in courtesy that some of the modern day stars would do well to study...

There was a huge ice-skating rink near our hotel which lured us to try our luck on skates. In St. Louis I had done some ice-skating; we had a lovely rink, grassed in, with a sort of promenade around it, tables at which you would warm up with hot chocolate, and a palm-filled lobby in which boys and girls paired off. Most of my skating had been done with a partner, on whom I relied rather heavily. I had never been one of those intrepid girls who spun in the center of the ice, short skirts swirling, but was sensibly content to go round and round, hands interlocked with some strong-ankled boy, as waltz after waltz poured from a hidden victrola.

At the Colorado Springs rink, in 1942, it wasn't much different. Inspired by the Skaters Waltz, I wobbled around once or twice, then joined up with Clark, who was also wobbling, with the idea that four ankles might manage better than two.

While we were getting our breath after a dazzling display of staying erect for three whole circuits—taking care never to get too far from the railing—a young G.I. skated up to Clark and respectfully requested the Major's permission to ask me to skate with him. Graciously, I accepted. The handsome young man looked rather slight, but strong enough, I hoped, to get me around a few times. In pre-scribed fashion we linked hands and pushed off for the one-two-three-change-feet-glide I was getting to do quite well.

Suddenly, to my utter disbelief, we were in the center of the rink. To my further disbelief, I was swinging around in a circle. Before I could explain that I didn't know how to skate on one leg, I was doing it. As my young partner drew me back to him in a swooping swerve, he whispered, "Just do what I tell you. I won't let you fall."

He had me by one hand, then the other, around the waist, on the shoulder; and all the time he was whispering, left leg straight out, skates together, lean back on me... and like an automaton, but a happily terrified exhilarated automaton, I swirled, I swooped, I glided and spun, and I ended in a magnificent pirouette, caught by my partner in the knick of time to take a bow.

I was brought out of my trance by the sound of applause, and straightened up to see a ring of skaters lined up at the railing. We had the whole rink to ourselves, for how long I have no idea. My knees started to tremble, and I had to hang on for dear life to my soldier as he returned me to my group who were staring in disbelief. Then I re-joined Clark who said accusingly, "You didn't skate that way with me!"

I later found out who my young partner was: a contender for the next Olympics, and who might well have made it had he not gone down in the English Channel in a flaming B-17.

As I'm remembering Clark, it doesn't seem fair that he should have died just when he did. He had come home from the war unharmed, had weathered that ill-begotten marriage to Lady Sylvia Ashley, and had had the good fortune to find Kay Spreckles, who was just right for him. There was no doubt, seeing them together, that Clark was once more a happy man.

When Kay became pregnant, Clark was even happier. He told John—who, of course, told me—that he was abso-lutely certain it was going to be a boy, the son he had always wanted. I remember when he came over to see our baby, Timothy, for the first time, how he clucked at him and touched his little fingers, and said, One of these days, I'll have a youngster like you to take hunting and fishing.

But he never did. As everyone knows, Kay did have a boy—born posthumously.

My mind goes back to an evening during the war, an evening at their house just a week or so before Carole went off on the War Bond selling trip from which she never returned. John and Clark were downstairs having a drink and talking shop, so I went upstairs to see Carole. She was in bed, having just come home from the hospital where she had had what she referred to as very very minor surgery. She was enthused about her coming junket, and when I asked if it was wise to fly so soon after her session in the hospital, minor as it may have been, she laughed and said, "Oh, it was nothing. Just one of those little readjustments we girls sometimes have to have... you know, so we can have a baby."

"Oh, that's wonderful," I said, and Carole said, "Pops thinks so too."

Then we went on to other things... girl talk. She hadn't actually said she was pregnant, she might just have had a little "adjustment," as she called it, in the hope of being. But when we got word that dreadful night that Carole's plane was lost and John rushed over to Clark to help him

193

through his agonized waiting, I couldn't help thinking poor Carole—she might have given him a son.

But the Fates wouldn't permit it. When I heard of his death, I had a mental picture of them, Clotho, Lachesis, Atropos, sitting around and discussing him.

Clotho says, Look, girls, he already has everything a man could want—fame, fortune, a good marriage. You know our rule, no one can have everything. Then Lachesis says, That's all very well, but I've heard you say a thousand times that rules are made to be broken. Then Atropos chimes in, we all know you've always had a soft spot for that man, but you have to have a better reason than that for breaking the rules. Atropos says I agree, and Clotho says firmly, It's decided. Two to one. We keep the rules.

No one can have everything!

Kay and "John" Clark Gable

CHAPTER THIRTY ONE

One day, when I was in my Riverside Drive apartment, Leonard Sillman called to suggest that I join him and a friend on a trip to Bermuda. Leonard was producing that smash revue, *New Faces*, which introduced Imogene Coca, Henry Fonda, and a host of other talented youngsters to an enthusiastic public, and wanted to relax on a beach and savor his triumph.

I would have loved to have gone with him; I was longing to get back to my beloved California to see more of my brother, Winston, who, safely back from the South Pacific, was again writing great movies, and to get rid of my New York pallor with some California sun. But as long as I couldn't yet go home, Bermuda would have been the next best thing. I had the time; I had finished the libretto of *Music in My Heart*, a sort of operetta based on the life of Tschaikowsky, using all of his glorious music. Rehearsals wouldn't start for a few weeks as they were still casting. My son, Timothy, had been entered in a fine kindergarten nearby and Frederee was there to take care of him. Everything was perfect for a holiday in Bermuda. There was only one drawback: I didn't have enough money, not even a credit card. (I don't think they had yet been invented, or I'm sure I would have had one.)

Leonard had told me, if I changed my mind, to come to the Eagle's Nest where he and Frank, his friend, would be staying, but it wasn't my mind that needed changing, it was my bank account. I grumped around the apartment all day, looked out at the cloudy sky, and felt very abused. As things were, I couldn't even go on a shopping spree, the feminine panacea for all ills.

The next morning I awakened to another cloudy, drizzly day, and while I was rather gloomily finishing my breakfast waffle with syrup and bacon the phone rang. Frederee answered it, and though I shook my head, meaning for her to say I wasn't in, she handed me the phone anyway, saying firmly, "You better talk to him. It's that insurance man."

I was immediately ready to put up a fight. I knew I had paid my insurance premium; that was one of the reasons I was so short of funds. Then something occurred which has to be called a miracle. Has anyone ever heard of an insurance company that *returns* money to its policy holders? Paying off (relunctantly) valid claims, yes. But actually giving money *back*? Never.

Very apologetically, Mr. Osborne told me that through some unheard of error—a new girl in the office, probably... he simply couldn't understand how it happened... it never had before... through someone's carelessness, no doubt—I had been grossly overbilled, and I had a refund due me of nearly $1,500, a check for which would be immediately forthcoming. In fact, to make up for any inconvenience this might have caused me, he, Mr. Osborne, would bring me the check in person that very afternoon.

As if this were not miraculous enough, consider the timing. The next day about noon, Leonard and Frank met me at the Bermuda airport, and by three o'clock I was on Elbow Beach.

While I was chatting with a group of tourists, the boys came over and practically dragged me away. As soon as we were out of earshot, they told me there was the best-looking Englishman sitting all alone, you could tell he was English by the way he talked, sort of like David Niven, and don't say we never did anything for you, he's absolutely gorgeous, we've been talking to him, and really, Pat, why don't you go over and get acquainted.

All this time we're walking down the beach toward the gorgeous Englishman—who was actually a Scotsman—and I was beginning to feel like a call girl.

Here's where our stories differ; the gorgeous Scot maintained that I deliberately tripped over his feet. I maintained that he thrust his legs out and tripped me. But that's about the only difference of opinion we ever had in the next forty years. For of course I married him—not right away, but as soon as possible. From now on, when I mention "My husband" I am speaking of my brawny Scot, Effingham Smith Deans.

My dearest Frederee.

Mr. and Mrs. E.S. Deans.

Jackie Coogan, Patsy Ruth Miller and Ray Bradbury at The Academy of Motion Pictures tribute to Lon Chaney.

CHAPTER THIRTY TWO

Hollywood, my Hollywood, has aged quite differently than I would have expected. The producers and moguls of my day, Sam Goldwyn, L.B. Mayer, Jack Warner, C.B. deMille, and others of that ilk, are gone, and they have not been replaced by men who care greatly about the pictures they make, or who are in love with movie making, as they were. The producers of those days felt a sense of responsibility toward what they thought of as "their public". The New York money men who now run the studios are only interested in the bottom line. There's nothing against showing a profit; all the producers wanted to make money on their pictures, but it's the means used to make money that matters. At least it did in those days.

They all had their trademarks: Sam Goldwyn hated ugliness. He wanted to make only beautiful pictures with beautiful people in beautiful stories, and his pictures always made money.

L.B. Mayer loved beautiful pictures too, especially musicals with beautiful music in them. He would have been horrified at most of what they call "music" today.

C.B. deMille loved eye-filling spectacles and glamour. There was never anything ugly or sordid in his films. And the public ate them up.

Jack Warner went more for action pictures, which sometimes contained violence, but it was clean-cut violence, not slimy or degenerate. One thing Jack Warner would not tolerate—a slur of any kind on his country. In fact, he was accused of being a "super patriot", whatever that means, and proudly admitted it. His flag waving didn't offend the public, it delighted them.

Even Harry Cohn, of Columbia Pictures, who perhaps didn't have the greatest taste in the world, cared tremendously about turning out good movies that everyone in the family could enjoy.

Some of the credit for clean entertainment must be given to the Great American Public of those days. Moviegoers didn't want ugly stories about ugly people doing ugly things to each other. An occasional "horror" film was okay; you knew in advance what you'd see, and it didn't pretend to be real. A tear jerker now and then was fine, so long as it ended happily. Just stay away from indecency; that embarrassed the audience. It would seem that movie viewers as well as the men who make them, are different today.

The resurgence of interest in old movies intrigues me. It seems to be on the increase, judging by the mail I receive, asking about everything imaginable; did I know so-and-so, which director did I like best, how much did the cameraman have to do with the lighting—what was Lon Chaney's hump made of in *The Hunchback*—and dozens of other questions. These letters are not from Senior Citizens; most of the writers are in their twenties or thirties—some even sound younger. Lon Chaney seems to be of particular interest this year, which rather surprises me. Not that he wasn't a splendid actor, just that he was such a private person that I never thought of him as being the subject of many books, as he now is.

Could it be that people are tired of violence and sordid sex, and are unconsciously yearning for the sheer entertainment of the old-time movies? Could it be that they would welcome Love and Romance and good clean fun again? In other words-ENTERTAINMENT, which is what show biz is all about. Whatever the reason, the study of old movies is now the "in" thing.

Numerous colleges and universities give classes in old films and film making, and I'm told the classes are filled with young students. It's hard to think of myself and my fellow actors as deserving all this attention, and I'm sure none of us ever dreamed that we would be referred to as creators of a new "art form". Nor did we regard ourselves as pioneers in an infant industry because to us the industry had been in its infancy when we were in ours. We were just actors, doing our stuff in front of a camera instead of on a stage. Just a branch of show biz... While it's true that being movie actors made us feel a little special at times, it didn't go so far as to make us think of ourselves as objects of historic interest to future generations.

For directors the trail had been blazed by D.W. Griffith, but naturally, with the improvements in cameras, lighting, and technical equipment they developed new techniques. I seriously doubt that any of them foresaw that their methods of directing would become subjects of profound study, analysis, and even psycho-analysis, as they are today. Classes have weighty discussions dealing with "over-narrativization" and "under-narrativization"; at a guess I'd say that means too much or too little talk... So why not just say it that way?

Then there's "valorize". The dictionary says it means "to fix or control the price by valorization." Huh?

And how about "diogesic?" Try this on for size: Diogetic and non-diogetic elements". Does anyone out there know what that means? And don't forget about "probing the psychic depths," and "problematic possibilities."

Analysis can be overdone. If you stand up close to an oil painting, scrutinizing every square inch through a magnifying glass, you'll only see the brush strokes; you won't see the picture at all.

My brother, who has been writing movies ever since he left college, once found himself so annoyed by all this analysis that he stood up—or so I was told—and said, "This is a lot of—." But I'd better let him tell it in his own words—and in his own restrained fashion.

Introducing my brother, Winston Miller, who will now take over the typewriter:

I've read books about directors in which the author on the Academy Committee charged with selecting the nominees for best documentary short subject. One of the candidates for selection was about famous directors. Sample scenes by each director were shown, while the narrator analyzed the scenes in depth for symbolism, revelations of the director's personal philosophy, and so forth.

The first scene shown was from a picture called *My Darling Clementine*, a Western directed by John Ford. The scene showed Henry Fonda, as Wyatt Earp, walking away from the camera with Cathy Downs. Ford kept the camera on them as they walked toward a distant wooden building under construction on the outskirts of Tombstone, Arizona.

The narrator explained at great length some of the inner meanings revealed by the way Ford shot this scene, a fairly unimportant one. It typified Man's insignificance against the vastness of Nature, etc., etc., and so on.

It so happened that I wrote *My Darling Clementine*, and knew the reason Ford kept the camera on Fonda as he walked down that long dusty street. It was because he got a kick out of the way Fonda walked... arms hanging motionless, straight down, instead of with the usual swinging motion. It amused Ford to watch him... as simple as that.

While it's true I rose to my feet and set the narrator straight, I did not jump up and say what my sister infers that I said. I may have thought it, but I don't believe I said it. However, as Ford often said—or is quoted as having said—When there's a conflict between fact and legend—shoot the legend.

Winston Miller discusses a scene with Charlton Heston

197

Patsy, Esther Ralston and Laura LaPlante.

CHAPTER THIRTY THREE

A long time ago, when my years were merely three score and ten, a friend called me to ask if there was really life after seventy. I assured her that there was, but she seemed doubtful.

"I'm not even there yet," she complained, "but I find I can't do lots of things I used to do, and most of the things I can do, I don't enjoy any more."

"It all evens out," I tried to tell her, but she would have none of it.

She didn't mind the grey hairs, she said, that could be changed, but she resented the wrinkles. She didn't mind not being able to wear a bikini, she never liked them anyway, but she hated not being able to walk on four-inch spike heels, without tottering. Getting old was a damn bore, she said sadly, and she couldn't understand why the hell I was so damn cheerful about it. I knew she wouldn't listen to any comforting words, so I told her someone was at the door, and hung up. Then I sat down and wrote her this letter:

> Listen, you dope; seventy can be a wonderful age providing you're sound of limb and bank account, which, thanks be to God, you and I are. Seventy has many delights, the nicest of which is to be told you don't look it. If you keep your figure, more or less, and don't overdo the makeup, you can get away with an awful lot. In fact, it's possible at seventy to have more fun than when you were seventeen, because you're no longer inhibited or self-conscious or trying to "find yourself." If you haven't "found yourself" by the time you're seventy, you might as well stay lost.
>
> Also, if you've had your wits about you and noticed what's going on, you can no longer be taken by surprise by anything that happens. That gives you an edge on younger people who generally aren't prepared for the amazing things that can happen to them, and waste valuable time getting over their surprise.
>
> One thing I must warn you against, darling, beware the pit of nostalgia into which some of us fall. Nothing is the same as it was, and it's never going to be. . . including us. Change is the one thing you can depend on.
>
> So you can't do all the things you did when you were a mere chit of twenty, or thirty, or forty. . . who needs it? So you don't skippity hop up and down the stairs. . . who wants to! What you do is say, "Darling, run upstairs for me and bring me my reading glasses," or "There's a dear, bring your poor old grandmother another Scotch and soda," or "Officer, I honestly didn't see that No Parking sign. . . My, you're very young to be an

officer, aren't you? And would you mind terribly if I park here anyway? It's so far to walk." Believe me, you'll park there for as long as it takes you to do your shopping.

But best of all is knowing that you've made it this far when so many of us haven't.

Love and kisses, youngster,
Pat

I must just add one paragraph:

The day before Laura la Plante's birthday, I called her from Connecticut. Laura and I had been casual friends for many years, until working together in a picture with Edward Everett Horton. After being together on the set for six weeks, we became dear, close friends, and we have remained so. I love Laura; she is not only sweet and amiable, she is witty, with a dry humor that is unexpected in one so pretty. So I called to wish her a happy birthday. I knew it would be her sixtieth, as she was just two months older than I, and my sixtieth was looming on the horizon. As soon as she said hello, I sang out, Happy Birthday tomorrow, and many happy returns.

But Laura wasn't happy. In fact, she was despondent. She said she hadn't minded forty, really, although lots of women did; she had managed to ignore fifty—but SIXTY! That was really getting old.

"Just wait till you turn sixty, and see how you feel," she said. I didn't think I'd feel so much different than I did at fifty—nine, but she seemed determined to be unhappy about it, so I asked about the weather—warm out there, cold back here—said to give my love to Irving, her husband, and hung up.

The next morning, about seven o'clock California time, the phone rang and it was Laura, laughing so hard I couldn't understand her for the first few seconds. When she got control of herself, she told me what had happened. She had awakened early on her natal day to see Irving stretched out beside her, his head propped up on one hand, staring down at her. She was startled, even a little frightened, and said, "My goodness, what's the matter?"

Irving gave a little tsk, tsk, and said, "I never thought I'd find myself in bed with a sixty-year-old dame!" Laura burst out laughing and couldn't wait to call me, still laughing. And that was the end of her birthday trauma.

The Eighties, which I'm now in the midst of, aren't all that different from the Seventies, providing you can still get around under your own steam, and that you have all your marbles. Maybe you walk a little more slowly—but what's the hurry? Maybe you don't feel like having a night on the town—but it's the same town you've already had many a night on—so what's the big deal?

And there's one other terrific advantage; you don't have to pretend not to be tired when you are.

Before I sign off I'd like to clear up one point: once I stopped being a movie actress I never, ever, attempted a "comeback."

The Congressional Archive, which supposedly lists all the movies ever made, does not mention the two I made at the Whitman Bennett Studio in Yonkers, but does list a picture called *Quebec*, referring to it as my "comeback" attempt. Naturally, the film historians who write books about all us old silent movie stars, include *Quebec* in their lists of my films. And I'm sick and tired of it.

The simplest way to explain what happened is to quote a magazine article published back in the 60's. Here it is, verbatim:

In 1951 one day Mr. Deans called Miss Miller in New York from Montreal. He was there on a business trip and had run into a Hollywood movie company making *Quebec*, a costume film in color starring John Barrymore Jr. and set in the Canada of the 1930's. The director happened to be George Templeton, an old friend of Miss Miller's from Hollywood.

Mr. Templeton talked with her over the phone and asked her to come up and see some of the old crew whom she hadn't seen in years. She had such a good time at the reunion that she decided to go out on location with the crew. While there, Mr. Templeton asked her to do a bit in the film so he wouldn't have to go out and hire somebody. She agreed—but only on condition that it would just be for fun, as a favor: there was to be no mention of her name.

She was made up to look like an old peasant woman and given two lines of dialogue to speak in a French-Canadian accent. Later, back in New York, she was surprised to receive a check for her services.

'You can imagine my horror,' says Miss Miller, 'when, after the picture was released, I heard from a friend (friend?) that my name was in the cast, that I looked simply awful, and that the picture was one of the worst ever made. I never saw it, but I understand my friend's comment was an understatement.'

She shudders to think that some people might have taken it for granted that she did that tiny "bit" in Quebec as a comeback. . ."

As *Quebec* has been listed as my "comeback" in so many of the books by film historians, I'm afraid that quite a number of old movie buffs believe it. It's not really important enough to spend time denying it, but I'm going to anyway, for the sake of my vanity. There I was, made up to look old and peasanty, with gray hair and wrinkles, and the public was told it was *ME*. Gee whiz—I was only forty-seven years old. Even without false eyelashes and all those skin creams they advertise, no one in good health looks *that* old at forty-seven. If I had looked like that, the Mr. Deans mentioned in the article wouldn't have called me from Quebec, much less married me.

George Templeton, when I used to know him, was known as Dink Templeton, the great football player; he played on the Trojan All-American team during their finest years. After graduating, Dink went to work for one of the studios, and the last I had heard of him, he was an assistant director. Until he called from Montreal, I hadn't known he was a director. (If you can believe the reviews, there may have been some doubt about that).

One other thing I'd like to make clear-I didn't take a job away from another actress. They weren't going to send for anyone to do that bit, they were just going to let one of the bit players double in brass. Dink said if I wanted to do it as a gag, he'd put me down as a member of the company and I'd have my few nights in the hotel free. Why not? They'd taken the whole floor, and there were plenty of rooms. That's all I thought I was getting.

I was pleasantly surprised to receive a check in the mail, but, unpleasantly surprised to learn that my name was listed in the cast of characters, was actually advertised outside the theatre where *Quebec* was playing. I still can't figure out why. My name couldn't have had much value by that time, and it wasn't even a "cameo" role—it was just a two line bit.

Maybe my old friend Dink Templeton gave me a screen credit for old times' sake, or perhaps he thought he was doing me a favor. But let's just leave it out of the books from now on, shall we, fellas? Thanks.

On location with film critic and television personality Leonard Maltin at Universal Studios, 1988

200

Effingham Smith Deans

CHAPTER THIRTY FOUR

With the exception of my son, Timothy, my marriage to my handsome Scot was the greatest thing that ever happened to me. I never did get back to California, except for visits, but I went just about every other place you can think of and loved every minute of it. They were business trips, which didn't keep them from being fun; business combined with pleasure is a nice way to go. Our meeting, as I have reported, was something of a miracle; that we were never bored in each other's company might well be considered something of an additional miracle.

One of those trips is worth reporting, before I leave forever my tales of the ubiquitous movie industry.

A few years ago, before Lebanon was engulfed in a ghastly war, we stopped off in Beirut on our way from Hong Kong to London. Beirut was a lovely city, clean, prosperous, very European. That was the one thing that was rather disappointing; it was more French than Lebanese. The restaurants were excellent; mostly French cuisine, and who's to cavil at that? The men looked more British in their manner of dress, but the women all seemed to have been clothed by French coutouriers. Even the cab drivers, wearing cords and jeans, drove like French taxi drivers, depending largely on brakes and horns.

One morning, looking out the window of our magnificent hotel on the waterfront, I saw a group of *real* Lebanese in the little park across the street. The women wore veils and had bare midriffs; the men in flowing desert robes and caftans, wore tarboushes on their heads and looked just as I had always pictured them.

Grabbing my camera and calling to Eff to come along, I fairly ran down the marble stairs, not even waiting for the elevator. I dashed out to the street and crossed to the park against the traffic, praying that they would still be there.

They were still there—the lovely girls, the desert tribesmen—and the reflectors, the Movie camera and the crew. They were making a movie: a costume picture.

As my braw Scot was a sailor we bought a house in Stamford, Connecticut, right on Stamford Harbor, and when we weren't traveling we sailed on Long Island Sound. From boats to horses and back to boats; a neat parlay.

I don't want to sound mawkish, but I am truly grateful for my good fortune: to have lived in and been a part of Hollywood in its loveliest days, to have known and been friends with so many wonderful people, to have had a family whom I loved, a son I adore, and to have topped it all with my beautiful Effingham Smith Deans, called E.S. by his friends, and Eff darling by me.

But the day finally came when he had to leave. He went quietly, gently, with the courtliness with which he had lived, and he left me with this to remember:

The way to meet the Great Hereafter
Is with Faith in God—and laughter.

FINIS

Winston and Patricia Miller.

Visiting the "Hunchback" sets over 60 years later, Winston Miller became one of the top film writers in Hollywood, later producing television shows such as "The Virginian" for Universal Studios.

"The Hollywood Hotel" being torn down in 1957.

The HUNCHBACK of NOTRE DAME
UNIVERSAL SPECIAL PRODUCTION
6-5

THE FILMS OF PATSY RUTH MILLER

Compiled by:
Jeffrey Carrier

All information is this filmography was obtained from the American Film Institute Catalog.

Assistance in locating stills was supplied by Mary Corliss and her staff at the Museum of Modern Art Film Stills Archive, The New York Public Library at Lincoln Center, The British Film Institute, Kevin Brownlow, The University of Wyoming American Heritage Center, John E. Allen, Jerry Ollinger's Movie Material, Cinemabilia, Eddie Brandt's Saturday Matinee and Patsy Ruth Miller.

ONE A MINUTE
1921 A Thomas H. Ince Production
Released through Paramount
Cast
Jimmy Knight, Douglas MacLean; *Miriam Rogers*, Marian De Beck; *Jingo Pitts*, Victor Potel; *Silas Rogers*, Andrew Robson; *Grandma Knight*, Frances Raymond.
Credits
Jack Nelson (Director); Thomas H. Ince (Supervisor); Joseph Franklin Poland (Scenarist); Bern Cann (Photographer).
Synopsis
When Jimmy Knight (MacLean) undertakes to operate a drugstore left him by his father, he finds the store's methods old-fashioned, and a syndicate headed by Silas Rogers (Robson), offers to buy him out. But in order to impress Rogers' daughter, Miriam (De Beck), he determines to be a success by selling a cure-all medicine of his father's invention, and he begins by making several extraordinary cures. The syndicate members obtain a restraining warrant from Pure Food and Drug inspectors, and Jimmy is tried. But when the judge has a sudden attack of gastricitis, the medicine relieves him and Jimmy is declared innocent. He is later elected mayor and wins Miriam.
Reviews
"Thomas Ince has turned out a highly amusing comedy for Douglas MacLean in this Paramount feature, handled along farcical lines and at times running into almost burlesque." – *Variety*
Notes
Patsy Ruth Miller was an unbilled extra in two scenes, first as one of seven stenographers and second, as a telephone operator. She was given a brief close-up in the second scene.

CAMILLE
1921 A Nazimova Production
Released through Metro Pictures
Cast
Camille/Marguerite Gautier, Nazimova; *Armand Duval*, Rudolph Valentino; *Count De Varville*, Arthur Hoyt; *Prudence*, Zeffie Tillbury; *Gaston*, Rex Cherryman; *Duke*, Edward Connelly; *Nichette*, Patsy Ruth Miller; *Olimpe*, Consuelo Flowerton; *Monsieur Duval*, William Orlamond.
Credits
Ray C. Smallwood (Director); Nazimova (Producer); June Mathis (Scenarist); Rudolph Bergquist (Photographer); Natasha Rambova (Art Director).
Synopsis
Armond Duval, a young and unsophisticated law student, falls passionately in love with Marguerite Gautier (Nazimova), known as Camille, a notorious Parisian courtesan. Armand forsakes his family and career. Marguerite abandons her friends for him, and they pass the days happily in a country retreat, but they soon find themselves without money. Armond arranges for Marguerite to receive his small legacy and, unknown to him, Marguerite plans to sell all her possessions. Armand's father learns of the situation and determines to save the family name from disgrace. He persuades Marguerite to give up Armand, and she reverts to her former life of debauchery. Visiting a gambling house, she encounters Armand, believing himself abandoned for the wealth of Count de Varville, whom Marguerite has been seen with, he denounces her before the crowd and she returns to her home ill and alone. Marguerite soon dies alone in her room, clasping Armand's only gift, a copy of *Manon Lescaut*.
Reviews
"Before and throughout the unfolding of the picture, Nazimova had disclosed the finest acting with which the silver screen has been graced. Instead of the sinuous, clinging Nazimova, she appeared an actress almost new-born for the part. The surrounding company is excellent... 'Camille' will, it is safe to assume, attain wide popularity, holding as it does all the elements of success, augmented by the mastery and superb artistry of Nazimova." – *Variety*

"Nazimova's portrayal is... at times exceedingly interesting, Rudolph Valentino... does excellently and at times takes the picture away from the star. The settings, designed by Natacha Rambova, are very unusual and exceedingly worthwhile. Should bring in a tremendous lot of money at the box office." – *Wid's Daily (Film Daily)*
Notes
In her first billed role, Patsy Ruth Miller attracted little critical attention as Camille's shop girl friend, whose romance with Gaston provided the film with a minor sub-plot, but appearing in a Nazimova production was an auspicious beginning for her career, as Nazimova's films were quality productions and attracted a lot of attention. The film still survives and is often screened at universities where Rambova's art deco interiors still fascinate.

207

HANDLE WITH CARE
1922 A Rockett Production
Distributed by Associated Producers
Cast
Jeanne Lee, Grace Darmond; *Ned Picard*, Harry Myers; *Phil Burnham*, James Morrison; *David Norris*, Landers Stevens; *Peter Carter*, William Austin; *MacCullough*, William Courtleigh; *Marian*, Patsy Ruth Miller.
Credits
Philip Rosen (Director); Al Rockett, Ray Rockett (Producers); Will M. Ritchie (Scenarist); Philip Hurn (Photographer).
Synopsis
Although five of her suitors declare they would die for her, Jeanne Lee (Darmond) marries young lawyer David Norris (Stevens). Two years later, absorbed in an important law suit, David forgets their wedding anniversary, and when reprimanded for his neglect, he agrees to give Jeanne a divorce if one of her former suitors will elope with her. Jeanne picks up Phil Burnham (Morrison) on his morning walk and recalls old times, but when asked to elope, he confesses to being engaged. Ned Picard (Myers), at first staggered by her proposition, consents, but then accepts David's offer of $10,000 to call it off. Jeanne is prepared to relent until she sees David kissing Marion (Miller), his pretty ward. David later follows Jeanne to the office of Peter Carter (Austin), and author of books on marriage who declares his love for her, but when threatened by David with a gun, his cowardly cries for mercy prove him unworthy. MacCullough, the last of her ex-suitors, almost carries Jeanne off but proves to be Marion's new husband and brings about a reunion of Jeanne and David.
Reviews
"... better than the ordinary run of program features. The locations and the sets are particularly good and the photography splendid." – *Variety*
Notes
Handle With Care was an ordinary feature in every respect; even the cast was mostly an undistinguished one, with the possible exception of Harry Myers, whose best role as Charlie Chaplin's inebriated benefactor in *City Lights* was still ten years away.

WHERE IS MY WANDERING BOY TONIGHT?
1922 A B.F. Zeidman Production
Distributed by Equity Pictures
Cast
Garry Beecher, Cullen Landis; *Silas Rudge*, Carl Stockdale; *Veronica Tyler*, Kathleen Key; *Martha Beecher*, Virginia True Boardman; *Lorna Owens*, Patsy Ruth Miller; *Stewart Kilmer*, Ben Deeley; *R. Sylvester Jones*, Clarence Badger, Jr.
Credits
James P. Hogan, Millard Webb (Directors); B.F. Zeidman (Producer); Gerald C. Duffy (Story, Scenario); David Abel (Photographer); Henry Scott Ramsey (Art Direction).
Synopsis
Garry Beecher, forgetting his mother and sweetheart, Lorna (Miller), falls in love with Veronica (Key), a chorus girl, and heads for the city. Finding her with a millionaire, he returns home and robs his former employer, then returns to Veronica and begins a career of reckless spending. When he is unable to pay for a diamond necklace, Garry is threatened with arrest and betrayed by Veronica; he is convicted of grand larceny and sentenced to ten years' imprisonment. To help mend the broken heart of Garry's mother, Lorna sends her letters ostensibly written by him.
In prison, Garry saves the warden from an attack by one of the prisoners, but when a prison break is planned, Garry follows the escaping prisoners aboard a speeding locomotive and rescues the warden just as a freight train is sighted coming in the opposite direction. Grateful for having his life saved, the warden gives Garry a full pardon. He returns to the open arms of his mother and his faithful sweetheart, Lorna.
Reviews
"As a feature, it isn't quite in the special class, although it will prove a fairly entertaining picture... Its principle trouble at present is that it is too long. With judicious cutting, the value will be enhanced 50 percent. One thing the producers did do was to pick a very fair cast. Cullen Landis is a clever juvenile. Ruth 'Patsy' Miller... was the little country miss delightfully."
– *Variety*

"'Mother Love' theme dominates, but enough sure-fire hokum, including a runaway engine, to make it a box office bet. Generally the cast is good and the types are excellent." – *Film Daily*
Notes
Only in her third film, Patsy was moving up the cast list and was finally being noticed by the major critics. By the time of this film's release, she had already signed with Goldwyn.

WATCH YOUR STEP
1922 A Goldwyn Picture
Cast
Elmer Slocum, Cullen Landis; *Margaret Andrews,* Patsy Ruth Miller; *Russ Weaver,* Bert Woodruff; *Lark Andrews,* George Pierce; *Lon Kimball,* Raymond Cannon; *Jennifer Kimball,* Gus Leonard; *Constable,* Henry Rattenbury; *Henry Slocum,* John Cossar; *Ky Wilson,* Joel Day; *Detective Ryan,* L.J. O'Connor; *Mrs. Spivey,* Lillian Sylvester; *Lote Spivey,* L.H. King; *Mrs. Andrews,* Cordelia Callahan; *Mrs. Weaver,* Alberta Lee
Credits
William Beaudine (Director); Julien Josephson (Story/Scenario); John J. Mescall (Photographer)
Synopsis
Elmer Slocum has just served a jail sentence for speeding, and on his first day out, he encounters a physician whose car has broken down, and he offers to drive him to his waiting patient. He is pursued by motorcops for speeding, wrecks his car in a closed street, and knocks down and believes he has killed a policeman.
He secretly boards a freight train and makes his way to a small town in Iowa where he meets Margaret Andrews (Miller), daughter of the town's richest citizen, and is given a job by storekeeper Russ Weaver. But Margaret's father and her suitor, Lon Kimball (Cannon) are suspicious of him, and when a detective hired by his own father finds him, Lon is glad to be rid of his rival. But the detective has good news: the policeman is alive, and Elmer is free to accept the attentions of Margaret.
Reviews
"Every once in a while a motion picture comedy bobs up which is so joyous and naturally gay that it makes photoplay going less of a duty and more of a pleasure. Of such is *Watch Your Step.*" – *New York Herald*

"...an all around agreeable piece. Patsy Ruth Miller is a pretty and pleasing leading lady." – *Film Daily*
Notes
As part of their No Star Policy, which Goldwyn began in 1922, several young screen players were signed and put into films in which no one received star billing. These were generally quiet, gentle films which relied on their charm and good production values to attract an audience. Colleen Moore and Cullen Landis were also signed under that policy. It didn't promote stardom, however, but did their careers no harm.

THE FIGHTING STREAK
1922 A Fox Picture
Cast
Andrew Lanning, Tom Mix; *Ann Withero,* Patsy Ruth Miller; *Charles Merchant,* Gerald Pring; *Jasper Lanning,* Al Fremont; *Bill Dozier,* Sidney Jordan; *Hal Dozier,* Bert Sprotte; *Chuck Heath,* Robert Fleming
Credits
Arthur Rosen (Director/Scenario); Dan Clark (Photographer)
Synopsis
Andy Lanning (Mix), a peace-loving blacksmith, rescues Ann (Miller), the fiancee of Charles Merchant (Pring), from a run-away train. When the town bully teases Andy and picks a fight with him, Andy knocks him unconscious and, thinking he has killed him rides into the hills where he joins a band of outlaws. Merchant, jealous of Ann's admiration of Andy, bribes the sheriff to go in search of Andy and kill him. The two have a confrontation, and the sheriff is killed, but Andy later saves the new sheriff's life and forces him to listen to his story.
Meanwhile, Ann, who has broken off her engagement with Merchant, engages a lawyer to defend Andy, and she returns to find her awaiting him.
Reviews
"Lovers of western stuff and Mix fans will relish this picture, which contains some thrills, although not the best of the later Mix releases by a long shot. Patsy Ruth Miller... turned in a capable performance, registering lightly in the conventional ingenue role." – *Variety*

"The development is somewhat anti-climatic, but the director has managed to hold the interest pretty well throughout. The romance is rather slight, but there is the usual number of fights and daring escapes with one rescue getting the picture off to a fairly exciting start." – *Film Daily*
Notes
Westerns were considered good training ground for young, up-and-coming actresses at that time, and appearing opposite Mix increased her popularity by introducing her to the fans of action films. Patsy saw quite a bit of action herself while making the picture as she did much of her own stuntwork. She made two other westerns, another with Mix, and one with Hoot Gibson, but after a sprained ankle, several bruises, and having to share love scenes with a horse, she was glad to leave the sagebrush behind.

FOR BIG STAKES
1922 A Fox Picture
Cast
"Clean-Up" Sudden, Tom Mix; *Dorothy Clark,* Patsy Ruth Miller; *Scott Mason,* Sid Jordon; *Rowell Clark,* Bert Sprotte; *Roman Valdez,* Joe Harris; *Sheriff Blaisdell,* Al Fremont; *Tin Horn Johnnie,* Earl Simpson; *Tony, a horse,* himself.
Credits
Lynn Reynolds (Director/Story); Ralph Spence (Titles/Film Editor); Dan Clark (Photographer).
Synopsis
"Clean-Up" Sudden (Mix), a stranger in town, incurs the wrath of Scott Mason (Jordon) and wins the love of Dorothy Clark (Miller) while punishing a crooked sheriff and cleaning up the ranch of Rowell Clark (Sprotte). Dorothy's father, Mason ties Dorothy to a tree, sets fire to the ranch, but is unable to escape in time and perishes in the fire. "Clean-Up" rescues the girl, though he cannot save the buildings, and reveals himself as the rightful owner of the ranch.
Reviews
"...provides plenty of action of the sort that Mix admirers like." —*Film Daily*

"Supporting Mix is Patsy Ruth Miller, a youthful miss rapidly coming to the fore as an ingenue leading woman. She was a good selection to provide the necessary interest in the love angle of the story." —*Variety*

TRIMMED
1922 A Universal Picture
Cast
Dale Garland, Hoot Gibson; *Alice Millard,* Patsy Ruth Miller; *John Millard,* Alfred Hollingsworth; *Young Bill Young,* Fred Kohler; *Nebo Slayter,* Otto Hoffman; *Judge William Dandridge,* Dick La Reno; *Lem Fyfer,* R. Hugh Sutherland.
Credits
Harry Pollard (Director); Arthur F. Statter, Wallace Clifton (Scenario); Sol Polito (Photographer).
Synopsis
Returning from service in the AEF, Dale Garland (Gibson), is given a rousing reception by his townsmen. County political boss Nebo Slayter (Hoffman), persuades the community to nominate Dale for sheriff —thinking he can easily manipulate him —against John Millard (Hollingsworth), the incumbent, who refuses political compromises. Dale easily wins and pledges to give the community an honest deal. Millard's daughter, Alice (Miller), who is Dale's childhood sweetheart, learns of Slayter's dishonest schemes and sees his men murder a moonshiner whom they had been furnishing protection. She informs Dale, who tracks down the slayers and arrests them after a battle. Meanwhile, the deputies arrest the slain man's accomplices, who implicate the political ring, and Dale jails them all. His honesty wins Alice's love.
Reviews
"...will fulfill all the demands of the admirer of westerns and gain some more friends of the star (Gibson)." —*Film Daily*
Notes
The most distinguished name associated with this picture is Sol Polito, whose fine reputation as a photographer is due mainly to his outstanding black and white work for Warner Brothers during the 30s and 40s.

REMEMBRANCE
1922 A Goldwyn Picture
Cast
John P. Grout, Claude Gillingwater; *Mrs. Grout,* Kate Lester; *Mab,* Patsy Ruth Miller; *Seth Smith,* Cullen Landis; *George Cartier,* Max Davidson; *Beatrice,* Esther Ralston; *J.P. Grout, Jr.,* Richard Tucker; *Ethelwood Grout,* Dana Todd; *Julia,* Nell Craig, *Mrs. Frish,* Helen Hayward.
Credits
Rupert Hughes (Director/Screenplay); Cedric Gibbons (Art Director); Norbert Brodin (Photographer).
Synopsis
John P. Grout (Gillingwater) collapses under the strain of trying to make enough money to keep his greedy family happy. Only his favorite daughter, Mab (Miller), remains unimpressed by possessions and social status. She falls in love with Seth Smith (Landis), a clerk in her father's department store.
While Grout hovers near death, unable to supply the family with money, they begin to change their attitude. He recovers in time to save himself from financial ruin, the family reduces its demands on him, and Seth becomes a successful businessman.

210

Reviews

"It lacks the keenly pictorial treatment with which Mr. Hughes has vivified obvious stories before. Perhaps he had not yet got his hand in as a director, as well as an author. Certainly no discriminating director would permit, or induce, such capable players as Claude Gillingwater and Kate Lester to overact as they frequently do." – *The New York Times*

"The author has written a very human story and in transferring it to the screen, has succeeded in bringing out the human side of it through a deft combination of humor and pathos that brings laughs and possibly tears, in a true to life fashion." – *Film Daily*

"The support of this picture is a delight, especially the work of Patsy Ruth Miller as the younger daughter, and Cullen Landis as the clerk." – *Variety*

Notes

This was Patsy's third and last film with Cullen Landis, a popular juvenile lead who never developed into a major star. He does have the distinction of appearing in the first all-talking film, The Lights of New York, in 1928.

FORTUNE'S MASK
1922 A Vitagraph Picture

Cast
Ramon Olivarra, alias Dicky Maloney: Earle Williams, *Pasa Ortiz:* Patsy Ruth Miller, *Losada:* Henry Herbert, *General Pilar:* Milton Ross, *Madame Ortiz:* Eugenie Ford, *Vicenti:* Arthur Travers, *Esperacion:* Frank Whitson, *Chief of Police:* Oliver Hardy, *Captain Cronin:* William McCall

Credits
Robert Ensminger (Director), C. Graham Baker (Scenario), Steve Smith (Photographer)

Synopsis
Dicky Maloney, an Irish newcomer to a Central American town, wins the hearts of the people and the love of Pasa Ortiz with his charm and daring deeds against the army. He finally reveals himself as the son of a deposed president, successfully leads a revolution, and becomes president himself.

Reviews
"On the screen the story lacks speed, and Williams seems a little too heavy and mature for the role of the hero, but otherwise it is good picture material. Patsy Ruth Miller is cute and manages to make much of the little Spanish girl." – *Variety*

Notes
Earle Williams, the film's star, was nearing the end of his prime as a matinee idol, which he had been since the early 1910's.

OMAR THE TENTMAKER
1922 A Richard Wally Tully Production
Released through First National

Cast
Omar: Guy Bates Post, *Shireen:* Virginia Browne Faire, *Nizam ul Mulk:* Nigel De Brulier, *The Shah of Shahs:* Noah Beery, *Shah's Mother:* Rose Dione, *Little Shireen:* Patsy Ruth Miller, *Hassan:* Douglas Gerrard, *The Christian Crusader:* Maurice "Lefty" Flynn, *Little Mahniss:* Will Jim Hatton, *Imon Mowattak,* Boris Karloff, *Omar's Father:* Edward M. Kimball, *The Executioner:* Walter Long

Credits
James Young (Director), Richard Walton Tully (Adaption), Wilfred Buckland (Art Director), George Benoit (Photographer)

Synopsis
The student Omar (Post) loves and secretly marries Shireen (Faire), but she is taken away by the Shah of Shahs to join his household. For spurning the Shah, Shireen is thrown into a dungeon, then sold into slavery when her child is born.
Years pass. Omar's boyhood friends, Nizam and Hassan (De Brulier and Gerrard), have become Grand Vizier and Governor respectively, and Omar has brought up Little Shireen (Miller), whom he believes to be the daughter of the Shah (Beery). When Omar is arrested and tortured for sheltering a Christian crusader (Flynn), who has also fallen in love with Little Shireen, Nizam frees Omar, punishes Hassan for ordering the torture, and reunites Shireen with Omar and their daughter.

Reviews
"There are sufficient elements in 'Omar' to make it sure fire as a box office picture in the general release way. It may not be unwise to predict that 'Omar' will shoot the gross ahead of the general release for this is a spectacle of a film production as well as holding a story set in curious climes for the native American." – *Variety*

"Despite its excessive gorgeousness in costumes and trappings, it is just a movie with a Persian background." – *Film Daily*

Notes
After eight consecutive films in which she was featured, she was relegated to a supporting role in this screen adaption of the popular Broadway play, but by the time of the picture's release, she had already completed another film, in which she had the leading female role, and was preparing for another.

THE GIRL I LOVED
1923 A Charles Ray Production
Distributed by United Artists
Cast
John Middleton, Charles Ray; *Mary*, Patsy Ruth Miller; *Willy Brown*, Ramsey Wallace; *Mother Middleton*, Edythe Chapman; *Neighbor Silas Gregg*, William Courtwright; *Betty Short*, Charlotte Woods; *Neighbor Perkins*, Gus Leonard; *Hired Man*, F. B. Phillips; *Minister*, Lon Poff; *Hiram Lang*, Jess Herring; *Ruth Land*, Ruth Bolgiano; *Organist*, George F. Marion.
Credits
Joseph De Grasse (Director); Harry L. Decker (Film Continuity); Edward Withers (Titles); Albert Ray (Adaption); George Rizard (Photography); George Meehan (Assistant Photographer); Robert Ellis (Art Direction); Stanley Partridge (Costumes); Edward Withers (Special Effects).
Synopsis
An only child, John (Ray) first resents Mary (Miller) an orphan adopted by his mother (Chapman), then gradually softens, feels brotherly affection, and finally falls in love with her. But before John can bring himself to propose to Mary, she announces her engagement to Willy Brown (Wallace). With much difficulty, John accepts his loss, keeps it to himself, and gives the bride away to Willy.
Reviews
"A typical Charles Ray production with Ray doing his country lad, which is best. It is quite as good as anything he has done from a standpoint of sentiment." – *Variety*

"(Charles Ray) is a capable young actor, but he seems to have underrated his age before the camera when he plays the first part of the picture. He goes through all the antics employed by a spoiled girl, and obviously this particular first part ought to be taken by a boy much younger than Ray can make himself, even on the screen." – *The New York Times*

"The most beautiful, romantic, poignant and harrowing picture we ever saw was *The Girl I Loved*. The performance of Charles Ray in that was inspired, and since then, we can think of only one film which has equalled it – that of Betty Bronson in Peter Pan." – *The New York Tribune* (March, 1925)
Notes
Based on James Whitcomb Riley's autobiographical poem, only one print is known to have survived of The Girl I Loved, an edited version housed in a Brussels Archive. Several scenes are missing, including a dramatic dream sequence in which John kills his rival, shouting "You've stolen the girl I loved!" And the subtitles are a mixture of different languages, but even in that inferior form, it still has great beauty and charm.

SOULS FOR SALE
1923 A Goldwyn Picture
Cast
Remember Steddon, Eleanor Boardman; *Frank Claymore*, Richard Dix; *Robina Teele*, Mae Busch; *Leva Lemaire*, Barbara LaMarr; *Tom Holby*, Frank Mayo; *Owen Scudder*, Lew Cody; *Jimmy Leland*, Arthur Hoyt; *Lady Jane*, Aileen Pringle; *Velma Slade*, Eve Southern; *Pinky*, William Haines; As Themselves: T. Roy Barnes, Barbara Bedford, Hobart Bosworth, Charles Chaplin, Chester Conklin, Robert Edeson, Claude Gillingwater, Dagmar Godowsky, Raymond Griffith, Elaine Hammerstein, Alice Lake, Bessie Love, June Mathis, Patsy Ruth Miller, Marshal Neilan, Fred Niblo, Anna Q. Nilsson, ZaSu Pitts, Milton Sills, Anita Stewart, Erich von Stroheim, Blanche Sweet, Florence Vidor, King Vidor, Johnnie Walker, George Walsh, Kathlyn Williams, Claire Windsor.
Credits
Rupert Hughes (Director/Producer/Adaptor); John Mescall (Photographer).
Synopsis
Remember Steddon (Boardman), the daughter of a small town minister, married Owen Scudder (Cody), but has second thoughts when their train crosses the desert on the wedding night, and she gets off quietly when it stops for water. A movie company on location finds her a few days later in poor condition and takes her to Hollywood. Because she has heard bad things about movie people, she at first rejects the urgings of director Frank Claymore (Dix) and star Tom Colby (Mayo) to work in motion pictures, but she eventually makes the rounds of the studios (Famous Players-Lasky, Metro, Fox, Robertson-Cole, Pickford-Fairbanks, and Goldwyn) in search of a job, and sees many well-known directors and actors at work, including Stroheim, Chaplin, Blanche Sweet and Patsy Ruth Miller.
She finally gets her chance from Claymore, works hard, and steadily rises to fame. Claymore and Holby become rivals for her affections. Meanwhile,

Scudder, who has been searching for her, comes to Hollywood to assert his marital claims, bringing about the climax in which there is an enormous fire. Scudder is killed by a wind machine he has aimed at Claymore, and Remember chooses Claymore over Holby.

Reviews

"A cleanup for the box office. Movie fans will eat it up. Most of the shining lights of Hollywood, including Chaplin, [have] bits..." – *Film Daily*

"Rupert Hughes as a director has topped everything he ever did, even as an author, in this picture. It is also a remarkable piece of propaganda for Hollywood, the picture industry as a whole, and its clean-living acting people as well." – *Variety*

Notes

Miss Miller doesn't include this in her list of films, but since she did appear in it, if even for a few seconds as herself, it is worthy of inclusion in this filmography. The gruesome death of Scudder was based on an incident which occurred during the filming of *Remembrance*. While a night scene was being filmed Patsy apparently took a step in the wrong direction and narrowly escaped being hit by the huge blade of a wind machine.

THE HUNCHBACK OF NOTRE DAME
1923 A Universal - Jewel Picture

Cast

Quasimodo, Lon Chaney; *Esmeralda*, Patsy Ruth Miller; *Clopin*, Ernest Torrence; *Phoebus*, Norman Kerry; *Jehan*, Brandon Hurst; *Gringoire*, Raymond Hatton; *Dom Claude*, Nigel De Brulier; *Louis XI*, Tully Marshall; *Madame de Gondelaurier*, Kate Lester; *Godule*, Gladys Brockwell; *Marie Queen of the Gypsies*, Eulalie Jensen; *Monsieur Neufchatel*, Harry Van Meter; *Fleur de Lys*, Winifred Bryson; *Judge of Court*, John Cossar

Credits

Wallace Worsley (Director); Jack Sullivan, William Wyler (Assistant Directors); Edward T. Loew (Scenario); Perley Poore Sheehan (Adaption); Robert Newhard (Photographer); Tony Kornman (Additional Photography); E. E. Sheeley, Sydney Ullman (Art Direction); Maurice Pivan, Edward Curtis (Film Editors)

Synopsis

Quasimodo, the inarticulate, deformed bellringer of Notre Dame Cathedral (Chaney), is prevailed upon by Jehan (Hurst), the Arch-Deacon's evil brother, to kidnap the fair Esmeralda (Miller), the ward of Clopin, King of the Beggars (Torrence). She is rescued by the dashing Phoebus, Captain of the King's Guard (Kerry) and taken under his wing. Quasimodo is sentenced to be whipped in the public square, and while he is suffering, Esmeralda pities him and gives him a drink of water.

The romance between Phoebus and Esmeralda attracts the attention of Jehan, who, raging with jealousy and lust for Esmeralda, stabs Phoebus while he and Esmeralda are alone together in a garden. Esmeralda is blamed and is sentenced to die. She is to be hanged and Quasimodo, watching from the cathedral tower, recognized the girl who befriended him, and swings down on a rope and rescues her. She is given refuge in the cathedral and watched over by Quasimodo.

Fearing that she will be taken from the Cathedral and hanged, Clopin and his army of beggars, storm Notre Dame to rescue her. Quasimodo, single-handed, attacks the angry mob with streams of molten lead poured from the roof. Phoebus, who was not killed but only wounded by the stabbing, rides with his men to save the Cathedral and Esmeralda. But while Quasimodo was fighting off the attackers below, the evil Jehan was attempting to carry off Esmeralda. The deformed bellringer discovers just in time and throws him from the tower but not before being fatally stabbed. Phoebus and Esmeralda are reunited and Quasimodo, watching them leave, approving of their love, rings the bells, announcing his own death and the happiness of the two lovers.

Reviews

"A picture as beautiful, as profoundly stirring as anything that the erratic movie industry has ever produced... An indisputably fine achievement. Patsy Ruth Miller is a personable heroine—evincing a power of emotion that is genuine and well controlled." – *The New York Herald*

"One of the really big pictures of the year—for that matter, of many years, with Chaney giving a remarkable performance. Ernest Torrence also gives a fine performance and Patsy Ruth Miller is splendid." – *Film Daily*

"Patsy Ruth Miller is Esmeralda, a sweetly pretty girl carrying her troubles nicely enough for the heavy work thrust upon her and with the absence of heavy emoting not so noticeable through her opposites not being always as emotional as they should have been either. *The Hunchback of Notre Dame* is a two-hour nightmare. It is murderous, hideous and repulsive. No children can stand its morbid scenes, and there are likely but few parents seeing it first who will permit their young to see it afterward." – *Variety*

"Naturally there is much in this picture which is not pleasant, (but) it is, however, a strong production, on which no pains or money have been spared

to depict the seamy side of old Paris. Patsy Ruth Miller has the part of Esmeralda, a truly pretty, chubby girl whose only fault is the over-decorating of her upper lip, which was too perfectly 'bowed.' However, her acting is unusually good in the many difficult scenes in which she has to appear."
– *The New York Times*

Notes
Originally 12 reels in length, its running time was shortened after its initial roadshow release (it still ran 120 minutes), one of the casualties of the cuts being Ernest Torrence, whose role of the beggar King Clopin, considered by many to be as great as Chaney's, was shortened.
The first version of Victor Hugo's novel was made in 1915 with Theda Bara. It lacked the spectacle and superior production values of the Chaney version, which is generally considered the definitive screen adaption of the novel. It has since been re-made three times: in 1939 by RKO with Charles Laughton and Maureen O'Hara, by Allied Artists in 1957 with Anthony Quinn and Gina Lollobrigida and as a made for television movie with Anthony Hopkins and Lesley-Anne Down in 1982.

THE DRIVIN' FOOL
1923 A Regent Picture
Distributed by W.W. Hodkinson Corporation
Cast
Hal Locke, Wally Van; *Sylvia Moorehead,* Patsy Ruth Miller; *John Moorehead,* Alec B. Francis; *Henry Locke,* Wilton Taylor; *Richard Brownlee,* Ramsey Wallace; *Howard Grayson,* Wilfred North; *Horatio Jackson Lee St. Albans,* Jesse J. Aldriche; *John Lawson,* Kenneth R. Bush.
Credits
Robert J. Thornby (Director); Walter Anthony (Titles); H.H. Van Loan (Adaption); A.J. Stout, Steve Rounds (Photographers); Emile De Ruelle (Assistant Director).
Synopsis
Having an appointment with Sylvia Moorehead (Miller), his fiancee, at 8 p.m., Hal Locke (Van) drives 60 miles an hour to his home in San Francisco, where he has just enough time to shower and change into his dinner jacket. Sylvia is about to bemoan his tardiness when he arrives, punctual to the dot. A generally worthless scamp, Hal's sole asset is his love for lovely Sylvia. The only he can do is drive his roadster beyond the speed limit, which he often does. His father (Taylor) is an official of the Golden Gate Packing Company, and his hope that Hal will settle down and work for the company dwindles day by day. The New York firm of Grayson and Company are jealous of the successful California company, and through a techicality, scheme to take it over. They hold a contract, which stipulates if a check for $500,000 is not delivered to them on a certain date, by noon, they will assume control of the company. A letter containing the check is supposed to have been mailed in time, but a representative for the New York firm, in San Francisco, delays the mailing until it is too late for the letter to arrive in time. On the day the letter is finally to be mailed, the entire railroad system is paralyzed from coast to coast (there was no air mail in those days). The hitherto worthless Hap steps in and offers to deliver the check to the Wall Street firm by driving across the country. He sets off immediately, and his father, fiancee and doubtful father-in-law to be, keep track of his progress and plot his course on a map. He overcomes a series of obstacles and arrives in New York on the appointed day just before noon. He finds the building and delivers the check just as the clock strikes twelve; after which a policeman arrests him for breaking most of the New York speed laws.
Reviews
"To those who delight in speeding automobiles, with agreeable suspense, plenty of fair comedy, in spite of impossible incidents, *The Drivin' Fool* will prove entertaining... A very good film of its kind, and one filled with fun."
– *The New York Times*

"A lively entertainment that goes along at a great pace... a sure-fire number that has pep and good humor." – *Film Daily*

NAME THE MAN
1924 A Goldwyn Picture
Cast
Bessie Collister, Mae Busch; *Victor Stowell,* Conrad Nagel; *Fenella Stanley,* Patsy Ruth Miller; *Alick Gell,* Creighton Hale; *Christian Stowell,* Hobart Bosworth; *Isabelle,* Aileen Pringle; *Governor Stanley,* Winter Hall; *Dan Collister,* De Witt Jennings; *Lisa Collister,* Evelyn Selbie; *Constable Cain,* Mark Fenton; *Coroner,* Cecil Holland; *Sharf,* Lucien Littlefield; *Taubman,* William Orlamond.
Credits
Victor Seastrom (Director); June Mathis (Editing Director); Paul Bern (Scenario); Charles Van Enger (Photographer).
Synopsis
Victor Stowell (Nagel), son of the Deemster of the Isle of Man, is engaged to Fenella Stanley (Miller). He becomes involved in an intrigue with local girl

Bessie Collister (Busch), becomes the Deemster upon his father's death, and is forced to try Bessie for killing her illegitimate child. When Bessie refuses to name the father of the baby, Fenella and Alick Gell (Hale), who loves Bessie, guess that it is Victor. Bessie is condemned to die, but Victor helps her to escape to meet and marry Alick. He then confesses all, serves a jail sentence, and marries Fenella at the expiration of the term.

Reviews

"Tremendous drama. Magnificently produced. Great entertainment for women patrons. Seastrom's direction is superb. Keep your eye on Seastrom. He is liable to do some things that will make him one of the most important directors in this country. Patsy Ruth Miller, of The Hunchback fame, has a saccharine role." – *Film Daily*

"Almost safe to predict this early in 1924 that when the year ends, this picture is going to be marked up among the screen achievements of the period." – *Variety*

Notes

This was the first American film directed by Swedish director Victor Seastrom, who went on to become one of the most important directors of the 1920's, bringing such films as *He Who Gets Slapped*, *The Tower of Lies*, *The Scarlet Letter*, *The Divine Woman* and *The Wind* to the screen before he returned to his native country. The role of Victor Stowell was first given to Joseph Schildkraut, but after only a few days of filming, he was replaced by Conrad Nagel.

MY MAN
1924 A Vitagraph Picture

Cast

Sledge, Dustin Farnum; *Molly Marley*, Patsy Ruth Miller; *Dicky Reynolds*, Niles Welch; *Fern Burbank*, Margaret Landis; *Bert Glider*, ?George Webb; *Henry Peters*, William Norris; *Mrs. Peters*, Edith Yorke; *Jessie Peters*, Violet Palmer; *Christopher Marley*, Sidney De Gray

Credits

David Smith (Director); Donald Buchanan (Scenario); Steven Smith, Jr. (Photographer)

Synopsis

A political boss named Sledge (Farnum) meets the daughter (Miller) of a wealthy opponent (De Gray). Sledge determines to win Molly although she is already engaged to Bert Glider (Webb), a lounge lizard intending to exploit Molly for her money. Unable to convince Molly of Glider's nefarious motives, Sledge kidnaps her on her wedding day and contrives to make it appear that Mr. Marley has lost all his investments. Glider cancels his marriage plans, Sledge returns Marley's money to him, and marries Molly himself.

Reviews

"The picture is a hackneyed familiar, not particularly well cast, with Patsy Ruth Miller running away with whatever acting honors there were." – *Variety*

"With a modest and brief title such as *My Man*, one anticipates an afternoon or evening with the Apaches in the Paris Underworld and that the orchestra will be constantly dwelling on the bars of *Mon Homme*. But from the instant the film presentation strikes the screen, it is obvious that the time is going to be spent amid transportation quarrels in Ringville, as one is so informed through the medium of verbose and trite subtitles." – *The New York Times*

"Rather good direction and interesting players help cover up conventional 'Give me your daughter or I'll ruin you' plot." – *Film Daily*

THE YANKEE CONSUL
1924 A Douglas MacLean Production
Distributed by Associated Exhibitors

Cast

Dudley Ainsworth, Douglas MacLean; *Margarita*, Patsy Ruth Miller; *Jack Mottell*, Arthur Stuart Hull; *Leopoldo*, Stanhope Wheatcroft; *Donna Theresa*, Eulalie Jensen; *Purser of S.S. President*, L.C. Shumway; *John J. Doyle, Secret service Agent*, Fred Kelsey; *Don Rafael Doschado*, George Periolat; *Admiral Rutledge, USN*, Eric Mayne; *Servent*, Bert Hadley

Credits

James Horne (Director); Raymond Cannon (Scenario); Raymond Griffith, Lewis Milestone (Adaption); Max DuPont (Photographer); George W. Crane (Film Editor)

Synopsis

Last minute confusion causes travel agent Dudley Ainsworth (MacLean) to pose as Abijah Boos, American Consul to a South American country. On a passenger ship bound for Rio, he meets Margarita Carrosa (Miller) and becomes involved in a conspiracy involving Margarita and some thieves intent upon stealing a chest of gold from the consulate in Rio. Landing in Rio, Ainsworth notifies the US Navy, then rushes to a castle

215

outside the city where Margarita is being held captive. He dashingly rescues Margarita, captures the thieves, greets the summoned Admiral (Mayne), who arrives accompanied by the real Yankee Consul (Pertolat), and finds out that the adventure was all a joke perpetrated by his friends.

Reviews

"One of the funniest pictures it has been our pleasure to see in some time. Douglas MacLean, who officiates in the leading character, keeps on a hop, skip and a jump throughout this picture, which is equipped with fine interior sets and startlingly beautiful exteriors. Apparently no cost has been spared to make the scenes worthy of the comedy. There is a great, wide stairway, rooms large enough for Alan Dwan, fascinating views of an old chateau, and a wonderful, winding hilly motor road, which reminded us of the lower Corniche on the French Riviera... Miss Miller is appealing as the heroine." – *The New York Times*

"The cast supporting the star is a corking one and the direction carries the story along in great shape without a single dull moment." – *Variety*

Notes

This was Patsy's second film with Douglas MacLean, but her first as his leading lady. She has been merely an extra in the 1920 *One A Minute*. This was a typical MacLean production, with the star getting most of the screen time and Patsy providing the love interest. The film greatly benefited from the work of the adaptors, Raymond Griffith and Lewis Milestone. Griffith was a fine film comedian and Milestone, who began as an editor, then graduated to writing, became a fine director, earning much praise for his films, among them *All Quiet on the Western Front* (1930) and *Of Mice and Men* (1939).

THE BREAKING POINT
1924 A Famous Players - Lasky Picture
Distributed by Paramount

Cast

Beverly Carlysle, Nita Naldi; *Elizabeth Wheeler*, Patsy Ruth Miller; *Judson Clark*, Matt Moore; *Dr. David Livingstone*, George Fawcett; *William Lucas*, John Merkyl; *Fred Gregory*, Theodore von Eltz, *Lucy Livingstone*, Edythe Chapman; *Louis Bassett*, Cyril Ring; *Sheriff Wilkins*, W.B. Clarke; *Joe*, Edward Kipling; *Harrison Wheeler*, Charles A. Stevenson.

Credits

Herbert Brenon (Director); Edfrid Bingham, Julie Herne (Scenario); James Howe (Photography).

Synopsis

Assuming that he has killed the husband of the woman he loves, Judson Clark (Moore) flees through a blizzard to a lonely cabin, where he nearly dies. When he recovers, he has lost his memory and is believed to be dead until an actress (Naldi) recognizes him. Following many adventures, the real killer confesses. Clark regains his memory and the woman he loves (Miller).

Reviews

"Frequent coincidence in plot development makes this a bit absurd at times, but quick comedy relief ususally saves the situation. Pretty good audience picture in spite of flaws that may be picked up in it. Patsy Ruth Miller pretty as the eventual bride." – *Film Daily*

"The novel was a best seller, the play failed to cause a stir, but the picture should split the difference, with the odds favoring a like reception for the film as was given the book. The actual story is above the average celluloid menu and, portrayed by a smooth working cast, working under sane supervision, the total result of this intricate theme is satisfying." – *Variety*

Notes

Herbert Brenon, was one of the most important directors Miss Miller worked for. During 1910's he was rivalling Griffith with spectacles starring Annette Kellerman (*Daughter of the Gods*), and during the 1920's, directed the popular *Beau Geste* and the first version of *The Great Gatsby*, but his greatest achievement was probably the two Betty Bronson fantasies he directed for Paramount: *Peter Pan* (1924), and *A Kiss for Cinderella* (1926). James Howe, the photographer, is best known as James Wong Howe the cinematographer responsible for the fine pictorial quality for scores of Hollywood films through the 1950's, *King's Row* and *The Old Man and the Sea* being two of them.

DAUGHTERS OF TODAY
1924 A Sturgeon-Hubbard Picture
Distributed by Selznick

Cast

Lois Whittal, Patsy Ruth Miller; *Ralph Adams*, Ralph Graves; *Mabel Vandegrift*, Edna Murphy; *Peter Farnham*, Edward Hearn; *Reggy Adams*, Philo MacCullough; *Dirk Vandegrift*, George Nichols; *Ma Vandegrift*, Gertrude Claire; *Leigh Whittal*, Phillips Smalley; *Lorena*, ZaSu Pitts; *Calvan*, H.J. Herbert; *Flo*, Dorothy Wood; *Maisie*, Marjorie Bonner.

216

Credits
Rollin Sturgeon (Director) Lucien Hubbard (Story), Milton Moore (Photographer)
Synopsis
Country girl Mabel Vandegrift (Murphy) enrolls in a fashionable city college and there joins a fast-moving crowd led by flapper Lois Whittal (Miller). During a house party Reggy Adams (MacCullough) tries to force his attentions on her, but she escapes. Later, when he is found dead, she is accused of murdering him. Her country sweetheart Peter Farnham (Hearn) solves the mystery and all ends happily.
Reviews
"There is nothing particularly original about [the picture]. In it one sees many of the overworked situations and old ideas presented years ago in a similar type of picture. Patsy Ruth Miller and Edna Murphy seem to be having a jolly time in this production." —*The New York Times*

"Another girl-of-today story with a moral. Has some good heart interest touches. Jazzy enough to satisfy the jazz hounds. At times daring." —*Film Daily*

"The direction is uninspired, and the acting without a single high spot, even from Patsy Ruth Miller, who seems to take second place in the story to Edna Murphy." —*Variety*
Notes
This film was Irving Thalberg's first attempt at independent production. However, when he and his partner, Lucien Hubbard, were offered twice their investment of $30,000 for the rights to the film by Lewis J. Selznick, they took the cash and the film went on to earn over $750,000.

A SELF-MADE FAILURE
1924 A J.K. MacDonald Production
Distributed by First National
Cast
John Steele, Matt Moore; *Breezy*, Lloyd Hamilton; *Alice Neal*, Patsy Ruth Miller; *Sonny*, Ben Alexander; *Grandma Neal*, Marry Carr; *Cyrus Cruikshank*, Sam De Grasse; *Spike Malone*, Chuck Reisner; *Pokey Jones*, Victor Potel; *Dan*, Dan Mason; *The Constable*, Harry Todd; *Mrs. Spike Malone*, Alta Allen; *Waitress*, Doris Duane; *Vernon*, Joel McCrea
Credits
William Beaudine (Director); Violet Clark, Lex Neal, John Grey (Scenario); Tamar Lane (Adaption); J.K. MacDonald (Story); Ray June, Ramey McGill (Photography), H.P. Bretherton, Beth Matz (Editors)
Synopsis
Breezy (Hamilton), a kind but illiterate tramp, accompanied by a boy, Sonny (Alexander), and a dog, hops off a freight train at a health resort, and there is mistaken for a German masseur by a sanatarium proprietor. Still assumed to be the masseur, he discovers that the hotel owner, Cyrus (De Grasse), has stolen the mineral spring from a boardinghouse keeper (Carr) and while romancing her granddaughter (Miller), succeeds in restoring the property to her.
Reviews
"Sure fire comedy with great score of laughs. Fine combination of situations that include some good heart-interest touches. It is really delightful, wholly amusing... can't fail to win laughs as a box office attraction." —*Film Daily*
Notes
William Beaudine is one of the most under-rated of the silent film directors, but his work was consistently good, and one has only to watch Pickford's *Sparrows* (1926) to see that his talent was abundant. Ben Alexander is best known, not as a 20's child actor, but as Jack Webb's first patrol partner in 1950's TV series *Dragnet*.

GIRLS MEN FORGET
1924 A Principal Picture
Cast
Russell Baldwin, Johnnie Walker; *Kitty Shayne*, Patsy Ruth Miller; *Jimmy Masson*, Alan Hale; *Lucy*, Mayme Kelso; *Aunt Clara*, Carrie Clark Ward; *Michael Shayne*, Wildred Lucas; *Mrs. Baldwin*, Frances Raymond; *Ruby Thomas*, Shannon Day
Credits
Maurice Campbell (Director); Percy Heath, Maurice Campbell (Scenario); Allen Siegler (Photographer); Glenn Kershner (Additional Photography).
Synopsis
Kitty Shayne (Miller), a cut-up who is the life of every party she attends, discovers that the men in her life invariable pass her up to marry timid and retiring girls. Kitty decides to change, and goes to live with an aunt (Ward) in a distant town, assuming there the role of a modest young woman. She is intent on finding herself a husband, and soon she meets and falls in love with Russell Baldwin (Walker), a proper young man who hates jazz babies. When she and Russell become engaged, Mrs. Baldwin (Raymond) gives a party to celebrate the occasion, but the affair is a lifeless one until Kitty can

stand it no longer. To save her future mother-in-law from the heartbreak of social embarrassment, she becomes the life of the party and Mrs. Baldwin's gathering is hailed a smashing success. Russell, however, is disgusted with Kitty until she explains that she did it only to please his mother, and they are reconciled.
Reviews

"So ridiculous it can't displease, but because of the spineless thesis, it won't make much of an impression anywhere. It has a share of mild amusement and those few laughs provided are all that saves it from being an almost worthless affair." – *Variety*

FOOLS IN THE DARK
1924 An RC Picture
Distributed by FBO
Cast
Percy Schwartz, Matt Moore; *Ruth Rand*, Patsy Ruth Miller; *Kotah*, Bert Grasby; *Dr. Rand*, Charles Belcher; *Diploma*, Tom Wilson; *Julius Schwartz*, John Steppling.
Credits
Al Santell (Director); Bertram Millhauser (Story/Adaption); Leon Eycke, Blake Wagner (Photography).
Synopsis
Young Percy Schwartz (Moore), is in love with Ruth (Miller), the daughter of a well-known doctor (Belcher), but when he asks Dr. Rand for permission to marry his daughter, he finds himself the prisoner of a mad scientist (Grasby). Assisted by Diploma (Wilson), a negro streetcleaner, he makes his escape and rescues Ruth who has been taken captive by evil plotters with the aid of a seaplane and the timely arrival of marines.
Reviews

"Clever nonsense. The producers call it a melodramatic farce, but whatever one decides to term this production, it is thoroughly entertaining, with really good subtitles and spirited acting. (It is) like a serial packed into seven reels." – *The New York Times*

"A good combination of thrills, comedy and mystery that will probably serve exhibitors very well. Patsy Ruth Miller is pleasing and Matt Moore is good as the hero." – *Film Daily*

"Corking mystery comedy, ranking in entertainment value with Griffith's *One Exciting Night*. It is all doughty stuff, well played and directed. – *Variety*
Notes
The title *Fools in the Dark* refers to movie audiences whom Matt Moore's character aspired to entertain by writing motion picture scenarios.

THE BREATH OF SCANDAL
1924 A B.P. Schulberg Production
A Preferred Pictured
Cast
Sybil Russell, Betty Blythe; *Charles Hale*, Lou Tellegen; *Marjorie Hale*, Patsy Ruth Miller; *Bill Wallace*, Jack Mulhall; *Helen Hale*, Myrtle Stedman; *Clara Simmons*, Phyllis Haver; *Gregg Mowbry*, Forrest Stanley; *Sybil's husband*, Frank Leigh; *Atherton Bruce*, Charles Clary.
Credits
Louis Gasnier (Director); Eve Unsell (Scenario); Harry Perry (Photographer).
Synopsis
When Charles Hale (Tellegen) is visiting his mistress, Sybil Russell (Blythe), he is shot in the arm by Sybil's estranged and outraged husband (Leigh). Hale's daughter, Marjorie (Miller), is so shocked to discover her father's philandering in such an abrupt fashion that she leaves her plush home and goes to the slums to do settlement work. Marjorie, who is engaged to the district attorney (Mulhall), is there placed in a compromising position by her father's assailant, who intends to revenge himself upon the entire Hale family. The DA breaks off his engagement with Marjorie, however she is reconciled to her father, who has given up Sybil.
Mrs. Hale (Stedman), generally engaged in social activities, returns from a convention and is happily reunited with her husband and daughter. Meanwhile, the DA learns that Marjorie was the victim of Russell's scheme and he asks Marjorie to take him back, which she gladly does.
Reviews

"Cheek to cheek poses are popular with L. Gasnier (the director) in his current film. Mr. Gasnier obviously hopes to stir the emotions of his audience with close-ups of women's heads moving slowly while tears drop from their right eyes. Everybody is well dressed in this production, no matter what happened, or where they go. Patsy Ruth Miller has given far better performances. – *The New York Times*

"New type of flapper story with box office appeal and aided therein with fine cast." – *Film Daily*

218

"The subject has been both dressed up and given an imposing production while the names in the cast should mean something for selling value. The players do much to sustain the script, and in this respect Patsy Ruth Miller and Lou Tellegen are outstanding. Miss Miller upholds a well-established reputation in an 'unsophisticated' role." – *Variety*

THE WISE VIRGIN
1924 A Peninsula Picture
Distributed by Producers Distributing Corporation
Cast
Billie Farrington, Patsy Ruth Miller; *Bob Hanford*, Matt Moore; *Mrs. John Farrington*, Edythe Chapman; *Count Ricardo Veruno*, Leon Barry; *Ethie Green*, Lucy Fox; *Thomas Green*, Charles A. Stevenson.
Credits
Lloyd Ingraham (Director); Elmer Harris (Supervisor/Writer); Joseph Walker (Photographer); Una Hopkins (Art Direction); Earl Sibley (Technical Director)
Synopsis
Although Billie Farrington's aunt (Chapman) wishes her to marry Bob Hanford (Moore), the manager of her ranch, Billie (Miller) is interested only in Count Veruno (Barry), a fake nobleman. Mrs. Farrington becomes seriously ill, and Billie gives in and weds Bob to please her aunt, but treats him with chilly reserve.
When Mrs. Farrington recovers, she learns of the Count's masquerade and halfcaste birth and gives a reception to which she invites Veruno's Burmese mother. Billie runs away, is kidnapped by Veruno, and is then rescued by Bob whose rugged honesty she finally appreciates.
Notes
Made for the small, independent Peninsula studios in San Francisco, *The Wise Virgin* was not reviewed in any major publication and obviously did not get a wide distribution.

THE GIRL ON THE STAIRS
1924 A Peninsula Picture
Distributed by Producers Distributing Corporation
Cast
Dora Sinclair, Patsy Ruth Miller; *Frank Farrell*, Niles Welch; *Dick Wakefield*, Freeman Wood; *Agatha Sinclair*, Frances Raymond; *Joan Wakefield*, Arline Pretty; *Manuela Sarmento*, Shannon Day; *Jose Sarmento*, Bertram Grassby; *Wilbur*, Michael Dark; *Dr. Bourget*, George Periolat.
Credits
William Worthington (Director); Elmer Harris (Adaption); Joseph Walker, Charles Kaufman (Photography)
Synopsis
Discovering that Dick Wakefield (Wood), with whom she has been carrying on a flirtation, is married, Dora Sinclair (Miller) begins seeing and becomes engaged to Frank Farrell (Welch). But when Wakefield refuses to return her love letters, his wife walks out on him.
While sleepwalking one night, Dora enters the Wakefield home in an unsuccessful and unconscious attempt to retrieve the letters. The next morning Wakefield is found murdered and Dora, who was seen leaving the house, is accused of the crime. Farrell undertakes her defense and calls Dr Bourget (Periolat) to the stand. Bourget hypnotizes her and she recalls the events of the night of the crime, revealing that she had seen Jose Sarmento (Grassby), an insanely jealous South American, kill Wakefield for flirting with Senora Sarmento (Day). Dora is freed and she and Frank marry.
Reviews
"An interesting murder mystery. If one accepts the theory that the subconscious mind directs the activities of sleepwalkers and that the somnambulists do not remember anything they do while in the coma, but if put to sleep by artificial means, will reveal the promptings of the subconscious mind, the picture is credulous. Whether one admits its plausibility or not, it is an engrossing picture, admirably cast and directed and sumptuously produced. A corking good feature for the second run houses. Miss Miller is girlishly appealing and convincing throughout."
– *Variety*

THOSE WHO JUDGE
1924 A Banner Production
Cast
Angelique Dean, Patsy Ruth Miller; *John Dawson*, Lou Tellegen; *Kitty Drexel*, Mary Thurman; *Shirley Norton*, Flora le Breton; *Henry Dawson*, Edmund Breese; *Bob Dawson*, Walter Miller; *Chapman Griswold*, Cort Albertson.
Credits
Burton King (Director) Harry Chandlee (Adaption)

Synopsis
In spite of Angelique Dean's (Miller) seeming friendship with Chapman Griswold (Albertson), a society bum, John Dawson (Tellegen), falls in love with her and asks the charming and mysterious "widow" to marry him. John then learns from Griswold that Angelique has never been married. When John breaks off the engagement, Angelique is forced to accept Griswold's proposal of marriage, fearing that he will expose the fact that she had been involved in a mock marriage with Major Twilling, a Brittish Officer. However, when John learns that Angelique had sacrificed her reputation in order to protect Twilling from scandal, he prevents her marriage to Griswold and marries her himself.

Reviews
"Fairly good story even though it isn't entirely new. Better development would have helped sustain the interest more completely. Drags badly at times. Patsy Ruth Miller pleasing and pretty." –*Film Daily*

Notes
Lou Tellegen had been Sarah Bernhardt's leading man and lover, and by the mid 1920's was a bit too mature to be the romantic lead of Patsy Ruth Miller. He was better suited to playing fatherly roles, as he had done in Miller's *The Breath of Scandal*, the same year.
1924 was Patsy's busiest year on screen, appearing in 12 features. Naturally, they all weren't *made* in 1924, some had been made in 1923, but having 12 Patsy Ruth Miller pictures released in one year proves that movie-making in the 1920's does not compare with movie-making in the 1980's.

BACK TO LIFE
1925 A Postman Picture
Distributed by Associated Exhibitors

Cast
Margaret Lothbury, Patsy Ruth Miller; *John Lothbury*, David Powell; *Wallace Straker*, Lawford Davidson; *Iuzie Porter*, Mary Thurman; *Arthur Lothbury*, George Stewart; *Henry Porter*, Frederick Burton; *Sonny Lothbury*, Frankie Evans.

Credits
Whitman Bennett (Director); Harry Chandlee (Scenario); Edward Paul (Photography).

Synopsis
During the World War, John Lothbury (Powell) joins the French Air Force as a pilot and is later reported dead by the French government. John's brother Arthur (Stewart), who has embezzled $10,000 from Wallace Straker (Davidson) blames the theft on John and Margaret (Miller), John's widow, married Straker to avoid a posthumous scandal involving her late husband. With Margaret still secretly mourning him, John returns to the United States from a German prison camp. Going back to his small hometown, he discovers that Margaret has remarried. He calls on her, introducing himself as a friend of her late husband's. She doesn't recognize him because his face was disfigured in the war and plastic surgery has altered his appearance. He eventually works himself into the presidency of an aircraft company which is a rival to Straker's firm, and when Straker finds himself in financial difficulties, John helps out in order to protect Margaret.
Straker learns of John's true identity, and in a drunken rage goes after him with a gun. He is about to shoot when stricken with a fatal heart attack. John and Margaret are reunited and he is cleared of all guilt in the theft of Straker's money.

Notes
Back To Life is indeed an obscure picture with stills and reviews difficult to find.

HER HUSBAND'S SECRET
1925 A Frank Lloyd Production
Distributed by First National

Cast
Elliot Owen, Antonio Moreno; *Judy Brewster*, Patsy Ruth Miller; *Mrs. Pearce*, Ruth Clifford; *Ross Brewster*, David Torrence; *Leon Kent*, Walter McGrail; *Pansy La Rue*, Phyllis Haver; *Mrs. Van Tuyler*, Pauline Neff; *Irene Farway*, Margaret Fielding; *Young Elliot Owen*, Frankie Darro; *Miss Van Tuyler*, Frances Teague.

Credits
Frank Lloyd (Director); J.G. Hawks (Adaption); Norbert Brodin (Photography).

Synopsis
To relieve the monotomy of homelife, Leon Kent (McGrail) throws a wild party. Distracted by the noise and drunken revelry, Mrs. Kent (Clifford) leaves the house with her young son (Darro) and goes to the house of sympathetic neighbor Ross Brewster (Torrence), a wealthy banker. The following morning, Kent becomes enraged to discover that his wife has spent the night with Brewster, and he divorces her, taking their young son with him. For 25 years, Mrs. Kent, known by her maiden name of Pearce,

and Brewster maintain a beautiful relationship, although they never marry. Brewster's daughter by an earlier marriage, Judy (Miller), returns home from college with Elliot Owen, a young man whom she introduces as her fiancee. Brewster soon discovers that Owen is guilty of fraudulent investment-promotion, and Owen discloses that he has been married to Judy for the past three months. Brewster refuses to help Owen and hints that the best and most honorable thing for him to do would be to kill himself. Owen then reveals that he is the son of Mrs. Pearce, but Brewster still refuses to help him. Overcome with remorse, Owen jumps from a cliff. He isn't killed fortunately, and Brewster does help him to regain spiritual and physical health. Judy gives birth to a child and Brewster takes Owen in the banking business with him.

Reviews

"It quite thoroughly fills the demand for something 'new' in the movies, the interest is well sustained and there has been no time expended upon unnecessary detail. Has splendid heart interest and other qualities of appeal. Excellent cast, all well-suited and capable. Patsy Ruth Miller is a beautiful heroine." —*Film Daily*

"One of the comparatively few First National that failed to make the first-run grade around New York. The reason is that it is draggy, unimportant, but fairly interesting in its story and treatment and surely no worse than a good many features seen at the Broadway houses... Frank Lloyd has endeavored to produce a film without tricks, and the straightforward method of direction is convincing for the most part. But he erred in allowing the picture to run more than a quarter of an hour overtime." — *Variety*

Notes

The accepted length of the average movie in 1925 was apparently 60 minutes, at least to the film reviewer for *Variety*, because *Her Husband's Secret* was only 77 minutes long, quite short by today's standards. Miss Miller worked for several fine directors, and Frank Lloyd is definitely one of them, although he is best known today for his 30's work — *Berkeley Square*, *Mutiny on the Bounty*, and *Maid of Salem*.

RED HOT TIRES

1925 A Warner Brothers Picture

Cast

Al Jones: Monte Blue, *Elizabeth Lowden*: Patsy Ruth Miller, *Hon. R. C. Lowden*, Fred Esmelton; *George Taylor*, Lincoln Stedman; *Coachman*, Charles Conklin; *Al Martin*, Jimmy Quinn; *Crooks*, Tom McGuire, William Lowery, Malcolm Waite.

Credits

Erle C. Kenton (Director); Edward T. Lowe, Jr. (Scenario); Gregory Rogers (Story); Charles J. Van Enger (Photography)

Synopsis

The first time Al Jones (Blue) sees Elizabeth Lowden (Miller), he becomes so distracted that he runs his car into a steamroller. The second time he sees her, Elizabeth's car frightens his horse, causing him to fall. She rushes him to a hospital, and her father (Esmelton), who is the local chief of police, throws her into jail on speeding charges. Al becomes argumentative for this injustice and soon joins Elizabeth behind bars. He is soon released, and in an effort to get back in, arouses the enmity of a gang of crooks. The gang later kidnaps Elizabeth and Al rescues her. Overcoming his fear of automobiles, Al drives away with Elizabeth in a speedster to elope.

Reviews

"Fully three-quarters of *Red Hot Tires* is enjoyable, and the latter chapters are only weakened by the not unusual inclusion of speeding cars dashing before a locomotive or through signboards. Monte Blue and Patsy Ruth Miller, who figure in the principle roles, give an excellent account of themselves." — *The New York Times*

"A comedy that is good in spots, but has not the continued laughs to make it a touring success." — *Film Daily*

Notes

Miss Miller moved from Goldwyn, where she had been since 1922, to Warner Brothers in 1925, and her first film for the Brothers Warner set the tone for most of her later films for that studio—comedies. She was quickly teamed with Monte Blue in three other pictures, all on the light side, and all well received.

HEAD WINDS

1925 A Universal Picture

Cast

Peter Rosslyn: House Peters, *Patricia Van Felt*, Patsy Ruth Miller, *John Templeton Arnold*, Richard Travers, *Winthrop Van Felt*, Arthur Hoyt, *Theodore Van Felt*, William Austin; *Nurse*, Lydia Yeaman Titus; *Wu Lung*, Togo Yamamoto.

Credits
Herbet Blanche (Director), Edward T. Lowe, Jr. (Screenplay), John Stumar (Photography).

Synopsis
Peter Rosslyn, a sturdy gentleman yachtsman in love with irresponsible and vivacious Patricia Van Felt (Miller), does not propose to her in the hope that in time she will mature. When Peter learns, however, that she plans to marry Templeton Arnold (Travers), a fortune hunter, he arranges for her to be brought aboard his yacht where he impersonates Arnold by swathing his head with bandages. A minister is brought on board and Patricia marries Peter, still thinking him to be Arnold. Peter takes off the bandages in private and Patricia is stunned, thinking herself kidnapped. She tries to escape in a rowboat but is brought back to the yacht by its Chinese crew. She becomes ill and learns from her nurse that she is really married to Peter. When she recovers, she and Peter are reconciled and begin married life in earnest.

Reviews
"Romance that spread one good situation for five reels and then winds up with an action finish that might well have come before. Miss Miller is pretty and makes an interesting heroine."

Notes
House Peters 25 years older than his co-star, had been in films since 1913, and his popularity was beginning to wane, however, he still held enough sway at the box office to insure a successful run.

LORRAINE OF THE LIONS
1925 a Universal Picture

Cast
Lorraine, Patsy Ruth Miller; *Don Mackay*, Norman Kerry; *Bimi*, Fred Humes; *Lorraine (at 7)*, Doreen Turner; *Colby*, Harry Todd; *Hartley*, Philo MacCullough; *Livingston, Sr.*, Joseph J. Dowling; *Livingston, Jr.*, Frank Newberg; *Mrs. Livingston*, Rosemary Cooper

Credits
Edward Sedgwick (Director), Isadore Bernstein, Carl Krusada (Scenario), Isadore Bernstein (Story), Virgil Miller (Photographer).

Synopsis
John Livingston (Newberg), who is married to a circus performer, is disowned by his wealthy father (Dowling), but he does offer to care for his little granddaughter, Lorraine (Turner). John agrees and the girl is put on a boat bound for the United States. But the ship sinks during the voyage, stranding Lorraine on a desert island, where she is cared for by lions and a gorilla (Humes) whom she names Bimi. She grows to maturity with a wild and wholly natural grace.

Don Mackay (Kerry), a fortune teller, is eventually sought out by Lorraine's wealthy grandfather, and through his mysterious methods, is convinced that Lorraine is not only still alive, but tells where she can be found. Livingston mounts an expedition to the island and returns to civilization with the mature Lorraine (Miller) and her pet gorilla, Bimi. During a formal dinner Lorraine is ill at ease, and Bimi, who misbehaves only in protection of Lorraine, is caged. Bimi escapes from his prison later that night during a thunderstorm and carries Lorraine off. Don rescues her and Bimi attacks him. Bimi is shot and killed, leaving Lorraine alone to mourn for him. Don prepares to go, and Lorraine, who has fallen in love with him, announces that she intends to go along.

Reviews
"Unusual sort of story that may entertain from a novelty standpoint, but it's far fetched and possibly a bit too 'novel' for some tastes. Patsy Ruth Miller is the outstanding character and performance as well. And at that she's too pretty to tog out in a bearskin bathing suit and be made to imitate her jungle friends." – *Film Daily*

"One of the features of Universal's Second White List, which means it will be given a special plug in exploitation and salesmanship. From a strictly point of view (and assuming that audience is not too discriminating) it should be quite a box office success. Though utterly ridiculous, it is very well done and never becomes stupid or boring. ... Miss Miller's (acting is not a) true interpretation of how a girl who has been brought up with lions and monkeys would disport herself, but she is always cute and appealing."
– *Variety*

Notes
Lorraine of the Lions was one of Miss Miller's most unusual films, and still survives, although in a slightly edited version. Edward Sedgwick was one of the 1920's most prolific directors, moving from westerns starring Tom Mix and Hoot Gibson, to comedies at MGM including a string of Buster Keaton vehicles.

ROSE OF THE WORLD
1925 A Warner Brothers Picture
Cast
Rose Kirby, Patsy Ruth Miller; *Jack Talbot*, Allan Forrest; *Edith Rogers*, Pauline Garon; *Clyde Bainbridge*, Rockliffe Fellowes; *Cecilia Kirby*, Barbara Luddy; *"Gramp" Tallifer*, Alec B. Francis; *Mrs. John Talbot*, Helen Dunbar; *Sally Towsey*, Carrie Clark Ward
Credits
Harry Beaumont (Director); Julien Josephson (Scenario); Dorothy Farnum (Adaption); David Abel (Photographer); Frank Strayer (Assistant Director)
Synopsis
Wealthy Jack Talbot falls in love with Rose Kirby, a girl living in reduced circumstances, but, through fear of his mother's disapproval, does not marry her. Rose later marries Clyde Bainbridge (Fellowes), a rotter who knows that, under the terms of a secret contract, Rose will inherit the Talbot ironworks. Rose finds the contract but, mistrusting her husband, does not make use of it. Talbot marries a vamp (Garon) who later dies in childbirth. Clyde is killed by Rose's demented grandfather, and Rose and Talbot are reunited to find a long-delayed happiness.
Reviews
"... an incredibly dreary picture, in which the bromidic touch is superbly delineated. Patsy Ruth Miller is attractive in the role of the heroine." – *The New York Times*

"A real reliable program feature that will make itself especially interesting to women. It's full of sentimental intrigue, weaves in and out of plot and schemes, with an overdose of love interest, also kissing – but it's clean." – *Variety*

"Patsy Ruth Miller is a real saving grace with her beauty and pleasing manner." – *Film Daily*

HOGAN'S ALLEY
1925 A Warner Brothers Picture
Cast
Lefty O'Brien, Monte Blue; *Patsy Ryan*, Patsy Ruth Miller; *Michael Ryan*, Willard Louis; *Dolly*, Louise Fazenda; *A Stranger*, Ben Turpin; *His Friend*, Charles Conklin; *Jewish Clothier*, Abie O Murphy; Max Davison, *The Texas Kid*; Herbert Spencer Griswold, *Battling Savage*; Frank Hagney, *Mother Ryan*, Mary Carr; *Al Murphy*, Frank Bond
Credits
Roy Del Ruth (Director); Daryl Francis Zanuck (Adaption); Charles Van Enger (Camera); Willard Van Enger (Assistant Camera); Clarence Kolster (Film Editor); Ross Lederman (Assistant Director)
Synopsis
Lefty O'Brien (Blue), a pugilist, becomes engaged to ex-tomboy Patsy Ryan (Miller) against the wishes of her father, Michael (Louis). They both live in a Jewish/Irish neighborhood on New York's East Side known as "Hogan's Alley." Lefty defeats Battling Savage (Hagney) for the championship, breaking his left hand and leaving his opponent close to death. Lefty seeks refuge from apprehension from the police, but Michael turns out both Lefty and Patsy. Patsy is injured and Lefty calls in wealthy Dr. Emmet Franklin who takes more than a professional interest in Patsy. Lefty breaks in and Patsy returns his ring. The doctor invites father and daughter to his mountain lodge but leaves Michael stranded at the station. Michael and Lefty pursue the train in an automobile. The car and train collide, and the engineer abandons the train, leaving a part of it to run away. Lefty rescues Patsy with the aid of an airplane, and the two settle down to married life, and to Michael's pleasure make their living in plumbing.
Reviews
"The narrative is one of those weird mixtures which were in great favor years ago, so the comic situations are of the chestnut variety. Monte Blue is starred. He has stepped down from appearing in Ernst Lubitsch's productions, and is quite out of his element in this offering, as is Patsy Ruth Miller." – *The New York Times*

"East Side story with heart interest and dizzy melodrama. Good old hokum gets popular vote, as usual. Patsy Ruth Miller does a Mary Pickford 'Little Annie Rooney' role, but is too grown up and sophisticated to get it over with realism." – *Film Daily*

"Miss Miller is unquestionably cute at moments, and her charm will do much to overbalance many of the crude bits that are introduced. But neither she nor anything else can make *Hogan's Alley* other than a typical program feature." – *Variety*
Notes
Miss Miller worked several times with Roy Del Ruth, a former journalist who entered the film industry in 1915 as a gag writer. He later found himself at Warner Brothers directing atmospheric dramas, and then at MGM where he directed lavish 30's musicals, among them *Born to Dance*.

223

THE FIGHTING EDGE
1926 A Warner Brothers Picture
Cast
Juan de Dios O'Roarke, Kenneth Harlan; *Phoebe Joyce*, Patsy Ruth Miller; *Gillette*, David Kirby; *Chuck*, Charles Conklin; *Taggert*, Pat Hartigan; *Bailey*, Lew Harney; *Simpson*, Eugene Pallette; *Hadley*, Pat Harmon; *Joyce*, W.A. Carroll.
Credits
Henry Lehrman (Director); Edward T. Lowe, Jr., Jack Wagner (Adaption); Allan Thompson (Photography); Robert Laprell (Additional Photography); Clarence Kolster (Film Editor); Sandy Roth (Assistant Director).
Synopsis
A government agent named Joyce (Carroll) is imprisoned in a ranch house by a gang of smugglers. Juan O'Roarke (Harlan), another agent, is then reassigned to the case, going across the Mexican border disguised as a half-breed. He meets Joyce's daughter, Phoebe (Miller), and together they work their way into the smuggler's ranch house. With the aid of the cook, they free Joyce and make their way to the U.S. border. The smugglers follow and the four take refuge in a deserted house. They are surrounded, but before they are captured, the U.S. Army arrives and drives off the smugglers. Phoebe and Juan, who have fallen in love, are married.
Reviews
"Some spine-tickling and reckless automobile riding is well done and holds most of the picture's thrills. Just a rough one, but will please on the outlying circuits."
Notes
Kenneth Harlan, Miss Miller's leading man in two consecutive films, was signed by D.W. Griffith in the late teens and went on to become one of the 20's most popular matinee idols. In later years he was both a theatrical agent and restaurateur.

THE KING OF THE TURF
1926 An FBO Picture
Cast
John Doe Smith, Kenneth Harlan; *Kate Fairfax*, Patsy Ruth Miller; *Colonel Fairfax*, George Irving; *Tom Selsby*, Al Roscoe; *Letitia Selsby*, Kathleen Kirkman; *Martha Fairfax*, Mary Carr; *Martyn Selsby*, David Torrence; *Red Kelly*, Dave Kirby; *Soup Conley*, William Franey; *Dude Morlanti*, Eddie Phillips.
Credits
James P. Hogan (Director); J. Grubb Alexander (Continuity); John C. Brownell, Louis Joseph Vance (Adaption); Jules Cronjager (Photography); Frank Geraghty (Assistant Director).
Synopsis
Col Richard Fairfax (Irving), a courtly southern horsebreeder, is framed on a charge of embezzlement by Martyn Selsby (Torrence), his business partner, and sentenced to jail. Selsby soon dies of apoplexy, but not before dictating a full confession to exonerate Fairfax. Selsby's wife (Kirkman) is afraid of scandal and hides the document in a wall safe.
Time passes. The Colonel serves out his sentence and returns home in the company of four friends he has made in prison: John Doe Smith (Harlan), a horsetrainer gone astray, Red Kelly (Kirby), Soup Conley (Franey), and Dude Morlanti (Phillips). Selsby's son Tom (Roscoe), who is infatuated with the Colonel's daughter, Kate (Miller), offers to give her his father's confession if she will marry him. Smith overhears this proposal and with the help of his former cellmates, recovers the confession. The Colonel is cleared, and his horse, entered in an important race, wins a gold cup. Kate and John Doe hit it off just fine.
Reviews
"The hero's name is John Smith. Even with such a disadvantage, this film is a good, interesting and well-made feature, suitable for the smaller houses and those playing combination vaudeville bills." – *Variety*

WHY GIRLS GO BACK HOME
1926 A Warner Brothers Picture
Cast
Mary Downey/Marie, Patsy Ruth Miller; *Clifford Dudley*, Clive Brook; *A model*, Jane Winton; *Sally Short*, Myrna Loy; *John Ross*, George O'Hara; *Joe Downey*, Joseph Dowling; *Three in Badger Game*, Herbert Pryor, Virginia Ainsworth, Brooks Benedict.
Credits
James Flood (Director); Sonya Hovey (Scenario); Walter Morosco (Adaption); Catherine Brody (Story); Charles Van enger (Photography); Frank Kessan (Assistant Camera man); Ross Lederman (Assistant Director).
Synopsis
Smalltown girl Mary Downey (Miller) becomes infatuated with New York actor Clifford Dudley (Brook) when he visits her town in a road show. Although he encourages Mary's flirtation, he is astonished to learn – when

she follows him to New York — that she considers herself engaged to him. Sally Short (Loy), his leading lady, tries to comfort the disillusioned girl and gets her a chorus job. When Mary overhears a derogatory remark about Dudley, she defends him, declaring she is his fiancee. As a result, she becomes notorious, gets a promotion in the show, and, now known as Marie, has a success rivaling Dudley's.

When John (O'Hara), her smalltown sweetheart, comes to town, Marie realizes that it is John, not Dudley, whom she truly loves, and returns home. Though received with suspicion from the townsfolk, she is accepted when she contributes money for a church.

Reviews

"As the picture has been produced with a keen sense of humor, it is deserving of a loftier, or at least more conservative title. Miss Miller gives a really clever characterization of Marie. She blossoms from an unsophisticated lass into a dazzling actress with agreeable sincerity in the respective chapters." — *The New York Times*

"This picture may please the women — perhaps the girls more so than their elders. Therein lies its only strength." — *Variety*

Notes

Clive Brook, Miss Miller's co-star in this film, is better known today as a reliable leading man of the 30's, when he epitomized stiff-upper-lipped suavity, most notably in Dietrich's *Shanghai Express* and the academy award winning *Cavalcade*. And Myrna Loy, who had a minor role, didn't remain in the background very long. She moved from Warner Brothers to MGM and became one of their biggest stars. This was the first of two Patsy Ruth Miller films in which Loy had small parts. They appeared as equals in the 1929 *Show of Shows*.

OH! WHAT A NURSE!

1926 A Warner Brothers Picture

Cast

Jerry Clark, Sydney Chaplin; *June Harrison*, Patsy Ruth Miller; *Clive Hunt*, Gayne Whitman; *Capt. Layde Kirby*, Matthew Betz; *Mrs. Clark*, Edith Yorke; *Big Tim Harrison*, David Torrence; *Eric Johnson*, Ed Kennedy; *Mate*, Raymond Wells; *Editor of the Gazette*, Henry Barrows.

Credits

Charles Reisner (Director), Daryl Francis Zanuck (Adaption), John Mescall (Photography), Nelson Larabee (Additional Photography), Sandy Roth (Assistant Director).

Synopsis

Cub reporter Jerry Clark (Chaplin) substitutes for Dolly Wimple, the editor of an advice to the lovelorn column, and advises wealthy June Harrison (Miller) not to marry Clive Hunt (Whitman), a man whom she does not love. This advise maddens June's penniless uncle, political boss Tim Harrison (Torrence), who is in league with Hunt to get his hands on June's fortune. After a series of mad adventures involving rumrunners and female impersonators, Jerry saves June from a forced marriage with Hunt and marries her instead.

Reviews

"Mr. Chaplin errs in using his so-called gags too frequently in this obstreperous mileage of slapstick, in which it is true that not a single lemon meringue pie is thrown. Patsy Ruth Miller is calm and attractive during the feverish moments of this production." — *The New York Times*

"Starts off in fine style and brings in a great lot of laughs. Good audience material. Patsy Ruth Miller pleasing but well in the shade, giving Chaplin a free rein." — *Film Daily*

Notes

Sydney Chaplin, Charlie's less famous half-brother, had been considered the more talented of the two when they began their respective careers, but Charlie developed his own unique style and far surpassed his brother who today is almost totally forgotten. Probably his biggest success was the 1925 *Charley's Aunt* in which he appeared in drag. He attempted to cash in on its popularity in this follow-up with Miller, but it wasn't nearly as successful.

SO THIS IS PARIS

1926 A Warner Brothers Picture

Cast

Dr. Giraud, Monte Blue; *Mrs. Giraud*, Patsy Ruth Miller; *Georgette Lalles*, Lilyan Tashman; *M. Lalles*, Andre de Baranger; *Maid*, Myrna Loy; *Cop*, Sidney D'Albrook.

Credits

Ernst Lubitsch (Director), Hans Kraly (Adaption), John Mescall (Photography), Bert Shipman (Assistant Cameraman), George Hippard (Assistant Director).

Synopsis

To relieve the boredom of their marriage, the Lalles (de Baranger and Tashman), a young dancing couple, are constantly on the alert for a new flirtation. One morning Dr. Giraud (Blue) comes to their apartment with the intent of thrashing M. Lalles with his cane for entrancing his wife by practicing a dance in front of an open window in a shiek's costume, but his temper quickly cools when he recognizes Georgette has a former sweetheart. They become involved in a flirtation and Dr. Giraud tells his wife a fantastic story to cover up his long absence, saying he broke his cane over M. Lalle's head. M. Lalle, however, returns the doctor's cane intact and begins a counter flirtation with Mrs. Girard, and tells her about her husband's philandering.

Driving to meet Georgette, Dr. Giraud is arrested for speeding. Meanwhile, M. Lalle has come to visit Mrs. Giraud, and when officers arrive to take the doctor to jail, he impersonates the doctor to save Mrs. Giraud's reputation. Later, she hears on the radio that Dr. Giraud and Georgette Lalles have won a Charleston contest at a ball. She goes there and finds the doctor intoxicated. After a number of amusing tiffs, Georgette finds a new admirer and the Giraud's are reunited.

Reviews

"Lubitsch rings the bell again. His tour de force is an extraordinarily brilliant conception of an eye-full of a Charleston contest, with vibrant kaleidoscopic changes from feet and figures to the omnipotent saxophones. This dazzling episode is like the dream of a man after drinking more than his share of wine at such an event. Patsy Ruth Miller is much more impressive than she has been in the past. – *The New York Times*

"Miss Miller admirably brings out the coy, romantic nature of Suzanne. (The dance scene) is the wildest revel of kicking legs ever seen on the screen." – *The New York Telegram*

"Patsy Ruth Miller has range and much expression." – *Variety*

Notes

Of Miss Miller's 71 films, this one competes with *The Hunchback* as far as quality and lasting fame is concerned. Now available on video cassette, as is the Chaney film, *So This is Paris* is still immensely enjoyable to watch. Ernst Lubitsch, one of the finest directors in motion picture history, brought to the screen a film which was voted one of the ten best of the year. And Miss Miller's performance was one of her best, beautifully controlled and finely tuned to every nuance of the flirtatious Suzanne.

PRIVATE IZZY MURPHY
1926 A Warner Brothers Picture

Cast

Izzy Murphy, George Jessel; *Eileen Cohannigan*, Patsy Ruth Miller; *Sara Goldberg*, Vera Gordon; *The Shadchen*, Moe Ginsburg; *Natt Carr; Jacob Goldberg*, William Strauss; *The Monohan Kid*, Spec O'Donnell; *Cohannigan*, Gustav von Seyffertitz; *Robert O'Malley*, Douglas Gerrard; *The Attorney*, Tom Murray.

Credits

Lloyd Bacon (Director); Philip Lonergran (Adaption); Raymond Schrock, Edward Clark (Story); Virgil Miller (Camera); Walter Robinson (Assistant Cameraman); Sandy Roth (Assistant Director).

Synopsis

Isadore Goldberg (Jessel), an enterprising Russian Jew, comes to the United States and establishes himself in the delicatessen business so that one day he can send for his parents. Forced to vacate his store, Izzy relocates in an Irish neighborhood. There, after he changes his surname to Murphy, his business prospers. While waiting for a subway train, Izzy recovers a girl's handkerchief. He later meets the owner in his store and learns that her name is Eileen Cohannigan (Miller) from whose father he buys foodstuffs. Izzy sends for his parents, and after their arrival, he embarks for France with an all-Irish regiment and inspires his comrades to deeds of valor. He is welcomed home by Cohannigan, but when Cohannigan learns that he is Jewish, he denounces his daughter for loving him. With the aid of his service buddies, however, Izzy and Eileen head for the city hall to be married.

Reviews

"A dignified fourth cousin of *Abie's Irish Rose*. It is a feature that has a decided inclination to be melonchaly and to emphasize this mood there is a wealth of tearful close-ups. Patsy Ruth Miller is docile and affectionate." – *The New York Times*

"The whole treatment here of the subject is crude. It's all cheap, hip hurrah melodrama." – *Variety*

Notes

Actor, singer, songwriter, producer, and all-around entertainer George Jessel made his big screen debut in *Private Izzy Murphy*, but he failed to become as big a celluloid star as he was on the stage, where he had been appearing in vaudeville since the age of 11. He became even more famous in the 40's as a radio personality and later earned the name of America's "Toastmaster General" due to his compulsive telling of jokes and anecdotes. He died in 1981.

"SO THIS IS PARIS" an ERNST LUBITSCH Production

"PRIVATE IZZY MURPHY" starring GEORGE JESSEL

HELL-BENT FOR HEAVEN
1926 A Warner Brothers Story
Cast
Jude Lowrie, Patsy Ruth Miller; *Sid Hunt*, John Harron; *Andy Lowrie* Gayne Whitman; *Rufe Pryor*, Gardner James; *Dave Hunt, Sid's Grandfather*, James Marcus; *Matt Hunt, Sid's Father*, Wilfred North; *Meg Hunt, Sid's Mother*, Evelyn Selbie.
Credits
J. Stuart Blackton (Director); Marian Constance Blackton (Adaption); Nicholas Masuraca (Photography); William Adams (Assistant Cameraman); William McGann (Assistant Director).
Synopsis
When Sid Hunt (Harron) returns to his Carolina mountain home from the war and is welcomed as a hero, Rufe Pryor (James), a hired man who covets Sid's sweetheart, Jude Lowrie (Miller), and is envious of Sid's courage and honesty, determines to bring about his downfall. Under the guise of a psalm-singing religious fanatic, Rufe rekindles a feud between the Hunts and Lowries, and when his methods fail to take effect, he proceeds to dynamite a dam.

The escaping water floods the countryside and pours into a cellar where Andy (Whitman), Jude's brother, is caught along with Sid. When Rufe sees Jude helpless in the water, he frees the men so they can rescue her, but he is swept away by the torrent and Jude and Sid are happily reunited.
Reviews
"For the most of its length, the film ... possesses a fine dramatic quality, capital acting, adroitly sketched scenes and stirring suspense. The latter chapters are weakened by the unnatural actions of at least two of the characters and some exaggerations. For instance, there are two men up to their waists in water in a cellar, and it hardly seems the time or the place to discuss forgiveness regarding a little shooting incident. Patsy Ruth Miller is sincere and sympathetic as Jude..." – *The New York Times*

"... has been handled along the lines of the average, old-fashioned screen meller with the usual floods that no longer have a novelty on the screen. What the Warners should have done ... is to have announced a new star in Gardner James and sat back and heard the critics rave ..." – *Variety*
Notes
Hell-Bent for Heaven had been a Pulitzer prize winning play and was adapted into a well-received motion picture, especially praised for its flood climax. It was in capable hands with J. Stuart Blackton directing. One of the industry's very first directors, he was responsible for probably the first propaganda film, *Tearing Down the Spanish Flag*, shot during the Spanish-American War in 1898. According to many film historians, Blackton is next to Griffith in being the most innovative and creative force in the development of the motion picture art. He was one of the earliest animators and pioneered the single-frame technique in cinema animation. He established the Vitagraph Company in 1897 and retired when it was absorbed by Warner Brothers in 1926. He directed only one other film after *Hell-Bent for Heaven*.

BROKEN HEARTS OF HOLLYWOOD
1926 A Warner Brothers Picture
Cast
Betty Anne Bolton, Patsy Ruth Miller; *Virginia Perry*, Louise Dresser; *Hal Terwilliger*, Douglas Fairbanks, Jr.; *Marshall*, Jerry Maley; *McLain*, Stuart Holmes; *Molly*, Barbara Worth; *Sheriff*, Dick Sutherland; *Director*, Emile Chautard; *District Attorney*, Anders Randolph; *Chief of Detectives*, George Nichols; *Defense Attorney*, Sam De Grasse.
Credits
Lloyd Bacon (Director); C. Graham Baker (Scenario); Raymond Schrock, Edward Clark (Story); Virgil Miller (Camera); Walter Robinson (Assistant Camera); Clarence Kolster (Film Editor); Ted Stevens (Assistant Director).
Synopsis
Virginia Perry, a former actress, leaves her husband and child to return to Hollywood, but having dissipated her beauty and seeking solace in drink, finds herself another "has been" on the fringe of movie circles. Her daughter, Betty Anne (Miller), wins a national beauty contest, the prize being a chance to become a film star and en route to Hollywood, meets Hal (Fairbanks), another contest winner. Both fail in their first screen attempts and turn to Marshall (Maley), an unscrupulous trickster, who enrolls them in his acting school. Molly (Worth), a movie extra, induces Betty Anne to attend a wild party. She is arrested in a raid, and Hal, in order to raise bail, takes a stunt job in which he is badly hurt. Betty Anne seeks the aid of star actor McLain (Holmes), who obtains her for the leading female role in his next film. Virginia, who is cast as her mother, keeps silent about their relationship until the film is completed.

Marshall makes an advance to Betty Anne, and fearing for her daughter's safety, Virginia shoots him while in a drunken stupor and is arrested. At the trial, Betty Anne's testimony saves her mother, who is then happily reunited with her daughter and Hal.

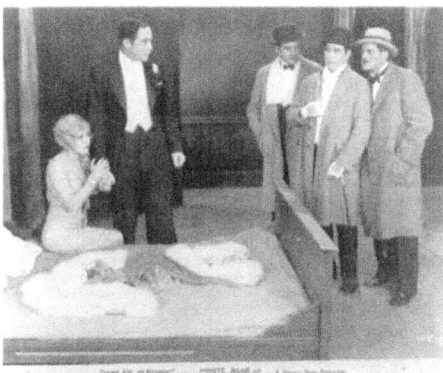

Reviews

"A very likely box office bet. Patsy Ruth Miller is appealing and always pleasant as the little New England girl. Douglas Fairbanks, Jr. does very well though he hardly seems a suitable lead for Patsy." – *Film Daily*

"Here is a picture that should be taken up by the parents and mother's associations in every town that it plays. It is a picture produced with a purpose, the purpose being that youngsters must not expect to go to Hollywood and become screen stars overnight. Patsy Ruth Miller and Douglas Fairbanks, Jr. contribute corking juvenile performances." – *Variety*

Notes

Douglas Fairbanks, Jr. is, in 1988, the only living leading man of Patsy Ruth Miller films. That is due, no doubt, to the fact that he is also the only leading man who was younger than she. In 1926, when *Broken Hearts* was filmed, Miller was 22, while Fairbanks was still in his teens. Miss Miller normally played opposite men who were several years older than she – Dustin Farnum was 30, House Peters was 25, Kenneth Harlan was 9 and Monte Blue was 14 years older.

THE WHITE BLACK SHEEP
1926 An Inspiration Picture
Distributed by First National

Cast
Robert Kincairn, Richard Barthelmess; *Zelie*, Patsy Ruth Miller; *Enid Gower*, Constance Howard; *El Rahib*, Gino Corrado; *Kadir*, Albert Prisco; *Dimos*, Sam Appel; *Colonel Nicholson*, Col. G.L. McDonnell; *Stanley Fielding*, Templar Saxe.

Credits
Sidney Olcott (Director); Jerome M. Wilson, Agnes Pat McKenna (Adaption); Violet E. Powell (Story); David Gobbett (Photography).

Synopsis
Robert Kincairn (Barthelmess), son of Col. Kincairn of the British Army, assumes guilt for a theft for which his fiancée is responsible, and is renounced by his father, joining the British forces in Palestine. While defending Zelie (Miller), a Greek dancer, from the unwelcome advances of El Rahib, a traitorous desert chieftain in the service of the British, Robert is, in turn, saved by Zelie, who revives his health. In the guise of a mute beggar, he enters El Rahib's camp and learns of his plans to attack the British; he is discovered and tortured, but he escapes and reveals el Rahib's treachery to his father. When the warring tribesmen are subdued, the Colonel discloses that Enid (Howard) has confessed her part in the theft, thus absolving Robert, who finds happiness with Zelie.

Reviews

"The scenic effects in this production would pass muster on any screen, but the story is quite another matter. The dancing girl, impersonated by Patsy Ruth Miller, looks as if she belonged to Brooklyn rather than the Sahara." – *The New York Times*

"Patsy Ruth Miller is extremely effective as the dancing girl. She looks beautiful and acts beautifully." – *The New York Tribune*

"Not entirely a pleasant theme. Barthelmess splendid and direction good but story is not always convincing." – *Film Daily*

"Sidney Olcott has turned out a picture that doesn't get anywhere outside of a couple of suspense scenes toward the end of it... Patsy Ruth Miller runs away with the picture as far as the story is concerned." – *Variety*

Notes

During her 11-year career in motion pictures, Miss Miller appeared with some pretty big and important male co-stars, but one of the most popular was Richard Barthelmess, an actor possessing good looks and a strong talent. It was certainly appropriate that he and Patsy appear in a film together; both were discovered by Nazimova, Barthelmess in 1916 and Miller in 1920. The Inspiration Company, which produced the film, had been founded in 1920 by Barthelmess and director Henry King.

WOLF'S CLOTHING
1927 A Warner Brothers Picture

Cast
Barry Baline, Monte Blue; *Minnie Humphrey*, Patsy Ruth Miller; *Johnson Craigie*, John Miljan; *Herbert Candish*, Douglas Gerrard; *Vanelli*, Lew Harney; *Vanelli's pal*, Ethan Laidlaw; *Hotel Manager*, J.C. Fowler; *Hotel Doctor*, Walter Rodgers; *Hotel Detective*, Arthur Millett; *Crook "Doctor"*, John Webb Dillon; *Millionaire*, Lee Moran; *Three Toughs*, Paul Panzer, Charles Heafeli, Jack Cooper; *Ship Captain*, Kally Pasha; *Two Sailors*, Jack Curtis, Edwin Sturgis.

Credits
Roy Del Ruth (Director); Darly Francis Zanuck (Screenplay); Byron Haskins (Camera); Willard Van Enger (Assistant Camera); Edward Sowders (Assistant Director).

Synopsis
Barry Baline (Blue), a New York City subway guard, is knocked unconscious on his first night off in months by the speeding car of Johnson Craigie (Mulan), who has just escaped from an insane asylum. While unconscious, Barry imagines himself exchanging places with Craigie, the millionaire; he attends a New Year's Eve ball and is drugged, is mistaken for Craigie by two blackmailers, and along with Minnie (Miller), a lady's maid, is taken to a dive on the east waterfront. Minnie is held as a hostage while Barry is sent to get the ransom money. After several exciting events, he obtains the money from Craigie, succeeds in cornering the gang on a barge, escapes from the police, and saves the passengers of a run-away subway from the demented Craigie. Awakening in the hospital, Barry finds that Minnie, the girl of his dreams, is his nurse.

Reviews
"Quite a hectic session. Story essays a series a wild proceedings by way of comedy which fails and seems inexcusable in spite of dream ending." – *Film Daily*

"One of the best Monte Blue starring features that has been out in a long while. For the average theatre, it may be a riot. . . In support of Blue, Patsy Ruth Miller looks great and handles herself cleverly." – *Variety*

"A rollicking comedy. Patsy Ruth Miller is attractive and capable in the leading feminine role." – *The New York Times*

Notes
Daryl Francis Zanuck, who wrote the screenplay not only for this film, but also for the Patsy Ruth Miller films, *Oh, What a Nurse!*, and *The First Auto* is not known today as a silent film scenario writer, but as a tough studio executive, first as Jack Warner's right hand man at Warner Brothers from 1928 until 1933, and as the Chief of Production at 20th Century-Fox from its founding in 1933 until 1956; however, he remained a top executive in the company, even serving briefly as president, until his retirement in 1971.

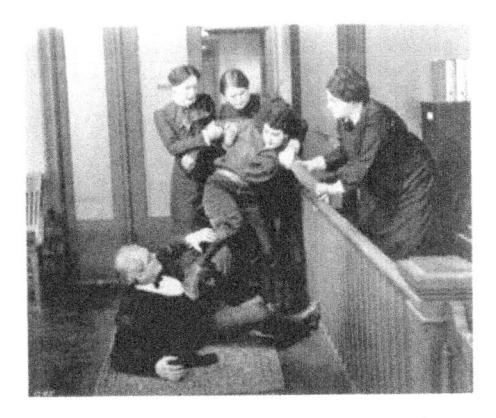

WHAT EVERY GIRL SHOULD KNOW
1927 A Warner Brothers Picture
Cast
Mary Sullivan, Patsy Ruth Miller; *Arthur Graham*, Ian Keith; *Dave Sullivan*, Carroll Nye; *Bobby Sullivan*, Mickey McBann; *Mrs. Randolph Lillian Langdon*; *Estelle Randolph*, Hazel Howell; *Madame Le Fleur*, Carmelita Geraughty

Credits
Charles F. Reisner (Director), Lois Jackson (Screenplay), Jack Wagner (Story), David Abel (Camera), Sandy Roth (Assistant Director)

Synopsis
Mary Sullivan (Miller), age 17, and her little brother, Bobby (McBann), who are both dependent on their older brother, Dave (Nye), are sent to an orphanage when Dave – though innocent – is convicted for transporting illegal liquor and sent to prison. As they are housed in separate buildings, Mary disguises herself in boy's clothing in an attempt to see Bobby, but she is discovered by a matron and taken to the superintendent. Touched by Mary's story, director Arthur Graham (Keith), a wealthy young philanthropist, adopts the two orphans, and they find happiness together. But their happiness is short-lived. Owing to the insinuations of a Mrs. Randolph (Langdon), Mary and Bobby run away, and Arthur is unable to find them.
Mary achieves prominence as a tennis player and Arthur is reunited with her at a match with Madame Le Fleur (Geraughty). Overruling her objections, he plans a speedy wedding, and as a wedding gift, uses his influence to obtain Dave's freedom.

Reviews
"Average fare. The development is obvious and unless (the audience is) over-blessed with tenderness, they won't feel many tugs at the heart strings. Patsy Ruth Miller is the plucky little heroine. She plays a good game of tennis, too." – *Film Daily*

"No credit here for anyone, taking in the director, and also the tennis match, about as poorly handled in method and execution as any athletic game could be. Nothing here but the title may be depended upon, other than Miss Miller's fame, and they will be disappointed in seeing her play this role." – *Variety*

THE FIRST AUTO
1927 A Warner Brothers Story
Cast
Bob Armstrong, Charles Emmet Mack; *Rose Robbins*, Patsy Ruth Miller; *Barney Oldfield, the master driver*, himself; *Hank Armstrong*, Russell Simpson; *Mayor Jim Robbins*, Frank Campeau; *Dave Doolittle*, William Demarest; *Steve Bentley*, Paul Kruger; *The Blacksmith*, Gibson Gowland; *Elmer Hays, the inventor*, E.H. Calvert; *Banker Stebbins*, Douglas Gerrard

229

Credits
Roy Del Ruth (Director); Anthony Coldeway (Scenario); Jack Jarmuth (Titles); Daryl Francis Zanuck (Story); David Abel (Camera); Ross Lederman (Assistant Director).

Synopsis
Hank Armstrong, an essentially old-fashioned man, is a lover of horses and deeply resents the new invention, the "horseless carriage," for which his son, Bob (Mack), has a particular fondness. When his son takes an interest in automobile racing, Hank disowns him and tinkers with a racing car so that it will explode, not knowing his son is to be the driver. Although Bob is not seriously hurt, Hank is cured of his automobile hatred, while Bob wins the love of Rose (Miller), the girl of his dreams.

Reviews
"Although there are sequences where the sentiment is somewhat strong, it is on the whole a vastly imaginative piece of work. Roy Del Ruth brings into the story some remarkable detail, much of which is informative as well as mirthful. Patsy Ruth Miller is charming." – *The New York Times*

"Mediocre release. Some good laughs where not intended. In places, almost burlesque." – *Film Daily*

Notes
The First Auto had the potential to be a quality film, and possibly a big money-maker, but its production ended in tragedy – the gruesome death of its male star, Charles Emmet Mack – and the remaining scenes had to be shot with a double. Some footage was probably scrapped all together. It's difficult to tell what the film might have looked like had Mack lived, because only a shortened version of the picture survives.

PAINTING THE TOWN
1927 A Universal Picture

Cast
Hector Whitmore, Glenn Tryon; *Patsy Deveau*, Patsy Ruth Miller; *Raymond Tyson*, Charles Gerrard; *Fire Commissioner*, George Fawcett; *Secretary*, Sidney Bracey; *Wilson*, Max Ascher; *Justice of the Peace*, Monte Collins.

Credits
William James Craft (Director); Harry O. Hoyt, Vin Moore (Adaption/Continuity); Albert Demond (Titles); Harry O. Hoyt (Story); Al Jones (Photography).

Synopsis
Patsy Deveau (Miller), a Follies girl, accompanied by Raymond Tyson (Gerrard), a city millionaire, is stopped by a policeman for speeding. While Raymond is paying the fine, Hector Whitmore (Tryon), a small town inventor, imagines he is making a hit with Patsy displaying his inventions, including a car that can travel 150 miles an hour and can stop in two car-lengths. She pretends to be flattered and casually suggest he see her in New York; he faithfully follows. Tyson persuades Patsy to play along, hoping to sell Hector's car to the fire department. His initial attempt at a demonstration is sabotaged. Patsy, however, disgusted with Tyson, pleads Hector's cause. He takes the commissioner on a perilous drive, refusing to stop until the contract is signed. Having proved the worth of his wonder car he wins the contract and Patsy as well.

Reviews
"As funny as they come." – *Film Daily*

"Feature honors are shared by Patsy Ruth Miller, whose name is more well known to the box office. She is the Follies dame with satisfying results, but overshadowed by her partner." – *Variety*

"(It) may be nonsensical from the viewpoint of its fractious narrative, but it possesses plenty of amusement. The work of the cast is highly commendable, especially that of a bright young man named Glenn Tryon." – *The New York Times*

Notes
This was the first of four comedies Patsy did with Glenn Tryon, who had been elevated by Universal from slapstick shorts to features, in an attempt to rival Harold Lloyd as a screen comedian. Unfortunately, his reputation failed to develope and by the end of the 1920's, Universal had lost interest.

SHANGHAIED
1927 A Ralph Ince Production
Released by FBO

Cast
Hurricane Haley, Ralph Ince; *Polly*, Patsy Ruth Miller; *Crawley*, Alan Brooks; *Bessie*, Gertrude Astor; *Ship's cook*, Walt Robbins; *Bronson*, H.J. Jacobson.

Credits
Ralph Ince (Director); Joseph P. Kennedy (Producer); J.G. Hawks (Adaption); Edward J. Montagne (Story); Joe Walker (Photography); Wallace Fox (Assistant Director).

Mary learns of the plotting, and with the help of Hiram and his plane, sets out for New York, but Hiram accidentally pilots Mary and her father across the ocean to Russia where he makes a forced landing. The success of the flight, however, saves the Sloan fortune.

Reviews

"For the most part, really funny. It slips up in spots, but not sufficiently to detract from the general entertainment qualities." – *Film Daily*

"...a curious mixture of low comedy, burlesque and melodrama. Patsy Ruth Miller is quite satisfactory." – *The New York Times*

"Glenn Tryon is in danger of being killed off as quickly as he was ballyhooed into stardom by Universal. Comedies need smart gag men and plenty of them. Story and situations here are weak. Titles are clever, but only occasionally." – *Variety*

SOUTH SEA LOVE
1927 An R-C Picture
Distributed by FBO

Cast

Charlotte Guest, Patsy Ruth Miller; *Fred Stewart*, Lee Shumway; *Tom Mallory*, Alan Brooks; *Bob Bernard*, Harry Crocker; *George Billways*, Barney Gillmore; *Moana*, Gertrude Howard; *Nahalo*, Everett Brown; *Joke Streeter*, Harry Wallace.

Credits

Ralph Ince (Director); Joseph P. Kennedy (Producer); Enid Hibbard (Continuity); George M. Arthur (Titles); Nick Musuraca (Camera); George M. Arthur (Film Editor).

Synopsis

Fred Stewart (Shumway) slaves for two years on the isolated island of Lamu Vita to send Charlotte Guest (Miller), a chorus girl, money for their future together. Meanwhile, Charlotte is approaching stardom through the efforts of her manager, Tom Mallory (Brooks), and by the means of Stewart's hard-earned money, while at the same time keeping reckless Bob Bernard (Crocker) on the string. When she tells Bob she is already married to a beachcomber in the Western Carolinas, Bob dramatically announces he will hunt Stewart down and kill him unless he agrees to divorce Charlotte. Stewart, shocked by her infidelity, decides to remain on the island and drink away his memories.

Bob arrives, but is stricken with fever, and Stewart cares for him. Together they plan revenge on the girl, whom they entice to the island. Both, however, are swayed by her charms, and when they fight, she attempts to drown herself. Stewart rescues her, Bob returns to the mainland, and she and Stewart remain on the island together.

Reviews

"Good action stuff, characterizations and tropic atmosphere. Plot far fetched but had good direction and acting. Patsy Ruth Miller screens handsomely." – *Film Daily*

"There is much melodrama in this film and many ludicrous titles. It looks very much as though the producers relied on the rain in the picture to make it interesting. Miss Miller cannot be accused of doing anything more for this picture than showing the South Sea natives the dernier cri of New York and Paris." – *The New York Times*

"Dull picture obviously designed to cut in on the South Sea thing, *Rain* and *Sadie Thompson*... Fairly capable cast struggles to no purpose with a discursive and rambling story." – *Variety*

RED RIDERS OF CANADA
1928 An FBO Picture

Cast

Joan Duval, Patsy Ruth Miller; *Sgt. Brian Scott*, Charles Byer; *Monsieur Le Busard*, Harry Woods; *Pierre Duval*, Rex Lease; *Nicholas*, Barney Furey.

Credits

Robert De Lacy (Director); Oliver Drake (Adaption/Continuity); Randolph Bartlett (Titles); William Byron Mowery (Story); Nick Musuraca (Photography); Jay Jones (Film Editor).

Synopsis

Canadian Mountie Sgt. Brian Scott (Byer) captures Le Busard (Woods), leader of a gang of fur pirates who murdered Joan Duval's (Miller) father, and takes him to Joan's cabin to spend the night. Le Busard escapes by tricking Joan into accompanying him to his hideout, where Joan's brother, Pierre (Lease), is being held prisoner. The treacherous pirate detains Joan and orders Pierre's death, but Scott arrives in time to save them. After a terrific fight, Pierre dies in his sister's arms from wounds inflicted by Le Busard, whom he has killed. Joan and Scott return to headquarters and marry after turning over Le Busard's henchmen over to the authorities.

Reviews

"It's ordinary. An uninspired version of the Old Northwest Mounted stuff. Lacks action and thrills, which only occur in weak climax. Patsy Ruth Miller has one of those 'walk-through parts.'" – *Film Daily*

"THE TRAGEDY OF YOUTH"   A Tiffany-Stahl Production

THE TRAGEDY OF YOUTH
1928 A Tiffany-Stahl Picture
Cast
Frank Gordon, Warner Baxter; *Paula Wayne*, Patsy Ruth Miller; *Dick Wayne*, William Collier, Jr; *Mother*, Claire McDowell; *Father*, Harvey Clarke; *Diana*, Margaret Quimby; *Landlady*, Billie Bennett; *Porter*, Stepin Fetchit.
Credits
George Archainbaud (Director); Olga Printzlau (Continuity); Frederick Hatton, Fanny Hatton (Titles); Albert Shelby Le Vino (Story); Faxon Dean (Photography); Burgess Beall (Set Design); Robert J. Kern (Film Editor).
Synopsis
Young newlywed Paula Wayne (Miller) turns to Frank Gordon (Baxter) when her husband, Dick (Collier), neglects her to practice bowling. Their affair ends when Dick pretends an attempt at suicide, and out of fear, Paula consents to a reconciliation. Frank departs on an ocean voyage that ends in disaster, but he returns alive and the lovers are reunited.
Reviews
"Should click with young folks. Nothing startlingly new, but it's the way it's handled by director and cast. Ending is happy but rather weak and has the romance they love." –*Film Daily*

"Produced in the best manner and neatly acted. Setting reflect atmosphere of elegance appropriate to the subject of modern married life among the wealthy." – *Variety*
Notes
Miss Miller shared the screen with two popular leading men in this film. Warner Baxter went on to tell Ruby Keeler that she was going out there a youngster but coming back a star in 42nd Street, and William "Buster" Collier was a handsome romantic lead who retired soon after silence gave way to sound.

WE AMERICANS
1928 A Universal Picture
Cast
Mr. Levine, George Sidney; *Beth Levine*, Patsy Ruth Miller; *Hugh Bradleigh*, John Boles; *Mr. Albertini*, Michael Visaroff; *Mr. Schmidt*, Albert Gran; *Phil Levine*, George Lewis; *Pete Albertini*, Eddie Phillips; *Mrs. Levine*, Beryl Mercer; *Mrs. Bradleigh*, Kathlyn Williams; *Mr. Bradleigh* Edward Martindel; *Helen Bradleigh*, Josephine Dunn; *Mrs. Schmidt*, Daisy Belmore; *Mrs. Albertini*, Rosita Marstini; *Pat O'Dougal*, Andy Devine; *Sara Schmidt*, Flora Bramley; *Korn*, Jake Bleifer
Credits
Edward Sloman (Direction/Co Screenplay), Carl Laemmle, Jr. (Supervision); Alfred A. Cohn (Adaption); Jackson J. Rose (Photography); Robert Jahns (Film Editor).
Synopsis
Hugh Bradleigh (Boles), the son of a socially prominent Jewish family, falls in love with Beth Levine (Miller), whose parents (Sidney, Mercer) are Russian Jewish immigrants. Pete Albertini (Phillips), the son of an Italian/American family, is engaged to Sara Schmidt (Bramley), whose parens are German immigrants. When the war with Germany breaks out, Hugh, Pete and Beth's brother, Phil (Lewis), all enlist. While overseas, Phil loses his life to save Hugh's, and Pete loses a leg. Returning from Europe, Pete marries Sara, and when Hugh announces his engagement to Beth, his parents (Martindel, Williams) object. All objections are dropped, however, when the Bradleighs meet Beth's parents and learn of Phil's sacrifice for Hugh.
Reviews
"The acting... is uncommonly good and the principals are particularly well suited to their respective roles. Miss Miller has changed her coiffure for her role, in which she is quite competent." – *The New York Times*

"... one of the best attributes is that after all the storm and strife, taking in the war, the film ends on a laugh title. This is the best titled U film that's been around in months. Patsy Ruth Miller has adopted an unbecoming coiffure to play the Jewish daughter, but it's in keeping, and no one is going to find fault with her performance." –*Variety*

"Not startlingly original, but has money-making possibilities. Many human touches throughout." –*Film Daily*
Notes
We Americans, sadly, has disappeared, but was one of Miss Miller's best films of 1928. The cast was particularly impressive. John Boles became more popular in the 30's when his good looks were enhanced by his rich speaking and singing voice. He starred with Shirley Temple in two films, and remained a popular leading man through the early 40's. Kathlyn Williams had been Selig's biggest star before World War I – she made film history in 1913 by appearing in the first serial – but she had gradually shifted to supporting roles and remained active as a character actress until the mid 30's.

232

TROPICAL NIGHTS
1928 A Tiffany-Stahl Picture
Cast
Mary Hale: Patsy Ruth Miller; *Jim*: Malcolm McGregor; *Harvey*: Ray Hallor; *Stavnow*: Wallace MacDonald; *Singapore Joe*: Russell Simpson.
Credits
Elmer Clifton (Director); Bennett Cohen (Story/Continuity); Harry Carr (Titles); John Boyle, Ernest Miller (Photography); Desmond O'Brien (Film Editor).
Synopsis
On a South Sea island, Harvey (Hallor) and his brother, Jim (McGregor), operate a pearl diving barge in partnership with Stavnow (MacDonald). Harvey becomes fresh with Mary Hale (Miller), a stranded opera singer working in a waterfront dive, and she knocks him cold. Stavnow sees the fight and robs Harvey of his pearls. Harvey regains consciousness and Stavnow kills him with a stone jar. Mary, who believes herself responsible, takes refuge with Jim, and they fall in love. He asks her to marry him, but she refuses. While diving, Stavnow's foot is caught in a giant clam, but before he dies, he signals to Jim that he is the one who killed Harvey. Jim and Mary are united.
Reviews
"Story material promising, but in the filming necessity of placating censor spoiled everything. Action is very slow. It winds through yards and yards... to get to the climax, which is over in a minute. Kick comes in a novel underwater sequence." – *Variety*

HOT HEELS
1928 A Universal Picture
Cast
Glenn Seth Higgins: Glenn Tryon; *Patsy Jones*: Patsy Ruth Miller; *Fannie*: Greta Yoltz; *Mr. Fitch*: James Bradbury, Sr.; *Tod Sloan, a jockey*: himself; *Manager Carter*: Lloyd Whitlock.
Credits
William James Craft (Director); Harry O. Hoyt (Scenario); Albert De Mond (Titles); Harry O. Hoyt (Story); Arthur Todd (Photography); Charles Craft (Film Editor).
Synopsis
Glenn (Tryon), owner of a small town hotel, is charmed by Patsy Jones (Miller), a dancer, and liquidates his assets to buy the stranded theatrical troupe to which she belongs. In answer to a telegram offering the group an engagement, Glenn takes the troupe to Cuba, only to find upon their arrival that the telegram was a trick. To recoup their losses, they enter 'Hot Heels,' their treadmill trick horse in the races and win the prize. Glenn then marries the dancing girl.
Reviews
"This could have been made into quite a strong number if more care had been employed in the story construction. At that, it is good audience entertainment, and gets plenty of laughs with broad comedy and heavy gagging. Patsy Ruth Miller fine decoration, and helps the star get laughs." – *Film Daily*

"An amusing farce. It begins by poking fun at the thundering race-track melodramas and ends by having a little fun with itself." – *The New York Times*

"It could have been a first runner if better judgment had been employed first by the writer and again by the story department. Just another chance muffed. Probably doesn't matter much, stories are so plentiful. One of the best bits of a long while was the Apache dance between Glenn Tryon and Patsy Ruth Miller." – *Variety*

BEAUTIFUL BUT DUMB
1928 A Tiffany-Stahl Picture
Cast
Janet Brady: Patsy Ruth Miller; *James Conroy*: Charles Byer; *Tad*: George E. Stone; *Beth*: Shirley Palmer; *Mae*: Greta Yoltz; *Ward*: William Irving; *Broadwell*: Harvey Clark.
Credits
Elmer Clifton (Director); J.F. Natteford (Story/Continuity); Frederick Hatton, Fanny Hatton (Titles); Desmond O'Brien (Film Editor); Arthur Ross (Assistant Director).
Synopsis
A romantic comedy of stenographer Janet Brady's (Miller) successful crusade to snare her boss, James Conroy (Byer). She learns that her personality has no appeal, so she drops her mannish clothes and blossoms into a sexy flapper. She develops sex appeal plus and though her boss is nonplussed at first, she wins him in the end.
Reviews
"Nice sexy offering with comedy highlights put over strong by work of Patsy Ruth Miller. She makes then an entertaining number." – *Film Daily*

233

"Patsy Ruth Miller does her best and Director Elmer Clifton tries to pep up things by working in a cabaret scene, but the staid dame who spruces up to make her boss and, of course, makes him, takes a terrifically long and uneventful 70 minutes to unreel." – *Variety*

MARRIAGE BY CONTRACT
1928 A Tiffany-Stahl Picture
Cast
Margaret, Patsy Ruth Miller; *Don*, Lawrence Gray; *Winters*, Robert Edeson; *Arthur*, Ralph Emerson; *Molly*, Shirley Palmer; *Father*, John St. Polis; *Mother*, Claire McDowell; *Grandma*, Ruby Lafayette; *Dirke*, Duke Martin; *Drury*, Raymond Keane.
Credits
James Flood (Director); John M. Stahl (Producer); Frances Hyland (Continuity); Paul Perez (Titles); Edward Clark (Story); Ernest Miller (Photography); L.R. Brown (Film Editor); Manny Baer (Music Score); Song: "When the Right One Comes Along," L. Wolfe Gilbert, Mabel Wayne; "Come Back to Me," Dave Goldberg, A.E. Joffe; Emmanuel Baer (Sound).
Synopsis
Margaret and Don (Miller, Gray) – an average American girl and boy – enter into a companionate marriage. Don goes philandering the first night after their honeymoon and Margaret leaves him. She finds that no decent man of her own class will marry her and finally enters into another companionate marriage with Dirke (Martin), a self-made man much beneath her social station. Margaret has children and is content, but Dirke leaves her at the end of the marriage contract. She then marries a rich old man, quickly divorcing him to marry Drury (Keane), a suave young fellow who soon runs through all her alimony. Margaret shoots him and is dragged away by the police. It all turns out to be a dream, however, and Margaret marries Don the next day in a church ceremony.
Reviews
"A winner. Exposes the bunk in the companionate marriage gag. Sexy, human, dramatic, timely. Great woman picture. Patsy Ruth Miller... gives one of her best performances." – *Film Daily*

"May possibly hold some interest for the extremely impressionable spectators. Others, depending upon their state of mind, may either frown or smile at it.... it has been produced with little imagination and little subtlety. Miss Miller works earnestly and parts of her performance are quite effective." – *The New York Times*

"Patsy Ruth Miller runs away with the picture in the playing, and easily. This is quite a picture for Miss Miller. In her make-up alone, simulating the different age periods of a girl of 19 to a grey-haired woman, she conveyed the proper age at all times, while the acting kept step." – *Variety*
Notes
With the success of *The Jazz Singer* in 1927, it was obvious to the motion picture companies that talking pictures were a must. Studios rushed to perfect recording systems and often injected otherwise silent films with musical effects. *Marriage by Contract* was advertised as having something unique – musical dialogue. According to program notes, "This is the first picture treated so as to accord musical significance to each character as he or she appears in the respective scenes. Each episode in the story has its corresponding musical theme and each character has his or her musical prototype." Despite this attraction, the film was not a major success.

THE GATE CRASHER
1928 A Universal-Jewel Picture
Cast
Dick Henshaw, Glenn Tryon; *Mara Di Leon*, Patsy Ruth Miller; *Hal Reade*, T. Roy Barnes; *Maid*, Beth Laemmle; *Jubb*, Fred Malatesta; *Zanfield, the stage manager*, Claude Payton; *Caesar, the actor*, Russell Powell; *Stage doorman*, Tiny Sanford; *Pedro, the waiter*, Al Smith; *Crook*, Monte Montague.
Credits
William James Craft (Director/Writer); Carl Krusada (Scenario); Albert De Mond (Titles); Vin Moore (Adaption); Jack Foley, William James Craft (Story); Al Jones (Camera); Charles Craft (Film Editor).
Synopsis
Dick Henshaw (Tryon), a bill poster in Swampscott, who is studying by mail to be a detective, is involved in an automobile accident with Mara Di Leon (Miller), a Broadway star, and quickly falls in love with her. She returns to New York and he to the pastepots. A few days later, Dick reads in the paper that Mara's jewels have been stolen, and he goes to New York to search for them. Dick eventually apprehends the thieves, Mara's maid and press agent (Laemmle, Barnes), recover the jewels, and convince Mara that there is more to him than poster paste and straw.
Reviews
"Scores neatly with comedy antics of Glenn Tryon. The story is just a lot of goofy nonsense but so well handled by director Craft that it becomes good entertainment all the way." – *Film Daily*

"Mildly amusing comedy romance." - *Variety*

Notes

In their last film together, Patsy and Glenn Tryon were as popular as ever, but Universal apparently felt that their effort to make Tryon a star had failed. He had to be content with only light leading role assignments until his career ended in the mid-30's.

THE FALL OF EVE
1929 A Columbia Picture

Cast

Eve Grant, Patsy Ruth Miller; *Mr. Mack*, Ford Sterling; *Tom Ford, Jr.*, Arthur Rankin; *Mrs. Ford*, Gertrude Astor; *Tom Ford, Sr.*, Jed Prouty; *Mrs. Mack*, Betty Farrington; *Cop*, Fred Kelsey; Hank Mann, Bob White.

Credits

Frank R. Strayer (Director); Harry Cohn (Producer); Frederick Hatton (Dialogue); Gladys Lehman (Adaption); Anita Loos, John Emerson (Story); Teddy Tatslaff (Photography); Harrison Wiley (Art Direction); George Rhein (Assistant Director).

Synopsis

Tom Ford, Jr. (Rankin) keeps secret his romance with his father's secretary Eve Grant (Miller). Ford, Sr. (Prouty) enlists Eve to entertain out-of-town buyer Mack (Sterling). When Mrs. Mack (Farrington) insists on joining the nightclub party, Eve is introduced as Mrs. Ford. A radio broadcast from the nightclub alerts the vacationing Mrs. Ford (Astor) that something is amiss when she hears that a certain dance tune has been requested by a Mr. and Mrs. Tom Ford. Ford calls his son to help extricate him from his difficulties with the boorish couple, and Ford, Jr. agrees to come only if Ford, Sr. will consent to his marriage. The party returns to the Ford home. The intoxicated Mr. Mack and his corpulent wife, having decided to stay the night, are about to go to bed when Mrs. Ford returns and calls the police, having seen an unfamiliar figure raiding her icebox. Ford, Jr. explains the situation to everyone's satisfaction and introduces Eve as his bride.

Reviews

"A film in which the producers reveal an overwhelming fondness for sound in stentorian volume. It is true that this film has a certain quality of mirth, but how welcome would be an occasional whisper of soft voice. Patsy Ruth Miller is sometimes quite good but now and again she lapses in her enunciation." - *The New York Times*

"Good cast carries the first three-quarters of the footage over to the last fraction, which is a machine gun for laughs and sends the audience out satisfied." - *Variety*

Notes

Fans of Patsy Ruth Miller heard her speak for the first time in this film, and although the Movietone system wasn't without fault, her voice was pleasing. The innovation of talking pictures was no handicap to Miss Miller, who was kept busy in 1929, appearing in eight films. This film also marked the talking debut of Ford Sterling, a slapstick comic dating back to the Keystone Comedies.

TWIN BEDS
1929 A First National Picture

Cast

Danny, Jack Mulhall; *Elsie Dolan*, Patsy Ruth Miller; *Ma Dolan*, Edythe Chapman; *Pa Dolan*, Knute Erickson; *Maizie Dolan*, Joycelyn Lee; *Bobby Dolan*, Nita Martan; *Tillie*, ZaSu Pitts; *Monty Solari*, Armand Kaliz; *Mrs. Solari*, Gertrude Astor; *Jason Treeohn*, Carl Levinus; *Mrs. Treeohn*, Alice Lake; *Pete*, Ben Hendricks, Jr.; *Red*, Eddie Gribbon; Edward J. Small, Bert Roach.

Credits

Alfred Santell (Director); F. McGraw Willis (Scenario/Titles/Dialogue); Sol Polito (Photography); LeRoy Stone (Film Editor).

Synopsis

Elsie Dolan (Miller), a telephone operator, by chance meets Danny Brown (Mulhall), a show doctor and song composer. They fall in love and are married. They rent an apartment, but their first night together is interrupted when Danny must go to the theatre and rehearse an understudy to go on for Monty Solari (Kaliz), the intoxicated star. Danny leaves the door open and Solari, who lives in the same building, wanders drunkenly into the apartment, puts on Danny's pajamas, and climbs into Danny's twin bed. Danny comes home and Solari is discovered, but everything is explained satisfactorally and the Browns go to Europe for the rest of their honeymoon.

Reviews

"...no better than it sounds and much worse than it might have been. The comedy is heavy and the romance is unconvincing." - *The Evening Graphic*

"A farce, or at least a comedy, the picture is in spots fair entertainment." - *The New York Times*

"Jack Mulhall parts company with Dorothy MacKaill in this one for Patsy Ruth Miller...(who) plays without the MacKaill flash but with pleasing sexy conservatism." - *Variety*

THE HOTTENTOT
1929 A Warner Brothers Picture
Cast
Sam Harrington, Edward Everett Horton; *Peggy Fairfax*, Patsy Ruth Miller; *Swift*, Douglas Gerrard; *Larry Crawford*, Edward Earle; *Alec Fairfax*, Stanley Taylor; *Mrs. Chadwick*, Gladys Brockwell; *May Gilford*, Maude Turner Gordon; *Perkins*, Otto Hoffman; *Ollie*, Edmund Breese.
Credits
Roy Del Ruth (Director); Harvey Thew (Adaption/Dialogue); Barney McGill (Photography); Owen Marks (Film Editor).
Synopsis
Mistaking Sam Harrington (Horton), who greatly fears horses, for a famous steeplechase rider, Peggy Fairfax (Miller) enthusiastically prevails upon him to ride the high-spirited Hottentot. Dumped, he covers up gamely, then narrowly escapes having to ride Peggy's horse in the steeplechase. She is so disappointed, however, that he buys Hottentot as a gift for Peggy, overcomes his fear, and rides the horse to victory.
Reviews
"...hilarious talking picture. The dialogue...is fast and funny. This is an example, it is to be presumed, of how really enjoyable a picture can be by having only good, clean fun. Miss Miller is sufficient and pretty as the heroine." – The New York Times

"...the dialogue is abundantly hoked, with some male members of the cast exaggerating this by inferior performance, [but] the theme is touched by the whip at the start. Patsy Ruth Miller...holds up a large part of the dialogue and is an attractive little thing in a riding habit." – Variety
Notes
The Hottentot, based on the play by Victor Mapes and William Collier, had first been filmed in 1922 with Douglas MacLean and Madge Bellamy. The 1929 talking version began an on-screen teaming of Miller and Horton that would last until 1931.

THE SAP
1929 A Warner Brothers Picture
Cast
Bill Small, the sap, Edward Everett Horton; *Betty*, Patsy Ruth Miller; *Jim Belden*, Alan Hale; *Jane*, Edna Murphy; *The Banker*, Russell Simpson; *The wop*, Jerry Mandy; *Mrs. Sprague*, Louise Carver; *Ed Mason*, Franklin Pangborn.
Credits
Archie Mayo (Director); Robert Lord (Screenplay/Dialogue); De Leon Anthony (Titles); Dev Jennings (Photography); Desmond O'Brien (Film Editor).
Synopsis
Bill Small (Horton), a smalltown inventor in South Dakota, is full of impractical ideas, though he is defended by his wife, Betty (Miller), against her sister, Jane (Murphy) and brother-in-law Ed Mason (Pangborn). When Ed confesses that he has been using the bank's funds for speculation, Bill, acting on a hunch, forces cashier Jim Belden (Hale) to confess that he has been doing the same thing. But Bill is humiliated when his shoe polish runs the shoes of Banker Sprague (Simpson). Ed and Jim aide him in appropriating $50,000, just as they are on the verge of being discovered, Bill reports that he has played the market and won, and he returns to his wife a hero.
Reviews
"Improbable story with lack of action. Reaches for entertainment in its gags, which are not hilarious but please. Nothing of histrionic elegance in the film. Horton holds nearly all the picture, which gets a whoop-up whenever Alan Hale sneaks in. Rest of the cast meander through in the standard manner." – Variety
Notes
The Sap was based on the play by William A. Grew, as was another Warner Brothers film version released in 1926. But despite being based on the same source, the films are completely different in plot. The 1926 film deals with a cowardly man who out of sheer terror fights splendidly in the war and returns to his hometown a hero, though he feels guilty and undeserving of the praise. This closely resembles the plot of the play, and there is evidence that the 1929 version was intended to follow the same storyline. Stills do exist of the assembled cast on a railroad platform wearing banners which proclaim Welcome Home Bill Small!

SO LONG LETTY
1929 A Warner Brothers Picture
Cast
Letty Robbins, Charlotte Greenwood; *Claude Davis*, Claude Gillingwater; *Harry Miller*, Grant Withers; *Grace Miller*, Patsy Ruth Miller; *Tommy Robbins*, Bert Roach; *Ruth Davis*, Marion Byron; *Sally Davis*, Helen Foster; *Clarence De Brie*, Hallan Cooley; *Joe Casey*, Harry Gribbon; *Judge*, LLoyd Ingraham; *Police Sargeant*, Jack Grey.

Credits
Lloyd Bacon [Director]; Robert Lord, Arthur Caesar [Adaption/Dialogue]; De Leon Anthony [Titles]; James Van Trees [Camera]; Jack Killifer [Film Editor]; Songs: "One Little Sweet Yes," "Beauty Shop," "Am I Blue?" "Let Me Have My Dreams," "My Strongest Weakness is You," Grant Clark, Harry Askt; Song: "So Long Letty," Earl Carroll; Song: "Down Among the Sugar Cane," Grant Clark, Charles Tobias.

Synopsis
Uncle Claude (Gillingwater), an eccentric millionaire, brings his flapper granddaughters, Ruth and Sally (Byron, Foster), to a fashionable beach hotel, where he is accosted by Letty Robbins (Greenwood), a beauty parlour solicitor. Infuriated by her tactics, he calls upon the "personality man" Harry Miller (Withers), a would-be singer who charms the girls. Claude rushes into the adjoining suite to find Clarence De Brie, a composer, who tries to induce him to produce his new opera. And back in his own suite, he encounters Joe Casey, who wants to give him swimming lessons, thus he decides to escape to the beauty salon. Later, Letty and Tom (Roach), her husband, decide to swap partners with their neighbors, Harry and Grace Miller (Miler). Complications ensue when Claude, who is Harry's uncle, arrives with his granddaughters. And when they are all booked in a raid on their "wild party," the judge finally straightens out matters.

Reviews
"The film is raucous and broad and the idea of an exchange of wives for a period of a week is not entirely new. But with the playful Miss Greenwood to carry it along its frivolous route, it manages to turn up as a cheery photoplay, with many entertaining moments." – *The New York Times*

"It's just a fair picture. Miss Greenwood and *So Long Letty* have been synonymous for almost 14 years, (and although) she remains the same smart comedienne... *So Long Letty* has lost its kick." – *Variety*

Notes
In *So Long Letty*, Miss Miller, for the first time since 1922 and *Omar the Tentmaker*, had a supporting role, but no one seemed to mind, or even notice, because 99 percent of the attention was, naturally, focused on Miss Greenwood. She was back to leading lady status with the release of her next film.

THE AVIATOR
1929 A Warner Brothers Picture

Cast
Robert Street, Edward Everett Horton; *Grace Douglas*, Patsy Ruth Miller; *Hobart*, Johnny Arthur; *Brown*, Lee Moran; *Gordon*, Edward Martindel; *Mrs. Jules Gaillard*, Armand Kaliz; *Sam Robinson*, Kewpie Morgan; *John Douglas*, Phillips Smalley; *Brooks*, William Norton Bailey

Credits
Roy Del Ruth [Director]; Robert Lord, Arthur Caesar [Scenario/Dialogue]; De Leon Anthony [Titles]; Chuck McGill [Photography]; William Holmes [Film Editor]

Synopsis
Wishing to assure the sale of a book of wartime experiences by an anonymous aviator, Brooks (Bailey), a publisher, and Brown (Moran), his publicist, decide to credit authorship to Robert Street (Horton), a highly successful writer. Though he detests aviation, knows nothing about the book in question, and finds the situation really embarrassing, Street agrees to lend his name to the publication and then retreats to a fashionable resort. Brown arrives, however, with Street's friends, John and Grace Douglas (Smalley, Miller), and he is thoroughly lionized. Street consents to pose for photographs in the cockpit of an airplane on the flying field. Frightened by the camera-flash, he accidentally starts the plane, takes off and gives an incredible demonstration, finally landing in a haystack. A race is arranged between Street and Gaillard (Kaliz), a French flyer, and after a series of hair-raising and hilarious complications, Street gives up his pose for the charms of Grace.

Reviews
"A hilarious audible production." – *The New York Times*

"It's a methodically plotted farce, but it's funny. Patsy Ruth Miller is nothing more nor less than Patsy Ruth Miller. She plays a secondary and necessarily wooden part in a somewhat wooden manner and lets it go at that." – *New York World*

"Peg this as a good one." – *Variety*

WHISPERING WINDS
1929 A Tiffany-Stahl Picture

Cast
Dora, Patsy Ruth Miller; *Jim*, Malcolm McGregor; *Eve Benton*, Eve Southern; *Jim's Mother*, Eugenie Besserer; *Pappy*, James Marcus

Credits
James Flood [Director]; Jean Plannette [Story/Continuity]; Charles Logue

(Dialogue); Harry Jackson, Jack MacKenzie (Photography); James Morley (Film Editor); Erno Rapee (Musical Score).

Synopsis

Jim (McGregor), a Maine fisherman who lives with his widowed mother, marries a neighborhood girl, Dora (Miller), when his sweetheart, Eve (Southern), goes to New York to become a pop singer. Dora is unsure of Jim's love for her until Eve, visiting them a year later, shows herself aloof and jaded. Dora later learns that Eve purposely assumed this attitude to make Jim forget about her and to insure Dora's happiness.

Notes

As no reviews of this film appeared in the major publications, it is likely that the film received a limited distribution and quickly disappeared. Not to discredit James Flood, who was a competent director, but by late 1929 silent films were just not profitable, and *Whispering Winds*, although it did have talking and singing sequences, was primarily a silent film.

SHOW OF SHOWS
1929 A Warner Brothers Picture
Cast (The Principals)
Master of Ceremonies, Frank Fay; *The Minister*, William Courtenay; *The Victim*, H.B. Warner; *The Executioner*, Hobart Bosworth; *Floradora Sextette*, Myrna Loy, Marion Nixon, Sally O'Neill, Patsy Ruth Miller, Lila Lee, Alice Day; *Waiter*, Ben Turpin; *Ice Man*, Heinie Conklin; *Street Cleaner*, Lupino Lane; *Plumber*, Lee Moran; *Father*, Bert Roach; *Hansom Cabby*, Lloyd Hamilton; *Pirates*, Noah Beery, Tully Marshall, Wheeler Oakman, Bull Montana, Kalla Pasha, Andres Randolph, Philo MacCullough, Otto Mattieson, Jack Curtis; *Hero*, Johnny Arthur; *Ladies*, Carmel Myers, Ruth Clifford, Sally Eilers, Viola Dana, Shirley Mason, Ethlyne Clair, Frances Lee, Julanne Johnston; *Ambrose*, Douglas Fairbanks, Jr., *Traffic Cop*, Chester Conklin; *Boys*, Grant Withers, William Collier, Jr., Jack Mulhall, Chester Morris, William Bakewell; *Girls*, Lois Wilson, Gertrude Olmstead, Pauline Garon, Edna Murphy, Jacqueline Logan; *Condemned Man*, Monte Blue; *Soldiers*, Albert Gran, Noah Beery, Lloyd Hamilton, Tully Marshall, Kalla Pasha, Lee Moran. (Additional Cast Members); Armida, John Barrymore, Richard Barthelmess, Sally Blane, Irene Bordini, Anthony Bushell, Marion Byron, Georges Carpentier, James Clemmons, Betty Compson, Helene Costello, Marceline Day, Louise Fazenda, Alexander Gray, Beatrice Lillie, Winnie Lightner, Harriette Lake (Ann Sothern), Lila Lee, Ted Lewis, Nick Lucas, Molly O'Day, Rin-Tin-Tin, E.J. Radcliffe, Sid Silvers, Alice White, Loretta Young.

Credits

John G. Adolfi (Director); Frank Fay, J. Keirn Brennan (Special Material); Bernard McGill (Photography); Esdras Hartley, Max Parker (Settings); Earl Luick (Costumes); Louis Geib (Technical Director); Frank N. Murphy (Electrical effects); Larry Ceballos, Jack Haskell (Dance Directors); George R. Groves (Recording Engineer)

Synopsis

A Musical revue with Frank Fay as Master of Ceremonies and featuring practically everyone under contract to Warner Brothers in various musical numbers and skits, including Winnie Lightner and a sexy rendition of "Singing in the Bathtub," a Floradora Sextette, Myrna Loy and Nick Lucas in an oriental routine featuring the song "Li-Po-Li," a rhythmic ballet number with 75 dancing girls in black and white costumes, highlighted by Louise Fazenda, John Barrymore reciting a scene from Shakespeare's *Richard III*, and as a finale, Betty Compson and Alexander Gray introducing 15 individual acts, culminating in a screen image of each of the film's stars singing "Lady Luck."

Reviews

"There is plenty to look at... but there are moments when the imposing hosts of dancing girls begin to pall. Not that scenes are lacking in imagination, but it is like having too much of a good thing." – *The New York Times*

"A pageant of color, splendidly interspersed with muscial numbers. It's box office anywhere." – *Film Daily*

Notes

Originally 124 minutes long *Show of Shows* was filmed entirely in technicolor with one brief black and white sequence. Warner Brothers was attempting, with this film, to outdo MGM's *The Hollywood Revue of 1929*, by using technicolor throughout and by casting only stars and featured players in every role, even down to the chorus. This offered an intriguing game of name-the-face, as over 70 famous (and almost famous) performers flitted by, often in groups of a dozen or more.

238

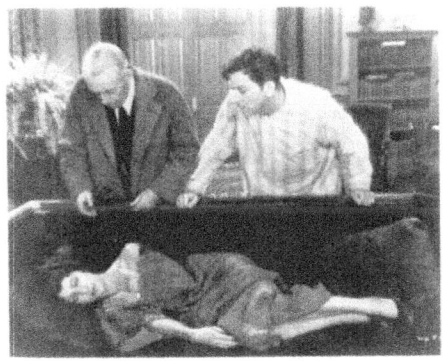

WIDE OPEN
1930 A Warner Brothers Picture
Cast
Simon Haldene, Edward Everett Horton; *Julia Falkner/Doris*, Patsy Ruth Miller; *Agatha Hathaway*, Louise Fazenda; *Agatha's Mother*, Vera Lewis; *Bob Wyeth*, T. Roy Barnes; *Trundle*, E.J. Ratcliffe; *Easter*, Louis Beavers; *Nell Martin*, Edna Murphy; *Faulkner*, Frank Beal; *Dvorak*, Vincent Barnett; *Doctor*, Lloyd Ingraham; *Office Boy*, Bobby Gordon; *Detective*, Fred Kelsey; *Office Worker*, Robert Dudley.
Credits
Archie Mayo (Director); James A. Starr, Arthur Caesar (Scenario/Dialogue); Alex Hurdley (Recording Engineer).
Synopsis
Simon Haldene (Horton), a timid bachelor, lives alone with his cat and works as a bookkeeper for the Falkner Phonograph Co. and though he offers many improvements, everyone—from Easter (Beavers), his maid, to Bob Wyeth (Barnes), the star salesman—treats him shabbily. He resents the attentions of women, particularly those of Agatha (Fazenda), a stenographer with an eye for romance whose marriage proposal is accidently recorded. But Doris (Miller), a stranger, finds his address and comes with her mother to demand that he marry her. When he refuses, she faints and is allowed to stay overnight. Doris gives Simon confidence in his ideas; he is promoted by Trundle (Ratcliffe), the general manager, and he gives Wyeth a scolding when he offends one of the ladies. Then Faulkner (Beal) introduces his daughter, Julia, whom Simon recognizes as Doris. Simon immediately proposes, and the two live happily together as man and wife.
Reviews
"Some of the dialogue is openly risqué. But the finale grants absolution to any prejudice formed in this respect.... *Wide Open* is good program entertainment. It is full of laughs and a few gasps for any audience."
– *Variety*

"Patsy Ruth Miller is competent as the pretty burglar." – *The New York Times*

THE LAST OF THE LONE WOLF
1930 A Columbia Picture
Cast
Michael Lanyard, Bert Lytell; *Stephanie*, Patsy Ruth Miller; *Varrel*, Lucien Prival; *Prime Minister*, Otto Matteson; *King*, Alfred Hickman; *Queen Maryland* Horne; *Camille, Queen's maid*, Haley Sullivan; *Master of Ceremonies*, Pietro Sosso; *Count von Rimpau*, Henry Daniel; *Hoffman* James Liddy.
Credits
Richard Boleslavsky (Director); Harry Cohn (Producer); Stuart Walker (Dialogue Director); Dorothy Howell (Scenario); James Whittaker (Dialogue); John Thomas Neville (Adaption); Ben Kline (Photography); Edward Jewell (Art Director); Edward Shulter (Technical Director); David Berg (Film Editor); Russell Malmgren (Sound Engineer); C.C. Coleman (Assistant Director).
Synopsis
When the King of Saxonia (Hickman) learns, through the Prime Minister (Matteson), that his wife has given a ring he gave her to Count von Rimpau (Daniel), he orders its retrieval. The Prime Minister commissions Michael Lanyard (Lytell), an American being held under arrest, to get it, offering him his freedom in exchange. Simultaneously, the Queen (Horne) sends Stephanie (Miller), her lady-in-waiting, to retrieve the ring, which she wants to wear at the Royal Ball. Varrel (Prival), a henchman sent to watch Lanyard follows on a train but is thrown off by Lanyard when he annoys Stephanie. With false credentials Lanyard gains admittance to the Embassy and steals the ring from a safe but, realizing he is suspected, replaces it and escapes. At his hotel he finds Varrel and overpowers him. Learning of the Queen's plight from Stephanie, he again steals the ring but is captured by Varrel. He escapes, however, and slips the ring on the Queen's finger at the ball, being rewarded with freedom and Stephanie's love.
Reviews
"A much drawn-out affair." – *Variety*

"Action is kept alive very nicely by the engrossing story. Satisfactory romantic melodrama in the popular vein." – *Film Daily*

LONELY WIVES
1931 A Pathe Production
Distributed by RKO
Cast
Mr. Smith/The Great Zero, Edward Everett Horton; *Mrs. Smith*, Esther Ralston; *Diane*, Laura La Plante; *Miss Minter*, Patsy Ruth Miller; *Andres the butler*, Spencer Charter; *Mrs. Mantel*, Maude Eburne; *Muzette, the maid*, Georgette Rhodes.

239

Credits
Russell Mack (Director); Walter DeLeon (Adaption); Edward Snyder (Camera); Robert Fellowes (Assistant Director).
Synopsis
Richard Smith (Horton) is a "Dr. Jekyll and Mr. Hyde" sort of character, a successful attorney by day and a philanderer by night. He tried unsuccessfully to endure the absence of his young wife (Ralston), and his mother-in-law (Eburne) moves in to remind him of his marital duties. His hard-boiled stenographer, Miss Minter (Miller), introduces him to her friend Diane (La Plante), a young actress whose husband leaves her at home alone every night. Smith suggests Diane meet him at the Whoopee Club, and just as he is about to leave he is visited at home by The Great Zero, a vaudeville impersonator who, unbeknownst to Smith, is the husband Diane has become bored with. Zero wants Smith's permission to include him among the local business men he impersonates, and Smith, in a scheme to conceal his rendezvous with Diane from his mother-in-law, persuades Zero to make up like Smith and spend the evening in his library. Everything is working well until Mrs. Mantel suddenly says she has a big surprise for her son-in-law; Mrs. Smith has returned home early from her vacation! Zero tries to escape, but ends up having to spend the night with Mrs. Smith. He tells her he is sick and sleeps in an adjoining room.

Mr. Smith returns home the following morning, after his wife has gone out for a walk and finds Zero preparing to leave. After a series of hilarious complications, Mrs. Smith finally admits that she was aware of the impersonation all the time. Everything is straightened out and everyone made happy.
Reviews
"One of the cleverest and most entertaining comedies of the season. Intelligent entertainment with Esther Ralston, Laura La Plante and Patsy Ruth Miller furnishing plenty of charm." – *Film Daily*

"...grows pretty warm at times, almost hot. Not in its scenes, but in its suggestions and through dialogue. The women play nicely." – *Variety*

"Patsy Ruth Miller, looking especially charming, gives an easy performance as Miss Minter."
– *The New York Times*
Notes
Miller, La Plante and Ralston were all leading silent film ladies finding their way into talkies. La Plante and Miller both retired the following year, and Ralston, although she continued to appear in films until the early 40's, usually had supporting roles.

NIGHT BEAT
1931 An Action Pictures Production
Cast
Johnny, Jack Mulhall; *Eleanor*, Patsy Ruth Miller; *Martin*, Walter McGrail; *Chill Scarpelli*, Harry Cording; *Weissenkorn*, Ernie Adams; *Featherstone*, Richard Cramer; *Italian*, Harry Semels.
Credits
George B. Seitz (Director); W. Scott Darling (Adaptor/Author/Dialogue); Byron Robinson (Film Editor); Jules Cronjager (Camera); James Stanley, Earl N. Crane (Sound Engineers).
Synopsis
In a city where racketeering has gained a foothold, gangster Johnny (Mulhall) comes to muscle in, only to discover that Martin (McGrail), the district attorney, is a pal from the world war. Martin is desperately trying to combat the gang who delight in shaking down small merchants. Martin invokes the aid of his old war buddy to help put the local gang out of business. Johnny agrees and turns his gangster methods against the gang members. He is not entirely sincere, however, until he falls in love with Eleanor (Miller), the DA's fiancee, then he decides to go truly straight.

Johnny finally does defeat the gang in a climactic shoot-out in a deserted warehouse, but loses his own life in the process, leaving the way clear for love to ignite again between Martin and Eleanor.
Reviews
"This film is the sort they should have made originally, for it pans the gangster element and shows graphically how the small-tradesmen have suffered at their hands. The story has a lot of original angles, and rings true... A great battle in a warehouse, and plenty of suspense and action along the way, plus a nice love element." – *Film Daily*

"Seldom... a very believable picture. A little different in some respects from similar pictures, but basically, it is weak talker fare." – *Variety*
Notes
Due, no doubt, to a restricted budget and limited distribution, *Night Beat* failed to make much of an impression, and today, is apparently totally forgotten. Perhaps if it had been made for a major studio, things might have been different. The director, George B. Seitz, when given more substantial material to work with could turn out a fine picture (he directed most of the Andy Hardy series).

240

THE PLAYS OF PATSY RUTH MILLER

STAGE WORK

Night Stick, Los Angeles, 1928.
It Pays To Advertise, Los Angeles, 1930.
A Man's Man, Los Angeles, 1931.
Rebound, San Francisco, Oakland.
Coquette, San Francisco.
Kempy, Los Angeles.
French Leave, Los Angeles.
Squaring the Circle, Los Angeles.
White Man, New York.

PLAYS WRITTEN AND PRODUCED

Windy Hill
Music in my Heart
Along came a Blackbird
Dona Elena

Squaring the Circle

Rehearsing for "Along came a Blackbird" at the Encino Ranch

A Man's Man

A MAN'S MAN

In the 20's Charles Ray and I worked together again, for the first time since *The Girl I Loved* in the play, *A Man's Man* which had a fairly successful run in New York City.

It was a powerful, sensitive play written by Patrick Kearney, who was a dear friend of mine. Some of his works that come to mind are *An American Tragedy*, *Elmer Gantry* and *Old Man Murphy*. In 1931 they revised *A Man's Man* but with the title *A Regular Guy*. I'm sure that had Patrick been less sensitive and more patient he would have continued a brilliant career, however, unable to follow up the revival of *A Man's Man* with another success, the damn fool committed suicide. Maybe there were other reasons as well, but who is to ever know?

I remember that I had such stage fright on opening night that I had just about decided I was going to get appendicitis or double pneumonia and send for an ambulance to take me home. A few minutes before curtain there was a knock at my dressing room door "Telegram for Miss Miller" said a voice. It was from Georgie Jessel and said: "Never mind Tootsie—stop—They can't put you in jail!" The thought that I couldn't be arrested for forgetting my lines so encouraged me that I actually enjoyed that first night.

Of all the plays I was in *A Man's Man* stands out in my memory because of one memorable performance.

To set the scene, I must go into some personal detail; I never wore a girdle, except on those occasions when the studio wardrobe designer insisted upon it to keep a tight skirt smooth, or to keep satin from wrinkling. In those days, before the blessed event of panty hose, I held up my stockings with a tiny garter belt and wore custom made batiste briefs, fastened with a little pearl button at the waist. They were cool, comfortable, and nonconfining, and as I didn't have a tummy I didn't need anything to hold it in.

At this particular performance, there were a number of my friends in the audience, among them Leatrice Joy and Helen Ferguson, so of course I wanted everything to go well, which it had for the first two acts.

Patrick Kearney

Then came the very dramatic climax in the third act. I was seated at the breakfast table listening to Charles, my husband, telling about someone's unfaithful wife, who had been seduced by the phoney promise of a movie career, and how all the guys down at the pool hall were laughing, through my nervousness, spilling my coffee, clinking the spoon against the saucer, my husband becomes suspicious and the scene mounts to a cresendo of realizations and denunciation.

He rises and starts pacing back and forth, threatening to go out and find my seducer, with me following him, begging forgiveness, and pleading with him not to fight my betrayer, who would kill him.

As I rose from the breakfast table I felt something cold sliding down my leg and knew, with indescribable horror, that it was the lone button holding up my panties. With both hands clutching my midriff—and the panties—I followed Charles in his interminable pacing, back and forth we went, he denouncing, me pleading, in what seemed an endless marathon. Fortunately, the curtain fell with me on my knees, sobbing contritely as I was forgiven, and I was able to scurry madly into the wings, let the damn panties drop—much to the amazement of the stage hands—and scurry back onstage for my bow.

243

Leatrice and Helen came back to my dressing room and both were profuse with their compliments. Leatrice said, in her soft Southern voice, "Patsy, darlin', you were wonderful. I declare I never saw such anguish—it was just tore me apart." Me too, I almost said—but I didn't.

Helen, too, was very complimentary. She told me that at one moment, when I just stood and gazed upward, it was almost as though I were praying. "It was very moving," she said. "It was a nice touch, really, very good acting." Acting, hell—I was praying; praying that the curtain would fall before my panties did.

Thus are great performances born. . .

Charles gave a magnificent performance, but there was one evening when he went up in his lines and started playing the third act while we were in the middle of the second. This was an easy thing to do, as the dialogue was purposely repetitious and some of the same phrases were used in both acts, but it presented an interesting problem; if he kept the bit in his teeth and galloped on to the third act curtain, our show would be over an hour early with nobody in the sold-out audience quite sure what had been happening. If I stopped coming in on cue, to warn him, he would assume that *I* had forgotten my own lines and would gallop even faster on his head-long flight to castastrophe.

All this flashed through my mind as I automatically responded with the third act speeches, which on my part consisted of little but, "Oh No Mel!" or "Oh please Mel!". Finally I just stood stock still, stamped my foot and shouted, "Mel, will you *please* shut up and listen to me!" His look of bewilderment as he heard this unexpected line almost made me burst out laughing. Fortunately it didn't (quite). I marched over to him, shook him by the shoulders, which I could barely reach, and said, "Now you just be quiet a second and listen to me." In the moments reprieve, while he was too startled to say anything I went into the lines which he had veered away from a dozen speeches ago. Being the trouper that he was, he caught on, plunged into proper reply, and we sailed into the second, not the third act curtain.

Hastily, during the intermission, we agreed to cut some of the third act lines which had already been spoken—lest the audience get the impression that they had heard it all before.

It wasn't the smoothest third act we ever gave, but nobody seemed to notice and we got our regular standing ovation.

WHITE MAN

White Man might conceivably be produced today—under another name, of course—but I doubt that it would be a hit. It was originally entitled *Harlem* and was written by Samson Raphaelson, and probably his only flop. Actually it was pretty good, but it dealt with a subject which was taboo in those days, and possibly still is; the problems faced by Blacks who are light enought of skin to pass as Whites. Raph had done extensive research, and the statistics on the number who actually "passed" was startling.

White audiences reacted strangely. As they realized that the actors, who were white, were portraying Blacks pretending to be white, they became uncomfortable, as though even if it were true they didn't want to hear about it.

Black members of the audience were hostile. They seemed to resent the play as a betrayal of one of their most closely guarded secrets.

The leading man was George Baxter who forgot that not only the show must go on—it *was* on! He became so engrossed in gossiping with a pal that the second act had been called and I was left on stage alone for something like four minutes, which doesn't sound like much, if it's all the time you have to catch a train, or prepare a box lunch for your child while the school bus is waiting, but it is an eternity under those conditions.

We were supposed to be in a suite in a Paris Hotel. The door to the hall was on one side and two doors leading to the bedrooms on the other; stage center was a French door presumably four flights up. At this particular performance I entered from the hall carrying some packages. George (his character named Richard in the play) was supposed to call to me from one of the bedrooms. I called back—he then entered—and we played our scene, which had a lot of plot in it.

The curtain rose, I entered—but there was no voice from the bedroom. There I was on stage with nothing to do, nothing to say, no one to say it to anyway—and a theatre of people staring at me. There are many more pleasant situations in which to find yourself; say, for example, going over Niagara Falls in a barrel. What does an actress do under those circumstances? I did everything but go into a soft-shoe routine. I lit a cigarette, I called "Richard" said to myself aloud, "He must be taking a shower", called again, a little louder this time—paced impatiently looked at my wrist watch, spoke aloud again, in a sort of soliloquy voice, "Richard had forgotten that we were to meet here?" Then I wondered audibly whether he had seen the Countess and gotten the account—all of these questions would have to be repeated if he ever showed up.

Suddenly muffled voices could be heard backstage—could be heard by me anyway, and probably by the first five rows of the audience. Then came a clatter of footsteps as George descended the iron steps from his dressing room. Then, as I turned to face the bedroom door, calling with a lilt in my voice, (I hoped) "Richard. Is that you?" Georgie Porgie burst on stage as though propelled by an irate stage manager's hand, if not foot—but he came through the door of the balcony! "Whatever were you doing out there!", I said and Mr. Baxter replied, "Huh?" I said "Did you drop in by parachute?" and he said "Oh no I was just taking a nap."

REBOUND

There was another *contretemps* in a play called *Rebound*. Written by Donald Ogden Stewart, written when he was still content to be amusing, and not out to remodel the world his way—his way being way out in left field. It was a sophisticated comedy about sophisticated people, thoroughly delightful while it was going on, forgotten by the time that you stopped for a sandwich on the way home.

I enjoyed doing it for several reasons. I love to hear an audience laugh, I had almost all the best lines, and it gave me a chance to wear some ravishing clothes. Including a glamourous backless evening gown in my favorite shade of turquoise, with all these illustrious oohs and aahs of appreciation when I made my first appearance, especially at matinees. (see copyright page for photo)

The leading man whose name I don't remember was very nice, very handsome, and a competent enough actor. He took direction well, didn't step on my laughs and didn't use too much aftershave lotion, but he did use too much of something on his hair, which had a tendency to curl and which he was determined to comb straight down.

The curtain was a tender scene. It ended with him on the floor, his head in my lap, as I gently stroked his hair and promised to be his forever, or something of the sort. I didn't so much mind having to have a towel handy to wipe my hands before taking our curtain call, but I did most emphatically object to having my dress cleaned after every performance.

Eight times a week his head lay in my lap; eight times a week I went back to the dressing room with a greasy spot on the front of my delicate elegant turquoise gown. Eight times a week Florence, my studio maid, cursed under her breath as she got out the Carbona.

Pleas, threats and entreaties were of no avail. Daily he promised to let the curls fly where they may—daily he laid a greasy kid's head on my lap. By the second week I had visions of my gown disintegrating!

One night I brought an enormous chiffon scarf to the theatre and swished it thoughout the first scene, then dropped it casually across the back of the chair I was later to be seated on. When the big moment came and he sank to the floor, his head about to drop in my lap, I stopped him with a gesture, reached back for the scarf, and carefully laid it across my knees. Then very deliberately, I pulled his head down and started stroking his hair. It got one of the biggest laughs of the evening and oddly enough it didn't hurt the scene, because it was quite in character with the part that I was playing. We kept it in, and my leading man had the grace to accept it with no comment, but he stopped asking me out for a bite of supper after the show.

Donald Ogden Stewart

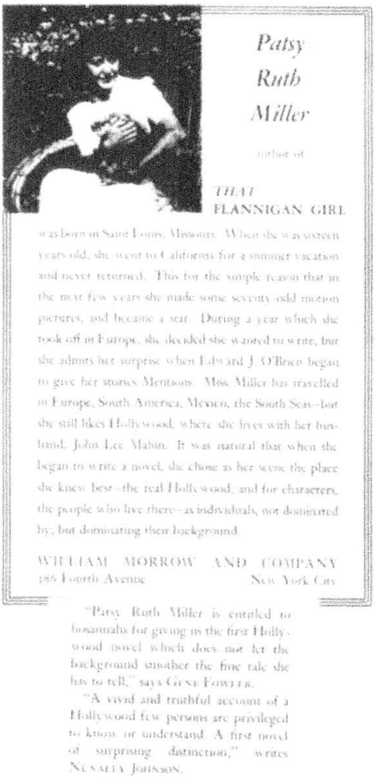

Patsy Ruth Miller

author of

THAT FLANNIGAN GIRL

was born in Saint Louis, Missouri. When she was sixteen years old, she went to California for a summer vacation and never returned. This for the simple reason that in the next few years she made some seventy-odd motion pictures, and became a star. During a year which she took off in Europe, she decided she wanted to write, but she admits her surprise when Edward J. O'Brien began to give her stories Mentions. Miss Miller has travelled in Europe, South America, Mexico, the South Seas—but she still likes Hollywood, where she lives with her husband, John Lee Mahin. It was natural that when she began to write a novel, she chose as her scene the place she knew best—the real Hollywood, and for characters, the people who live there—as individuals, not dominated by, but dominating their background.

WILLIAM MORROW AND COMPANY
386 Fourth Avenue   New York City

"Patsy Ruth Miller is entitled to hosannahs for giving us the first Hollywood novel which does not let the background smother the fine tale she has to tell," says GENE FOWLER.

"A vivid and truthful account of a Hollywood few persons are privileged to know or understand. A first novel of surprising distinction," writes NUNNALLY JOHNSON.

245

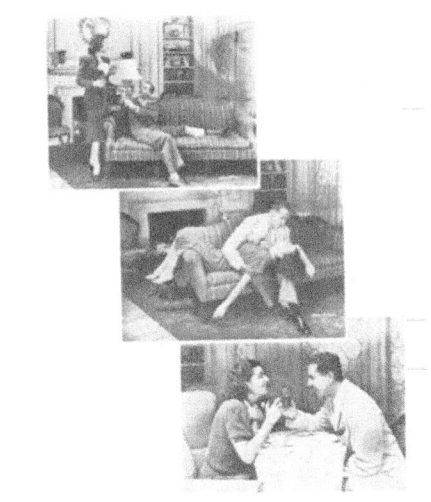

246

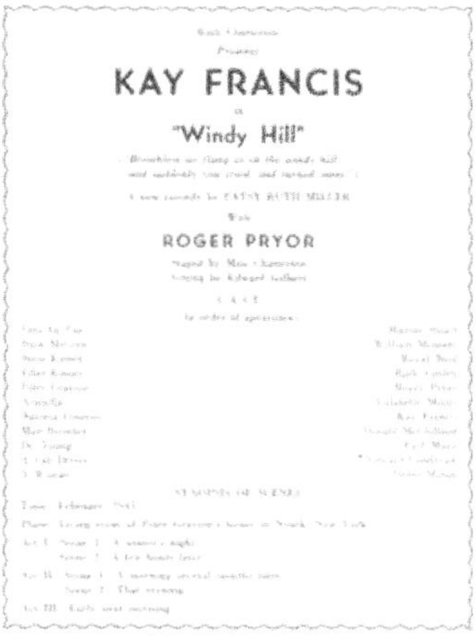

"Women at Work..."
By Patsy Ruth Miller

"Windy Hill" (let me tell you it basically a woman's play. Well, that's not surprising. I myself can very basically a woman. And strangely enough, I like other women and enjoy talking about them, although I am a bit leery about working with them. However, my agent who I damn, said to me that Ruth Chatterton was interested in directing and producing, and had read my play and liked it — Ruth and I had known each other since the good old days when we were both in pictures – oh, there, Ruth — remember? The net result: "We found for a while. Back of us was a little doubtful. 'Women working with women.' Well — lunching together, gossiping together, exchanging beaux and confidences, that was one thing, actually doing business together — that was something else again.

But to our amazement and delight, we have found as we clicked. I gave Kay and started with Ruth while we polished and edited and cut — and re-polished, and re-edited, and so on. Our only difference were climatic. Ruth is never cold. I am never hot. It was winter, a real typical New York winter. I am a Californian. It never gets cold in California. (Chamber of Commerce, please note.) Ruth would sit regally before the open window, clad in a silk blouse and slacks while I huddled over an hot typewriter, wrapped to the ears in sweaters, scarves, and foot warmers, trying to bat out last-hand dialogue. The moment Ruth left the room, I would make a mad dash to close the windows and turn on the heat. I had within more than thawed out, than, it would come I to Chatterton, and with a gay laugh, throw open the windows to let East River breezes freeze Sadi.

However I survived... assisted by hot continuous and encouragement. Then came the momentous moment of casting. Who looked the part, could play it, and would fit in with our furniture but not exclusively feminine group? With one accord, we said it together... Kay Francis! Kay had been interested from the beginning, just because her gals do have been trying to do something together. She had stopped over in New York several times on her way to entertain the troops in Europe, India and China, and had sort of let us in the only time, cheering.

Kay had been planning on going to the Pacific, but the idea of making a third appealed to her — As a matter of fact, I think she had been paid to take an extended rest before going on another tour as she had knocked herself out in Europe. At any rate! Little did we know. I've never to the old gag about "Women's work is never done." Never was a truer word spoken.

We opened in Montclair, N. J., with only a week's rehearsal. But what a week...! Just to make it a happy foursome, we could have placed bridge between acts — we also had a stage manager named Lillian — a pretty girl, and efficient as all get-out.

Getting "Windy Hill" ready for public presentation in a mere kind of life a girl's dormitory back-stage. Maybe there's some nagging that there would be with men living it, maybe we did take a little time out now and then to chat some clothes; but maybe we're having more fun too.

During working hours we are all evenly business women. But after hours... Vocal! I guess there's still a place in the world for men.

★ ★ ★ ★ ★

"Windy Hill" program courtesy Cody Morgan

INDEX

Adams, Charles, 168
Adolfi, John, 110*
Aitken, Max, 86
Allen, Woody, 141
Ameche, Don, 158*
Armstrong, Robert, 121*
Arnaz, Desi, 159
Asher, Irving, 146*, 150
Asher, William, 68A*
Ashley, Lady Sylvia, 176
Astor, Mary, 50
Auer, Leopold, 162
Auer, Mischa, 158, 159*, 160*, 161, 162*
Bacon, Lloyd, 97, 98, 100*, 110*
Ball, Lucille, 159
Banky, Vilma, 149, 152
Bard, Ben, 68A*
Barrymore, John Jr., 92
Barthelmess, Richard, 66*, 69*, 81*
Belmore, Lionel, 50*
Benchley, Robert, 77, 78, 87
Bennett, Constance, 77
Blackton, J. Stuart, 50*
Blue, Monte, 101*
Bradbury, Ray, 179*
Brando, Marlon, 124
Brennan, Walter, 23*
Brisbane, Arthur, 86
Brown, Joe E., 164*
Brownlow, Kevin, 48, 50
Buckingham, Tom, 121*, 124
Burr, Raymond, 124
Butler, Dick, 26*
Campbell, Alan, 78
Chaney, Lon, 43, 53*, 54-59, 123*, 180*
Chaplin, Charles, 64, 83, 84, 96, 164*
Chatterton, Ruth, 116
Cherryman, Rex, 33-35
Clark, Marguerite, 20
Cobb, Ty, 24*
Coca, Imogene, 177
Cohn, Harry, 179
Collier, Buster, 114
Colman, Ronald, 69*, 143
Connelly, Marc, 77, 78
Coogan, Jackie, 179
Courtleigh, William, 38, 39*
Coventry, Victor, 126, 128, 133*, 134
Crane, William, 24*
Crocker, Harry, 66, 71
Crosby, Bing, 165, 166
Crosland, Alan, 110*
Csepreghy, Bela, 152, 153
Csepreghy, Jeno, 152, 153, 155
Cummings, Constance, 143
Curtiz, Michael, 110*
Dale, Catherine Owen, 99
Dana, Viola, 20
Daniels, Bebe, 20, 25
Darmond, Grace, 38, 39
Davies, Marion, 82, 84*, 86, 87, 143
Davis, Mildred, 68B*, 109*, 111

Deans, Effingham Smith, 177*, 178, 182, 184*
De Baudigny, Madeline Bamburger, 88, 89
De Berenger, Andre, 102
Debove, Jean, 93
Deitrich, Marlene, 159
Del Ruth, Roy, 106*
De Mille, Cecil B., 114, 179
De St. Perrier, Jean, 135*, 136, 138, 141
De Ville Neuve, Noel, 135, 136, 138, 141
Donlin, Mike, 19*
Douglas, Donald, 108
Dove, Billie, 68B*, 109*, 111
Durbin, Deanna, 150
Duse, Eleonora, 28
Dwyer, Ruth, 68A*
Eagels, Jeanne, 77
Ebey, George, 77
Enright, Ray, 110*
Fairbanks, Douglas, 16, 17, 83, 111
Fairbanks, Douglas Jr., 37, 97, 143
Farrell, Charles, 50, 68A*, 111
Farrow, John Villiers 121*, 124, 137, 138*, 139-142
Farrow, Mia, 141
Ferguson, Helen, 68A*, 109*, 111, 121*
Fitzgerald, F. Scott, 51, 76*, 78*, 79*, 80, 81*
Fitzgerald, Zelda, 78*, 79*, 80
Flemming, Victor, 164*
Fonda, Henry, 177, 180
Forbes, Ralph, 51*, 77
Ford, Eugene, 46
Ford, Eugenia, 46
Ford, John 52*, 180
Francis, Kay, 116, 117
Fountain, Leatrice Gilbert, 95
Fox, Virginia, 68A*, 109*, 110, 121
Gable, Clark, 97, 121*, 158, 174*, 175*, 176*, 177*
Gable, Kay Spreckles, 174, 176, 177*
Gabor, Zsa, Zsa, 155
Gallery, Tom, 68A*
Garbo, Greta, 95*, 96*, 97*
Garnett, Tay, 119, 121*, 122*, 143, 144*, 147, 149*, 152, 153
Garon, Pauline, 109*
Geraghty, Carmelita, 83, 109*, 142*
Gerrard, Douglas, 14, 15*, 16, 17
Gilbert, John, 95*, 96*, 97*
Gleason, James, 121*, 158, 159
Gleason, Russell, 159
Glyn, Elinor, 86
Godowski, Leopold, 30
Goldwyn, Samuel, 179
Gowland, Gibson, 106*
Graham, Sheila, 81
Grant, Cary, 143
Green, Al, 110*
Green, George, 121*
Greenwood, Charlotte, 145*
Griffith, D.W. 180
Gump, Marcella, 125, 126, 128, 131, 132, 133*, 134, 136, 137-141
Hansen, Lars, 96*
Hardy, Oliver, 42B*, 64
Harlow, Jean, 121*
Hawks, Howard, 50, 164*

Hawks, Kenneth, 50, 66, 121*
Hay, Mary, 66
Hayes, Helen, 77, 78, 99
Hayes, William, 22*
Hayworth, Rita, 88
Hearst, William Randolph, 82*, 83, 86, 87
Henry, Clarence, 52*
Herriot, M., 93, 94
Heston, Charlton, 180*
Hitchcock, Tommy, 77
Holden, William, 115*
Holliday, Judy, 116
Hope, Gloria, 109*, 111
Horton, Clara, 109*
Horton, Edward Everett, 110*, 158*, 182
Hughes, Howard, 69, 70*
Hughes, Lloyd, 111
Hughes, Rupert, 69, 70*, 71
Huston, John, 103, 105*, 174
Ince, Thomas, 65*
Ingram, Rex, 27*
Ivano, Paul, 30*
Jackson, Cornwell, 52*, 151, 164*
Jannings, Emil, 127
Jessel, George, 67*
Johnston, Julanne, 68A*, 109*, 111
Jolson, Al, 100*, 158*
Joy, Leatrice, 95*
Kearney, Patrick, 66
Keaton, Buster, 24*, 64
Kennedy, Joseph, 116
Kerry, Norman, 56, 57, 59, 62*, 63*
Key, Kathleen, 68*
Khan, the Aga, 88, 89
Khan, Aly, 88
Kirkwood, James, 137
Knopf, Mildred, 90
Kress, Ray, 166
Kuhn, Bela, 153, 154
Laemmle, Carl, 53, 57, 58
Laemmle, Carl Jr., 51*
Landis, Cullen, 22, 54
La Plante, Laura, 68B*, 109*, 110*, 149, 150, 181*, 182*
La Rocque, Rod, 20, 143, 149, 152
Lasky, Jesse Jr., 73
Laurel, Stan, 64, 158
Lee, Lila, 18, 121*, 123*, 124, 135*, 136-142
Le Gallienne, Eva, 30
Leonard, Robert Z., 68B*, 111
Le Roy, Mervyn, 68B*, 111
Linder, Max, 96
Lindsay, Judge Ben, 114
Lloyd, Harold, 64, 65, 68B*, 111
Lombard, Carole, 159*, 174*, 175*, 176, 177
Loos, Anita, 86, 87
Love, Bessie, 18
Lubitsch, Ernst, 101*
Lyons, Eddie, 24*
Mac Arthur, Charles, 77, 78
Mack, Charles Emmett, 106*, 109
Mac Lean, Douglas, 64, 65*
Mahin, John Lee, 80, 116*, 122, 153, 158, 163*, 170, 174, 175*
Mahin, Timothy, 160, 163*, 166, 171*, 176, 177, 184
Maltin, Leonard, 183*

March, Frederic, 111
Markey, Morris, 163*
Marshall, Bart, 116*
Mathis, June, 26, 27*
May Wilbur, 66
Mayer, Louis B., 95, 97, 179
Mc Avoy, May, 24*, 68B*, 85*, 109*, 110, 112*
Mc Gregor, Malcolm, 52*
Miley, Jerry, 68B*
Miller, Winston, 19, 24*, 25*, 52*, 59*, 121*, 169, 177, 180*, 185*
Milton, Robert, 110*
Minter, Mary Miles, 24
Mitchum, Robert, 82
Mix, Tom, 43*, 44*, 45*, 46*, 47*
Monroe, Marilyn, 86, 172, 174, 177*
Moore, Colleen, 18, 111
Moran, Lee, 24*
Morgan, Frank, 153
Morris, Chester, 52*
Morris, Governeur, 124, 126
Morse, Kay, 148*
Murnau, F.W., 127, 129
Murphy, Dudley, 73
Murphy, Edna, 68B*, 109*, 111
Myers, Carmel, 68B*, 109*
Myers, Harry, 39
Nagel, Conrad, 103*
Nazimova, Alla, 20, 21*, 26-29, 30*, 32, 33*, 34, 35, 36*, 39, 41, 54
Negri, Pola, 29
Netcher, Townsend, 119
Niven, David, 143
Norton, Barry, 126*, 129, 133*, 134
Oakie, Jack, 83
O'Banion, Dion, 91
Oldfield, Barney, 106
Olmstead, Gertrude, 68B*, 109*, 111
O'Sullivan, Maureen, 141
Paddock, Charles, 68B*
Pagano, Ernie, 158
Pagano, Norma, 158, 167, 168, 170*
Parker, Dorothy, 77, 78
Parsons, Louella, 101*
Pasternak, Joesph, 149, 150*, 151
Pickford, Mary, 20, 37, 109*, 111
Pidgeon, Walter, 111
Pitts, Zazu, 68A*, 109*
Powell, William, 69, 159*
Pryor, Roger, 116
Raft, George, 104*
Ralston, Esther, 181*
Rambova, Natacha, 29*, 30*
Ray, Charles, 48*, 49*, 50, 51*, 54, 68
Reid, Wallace, 20, 25*
Rennie, Guy, 89, 90
Reynolds, Lynn, 46
Rich, Irene, 169
Rich, Lillian, 111, 68A*
Rodgers, Richard, 164*
Roland, Gilbert, 50
Roland, Ruth, 68B*, 109*, 111
Rosen, Art, 47*
Rosen, Phil, 39-41
Ross, Harold, 77
Russell, William, 68B*

Saunders, John Monk, 66, 68A*, 71, 72*, 73, 74*, 75
Schildkraut, Joseph, 77, 103*
Seastrom, Victor, 96*, 102*
Sedgewick, Ed, 62, 63*
Seiter, William, 68B*
Selleck, Tom, 97
Shepridge, John, (See Csepreghy, Jeno)
Shulter, C., 26*
Sillman, Leonard, 177
Smallwood, Ray, 26*, 33-35
St. John, Adela Rogers, 14
Stanwyck, Barbara, 158
Stewart, Anita, 68B*, 111
Stewart, Donald Ogden, 66, 82
Stewart, George, 111
Stewart, James, 159
Stiller, Mauritz, 96*
Sutherland, Eddie, 84
Swanson, Gloria, 115*, 116*
Talmadge, Constance, 86
Talmadge, Norma, 86
Tashman, Lilyan, 101*
Templeton, George, 182, 183
Thompson, Dave, 26*
Torrance, Ernest, 56
Tracy, Spencer, 164*
Tryon, Glenn, 23*, 158
Ustinov, Peter, 163*
Vale, Vola, 111
Valentino, Rudolph, 26, 27*, 29*, 30*, 31, 32, 33*, 42
Valli, Virginia, 109*, 111
Vanderbilt, William K., 128, 129
Von Gontard, Kay, 152, 153
Walker, Mayor Jimmie, 84*, 85
Wanamaker, Rodman, 77
Warner, Jack, 98, 179
Webb, Clifton, 66
Welles, Orson, 153
Wellman, William, 73*
Wheelock, Tommy, 168
White, Pearl, 111
Wills, Chill, 158*
Wilson, Lois, 24*, 68A*, 85*, 109*, 110, 121*
Windsor, Claire, 68B*, 109*, 111
Wolheim, Louis, 50
Woollcott, Alexander, 77
Worsley, Wallace, 54, 57, 58*, 59
Wray, Fay, 75
Wyler, William, 59
Yoltz, Greta, 23*
Zanuck, Daryl F., 68B*, 109, 110*

*Indicates Photograph

Made in the USA
Las Vegas, NV
02 February 2022